WHITAKER'S
WORLD OF
FACTS

RUSSELL ASH

WHITAKER'S WORLD OF FACTS

A & C Black • London

This edition published 2008
First published in 2005 by
A&C Black Publishers Ltd
38 Soho Square
London W1D 3HB
www.acblack.com

www.whitakersworld.com

Produced for A&C Black by
White-Thomson Publishing Ltd
210 High Street,
Lewes BN7 2NH

Illustrators Alan Baker (Illustration),
Julian Baker, KJA-artists

Heraldry consultant Henry Bedingfeld,
College of Arms
Religions consultant Martin Palmer,
ICOREC
Sports consultant Ian Morrison

A CIP catalogue record for this book
is available from the British Library.

ISBN 978-1-4081-0586-3

Printed and bound in China by
C&C Offset Limited

This book is produced using paper that
is made from wood grown in managed,
sustainable forests. It is natural,
renewable and recyclable. The logging
and manufacturing processes conform
to the environmental regulations of the
country of origin.

CONTENTS

CONTENTS

This latest edition of *Whitaker's World of Facts* has been updated from cover to cover. Inside, you will find thousands of amazing facts and hundreds of exciting pictures. Keep up-to-date with the most recent world record-breakers, the latest scientific breakthroughs, gadgets and gizmos from e-readers and iPhones to Blu-ray disks and atom-smashers, facts and figures about the environment, the people and the crucial events that shape our world.

Everything you want to know

Whitaker's World of Facts is divided into 20 sections - Space, Planet Earth, World History, Human Body to name but a few. It includes information on a huge range of subjects, with data from authoritative sources and specialists on every subject under the Sun - and beyond.

Inside information

Detailed lists and charts show global comparisons, while **special features** and **FactDisks** provide fast information, revealing everything from how much food you will eat in your lifetime to the highest-earning films and film stars, from the oldest people to the most popular names. You will discover an array of **oddities** from the number of ducks in the world to the countries where there are more sheep than people, the most dangerous things around the home to the world's tallest rubbish dump.

A section on **countries** gives essential information, including population, capital city and currency for every country in the world, as well as the flag of each one.

Timelines on subjects such as telecommunications, astronomy, wars and inventions give a see-at-a-glance overview and pinpoint important milestones up to the present day.

Useful maps, tables and formulae include conversions, mathematical symbols and scales, from Beaufort (weather) to Richter (earthquakes).

Other features

Web link boxes suggest useful websites to help you explore subjects further. **See also** boxes guide you to information on a particular subject elsewhere in the book. There is an extensive **index** at the back of the book, as well as a **list of sources**.

Whitaker's World Website

You can write to me with comments, suggestions and corrections at the publisher's address on page four or via the *Whitaker's World of Facts* website
www.whitakersworld.com

Russell Ash

About this book

Coloured bars identify each section of the book

Follow these *web links* for more information

One and Only boxes identify unique facts

Find cross-references throughout the book in these boxes

FactDisks highlight key facts

All new graphics used to illustrate facts and figures

Lists give you the latest facts and figures, dates and top tens for all kinds of subjects

Detailed information and statistics

Sample page 216 — AIR TRANSPORT

Aviation pioneers

John Alcock (UK, 1892–1919) and **Arthur Whitten Brown** (UK, 1886–1948)
On 14–15 June 1919, they completed the first ever non-stop flight across the Atlantic from Newfoundland to Ireland.

Samuel F. Cody (USA, c. 1861–1913)
The first person to fly in England, 16 October 1908.

Glenn Curtiss (USA, 1878–1930)
Rival to the Wright Brothers, Curtiss made the first public flight in the USA on 4 July 1908. He set up the first aeroplane manufacturing company in the USA.

Amelia Earhart (USA, 1898–1937)
The first woman to fly the Atlantic. She went on to establish many flying records but disappeared during an attempt to fly round the world.

Amy Johnson (UK, 1903–41)
She made the first solo flight from England to Australia in 1930.

Charles Lindbergh (USA, 1902–74)
The first pilot to fly solo across the Atlantic, from New York to Paris, 20–21 May 1927, in *The Spirit of St Louis*.

Harriet Quimby (USA, 1875–1912)
America's first female pilot. On 16 April 1912 she was the first woman to fly the English Channel – but on the day the sinking of the *Titanic* was reported, so her triumph was barely noticed.

Wilbur Wright (USA, 1867–1912) and **Orville Wright** (USA, 1871–1948)
The Wright brothers, two bicycle mechanics from Dayton, Ohio, made the first ever powered flights on 17 December 1903.

The Wright brothers demonstrate their Wright Model A plane

See also
Steve Fossett: page 153
Amelia Earhart: page 153

Concorde fact file

Concorde, the only passenger aircraft ever to fly faster than the speed of sound, was first named in a speech by General de Gaulle on 13 January 1963. The Anglo-French project began the following year.

- The first prototype Concorde was shown at the Toulouse Air Show on 11 December 1967.
- The first French flight took place on 2 March 1969.
- The first British flight took place on 9 April 1969.
- The first landing at London Heathrow was on 13 September 1970.
- The first Concorde landing in the USA was at Dallas-Fort Worth on 20 September 1973.
- The only Concorde crash was near Paris, 25 July 2000, when 109 passengers and crew and four people on the ground died.
- Concorde's last flight took place on 24 October 2004. All surviving BA and Air France Concordes are on public display in museums and airports in the USA, UK, France, Germany and Barbados.

First manned balloon flights

The first balloons worked on the principle that when air is heated, it rises. They were filled with hot air by burning things under them, such as paper, straw and wool – and even old shoes and rotten meat!

The balloons often caught fire and once the air cooled, they quickly came down. Soon after the first hot-air flights, people realized that the gas hydrogen could be used instead. Hydrogen is the lightest of all elements – almost 15 times lighter than air. Gas balloons can also be filled with helium, which is not as light as hydrogen but does not catch fire so easily. Most balloons today use hot air made by burning propane gas.

The first hot-air balloon flight
The Montgolfier brothers, Joseph and Etienne, tested their first unmanned hot-air balloon on 5 June 1783. On 21 November 1783, François Laurent, Marquis d'Arlandes and Jean-François Pilâtre de Rozier took off from the Bois de Boulogne, Paris, in a Montgolfier hot-air balloon. They travelled about 9 km (5.6 miles) in 23 minutes.

First hydrogen balloon flight
On 1 December 1783, Jacques Alexandre César Charles and Nicholas-Louis Robert made the first flight in a hydrogen balloon. They took off from the Tuileries, Paris, watched by a crowd of 400,000, and travelled 43 km (27 miles) north to Nesle in about two hours. Charles then took off again alone, so was the first ever solo pilot.

The Wright brothers
Orville Wright was the first person to fly a powered aircraft. He also became the first to fly a plane for more than one hour, on 9 September 1908 at Fort Meyer, Virginia, USA. His brother Wilbur became the first to fly for more than two hours, on 31 December 1908 at Auvours, France. On 20 May 1909 French pilot Paul Tissandier became the first person other than the Wrights to fly for more than an hour.

Sample page 217 — TRANSPORT AND TRAVEL

Breaking the sound barrier

Charles "Chuck" Yeager became the first person to break the sound barrier on 14 October 1947. His Bell X-1 rocket plane was dropped from a carrier aircraft above Muroc Dry Lake, California. At 12,800 m (42,000 ft) he reached a speed of 1,078 km/h (670 mph). He did not break the air speed record because only aircraft that take off and land under their own power are eligible. The speed of sound is not fixed and varies according to height and air conditions. In dry air at sea level the speed of sound is 1,229 km/h (263.67 mph), but at high altitudes, where air density is less, it is lower.

One and only
The only flight of the Hercules H-4 aircraft, known as the "Spruce Goose", took place on 2 November 1947. It was the largest flying boat ever built. It had the greatest wingspan (97.54 m/320 ft) of any aircraft and eight engines. Millionaire aviator Howard Hughes built and flew it himself, just 20 m (65.6 ft) above the water of Long Beach, California, USA. It travelled only 1.6 km (1 mile). The flight is recreated in the film *The Aviator* (2004).

www.flyingmachines.org [search]

First hot-air balloon flight

First British flight
On 27 August 1784 James Tytler, a doctor and newspaper editor, took off in a home-made balloon from Comely Gardens, Edinburgh. He reached an altitude of 107 m (350 ft) in a 0.8 km (0.5 miles) hop.

First Channel crossing
On 7 January 1785 Jean-Pierre Blanchard made the first Channel crossing in a balloon with Dr John Jeffries (the first American to fly). They also carried the first airmail letter. As they lost height, they had to reduce weight, so they threw almost everything overboard – including their clothes!

First flight in the USA
On 9 January 1793 in Philadelphia, Blanchard made the first balloon flight in America. He took a small black dog with him as a passenger.

The flight was watched by George Washington, who gave Blanchard a passport permitting his flight, which was the first pilot's licence and America's first airmail document.

First non-stop solo flight
US adventurer Steve Fossett made the first non-stop solo and fastest round-the-world balloon flight, 19 June to 3 July 2002.

Sample page 190 — TOYS AND GAMES

Valuable toys

Some wealthy collectors prize rare toys, especially those that are in good condition – in their original box, and never played with. These are just some of the toys that may have cost very little when they were made, but now sell for high prices.

- GI Joe prototype was sold by Heritage Galleries & Auctioneers of Dallas, Texas for $200,000 (£126,580) in 2003.
- A Kämmer and Reinhardt doll was sold at Sotheby's, London, on 8 February 1994 for £188,500 ($277,981).
- Titania's Palace, a doll's house with 2,000 items of furniture, was sold at Christie's, London, in 1978 for £135,000 ($258,728).
- Dingley Hall, a doll's house dating from 1877, was sold at Christie's, London, in 2003 for £124,750 ($211,938).
- A 1906 train set made by German toymaker Märklin was sold at Christie's, London, in 2001 for £113,750 ($165,290).
- A black mohair Steiff teddy bear, made in about 1912, was sold at Christie's, London, in 2000 for £91,750 ($132,157). It was one of only 494 black Steiff bears made as a mark of respect after the sinking of the *Titanic*. They are known as "mourning teddies".
- A tinplate clockwork motorcycle with Mickey Mouse and Minnie from about 1930 was sold at Christie's, London, in 1997 for £55,000 ($83,650).

"Teddy Girl" teddy bear made in 1904

Birth of Barbie
The first Barbie doll appeared in February 1959. It was made by Ruth and Elliot Handler, co-founders of American toy manufacturers Mattel, and they named the doll after their daughter Barbara. The doll was dressed in a black and white striped swimsuit, with sunglasses, high heels and gold hoop earrings. In the first year a total of 351,000 Barbies were sold at $3 (£1) each. The doll went on to become one of the bestselling toys of all time.

The first Barbie dolls, in the Barbie Museum, Palo Alto, California

Top Teddy
"Teddy Girl" is a teddy bear made by the German manufacturer Steiff in 1904. It was sold at Christie's, London, on 5 December 1994 for a record £110,000 ($171,600). A Japanese collector named Yoshiro Sekiguchi bought the bear for his teddy bear museum near Tokyo.

Toy-buying countries

Forecast sales of traditional toys (eg construction toys, model vehicles, indoor games, dolls and teddy bears) and video games in 2008 are estimated to average £16.9 ($33) for every person on the planet. There are huge differences between countries: North Americans spend the most and people in African countries the least per child.

USA $42,634,900,000
Toys world total $113,109,000,000
Other $41,591,700,000
UK £8,343,800,000
Japan $8,393,500,000
Germany $5,801,400,000
France $6,343,700,000

Sample page 191 — WORK AND HOME

Computer games

The first computer games were played on televisions and appeared in the 1970s. They were basic arcade games like PONG (1972), an electronic table-tennis game, and Pac-Man (1980), in which a yellow blob is steered round a maze, gobbling up everything in its path.

As computer technology advanced, games and consoles improved, with better graphics, sound and choice of themes. Second generation 8-bit games had removable cartridges, while the first 32-bit and 64-bit generation games could be played in 3D. Sixth and seventh generation games are more realistic than ever before and can be played online with anyone around the world. These are popular consoles of different generations.

First generation Atari PONG (1975)
Second generation Atari 2600 (1977)
Third generation Nintendo Entertainment System (1983), Nintendo Game Boy (1989)
Fourth generation Super Nintendo (1990), Sega Mega Drive (1988),
Fifth generation Nintendo 64 (1996), Sony PlayStation (1994)
Sixth generation Sega Dreamcast (1998), Sony PlayStation 2 (2000), Microsoft Xbox (2001)
Seventh generation Xbox 360 (2005), PlayStation 3 (2006), Nintendo Wii (2006)

Scrabble
Scrabble was invented in the USA during the 1930s by an architect named Alfred Mosher Butts. First he called it Lexiko, then It and Criss-Cross, before hitting on the name Scrabble. Well over 100 million sets have been sold in more than 120 countries. The numbers of letters included vary according to the language. In Dutch, for example, there are 18 Es, 10 Ns and two Js. The Slovak version has 41 different letters – more than any other version.

Monopoly®
Monopoly was invented in 1934 by an unemployed engineer called Charles Darrow, who lived in Philadelphia, USA. In his first version of the game he used street names from Atlantic City in New Jersey because he dreamed of going there, but could not afford the fare. The game was so successful that Darrow became a millionaire and spent the rest of his life travelling and growing rare orchids.

Monopoly was soon adapted for other countries, using street names from their main cities. The British version uses London place names and Mayfair is the most expensive street. There are also versions of Monopoly based on popular TV series, such as *The Simpsons*. Parkers, the US manufacturers of the game, print more Monopoly money than the US Treasury prints dollars.

Monopoly® around the world

Country	City*	Mayfair becomes
Australia	Canberra + state capitals	Kings Avenue
Canada	Vancouver + state capitals	Robson Street
China	Hong Kong	Victoria Peak
Egypt	Cairo	Shari Qasr El Nil
France	Paris	Rue de la Paix
Germany	Munich	Schlossallee
Ireland	Dublin	Shrewsbury Road
Netherlands	Amsterdam	Kalverstraat
New Zealand	Auckland	Queen Street
Portugal	Lisbon	Rossio
Russia	Moscow	Arbat
Singapore	Singapore	Queen Astrid Park
South Africa	Johannesburg	Eloff Street/Eloffstraat
Spain	Madrid	Paseo Del Prado
Switzerland	Zurich, etc	Paradeplatz
US	Atlantic City	Boardwalk

* Some feature streets from more than one city

Russian Monopoly board

Time

Millennium celebrations – 2,811 days late!

Ethiopians welcomed the year 2000 at midnight on 12 September 2007. The country's Christian Orthodox church uses a calendar that has 13 months and is seven years behind the rest of the world, most of which uses the Gregorian calendar.

The Universe in a year!

The American astronomer Carl Sagan (1934–96) first suggested a "cosmic calendar" as a way of helping people understand the history of the Universe. He put everything into the scale of a calendar year: the galaxies are formed over nine months and the Earth appears in September.

Human history is crowded into the last five minutes of the year. Recent time is divided into seconds and fractions of a second. So everything that happened in the last 475 years takes place in less than the last second of the last minute of the year.

The world in a single day

In one day (24 hours or 1,440 minutes or 86,400 seconds) the world turns once on its axis. During that time, on average:
364,478 people are born
151,650 people die

Earth's life in a year

1 Jan (midnight) Big Bang – Universe forms
15 Mar First stars and galaxies form
1 May Milky Way galaxy forms
8 Sep Sun forms
9 Sep Solar system forms
12 Sep Earth forms
13 Sep Moon forms
20 Sep Earth's atmosphere forms
1 Oct Earliest known life on Earth
7 Oct Earliest known fossils
18 Dec First many-celled life forms
19 Dec First fish
21 Dec First land plants; first insects
23 Dec First reptiles
24 Dec First dinosaurs
26 Dec First mammals
27 Dec First birds
28 Dec First flowering plants
28 Dec Dinosaurs extinct
31 Dec (11:55 pm)
Homo sapiens (modern humans)

The last day

11:59.50.487 pm Great Pyramid is built (2520 BC)
11:59.55.333 pm Great Wall of China is built (215 BC)
11:59.56.785 pm Roman Empire falls (AD 476)
11:59.58.026 pm Battle of Hastings (1066)
11:59.58.921 pm Columbus lands in America (1492)
11.59.59.pm Shakespeare writes his first plays (1588–90)
11:59.59.874 pm World War II ends (1945)
11:59.59.891 pm Mount Everest is climbed (1953)
11:59.59.924 pm Man lands on the Moon (1969)
Midnight Today

Royal Observatory, Greenwich; the "time ball" on the roof falls daily at 1.00 pm

Timetellers   1500 BC

The following are some landmarks in the history of telling the time.

1500–1300 BC Sundials are used in Egypt: as the Earth rotates, the gnomon – the upright part of the sundial – casts a shadow which moves to indicate the time.

c. 400 BC Water clocks are used in Greece: as water drains from a container, each level it reaches represents a period of time.

c. 890 In England people use candles marked with time intervals.

12th century The hourglass, familiar to us as an eggtimer, is used by monks to show times of prayer.

1325 The first clock with a dial is installed in Norwich Cathedral, England.

1335 The first clock to strike the hours is made in Milan, Italy.

1350 The oldest known surviving alarm clock is made in Würzburg, Germany.

1364 Clocks are first used in people's homes.

1386 The clock is installed in Salisbury Cathedral, England. This is the world's oldest clock in working order.

1462 The earliest description of a watch is written in Italy.

1641 The pendulum clock is proposed by Vincenzio Galilei, son of the astronomer Galileo.

1657 The first pendulum clocks are made in Holland.

Time zones

The Earth is constantly turning on its axis. If people everywhere set their clocks to the same time, midnight would be in the middle of the night on one side of the globe, but the middle of the day on the opposite side. To avoid this problem the Earth is divided into artificial time zones. These generally follow lines of longitude – imaginary lines running from the North to the South Pole. Some large countries, such as the USA, cover several time zones. Mainland USA is divided into Atlantic, Eastern, Central, Mountain, Pacific and Alaska zones, with Hawaii and other islands falling into further zones.

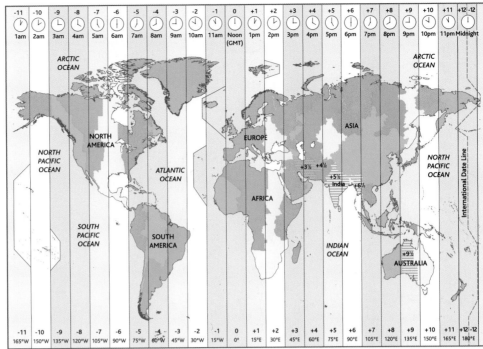

World time zones and the International Date Line

Since the Greenwich Prime Meridian (0°) was established in 1884, there have been 24 time zones, each of 15° longitude and an hour apart. Those to the east are ahead of Greenwich by one hour per zone. Those to the west are behind by one hour each. Some countries, such as India, have chosen zones halfway between those on either side, so that the whole country can use the same time.

Two sides of the Earth

The International Date Line

The Earth makes one complete turn in every 24 hours. In that time, each of the 360 degrees of longitude passes the Sun. This means that time progresses eastwards by four minutes for every degree of longitude.

The International Date Line is an imaginary line between the North and South Poles. It marks the end of one day and the start of another. Countries to the east of the Date Line are always a day ahead of those to the west. Travellers who cross the line gain or lose a day, depending on which direction they are going.

Most of the Date Line follows the 180° Meridian (on the opposite side of the globe from 0°, the Greenwich Meridian). The line generally passes through sea, but where it would pass through or near certain land areas, it is adjusted. It zigzags around islands, putting them either into the west or the east, and avoids dividing Siberia in north-east Asia into two time zones.

See also
Galileo Galilei: page 26

2008

c. 1665 The first watches with minute and second hands are made.

1759 John Harrison's marine chronometer is made. Accurate timekeeping at sea is important for calculating position, but previously the rolling of a ship had made it impossible.

1880 Greenwich Mean Time becomes the standard from which time around the world is set.

1880 The first practical wristwatches are made for the German navy.

1928 The first quartz crystal clock is made in the USA.

1949 The first atomic clock is built in the USA.

1957 The first battery watches are marketed in the USA.

1969 Quartz wristwatches are first sold in Japan.

1970 Digital watches and displays become widely used worldwide and can be made and sold cheaply.

2008 PARCS (Primary Atomic Reference Clock in Space), a super-accurate laser-cooled caesium atomic clock, is tested on the International Space Station.

 www.rog.nmm.ac.uk   search

Thor was the Scandinavian god of thunder and war. He is often shown brandishing a hammer. Thursday, or Thor's day, is named after him.

Names of months

The names of the months in English (as well as in many other languages) come from Latin words.

January
Januarius – this month was dedicated to Janus, the Roman god of doors. Janus had two faces, one looking back at the old year and the other looking forward to the new year.

February
Februarius – Februa was the Roman purification festival, which took place at this time of year.

March
Martius – from Mars, the Roman god of war.

April
Aprilis – from *aperire*, Latin for open, because plants begin to open during this month.

May
Maius – probably comes from Maia, the Roman goddess of growth and increase.

June
Junius – either from a Roman family name Junius, which means young, or perhaps after the goddess Juno.

July
Julius – after Julius Caesar. This month was named in Caesar's honour by Mark Antony in 44 BC. Previously this month was called Quintilis from the word *quintus*, five, as it was the fifth month in the Roman calendar.

August
Augustus – named in 8 BC in honour of Emperor Augustus.

September
September – from *septem*, seven, because it was the seventh month in the Roman calendar.

October
October – from *octo*, eight (as in octopus, which has eight legs), the eighth month in the Roman calendar.

November
November – from *novem*, nine, the ninth month in the Roman calendar.

December
December – from *decem*, ten, the tenth month in the Roman calendar.

Leap seconds

The rotation of the Earth is slowing down. This means that a solar day (the time it takes Earth to make one complete revolution) and the time shown by atomic clocks would gradually diverge. This problem has been solved by adding "leap seconds". There have been 22 leap seconds since 1972. The last one was added on 31 December 2005, which delayed New Year's Day 2006 by one second!

Naming the days of the week

The ancient Babylonians, then the Romans, named the days of the week after planets and other bodies they saw in the sky. Some names we know today come from the names of Scandinavian gods.

Monday
Moon's day

Tuesday
Tiu's day: Mars, the Roman god of war, was adopted in Scandinavian mythology as the warrior Tiu or Tiw.

Wednesday
Woden's day: the Roman god Mercury became the Scandinavian god Woden.

Thursday
Thor's day: like the Roman god Jupiter, Thor was a thunder god.

Friday
Freyja's day: like Venus, Freyja or Frigg was the goddess of love.

Saturday
Saturn's day

Sunday
Sun's day

How long does it take?

One beat of a fly's wing (1/1,000 second) 0.001 seconds
Flash of lightning (1/1,000 second) 0.001 seconds
One beat of a hummingbird's wing (80 times a second) 0.0125 seconds
Mouse heartbeat (10.8 times a second) 0.09 seconds
Blink of a human eye 0.33 seconds
Human heartbeat 1.0 seconds
Land speed record: car *ThrustSSC* travelling 1 km (0.62 miles)
2.9 seconds
**Record-breaking Jamaican athlete Asafa Powell to run 100 m
(328 ft)** 9.77 seconds
Bullet train to travel 1 km (0.62 miles) 13.75 seconds
Space Shuttle to travel 100 km (62 miles) 15 seconds
Light reaching Earth from the Sun 497 seconds

Watches at sea

At sea, the 24-hour day is traditionally divided into seven watches, during which some of a ship's crew are on duty.

8 pm to midnight
2000 to 0000

midnight to 4 am
0000 to 0400

8 am to noon
0800 to 1200

noon to 4 pm
1200 to 1600

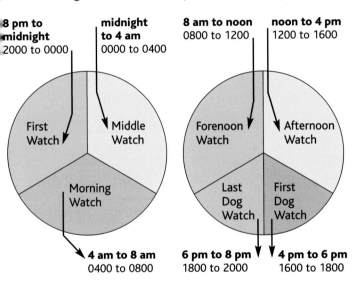

First Watch
Middle Watch
Morning Watch
Forenoon Watch
Afternoon Watch
Last Dog Watch
First Dog Watch

4 am to 8 am
0400 to 0800

6 pm to 8 pm
1800 to 2000

4 pm to 6 pm
1600 to 1800

www.physics.nist.gov/Genint/Time   **search**

Just a second

It will take you almost five seconds to read this sentence. During an average-length film more than 5,000 seconds will pass. In a lifetime of 80 years, there are more than 2.5 billion seconds – but you will spend more than 800 million of them asleep!

1 minute 60 seconds
1 hour 3,600 seconds
1 day 86,400 seconds
1 week 604,800 seconds
1 year 31,536,000 seconds

ThrustSCC set the first supersonic land-speed record, at 1,227.986 km/h (763.035 mph).

Time words

Here are some of the words used for units of time.

chronon
One-billionth of a trillionth of a second (the time a photon would take to cross the width of one electron at the speed of light)

femtosecond
0.000000000000001 of a second

picosecond
0.000000000001 (one-trillionth) of a second

nanosecond
0.000000001 (one-billionth) of a second

microsecond
0.000001 (one-millionth) of a second

millisecond
0.001 (one-thousandth) of a second; the blink of an eye takes 50–80 milliseconds

centisecond
0.01 (one-hundredth) of a second

second
1/60 of a minute

minute
60 seconds

hour
60 minutes

day
Sunrise to sunrise, or sunset to sunset, or midnight to midnight; 24 hours

week
Seven days; in Shakespeare's time, it was also called a sennight, or seven nights

fortnight
Two weeks (from the Old English for 14 nights)

month
Full Moon to full Moon; 1/12 of a year; 4 weeks, or 28, 29, 30 or 31 days, depending on month

bimester
Two months

trimester
A period of three months

year
365¼ days, 52 weeks, or 12 months

solar day
The time it takes for a place on the Earth directly facing the Sun to make one revolution and return to the same position (about 23 hours 56 minutes)

solar year
The time it takes for the Earth to make a complete revolution around the Sun, equal to 365.24219 solar days or 365 days, 5 hours 48 minutes, 45.51 seconds; also called a tropical year or astronomical year

leap year
366 days

decade
10 years; also called a decennium

century
100 years

millennium
1,000 years; also called a chiliad

bimillennium
2,000 years

era
A period of time measured from some important event

aeon or eon
A long period of time, usually thousands of years; in geology and astronomy it is one billion years

epoch
A geological era or very long period of time

See also
Geological time chart: page 34

THE CALENDAR

Gregorian calendar

The Gregorian calendar is the one most used nowadays. It is named after Pope Gregory XIII who introduced it in 1582. There is a leap year every four years (or more precisely, 97 leap years every 400 years). This means that the year corresponds closely with the astronomical year (365.24219 days) so that it gets just one day out of sync in every 3,300 years.

Calendar problems

Some non-Catholic countries such as Britain refused to adopt the Gregorian calendar at first. The Julian calendar previously used in Britain was based on a solar year, the time taken for the Earth to rotate around the Sun. This is 365.25 days, which is fractionally too long (it is actually 365.24219 days), so the calendar steadily fell out of line with the seasons. In 1752 Britain decided to correct this by abandoning the Julian calendar in favour of the Gregorian. By doing so, 3 September instantly became 14 September – and, as a result, nothing whatsoever happened in British history between 3 and 13 September 1752. Many people believed their lives would be shortened. They protested in the streets, demanding, "Give us back our 11 days!"

1 January 31 days	**5 May** 31 days	**9 September** 30 days
2 February 28 days*	**6 June** 30 days	**10 October** 31 days
3 March 31 days	**7 July** 31 days	**11 November** 30 days
4 April 30 days	**8 August** 31 days	**12 December** 31 days

* In a leap year, February has 29 days.

Time pyramid

The Mayan pyramid at Chichen Itza, Mexico, built around 1050, has four stairways, each with 91 steps and one platform. This makes a total of 365, the number of days in a year. The stairways also divide the nine terraces of each side of the pyramid into 18 segments, representing the 18 months of the Mayan calendar.

Mayan calendar

The Mayan people lived in the Yucatan area of present-day Mexico and the neighbouring region. They built many amazing pyramids and temples, and had an astonishing knowledge of astronomy.

Mayan culture had declined by the time Spanish invaders occupied their territory in the 16th century, but we know something about it from the remains found. The Haab or civil calendar of the Maya had 18 months made up of 20 days each. Five extra days were added at the year's end, known as Uayeb, giving a year of 365 days.

Chichen Itza, Mexico

Calendar timeline

Most of the world's countries and cultures use the Gregorian calendar, but some base their calendars on more ancient systems. Other countries have adopted an alternative calendar at some point in their history.

3761 BC Jewish calendar starts
2637 BC Original Chinese calendar starts
45 BC Julian calendar adopted by Roman Empire
AD 1 Christian calendar starts
79 Hindu calendar starts
597 Julian calendar adopted in Britain
622 Islamic calendar starts

1582 Gregorian calendar introduced in Catholic countries
1752 Julian calendar abandoned, Gregorian calendar adopted in Britain and its colonies, including America
1873 Japan adopts the Gregorian calendar
1949 China adopts the Gregorian calendar

Mayan months

1 Pop	**10** Yax
2 Uo	**11** Zac
3 Zip	**12** Ceh
4 Zotz	**13** Mac
5 Tzec	**14** Kankin
6 Xul	**15** Muan
7 Yaxkin	**16** Pax
8 Mol	**17** Kayab
9 Chen	**18** Cumku

Chinese calendar

Present-day China uses the Gregorian calendar for most purposes, but traditional festivals, such as Chinese New Year, take place according to the ancient Chinese calendar. Legend has it that this was started during the reign of Emperor Huangdi in 2637 BC, and relates to the positions of the Moon and Sun.

Chinese dragon

The ancient Chinese calendar follows a 60-year cycle which combines a heavenly stem and earthly branch, represented by a zodiac animal. The first year of the cycle is jia-zi, the second yi-chou, and so on; the 11th year is jia-xu, 12th yi-hai and 13th bing-zi. This continues until the 60th year (gui-hai) and then starts again. Each earthly branch is believed to be linked with certain qualities.

Calendars meet

The Islamic year is about 11 days shorter than a year in the Gregorian calendar. The Islamic calendar started 622 years later than the Gregorian so its date is behind. But because the year is shorter, the Islamic calendar is gradually gaining on the Gregorian. The two will eventually coincide – in the year 20874.

🔍 http://webexhibits.org/calendars **search**

Hebrew and Islamic calendars

The Hebrew (Jewish) and Islamic (Muslim) calendars are based on the lunar (Moon) cycle. Every month starts approximately on the day of a new Moon, or when a crescent moon is first seen.

The visibility of the Moon varies according to the weather so the start date cannot be determined in advance. Printed calendars may vary by a few days. Tishri/Muharram corresponds approximately with September/October in the Gregorian calendar, Heshvan/Safar with October/November, and so on.

Hebrew	Islamic	Hebrew	Islamic
1 Tishri	Muharram* (30 days)	**7 Nisan**	Rajab* (30 days)
2 Heshvan	Safar (29 days)	**8 Iyar**	Sha'ban (29 days)
3 Kislev	Rabi'a I (30 days)	**9 Sivan**	Ramadan † (30 days)
4 Tevet	Rabi'a II (29 days)	**10 Tammuz**	Shawwal (29 days)
5 Shevat	Jumada I (30 days)	**11 Av**	Dhu al-Q'adah* (30 days)
6 Adar	Jumada II (29 days)	**12 Elu**	Dhu al-Hijjah (29 days)

* Holy months   † Month of fasting

Indian calendar

The Indian calendar is based on the motions of the Sun and Moon and is dated from the so-called Saka Era, equivalent to AD 79. It is used for dating religious and other festivals, but the Gregorian calendar is used for official dates.

Month	Length	Gregorian calendar
1 Caitra	30 days*	22 March
2 Vaisakha	31 days	21 April
3 Jyaistha	31 days	22 May
4 Asadha	31 days	22 June
5 Sravana	31 days	23 July
6 Bhadra	31 days	23 August
7 Asvina	30 days	23 September
8 Kartika	30 days	23 October
9 Agrahayana	30 days	22 November
10 Pausa	30 days	22 December
11 Magha	30 days	21 January
12 Phalguna	30 days	20 February

* In a leap year, Caitra has 31 days and 1 Caitra = 21 March

Chinese calendar and Gregorian equivalents

HEAVENLY STEMS	EARTHLY BRANCHES	
1 jia	1 zi (rat)	11 xu (dog)
2 yi	2 chou (ox)	12 hai (pig or boar)
3 bing	3 yin (tiger)	
4 ding	4 mao (hare or rabbit)	
5 wu	5 chen (dragon)	
6 ji	6 si (snake)	
7 geng	7 wu (horse)	
8 zxin	8 wei (sheep or ram)	
9 ren	9 shen (monkey)	
10 gui	10 you (rooster)	

Zodiac animal	Gregorian calendar year beginning	Zodiac animal	Gregorian calendar year beginning
Ox	7 Feb 1997	Monkey	22 Jan 2004
Tiger	28 Jan 1998	Rooster	9 Feb 2005
Hare	16 Feb 1999	Dog	29 Jan 2006
Dragon	5 Feb 2000	Pig	18 Feb 2007
Snake	24 Jan 2001	Rat	7 Feb 2008
Horse	12 Feb 2002	Ox	26 Jan 2009
Sheep	1 Feb 2003	Tiger	14 Feb 2010

Space

Lunar landing

Work on NASA's new lunar lander, codenamed *Altair*, begins in 2009. The aim is to put humans on the Moon by 2018 – 46 years after the last *Apollo* mission. This artist's impression of the *Altair* (the name of a bright star) shows how the lander will look.

Twinkle twinkle little star...

Stars appear to twinkle because we see them through the layers of the Earth's atmosphere. Light is distorted as it passes through these layers, so that the amount we see changes constantly. Stars nearest the horizon seem to twinkle the most because the light is passing through a greater depth of atmosphere. Stars do not twinkle when viewed from space, so telescopes in space, such as the Hubble, give the best possible view of distant stars and galaxies.

Star facts

A star is a luminous body of gas, mostly hydrogen and helium. Stars generate light, which makes it possible for us to see them with a telescope or the naked eye.

Photographs all taken by the Hubble Space Telescope

Supergiant VY Canis Majoris

The Sun

● Brightest
Not counting the Sun, the brightest star as seen from Earth is Sirius, known as the dog star, in the constellation of Canis Major. It has a diameter of 149,598,020 km and is more than 24 times brighter than the Sun. The star LBV 1806–20 in the constellation of Sagittarius may be 40 million times as bright as our Sun, but dust clouds make it almost invisible from Earth.

● Largest
The largest star is VY Canis Majoris, which has an estimated diameter of about 1,950 times greater than the Sun. For comparison, if it were a football, the Sun would be no bigger than a pinhead.

● Nearest
Proxima Centauri, discovered in 1915, is 4.22 light years (39,953,525,879,212 km) from Earth. A spaceship moving at 40,000 km/h – which is faster than any human has yet travelled in space – would take more than 114,000 years to reach it.

● Supernovae
These are vast explosions in which a whole star blows up. They are extremely bright, rivalling for a few days the combined light output of all the stars in the galaxy. Supernovae are rare – the last one in our galaxy was seen in 1604 by the German astronomer Johannes Kepler.

● Quasars
These are extremely distant radio galaxies – galaxies giving out large amounts of radio energy – and the brightest objects in the Universe. Their radio emission is typically 1,000,000 to 100,000,000 times greater than that of a normal galaxy.

● Black holes
A black hole is a star that has collapsed into itself. It has a surface gravity so powerful that nothing can escape from within it.

Black Eye Galaxy

Swan Nebula

Monocerotis V838
(a red supergiant star surrounded by dust)

Travelling at the speed of light

In space, light travels at a speed of 299,792.46 km a second, or 1,079,252,956 km an hour. When we look at even the nearest star, we see light that left it more than four years ago. Here are the times it takes light to reach Earth from various bodies in space.

● Light years
A light year measures distance, not time. Distances in space are often described as light years, the distance light travels in a year.

Galaxy facts

Galaxies are groups of billions of stars held together by the force of gravity. Most are either spiral or elliptical, but some are irregular in shape.

● The Milky Way
This is the best-known galaxy. The word galaxy comes from the Greek for milk. Before telescopes were powerful enough to prove that they were made up of individual stars, galaxies looked like milky or cloudy areas in the sky. Our Solar System is only one of 100–200 billion stars in the Milky Way, which is 100,000 light years in diameter. The Sun and all the planets take about 200,000,000 years to complete one orbit around its centre.

● Brightest
The Large Magellanic Cloud, which is visible only in the southern hemisphere, is 170,000 light years from Earth and 39,000 light years in diameter.

● Largest
The central galaxy of the Abell 2029 galaxy cluster was discovered in 1990. It is 1,070 million light years distant and has a diameter of 5.6 million light years, 80 times the diameter of our own galaxy. It has a total light output equivalent to 2 trillion times that of the Sun.

● Nearest
Discovered in 1993, the Canis Major Dwarf galaxy is approximately 25,000 light years from the Solar System.

Small
Magellanic Cloud

Constellations

Groups of stars form patterns in the night sky, which are called constellations. There are 88 known constellations. The Sumerians, a Middle Eastern civilization, probably named them, about 5,000 years ago.

The largest is Hydra, the sea serpent, and the smallest is Crux Australis, the Southern Cross. Centaurus, the Centaur, has the most stars that can be seen with the naked eye (94). Others include Aquila, the Eagle; Canis Major, the Great Dog; and Orion, the Hunter.

Canis Major –
the Great Dog

Crux Australis –
the Southern Cross

Orion – the Hunter

Aquila – the Eagle

Moon 1.26 seconds
Sun 8 minutes 17 seconds
Furthest planet (Neptune) 4 hrs 21 mins when the planet is at its maximum distance from Earth
Nearest star 4.22 years
Distance at which the Sun would no longer be visible to the naked eye 60 years
Most distant star in our galaxy 62,700 years
From nearest body outside our galaxy 174,000 years
Furthest visible star 2,309,000 years
Most distant known quasar 14,000,000,000 years

www.astronautix.com   search

Solar System

The Solar System was formed about 4,560 million years ago. It is made up of the eight planets – Mercury, Venus, Earth, Mars, Jupiter, Saturn, Uranus and Neptune – as well as their moons, comets and other bodies. These all orbit our Sun, to which they are attracted by gravity.

Mercury

Mercury was named after the speedy messenger of the gods because it seemed to move more quickly than the other known planets. In 2004 NASA launched its MESSENGER probe, which is due to reach Mercury in 2011.

Diameter: 4,880 km
Mass: 3,302,000,000,000 tonnes
Average distance from Sun: 57,909,175 km
Rotation: 58.6462 days
Orbit: 87.969 days
Average temperature: +166.86°C
Moons: 0

Venus

In size, mass, density and volume Venus is the planet most similar to Earth. Venus rotates backwards, from east to west, so the Sun would appear to rise in the east and set in the west. In April 2006 the European Space Agency's *Venus Express* spacecraft reached Venus. Japan's Venus Climate Orbiter *PLANET-C* will be launched in 2010.

Diameter: 12,103.6 km
Mass: 48,690,000,000,000 tonnes
Average distance from Sun: 108,208,930 km
Rotation: 243.0187 days
Orbit: 224.701 days
Average temperature: +456.85°C
Moons: 0

See also
Planets visited by spacecraft: page 29

Mars

Several space probes have flown past or landed on Mars, providing information on its atmosphere and features, such as the volcano Olympus Mons. This stands 27 km high – more than three times the height of Mount Everest. The latest craft to visit the red planet is *Mars Reconnaissance Orbiter*, which began a four-year orbit in 2006. NASA's *Phoenix Mars* landed in May 2008 (see p. 27).

Diameter: 6,794 km
Mass: 6,421,900,000,000 tonnes
Average distance from Sun: 227,940,000 km
Rotation: 1.025957 days
Orbit: 686.98 days
Average temperature: -63°C
Moons: 2

Jupiter

Jupiter is the largest planet in the Solar System and is big enough to contain more than a thousand Earths. Four of its many moons were among the first ever astronomical discoveries made with a telescope, by Galileo in 1610. More were identified by later astronomers and in 1979 by the space probe *Voyager 2*. The NASA Juno mission to Jupiter is planned for launch in 2011.

Diameter: 142,984 km
Mass: 18,986,000,000,000,000 tonnes
Average distance from Sun: 778,412,010 km
Rotation: 9 hours 50 minutes
Orbit: 11 years 314 days
Average temperature: -150° C
Moons: 63

Earth

Earth is a watery planet – 70 per cent of its surface appears blue – and the only one that can support life. From space, astronauts have observed cities, forest fires, roads, airports, dams and other large structures, such as the Great Pyramid and the Great Wall of China.

Diameter: 12,756.3 km
Mass: 59,720,000,000,000 tonnes
Average distance from Sun: 149,600,000 km
Rotation: 0.99727 days
Orbit: 365.256 days
Average temperature: +15°C
Moons: 1

www.nineplanets.org   search

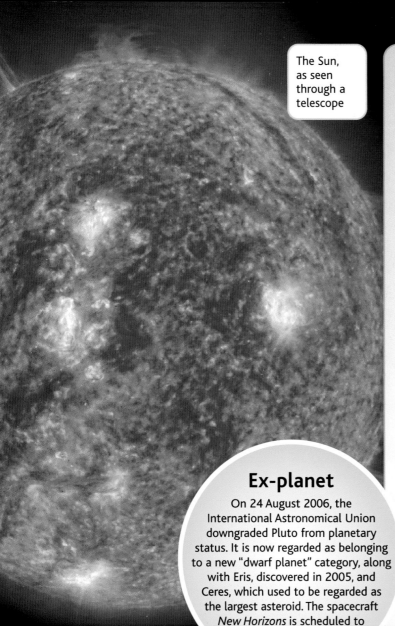

The Sun, as seen through a telescope

Sun facts

The Sun is 149,597,893 km from Earth and has a diameter of 1,391,940 km. This is more than 100 times larger than Earth. Its mass is equivalent to 99.98 per cent of the mass of the entire Solar System.

Elements
The Sun is mostly made up of two light gases, 75 per cent hydrogen and 23 per cent helium, with relatively small quantities of other elements – including metals such as gold. Helium was discovered in the Sun before it was detected on Earth. Its name comes from *helios*, the Greek word for sun.

Temperature
The Sun has a surface temperature of 5,880 K but it can be 56,000,000 K at its core. (K represents Kelvin, which is an astronomical temperature; it can be converted to Celsius by subtracting 273.16.) At the Sun's centre, nuclear fusion constantly changes hydrogen into helium, and the energy and heat released from this process rise to the surface. The yellow surface we see is called the photosphere.

The corona
The outermost layer of the Sun extends millions of kilometres into space but is visible only during eclipses. At a height of 75,000 km in the corona, the temperature may reach 2,000,000 K.

Rotation
The Sun rotates once every 25.4 days, but because it is not solid, the poles spin at a different rate, taking as much as 36 days to complete a single revolution.

Solar eclipses
When the Moon is between Earth and the Sun, it blocks out the light causing a partial or total eclipse. At this time, astronomers are able to observe the corona in detail.

Ex-planet
On 24 August 2006, the International Astronomical Union downgraded Pluto from planetary status. It is now regarded as belonging to a new "dwarf planet" category, along with Eris, discovered in 2005, and Ceres, which used to be regarded as the largest asteroid. The spacecraft *New Horizons* is scheduled to reach Pluto in 2015.

Saturn

Saturn and its rings are being examined by NASA/European Space Agency's *Cassini* probe, which reached it in 2004. In 2005 it released the *Huygens* probe to land on the surface of Titan and has continued to send back data from its flybys of Titan and other moons of Saturn.

Diameter: 120,536 km
Mass: 5,684,600,000,000,000 tonnes
Average distance from Sun: 1,426,725,400 km
Rotation: 10 hours 34 minutes
Orbit: 29 years 168 days
Average temperature: -139.5°C
Moons: 56

Uranus

All the satellites of Uranus are called after characters from either William Shakespeare's plays or Alexander Pope's poem *The Rape of the Lock*. Uranus has rings like those of Saturn, but they are visible only with a powerful telescope.

Diameter: 51,118 km
Mass: 868,320,000,000,000 tonnes
Average distance from Sun: 2,870,972,200 km
Rotation: 17 hours 17 minutes
Orbit: 84 years 4 days
Average temperature: -197.15°C
Moons: 27

Neptune

Neptune is the furthest body from the Sun. Surface winds are the strongest of any planet at up to 2,000 km/h. Neptune's year is so long that it has not completed an orbit round the Sun since its discovery and will not until 2011.

Diameter: 49,522 km
Mass: 1,024,700,000,000,000 tonnes
Average distance from Sun: 4,498,252,900 km
Rotation: 16 hours 7 minutes
Orbit: 164 years 298 days
Average temperature: -200.15°C
Moons: 13

Buzz Aldrin, walking on the Moon

The Moon's near side

Our Moon's far side
The far side of our Moon always faces away from Earth, so it was unknown until October 1959, when the Soviet *Luna 3* probe sent pictures of it back to Earth.

Moon facts

Earth's Moon is the most familiar and also the largest satellite in relation to its planet in the Solar System. It is the first body in the Solar System on which vehicles from Earth landed, and the only one to be explored by humans.

Diameter: 3,475.6 km

Distance from Earth: 406,711 km (furthest, 1912) to 356,375 km (closest, 1984), 384,403 km (average)

Mass: 734,556,000,000 tonnes; a person weighing 65 kg on Earth would weigh 10.79 kg on the Moon

Rotation: 27 days 7 hours 43 minutes 11.5 seconds

Surface temperature: -163˚C to +117˚C

Largest crater: South Pole Aitken (far side) 2,100 km diameter, 12 km deep (largest in the Solar System)

Asteroid facts

Asteroids are often called minor planets. They are lumps of rock orbiting the Sun, mostly in the asteroid belt between the orbits of Mars and Jupiter.

● Ceres was once considered the largest asteroid but it has been recently reclassified as a dwarf planet. It is 936 km in diameter and was found on New Year's Day, 1801. Since then thousands of asteroids have been found. Twelve of them are more than 250 km wide and 26 are larger than 200 km in diameter. As telescopes have improved, more and more small asteroids have been detected. There are probably about 100,000 asteroids larger than 1 km in diameter. Some experts think there may be as many as 1.2 million.

● Vesta, the fourth asteroid to be found (in 1807), is the only one bright enough to be seen without a telescope.

Part of the Bayeux Tapestry, showing Halley's comet top left

Halley's comet

British astronomer Edmond Halley (1656–1742) was the first to prove that comets travel in orbits, making it possible to calculate when they will next be seen from Earth. He predicted that the comet he saw in 1682 would return in 1759. It did and was named in his honour. The regular orbit of Halley's comet means that we can find historical accounts of its appearances going back more than 2,000 years. They were often believed to foretell great events.

240BC

25 May 240 BC Seen in China

10 October 12 BC Believed to mark the death of Roman general Agrippa

28 June AD 451 Believed to mark the defeat of Attila the Hun

20 March 1066 William (later William the Conqueror)

1450s

believed the comet foretold victory over King Harold at the Battle of Hastings. The comet and battle are later depicted in the Bayeux Tapestry.

9 June 1456 The defeat of the Turkish army by Papal forces was thought to be linked to the comet.

● Astronomers believe that, on average, one asteroid larger than 0.4 km strikes Earth every 50,000 years. Some 65 million years ago a 10 km diameter asteroid crashing to Earth may have been responsible for wiping out the dinosaurs. It would have caused a catastrophic explosion, affecting the climate and chemical composition of the atmosphere and destroying the plants and animals on which the dinosaurs fed. As recently as 1991 a small asteroid came within 170,600 km of Earth, the closest recorded near miss. On 30 Jan 2052 an asteroid is predicted to pass as close as 119,678 km.

● Toutatis (asteroid 4,179) was discovered in 1989. It is named after the Celtic god Toutatis, whose name is used as an oath by the comic strip character Astérix the Gaul. Toutatis measures 4.6 by 2.4 by 1.9 km. It passes Earth every four years and is one of the largest space objects to come so close to us. On 29 September 2004 Toutatis came within 1,555,818 km of Earth. Its next visit will be on 9 November 2008, when it will come within 7,524,773 km.

Titanic moon

Titan is the largest of Saturn's 34 moons. It is 5,150 km in diameter – larger than the planet Mercury. Dutch astronomer Christiaan Huygens discovered Titan in 1655. We still have no idea what its surface looks like because Titan has a dense atmosphere containing nitrogen, ethane and other gases which shroud its surface – not unlike that of Earth four billion years ago.

Information sent back by the space probe *Voyager 1* during 1980 and recent radio telescope observations suggest that Titan may have ethane "oceans" and "continents" of ice or other solid matter. *Cassini*, a space probe launched by NASA and the European Space Agency, arrived in Saturn's orbit on 1 July 2004. On 14 January 2005 it launched the *Huygens* probe on to the surface of Titan and sent back scientific data.

Neptune's moon

Triton, discovered in 1846, is the only known large moon in the Solar System with a retrograde orbit. It revolves around its planet (Neptune) in the opposite direction to the planet's rotation.

Comet Hale-Bopp as seen from Earth in 1997

Titan, the largest moon of Saturn

Comet Temple 1 as photographed by NASA's *Deep Impact* probe in 2005

Returning comets

More than 20 comets return more often than Halley. The most frequent visitor is Encke's comet, named after the German astronomer Johann Franz Encke (1791–1865). In 1818 he calculated the 3.3-year period of its orbit.

2000s

15 September 1682 Observed by Edmond Halley, who predicted its return

13 March 1759 The comet's first return, as predicted by Halley, proving his calculations correct

16 November 1835 The American author Mark Twain is born. He always believed that his fate was linked to that of the comet, and soon after it reappeared in 1910, he died.

10 April 1910 There was panic as many believed the world would come to an end.

9 February 1986 The Japanese *Suisei* probe, Soviet *Vega 1* and *Vega 2* and the European Space Agency's *Giotto* passed close to Halley's comet. Astronomers concluded that the comet is made of dust held together by water and carbon dioxide ice.

28 July 2061 Next due to appear. The orbit of Halley's comet is not exactly 76 years. Astronomers have to take into account the gravitational pull from planets when calculating its return.

www.spacetoday.org   search

Famous astronomers

John Couch Adams (Britain, 1819–92) studied the Leonid meteor shower and predicted the existence of Neptune, which was discovered in 1846.

Edward Emerson Barnard (USA, 1857–1923) discovered Barnard's Star and Amalthea, a moon of Jupiter.

Nicolaus Copernicus (Poland, 1473–1543) showed that the Sun was at the centre of the Solar System.

Galileo Galilei (Italy, 1564–1642) made important discoveries concerning gravity and motion. He built some of the first telescopes used in astronomy and used them to discover many previously unknown space objects.

George Ellery Hale (USA, 1868–1938) pioneered the astronomical study of the Sun and founded observatories, one with a major telescope named after him.

Edmond Halley (Britain, 1656–1742) predicted the orbits of comets, including the one that bears his name.

William Herschel (Germany/Britain, 1738–1822) built huge telescopes, compiled catalogues of stars and discovered moons of Saturn and Uranus.

Edwin Hubble (USA, 1889–1953) made important discoveries about galaxies. The Hubble Space Telescope was named in his honour.

Christiaan Huygens (Holland, 1629–95) discovered Saturn's rings and devised the wave theory of light.

Percival Lowell (USA, 1855–1916) was founder of the Lowell Observatory, Arizona. He predicted that a planet would be found in the region where Pluto was later discovered.

Charles Messier (France, 1730–1817) studied comets and eclipses, but he is best known for his catalogue of stars first published in 1774.

Isaac Newton (Britain, 1643–1727) is considered one of the greatest of all astronomers. His theories of gravity and the motions of planets revolutionized the subject.

Telescopes and observatories

The following are some of the world's most famous telescopes and observatories.

Royal Observatory, Greenwich, London
Founded by King Charles II in 1675, but atmospheric and light pollution in London reduced its efficiency. In 1884 the Prime or Greenwich Meridian, 0°, which passes through the Observatory, was adopted as the basis for all mapping and measurements. Longitude measurements refer to west or east of the meridian.

Herschel's "Forty-foot" reflector, Slough
A giant telescope built in 1788 with a 1.2 m (3.9 ft) mirror.

Birr Castle, Co. Offaly, Ireland
The Earl of Rosse's 1.8 m (5.9 ft) reflecting telescope, built in 1845, was used to discover the spiral form of galaxies. It was the world's largest until the opening of Mount Wilson.

Yerkes Observatory, Williams Bay, Wisconsin, USA
This 1 m (3.25 ft) telescope is the biggest refracting instrument made up to this time. It was completed in 1897.

Mount Wilson Observatory, California, USA
The telescope was installed in 1917 with a mirror size of 2.5 m (8.2 ft). It was the world's largest until the Hale.

Hale Telescope, Palomar Observatory, California, USA
The Hale's 5 m (16.4 ft) telescope was first used in 1949.

Jodrell Bank, Cheshire
Britain's first, and once the world's largest radio telescope, with a 76 m (249.3 ft) dish, began operating in 1957.

Arecibo Observatory, Puerto Rico
Completed in 1963, this is the world's most powerful radio telescope. Its uses include searching for pulsars and quasars and the search for alien life forms under the SETI (Search for Extra-Terrestrial Intelligence) programme. Its giant 305 m (1,000.65 ft) dish features in the final scenes of the James Bond film *Golden Eye* (1995).

Yerkes Observatory, Wisconsin, USA

Astronomy milestones

Astronomy is the scientific study of the Universe and the bodies it contains (excluding Earth). Astronomers are the scientists who study astronomy.

585 BC First prediction of eclipse of the Sun

130 BC Hipparchus calculates distance and size of Moon

AD 1543 Copernicus shows that the Sun is at the centre of the Solar System

1609 Johannes Kepler describes laws of planetary motion

1610 Galileo Galilei discovers moons of Jupiter

1655 Christiaan Huygens discovers Titan, moon of Saturn

1600s

1668 Isaac Newton builds first reflecting telescope

1687 Isaac Newton publishes theories of motions of planets, etc

1705 Edmond Halley predicts return of comet

1671–84 Giovanni Cassini discovers four moons of Saturn

1774 Charles Messier compiles star catalogue

1781 William Herschel discovers 7th planet, Uranus

1800s

1801 First asteroid, Ceres, discovered by Giuseppe Piazzi

1846 Johann Galle and Urbain Le Verrier discover 8th planet Neptune

1787–89 Herschel finds two moons of Uranus and two of Saturn

1839–40 First photographs of the Moon

1894 Flagstaff Observatory, Arizona, founded

1905 Einstein's Special Theory of Relativity first proposed

Hubble Space Telescope

The HST was launched in 1990 and orbits 600 km (372.8 miles) above Earth's atmosphere. It can photograph distant objects with ten times the detail possible with ground-based telescopes.

Keck I & II Telescopes, Mauna Kea Observatory, Hawaii, USA

The two Keck telescopes were opened in 1992–96. They are situated 4,000 m (13,123 ft) up a Hawaiian mountain, so above 40 per cent of the Earth's atmosphere. They are the world's most powerful ground-based instruments, with a 10.82 m (35.5 ft) total aperture made up of 36 hexagonal mirrors.

Hobby-Eberly Telescope, McDonald Observatory, Texas, USA

This telescope is designed to collect light for spectrum analysis rather than for visual exploration. It has been in operation since 1999, and has an overall diameter of 11 m (36.1 ft), making it one of the largest ever optical telescopes.

Large Binocular Telescope, Arizona, USA

The Large Binocular Telescope, completed in 2007, is the largest and most advanced optical telescope ever built. Sited at the Mount Graham International Observatory, it has two 8.4 m (27.5 ft) mirrors, giving a total area equal to one giant 11.4 m (37.4 ft) diameter mirror. It is expected to produce images as much as 10 times the resolution of those produced by the much smaller Hubble Space Telescope.

First telescopes

The first telescopes were made in 1608 by Dutchman Hans Lippershey. Galileo built his own soon after and used it to discover Jupiter's moons. The earliest type of telescope, known as a refracting telescope, produced a slight distortion of images (called aberration). Since about 1670, astronomers have used reflecting telescopes, which use mirrors that compensate for the distortion.

Hubble Space Telescope

1900s

1908 Giant and dwarf stars described

1923 Galaxies beyond the Milky Way proved

1927 Big Bang theory proposed

1930 Pluto discovered by Clyde Tombaugh

1959 First photographs of the far side of the Moon by Soviet satellite *Luna 3*

1961 First quasars discovered

1967 First pulsars identified

1971 Black hole first detected

1973 *Skylab* space laboratory launched

1976 Rings of Uranus are discovered

1977 *Voyager* deep space probes are launched

1971 *Mariner 9* spacecraft maps Mars

1980 *Voyager 1* explores Saturn

1978 Space probes *Pioneer 1* and *2* reach Venus

1985–89 *Voyager 2* discovers moons of Uranus and Neptune

2000s

1994 Comet Shoemaker-Levy observed crashing into Jupiter

1995 *Galileo* probe reaches Jupiter

1997 *Mars Pathfinder* lands

1997 *Cassini* probe launched to Saturn

1998 *International Space Station* construction starts

1999 Chandra X-Ray Observatory launched

2003 *Galileo* probe deliberately crash-landed on Jupiter

2006 *New Horizons* space probe launched to Pluto

2008 *Phoenix* mission to Mars landed on the planet

www.absoluteastronomy.com   search

SPACE EXPLORATION

Animal space pioneers

Before humans went into space animals were used to test equipment. The first animal to be sent up in a rocket – but not into space – was Albert 1, a male rhesus monkey, in 1948. He and his successor, Albert 2, died during the tests.

However, on 20 September 1951, a monkey and 11 mice were recovered after a launch in a US *Aerobee* rocket. Many further animal experiments were carried out before the first manned space flight.

Space dogs, and a cat
Laika, a female Samoyed husky, became the first animal in orbit after being launched by the USSR in *Sputnik 2* in November 1957. There was no way to bring her down and she died after ten days in space. Two female huskies, Belka and Strelka, orbited successfully in August 1960. Strelka later gave birth to puppies, one of which was given to US President John F. Kennedy. In October 1963, a French *Veronique AGI* rocket put a cat called Félix into space and returned him safely to Earth by parachute.

Monkey business
Able, a female rhesus monkey, and Baker, a female squirrel monkey, were launched by the USA in May 1959. They did not orbit and successfully returned to Earth. In November 1961 Enos, a male chimpanzee, completed two orbits and survived. The USSR's first space primates were monkeys Abrek and Bion, who orbited in December 1983 in one of a series of Bion satellite experiments.

Flying frogs
In November 1970, the USA's Orbiting Frog Otolith satellite (OFO-A) launched two bullfrogs into orbit for a week. In December 1990, Toyohiro Akiyama, a Japanese journalist, took six green tree frogs to the Soviet *Mir* space station to conduct weightlessness experiments.

Worldwide web
Arabella, a garden spider, went to the US *Skylab-3* in July 1973. She spent almost 60 days in orbit in an experiment to test the effect of weightlessness on her web-weaving skills.

A space menagerie
The *STS-90* mission of space shuttle *Columbia* (April/May 1998) contained the *Neurolab* – a space menagerie with 170 baby rats, 18 mice, 229 swordtail fish, 135 snails, four oyster toad fish and 1,514 cricket eggs and larvae.

In January 2006, an *Atlas V* rocket launched NASA's *New Horizons* probe on its 9-year journey to Pluto.

Can of worms
On 1 February 2003, space shuttle *Columbia STS-107* broke up on re-entry and its crew were killed. On-board animal experiments involving silkworms, spiders, carpenter bees, harvester ants and Japanese killfish were destroyed, but, amazingly, canisters of worms were found alive.

Long Duration Exposure Facility satellite (USA) orbited the Earth 34,422 times between 1984–90. Space Shuttle *Columbia* eventually brought it back to Earth.

Space junk

When satellites reach the end of their useful life, they may be deliberately directed back in such a way that they burn up as they re-enter the Earth's atmosphere or come down in the oceans or away from places where they could cause damage. So far, no one has been killed or seriously injured by space debris.

● **Returned to Earth**
The 69-tonne *Skylab* re-entered in 1979, scattering large chunks in the Australian desert, and Russia's *Mir* space station, which weighed 120 tonnes, came down in the Pacific.

● **Orbiting junk**
About 100–200 objects, each larger than a football, re-enter every year, but there are still many pieces of space junk in orbit. A survey carried out in June 2000 calculated that there are 90 space probes and 2,671 satellites still in space. There are as many as 100,000 objects between 1 and 10 cm in diameter and about 11,000 objects larger than 10 cm including parts of rockets: an *Ariane* rocket booster exploded in 1986, scattering 400 fragments large enough to be tracked. In 1991 space shuttle *Discovery STS-48* narrowly avoided a discarded Soviet rocket.

Artificial satellites

The USSR's *Sputnik 1* was the first artificial satellite to enter Earth's orbit. This 83.6 kg (184 lb) metal sphere transmitted signals back to Earth for three weeks before its batteries failed.

In 1958 the USA began to launch its own satellites. Five went into orbit. All of the earliest satellites have since crashed back to Earth, except *Vanguard 1* (USA, 1958) which is still in space – and likely to remain so for another 200 years.

Over the past 50 years, many more artificial satellites have been launched, with a greater range of uses.

Astronomy
The Hubble Space Telescope has been taking photographs of distant galaxies since 1990. In 2008 the Herschel Space Observatory is scheduled for launch. This new telescope will have the biggest mirror ever in space (3.5 m across).

Communications
Over 5,000 satellites have been launched to transmit telephone, radio and television signals around the world. Fewer than half are still orbiting, and many have stopped working.

Earth observation satellites
These transmit images of the weather and the Earth's environment. They helped to show the depletion of the ozone layer.

Military satellites
Governments use these "spies in the sky" for surveillance but their precise functions are secret.

Global Positioning System
This is a system of 24 linked satellites that allows people to pinpoint their exact position anywhere on Earth. The system is operated by the US Department of Defense and is used by aircraft and ships. GPS systems are now common in cars, too.

Space rockets

Thrust is the force required to lift a vehicle such as an aircraft or rocket off the ground. Rockets often have several stages. Each one provides a proportion of the thrust required to carry a satellite, space shuttle or other vehicle into orbit or into space, dropping away as their propellant has been used so that their weight no longer needs to be carried.

Planets visited by spacecraft

No human has yet set foot on any space body other than Earth and the Moon. But unmanned spacecraft have taken photographs, made scientific readings and gathered data from all the planets in the Solar System, either by flying past or landing.

Venus *Mariner 2* (USA) flyby 1962; *Venera 4* (USSR) landed 1967; *MESSENGER* (USA) flybys 2006, 2007

Mars *Mariner 4* (USA) flyby 1965; *Mars Pathfinder* (USA) landed 1997; *MER-A* and *MER-B* landed 2004; *Mars Reconnaissance Orbiter* (USA) in orbit 2006– ; *Phoenix Mars* (USA) landed in 2008; *Dawn* (USA) flyby 2009

Jupiter *Pioneer 10* (USA) flyby 1973; *Galileo* (USA) landed* 2003; *New Horizons* (USA) flyby 2007

Mercury *Mariner 10* (USA) flyby 1974; *MESSENGER* (USA) flybys 2008, 2009 and scheduled to orbit 2011

Saturn *Pioneer 11* (USA) flyby 1979; *Cassini/Huygens* (USA/ESA) orbiter/lander 2004/2005

Uranus *Voyager 2* (USA) flyby 1986

Neptune *Voyager 2* (USA) flyby 1989

* Deliberately destroyed entering Jupiter's atmosphere, rather than risk contaminating moon Europa with bacteria from Earth.

Manned space missions

During the 1950s, there was a "space race" between the USA and USSR to be the first country to send a human into space. NASA's *Mercury* missions were originally unmanned, or carried only animals. The USSR launched the first man into orbit in 1961.

Each country's subsequent space missions had different aims. The USA focused on Moon landings with their *Apollo* programme and later the re-usable space shuttle. The Soviets and later Russia concentrated on long-duration missions, with the *Mir* space station. The latest manned mission is the *International Space Station*, which is four times larger than *Mir*.

Mission	Country	Years
Mercury	USA	1959–63
Vostok	USSR	1961–63
Voskhod	USSR	1964–65
Gemini	USA	1965–66
Apollo	USA	1967–72
Soyuz	USSR	1967–76
Salyut	USSR	1971–82
Skylab	USA	1973
Apollo Soyuz	USA/USSR	1975
Space shuttle	USA	1981
Mir space station	USSR/Russia	1986–2001
International Space Station	USA, Canada, Japan, European Space Agency, Russia, Brazil	1998–
Shenzhou	China	2003–

International Space Station

STS-116 Patch design shows the names of the astronauts who went in *Discovery* to continue construction of the *International Space Station* in December 2006

Astronauts and cosmonauts

The word "astronaut" was first used in 1880 by the British writer Percy Greg. It was the name he gave to a spaceship in his novel *Across the Zodiac*. By the 1950s it was the word used for a space voyager. The Russian word is cosmonaut.

12 April 1961 First person in space Soviet cosmonaut Yuri Gagarin made a single orbit of Earth in *Vostok 1*, a flight that lasted 1 hour 48 minutes.

5 May 1961 First US astronaut America's first astronaut Alan B. Shepard Jr, entered space aboard *Mercury 3* but did not orbit during his 15 minute 22 second mission.

6 August 1961 First flight of over 24 hours Gherman S. Titov (USSR) in *Vostok 2* made the first flight of more than 24 hours. He was also the youngest ever astronaut at 25 years 10 months 25 days.

20 February 1962 First US orbit John H. Glenn Jr in the *Friendship 7* capsule made the first US orbit, completing three orbits in 4 hours 55 mins.

16 June 1963 First woman in space Valentina V. Tereshkova (USSR) in *Vostok 6* was the first woman in space. She spent 2 days 22 hours 50 minutes 8 seconds in space. She remains the youngest (26 years 3 months 10 days) woman in space.

18 March 1965 First space walk Aleskei Leonov (USSR) made the first space walk, from *Voskhod 2*. It took 24 minutes and it almost ended in disaster when his spacesuit ballooned. He was unable to return through the airlock until he reduced the pressure in his suit to a dangerously low level.

23 March 1965 First two-man US mission John Young and Virgil "Gus" Grissom made the first two-man US mission in *Gemini 3*.

3 June 1965 First US spacewalk Edward H. White II made a 36 minute spacewalk from *Gemini 4*.

24 April 1967 First space death After 18 orbits in *Soyuz 1*, Vladimir M. Komarov (USSR) died when his parachute got tangled and his capsule crash-landed.

24 December 1968 First manned spacecraft to orbit the Moon *Apollo 8* (followed in 1969 by *Apollo* missions 9 and 10) orbited the Moon but did not land.

All the men on the Moon

The human exploration of the Moon lasted just over three years and involved a total of six missions. In each, a pair of US astronauts went down to the surface in a LEM (lunar excursion module) while a third orbited in a CSM (command service module). The missions provided scientists with a huge amount of information about the Moon.

Astronaut	Spacecraft	Total EVA* hr:min	Mission dates
1 Neil A. Armstrong	Apollo 11	2:32	16–24 Jul 1969
2 Edwin E. "Buzz" Aldrin	Apollo 11	2:15	16–24 Jul 1969
3 Charles Conrad Jr	Apollo 12	7:45	14–24 Nov 1969
4 Alan L. Bean	Apollo 12	7:45	14–24 Nov 1969
5 Alan B. Shepard	Apollo 14	9:23	31 Jan–9 Feb 1971
6 Edgar D. Mitchell	Apollo 14	9:23	31 Jan–9 Feb 1971
7 David R. Scott	Apollo 15	19:08	26 Jul–7 Aug 1971
8 James B. Irwin	Apollo 15	18:35	26 Jul–7 Aug 1971
9 John W. Young	Apollo 16	20:14	16–27 Apr 1972
10 Charles M. Duke Jr	Apollo 16	20:14	16–27 Apr 1972
11 Eugene A. Cernan	Apollo 17	22:04	7–19 Dec 1972
12 Harrison H. Schmitt	Apollo 17	22:04	7–19 Dec 1972

* Extra vehicular activity: time spent out of the lunar module on the Moon. The six US *Apollo* missions above resulted in successful Moon landings. *Apollo 13*, 11–17 April 1970, was aborted and returned to Earth after an oxygen tank exploded.

Longest space walk

The record for the longest-ever spacewalk was broken from 10–11 March 2001, when mission specialists James Voss and Susan Helms stepped outside space shuttle *Discovery STS-102* to do construction work on the space station. Their EVA (extra vehicular activity) lasted 8 hours 56 minutes.

Astronaut Christer Fuglesang resumes construction work on the *International Space Station*, December 2006

Naming the space shuttles

Unlike space rockets, NASA's space shuttles, or orbiter vehicles, were designed to be re-used. Each has a name, but every mission on which it goes is given a unique number.

The acronym *STS* (Space Transportation System) has been used throughout the shuttle programme. The first nine flights were simply numbered *STS-1* to *STS-9*. A more complicated system was then used, but the original system of *STS* + number has been revived. They do not always follow numerical order, as a mission may be delayed and a later-numbered mission may take its place before it can be rescheduled.

The shuttles
Five space shuttles were built; *Discovery* (first launch 1984), *Atlantis* (1985) and *Endeavour* (1992) remain in service. *Challenger* was destroyed during its 10th mission on 28 January 1986 and *Columbia* was lost on re-entry from its 28th mission on 1 February 2003.

20 July 1969 First Moon landing Neil Armstrong and Edwin E. "Buzz" Aldrin became the first men on the Moon.

18 June 1983 First US woman in space Sally Ride was launched in the space shuttle *Challenger STS-7*, which was the first reusable space vehicle.

18 May 1991 First British astronaut Helen Sharman travelled to the *Mir* space station and spent a week in space.

29 June 1995 First space shuttle/space station docking Space shuttle *Atlantis STS-71* docked with the Soviet space station *Mir*.

26 September 1996 US endurance record On her 5th mission, US astronaut Shannon Lucid completed 188 days aboard the Russian *Mir* station, setting a world record for women. Lucid was born in China. She flew more missions than any woman and at 53 was the oldest female in space.

4 December 1998 International Space Station First stage of the *International Space Station* was established.

2 November 2000 First crew on ISS An American and Russian crew began living aboard the *International Space Station*.

28 April–6 May 2001 First space tourist US millionaire Dennis Tito became the first space tourist, paying $20 million for his Russian *Soyuz TM-32* flight to the *International Space Station*.

15–16 October 2003 First astronaut launched by China Chinese astronaut Lang Liwei made eight orbits of Earth in a *Shenzhou 5* spacecraft. China made its second flight, *Shenzhou 6*, with two astronauts on 12–16 October 2005.

2009 Virgin Galactic plans space tourism flights to over 100 km (62 miles) in *SpaceShipOne*, which carries six passengers at a cost of $200,000 per person.

2010 Last Space shuttle retires *Atlantis*, *Discovery* and *Endeavour* are to be progressively taken out of service and replaced by NASA's *Orion* spacecraft in a programme that will take astronauts back to the Moon and to Mars.

Planet Earth

Under the sea

The damage to coral reefs by global warming, pollution and fishing is threatening to destroy the fragile underwater life of the Earth. Without intervention 70% of the world's coral reefs will have died within 50 years. 2008 was International Year of the Reef – a worldwide campaign to raise awareness about the value and importance of coral reefs and threats to their sustainability.

ROCKS AND MINERALS

Layers of the Earth

The Earth is made up of a number of layers. At the top is the crust – the thinnest layer. Next is the mantle, then the outer and inner cores. The outer core is probably liquid and the inner core solid.

Ocean 3 km (1.9 miles)

Crust 21 km (13 miles)

Mantle 21–2,865 km (13–1,780 miles)

Outer core 2,865–5,125 km (1,780–3,185 miles)

Inner core 5,125–6,371 km (3,185–3,959 miles)

Inside the Earth showing the average depth of its layers

The largest meteorite craters

About 500 meteorites reach Earth every year. Many collision sites have been altered by weather over millions of years, and scientists are unsure whether some craters are actually the craters of extinct volcanoes. Those below are all agreed to be meteorite craters.

1 Vredefort, South Africa 300 km (186 miles) in diameter
2 Sudbury, Ontario, Canada 250 km (155 miles) in diameter
3 Chicxulub, Yucatan, Mexico 170 km (106 miles) in diameter
4 Manicougan, Canada 100 km (62 miles) in diameter
5 Popigai, Russia 100 km (62 miles) in diameter

The 10 degrees of hardness

The Mohs scale, named after German mineralogist Friedrich Mohs (1773–1839), is used for comparing the relative hardness of minerals. Each mineral on the scale can be scratched by the harder ones below it.

Mohs scale No.	Substance	Mohs scale No.	Substance
1	Talc	6	Orthoclase
2	Gypsum	7	Quartz
3	Calcite	8	Topaz
4	Fluorite	9	Corundum
5	Apatite	10	Diamond

Meteor Crater, Arizona

Geological time 2007

CENOZOIC ERA
Quaternary period
Recent/Holocene epoch: 11,000 years ago (y.a.) to present day – modern humans
Pleistocene epoch: 1,800,000 to 11,000 y.a. – humans

Tertiary period
Pliocene epoch: 5,000,000 to 1,800,000 y.a. – ape-like human ancestors
Miocene epoch: 23,000,000 to 5,000,000 y.a. – apes and whales

Oligocene epoch: 38,000,000 to 23,000,000 y.a. – cats and dogs
Eocene epoch: 54,000,000 to 37,000,000 y.a. – grasslands
Palaeocene epoch: 65,000,000 to 54,000,000 y.a. – large mammals

MESOZOIC ERA
Cretaceous period: 146,000,000 to 65,000,000 y.a. – flowering plants; dinosaurs became extinct
Jurassic period: 208,000,000 to 146,000,000 y.a. – birds and mammals
Triassic period: 245,000,000 to 208,000,000 y.a. – dinosaurs and flying reptiles

Uluru

The rock formerly known as Ayers Rock in Northern Territory, Australia, is believed to be the world's largest free-standing rock. It is made of sandstone and is 335 m (1,100 ft) high, 3.6 km (2.2 miles) long and 2 km (1.5 miles) wide. It was originally called after South Australian premier Sir Henry Ayers, but it is now known by the name given to it by local Aborigines, to whom it is sacred.

Rocks

There are three categories of rock – igneous, sedimentary and metamorphic.

● Igneous rocks originate deep in the Earth. They erupt from volcanoes as magma and cool or solidify as they rise to the upper layers. Basalt is an igneous rock and so is granite, a very hard rock often used in building. Pumice stone is a soft igneous rock that is ejected from volcanoes. As it cools, it often fills with so many air bubbles that it floats in water.

● Sedimentary rocks can be formed by deposits in water and occasionally by wind. Sandstone is a common example. Organic sedimentary rocks are formed by living plants and animals – coal comes from plant matter and limestone from the calcium from billions of plants and animals. Chemical sedimentary rocks occur when chemical processes take place and minerals are deposited.

● Metamorphic rocks are igneous or sedimentary rocks that have changed as a result of high temperatures or pressures. Slate used on roofs is a familiar example.

Giant meteorites

Many meteorites land in the sea and in unpopulated areas so they are never seen. The Hoba meteorite, the largest in the world, was found in Namibia in 1920. It measures 2.73 x 2.43 m (9 x 8 ft) and is 82 per cent iron and 16 per cent nickel. It weighs more than 60 tonnes. Second largest is the Tent, found in Greenland in 1894 and now known by its original Eskimo name, Ahnighito. This meteorite weighs about 57.3 tonnes and is on display in the New York Museum of Natural History.

🔍 www.webmineral.com **search**

Minerals

Minerals are naturally occurring substances with a definite chemical composition. Most mineral names end in "ite". Many have a practical use or contain a chemical compound or element that can be extracted and used commercially. Bauxite, for instance, is the main source of aluminium. Gems are minerals that are highly prized for their rarity or appearance, eg diamonds, sapphires, emeralds and rubies.

4,500,000,000 years ago

PALAEOZOIC ERA
Permian period: 286,000,000 to 245,000,000 y.a. – deciduous plants
Carboniferous Pennsylvanian period: 325,000,000 to 286,000,000 y.a. – reptiles
Carboniferous Mississippian period: 360,000,000 to 325,000,000 y.a. – winged insects

Devonian period: 410,000,000 to 360,000,000 y.a. – amphibians
Silurian period: 440,000,000 to 410,000,000 y.a. – land plants and insects
Ordovician period: 500,000,000 to 440,000,000 y.a. – corals and molluscs

Cambrian period: 544,000,000 to 500,000,000 y.a. – fish and shelled creatures

PRECAMBRIAN ERA
Proterozoic period: 2,500,000,000 to 544,000,000 y.a. – earliest fossils; jellyfish

Archaic period: 3,800,000,000 to 2,500,000,000 y.a. – living cells
Hadean period: 4,500,000,000 to 3,800,000,000 y.a. – environment unable to support life; from 4,500,000,000 or earlier – the Earth was formed

LAND FEATURES

Largest deserts

Deserts cover about a third of the world's land area. They range from extremely arid and barren sandy deserts (about four per cent of the total land surface of the globe), through arid (15 per cent) to semi-arid (just under 15 per cent).

Most deserts have features of all these, with one zone merging into the next, so the start and finish of any desert is not exact. Many of the world's largest deserts are broken down by geographers into smaller desert regions – the Australian Desert includes the Gibson, Great Sandy, Great Victoria and Simpson, for example.

1 Sahara, Northern Africa – 9,100,000 sq km (3,514,000 sq miles)

2 Australian, Australia (Includes Gibson, Great Sandy, Great Victoria and Simpson) – 3,400,000 sq km (1,313,000 sq miles)

3 Arabian Peninsula, Southwest Asia (Includes an-Nafud and Rub al Khali) – 2,600,000 sq km (1,004,000 sq miles)

4 Turkestan, Central Asia (Includes Kara-Kum and Kyzylkum) – 1,900,000 sq km (734,000 sq miles)

5 Gobi, Central Asia – 1,300,000 sq km (502,000 sq miles)

6 North American Desert, US/Mexico (Includes Great Basin, Mojave, Sonorah and Chihuahuan) – 1,300,000 sq km (502,000 sq miles)

The Devil's Marbles in the Australian desert

The highest mountain?

The height of mountains is usually measured from sea level. Mauna Kea in Hawaii is only 4,245 m (13,957 ft) above sea level, but it rises a total of 10,203 m (33,474 ft) from the floor of the Pacific Ocean, making its real height 1,353 m (4,439 ft) greater than Mount Everest!

Mount Everest, the world's highest mountain

Highest mountains

People used to think that Kangchenjunga in Nepal/India was the highest mountain. Then the Great Trigonometrical Survey of India measured all the country's land features. The survey was completed in 1852 and showed that Everest (then called Peak XV) was the world's highest mountain.

Everest's height was then reckoned to be 8,840 m (29,002 ft). This has since been adjusted as improved measuring methods have been used. The mountain's name was suggested in 1865 as a tribute to Sir George Everest, the Surveyor General of India, who had led the survey.

Everest (base moved to sea floor) *Mauna Kea*

sea level

sea floor

Highest mountains

1 Everest, Nepal/China – 8,850 m (29,035 ft)

2 K2 (Chogori), Pakistan/China – 8,607m (28,238 ft)

3 Kangchenjunga, Nepal/India – 8,598 m (28,208 ft)

4 Lhotse, Nepal/China – 8,511 m (27,923 ft)

5 Makalu I, Nepal/China – 8,481 m (27,824 ft)

Largest island

An island is a piece of land surrounded by water. Australia is so large it is a continent, not an island; otherwise it would rank first. The smallest island with country status is Pitcairn, at 4.53 sq km (1.75 sq miles).

1 Greenland (Kalaatdlit Nunaat)
– 2,175,600 sq km (840,070 sq miles)
2 New Guinea – 789,900 sq km (312,190 sq miles)
3 Borneo – 751,000 sq km (289,961 sq miles)
4 Madagascar (Malagasy Republic)
– 587,041 sq km (226,674 sq miles)
5 Baffin Island, Canada – 507,451 sq km (195,926 sq miles)
6 Sumatra, Indonesia – 422,200 sq km (163,011 sq miles)
7 Honshu, Japan – 230,092 sq km (88,839 sq miles)
8 Great Britain – 218,041 sq km (84,185 sq miles)
9 Victoria Island, Canada
– 217,290 sq km (83,896 sq miles)
10 Ellesmere Island, Canada
–196,236 sq km (75,767 sq miles)
11 Celebes, Indonesia – 179,000 sq km (69,100 sq miles)
12 South Island, New Zealand
– 151,971 sq km (58,676 sq miles)
13 Java, Indonesia – 126,900 sq km (49,000 sq miles)
14 North Island, New Zealand – 114,489 sq km (44,204 sq miles)
15 Newfoundland, Canada – 108,860 sq km (42,031 sq miles)
16 Cuba – 104,945 sq km (40,519 sq miles)
17 Luzon, Philippines – 104,688 sq km (40,420 sq miles)
18 Iceland – 102,819 sq km (39,699 sq miles)
19 Mindanao, Philippines – 94,630 sq km (36,537 sq miles)
20 Ireland 84,406 sq km (32,589 sq miles)
(Area excludes offshore islands)

Lowest places on land

Sea level is the average height of the sea at a point midway between high and low tides. The shore of the Dead Sea is the lowest exposed ground below sea level. Some land in Antarctica is 2,538 m (8,327 ft) below sea level, but is covered by a 2,100 m (6,890 ft)-deep ice cap.

1 Dead Sea, Israel/Jordan – 400 m (1,312 ft) below sea level
2 Lake Assa, Djibouti – 156 m (511 ft) below sea level
3 Turfan Depression, China – 154 m (505 ft) below sea level
4 Qattâra Depression, Egypt – 133 m (436 ft) below sea level
5 Mangyshlak Peninsula, Kazakhstan – 132 m (433 ft) below sea level

Geysers

Geysers are jets of boiling water and steam that erupt from beneath the ground where water is heated by volcanic activity. The name geyser comes from a hot spring called Geysir at Haukadalur, Iceland. Yellowstone National Park, Wyoming, USA has more geysers than anywhere else. There are 500 active ones including Steamboat, which erupts to a height of 120 m (374 ft), and Old Faithful, which erupts about every 91 minutes.

Geyser erupting in Yellowstone National Park

The seven continents

The Americas are named after the explorer Amerigo Vespucci (1451–1512). Africa was perhaps originally a Berber tribal name. This was adopted by the Romans as the name of their province and later spread to the whole continent.

The name of Europe may simply mean mainland. Asia is probably from the Assyrian, *asu*, meaning sunrise or east. Australis is Latin for southern; Australia, with New Zealand and other islands, is also considered as part of Oceania, a name invented by the geographer Conrad Malte-Brun (1775–1826). Antarctica is Greek for opposite the Arctic. Arctic comes from the Greek for bear, because the region lies under the stars of the Great Bear constellation.

North America
Land area:
24,349,000 sq km
(9,401,000 sq miles)
% of world total: 16.4

Europe
Land area:
10,498,000 sq km
(4,053,000 sq miles)
% of world total: 7.1

Asia
Land area:
43,608,000 sq km
(16,837,000 sq miles)
% of world total: 29.3

Africa
Land area:
30,335,000 sq km
(11,712,000 sq miles)
% of world total: 20.4

Australasia
Land area:
8,923,000 sq km
(3,445,000 sq miles)
% of world total: 6.0

South America
Land area:
17,611,000 sq km
(6,800,000 sq miles)
% of world total: 11.8

Antarctica
Land area: 13,340,000 sq km
(5,151,000 sq miles)
% of world total: 9.0

Niagara Falls

Longest river

The source of the Nile was discovered by Europeans in 1858 when British explorer John Hanning Speke reached Lake Victoria Nyanza, in what is now Burundi. About one hundred years later, in 1953, the source of the Amazon was identified as a stream called Huarco flowing from the Misuie glacier in the Peruvian Andes mountains.

By following the Amazon from its source and up the Rio Pará, it is possible to sail for 6,750 km (4,195 miles), which is slightly more than the length of the Nile. But geographers do not consider the entire route to be part of the Amazon basin, so the Nile is considered the world's longest river.

1 Nile* flows through Burundi, Dem. Rep. of Congo, Egypt, Eritrea, Ethiopia, Kenya, Rwanda, Sudan, Tanzania, Uganda – 6,695 km (4,158 miles)
2 Amazon flows through Peru and Brazil – 6,448 km (4,007 miles)
3 Chang Jiang (Yangtze) flows through China – 6,378 km (3,964 miles)
4 Huang He (Yellow) flows through China – 5,464 km (3,395 miles)
5 Amur flows through China and Russia – 4,415 km (2,744 miles)
* In 2006 the British and New Zealand Ascend the Nile team sailed from the mouth to the source of the river. Using Global Positioning, they measured their journey and came up with a total length 107 km (66.5 miles) longer than the official figure.

Greatest waterfalls

The flow of many waterfalls varies according to the season, and some have been reduced by building dams to harness their power for hydro-electric plants.

The flow of the Boyoma waterfall is equivalent to 17m. litres (36m. gall) a second – enough to fill more than 140,000 baths per second, or enough for every person on Earth to have two baths a day!

1 Boyoma (Stanley), Democratic Republic of Congo – 17,000 m³/sec (22,235 yd³/sec)
2 Khône, Laos † – 11,330 m³/sec (14,819 yd³/sec)
3 Niagara (Horseshoe), Canada – 5,830 m³/sec (7,625 yd³/sec)
4 Grande, Uruguay – 4,500 m³/sec (5,886 yd³/sec)
5 Paulo Afonso, Brazil – 2,800 m³/sec (3,662 yd³/sec)
(Based on volume of water)
† Also the widest waterfall at 10.8 km (6.7 miles)

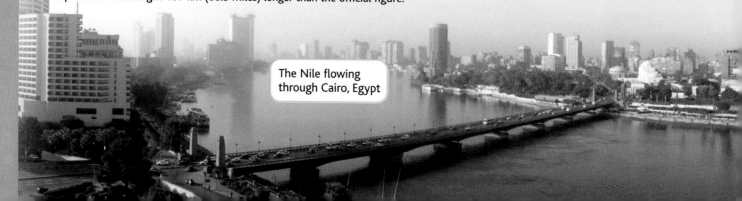

The Nile flowing through Cairo, Egypt

Highest waterfalls

Waterfalls form when a river or stream goes over a drop, often where softer rocks are eroded faster than harder ones. The drop is the distance from top to bottom of the waterfall.

1 Angel Falls, Carrao river, Venezuela – 979 m (3,212 ft)*

2 Tugela Falls, Tugela river, South Africa – 948 m (3,110 ft)

3 Ramnefjellsfossen, Jostedal Glacier, Nesdale, Norway – 800 m (2,625 ft)

4 Mongefossen Falls, Monge river, Mongebekk, Norway – 774 m (2,540 ft)

5 Gocta Cataracta, Cocahuayco river, Peru – 771 m (2,531 ft)

6 Mutarazi Falls, Mutarazi river, Zimbabwe – 762 m (2,499 ft)

7 Yosemite Falls, Yosemite Creek, California, USA – 739 m (2,425 ft)

8 Østre Mardøla Foss, Mardals river, Eikisdal, Norway – 656 m (2,152 ft)

9 Tyssestrengane Falls, Tysso river, Hardanger, Norway – 646 m (2,120 ft)

10 Cuquenán Falls, Arabopo river, Venezuela – 610 m (2,000 ft)

* Longest single drop 807 m (2,648 ft)

The Great Lakes

The Great Lakes are a group of five freshwater lakes in North America on the border between the USA and Canada. Superior is so called because it is higher upstream that the others. Huron takes its name from the name French settlers gave to a local Indian tribe (from *hure*, a boar's head). No one knows where the name Michigan comes from, but Erie and Ontario are both from the Iroquois language. Erie means cat, the animal the tribe used as its symbol. Ontario simply means beautiful lake.

1 Superior, Canada/USA – 82,414 sq km (31,820 sq miles)

2 Huron, Canada/USA – 59,596 sq km (23,010 sq miles)

3 Michigan, USA – 58,016 sq km (22,400 sq miles)

4 Erie, Canada/USA – 25,719 sq km (9,930 sq miles)

5 Ontario, Canada/USA – 19,477 sq km (7,520 sq miles)

Longest glaciers

During the last Ice Age, more than 30 per cent of the Earth's surface was covered by glaciers – frozen rivers of ice that move very slowly. Today, as much as 10 per cent is covered with glaciers.

The Lambert-Fisher Glacier is the longest in the world and was discovered (from the air) in 1956. The longest glacier in North America is the Hubbard Glacier, Alaska, which measures 146 km (91 miles). The longest in Europe is the Aletsch Glacier, Switzerland, at 35 km (22 miles).

1 Lambert-Fisher, Antarctica – 515 km (320 miles)
2 Novaya Zemlya, Russia – 418 km (260 miles)
3 Arctic Institute, Antarctica – 362 km (225 miles)
4 Nimrod-Lennox-King, Antarctica – 290 km (180 miles)
5 Denman, Antarctica – 241 km (150 miles)

Glaciers

Glaciers hold about 75 per cent of the world's fresh water. If all the glaciers melted, the world's sea level would rise about 70 m (230 ft).

Greatest rivers

The volume of water flowing from the mouth of a river varies according to the season. The figures given are highest averages. The outflow of the Amazon would fill almost two million baths every second.

1 Amazon flows into the South Atlantic, Brazil at 219,000 m³/sec (286,441 yd³/sec)
2 Ganges flows into the Bay of Bengal, Bangladesh at 43,900 m³/sec (57,419 yd³/sec)
3 Zaïre (Congo) flows into the South Atlantic, Angola/Congo at 41,800 m³/sec (54,672 yd³/sec)
4 Chang Jiang flows into the Yellow Sea, China at 31,900 m³/sec (41,724 yd³/sec)
5 Orinoco flows into the South Atlantic, Venezuela at 31,900 m³/sec (41,724 yd³/sec)
6 Plata-Paraná-Grande flows into the South Atlantic, Uruguay at 25,700 m³/sec (33,614 yd³/sec)
(Based on rate of discharge at mouth)

Lake fact file

● **Largest lake by volume and area**
The Caspian Sea (Russia, Kazakhstan, Turkmenistan, Azerbaijan and Iran) has a volume of 78,200 cubic km (18,760 cubic miles) and an area of 374,000 sq km (144,402 sq miles), making it the world's largest body of inland water. It would take 400 years for the entire contents of the Caspian to flow over Niagara Falls!

● **Largest freshwater lake by area**
Some geographers think that Lake Michigan and Lake Huron are one lake. They have a combined area of 117,612 sq km (45,410 sq miles) and have a larger area than half the world's countries.

● **Largest freshwater lake by volume and deepest lake**
Lake Baikal, Russia, contains 22,995 cubic km (5,517 cubic miles) of water. It has an average depth of 730 m (2,395 ft) and is 1,741m (5,712 ft) at its deepest point – deep enough to cover more than four Empire State Buildings piled on top of one another.

● **Fastest-shrinking lake**
In 1960, The Aral Sea (Kazakhstan and Uzbekistan) was 64,501 sq km (24,904 sq miles). Since then, feeder rivers have been diverted for irrigation and the lake has shrunk to about 28,000 sq km (10,811 sq miles). It is now in danger of disappearing.

www.geography.learnontheinternet.co.uk   search

Wave height scale

The wave height scale describes the sort of waves that sailors might meet at sea. Wave height varies according to wind speed. High waves can be very dangerous, especially to small boats which can be turned over and even smashed.

0 Glassy – 0.0 m (0.0 ft)
1 Calm – 0.0–0.30 m (0.0–1.0 ft)
2 Rippled – 0.30–0.60 m (1.0–2.0 ft)
3 Choppy – 0.60–1.2 m (2.0–4.0 ft)
4 Very choppy – 1.2–2.4 m (4.0–7.9 ft)
5 Rough – 2.4–4.0 m (8.0–13.0 ft)
6 Very rough – 4.0–6.0 m (13.0–20.0 ft)
7 High – 6–9 m (20.0–30.0 ft)
8 Very high – 9.0–14 m (30.0–45.0 ft)
9 Ultra high –14.0 m+ (45.0 ft+)

Huge waves breaking over a lighthouse in Havana, Cuba during a hurricane

Tsunami

The word tsunami comes from the Japanese *tsu* (meaning port) and *nami* (meaning wave). A tsunami is not a tidal wave, but a powerful surge of moving water caused by an earthquake or volcanic eruption beneath the sea bed.

There may be advance warning signs, such as bubbling water, a roaring noise and a sudden rise in water temperature. Tsunamis are rarely as high as tidal waves. However, powerful ones can cross huge distances, raising the sea level and destroying entire islands and coastal areas in their path. Lisbon, the capital of Portugal, was almost completely destroyed in 1755 by the combined effects of an earthquake, tsunami and fire. The worst recorded tsunami occurred in 2004 in South East Asia.

Animal survivors

Amazingly, few animals died in the tsunami that hit Sri Lanka and other areas in 2004. Elephants, buffalo and tigers, as well as smaller animals, moved to high ground in time. Scientists think that they sensed soundwaves and changes in air pressure in advance of the wave and this gave them time to escape.

Iceberg fact file

An iceberg is a large piece of ice that has broken away from a glacier or ice shelf. In the North Atlantic most came from Greenland glaciers, and in the South Atlantic from Antarctica.

● The word iceberg probably comes from the Dutch *ijsberg*, or ice hill.

● Icebergs float because they are made of fresh water, which is less dense than sea water.

● Seven-eighths of an iceberg is below the surface of the sea, hence the expression "the tip of the iceberg", which means that more is hidden than can be seen.

● The tallest iceberg measured was 168 m (551 ft) high. It was seen in 1958 off Greenland and was as tall as a 50-storey skyscraper.

● Icebergs less than 1 m (3.25 ft) high and 5 m (16.25 ft) wide are known as growlers because of the noise they make.

● Icebergs larger than growlers are called bergy bits; then they are graded small, medium, large or very large. Very large icebergs are those measuring more than 75 m (246 ft) high and 213 m (699 ft) wide.

● One of the biggest icebergs of recent times, known as B-15, broke away from the Ross Ice Shelf, Antarctica, in March 2000. It had an average length of 295 km (183 miles) and width of 37 km (23 miles), making it about the size of Jamaica!

● About 10,000 to 15,000 new icebergs are formed every year. The process is called "calving".

● The air trapped in icebergs is "harvested" and sold for use in drinks. It may be 3,000 years old.

● At least 500 incidents have been recorded of ships striking icebergs. The worst disaster involving an iceberg happened when the *Titanic* struck one on 14 April 1912 and 1,503 people died.

Longest coastlines

The coastline of Canada, including all its islands, is more than six times as long as the distance round the Earth at the Equator (40,076 km [24,902 miles]). Greenland (Kalaalit Nunaat) is not in this list as it is part of Denmark, not a separate country, but its coastline is 44,087 km (27,394 miles) long.

1 Canada – 265,523 km (164,988 miles)

2 USA – 133,312 km (82,836 miles)

3 Russia – 110,310 km (68,543 miles)

4 Indonesia – 95,181 km (59,143 miles)

5 Chile – 78,563 km (48,817 miles)

6 Australia – 66,530 km (41,340miles)

7 Norway – 53,199 km (33,056 miles)

8 Philippines – 33,900 km (21,064 miles)

9 Brazil – 33,379 km (20,741 miles)

10 Finland – 31,119 km (19,336 miles)

11 China 30,017 km (18,652 miles)

12 Japan 29,020 km (18,032 miles)

Deepest oceans and seas

The Pacific Ocean is the deepest ocean. Its greatest depth is 10,924 m (35,837 ft) with an average depth of 4,028 m (13,215 ft). The Indian Ocean is 7,455 m (24,460 ft) at its deepest point and has an average depth of 3,963 m (13,002 ft). The Atlantic Ocean comes next with a greatest depth of 9,219 m (30,246 ft) and an average depth of 3,926 m (12,880 ft).

Giant feather stars live 198 m (650 ft) deep in Cayman Trench, Caribbean.

Deep-sea trenches

There are about 20 deep trenches in the world's oceans. The eight deepest would be deep enough to submerge Mount Everest. The Marianas Trench is the deepest point in the deepest ocean, the Pacific. It was discovered in 1951 and explored in 1960 when Jacques Piccard (Switzerland) and Donald Walsh (USA) descended in their bathyscaphe *Trieste 2* to a depth that has since been calculated as 10,916 m (35,813 ft).

Oceans and seas

Ocean is the term used for the world's sea water, except for landlocked seas such as the Caspian.

More than 70 per cent of the planet's surface is occupied by oceans – the Pacific Ocean alone is more than 25 per cent larger than the planet's entire land area. Smaller divisions of some oceans are separately named as seas.

Pacific Ocean – 166,240,000 sq km (64,185,629 sq miles)

Atlantic Ocean – 86,560,000 sq km (33,421,006 sq miles)

Indian Ocean – 73,430,000 sq km (28,351,484 sq miles)

Arctic Ocean – 13,230,000 sq km (5,108,132 sq miles)

South China Sea – 2,974,600 sq km (1,148,499 sq miles)

Caribbean Sea – 2,753,000 sq km (1,062,939 sq miles)

Mediterranean Sea – 2,510,000 sq km (969,116 sq miles)

Bering Sea – 2,261,000 sq km (872,977 sq miles)

Gulf of Mexico – 1,542,985 sq km (595,749 sq miles)

Sea of Okhotsk – 1,527,570 sq km (589,798 sq miles)

East China Sea – 1,249,150 sq km (482,299 sq miles)

Sea of Japan – 1,012,945 sq km (391,100 sq miles)

Andaman Sea – 797,700 sq km (307,993 sq miles)

Hudson Bay – 730,380 sq km (282,001 sq miles)

Global warming is melting the world's ice shelves. As ice floes shrink and drift apart, polar bears are forced to swim up to 97 km (60 miles) between them in search of prey. Some never make it and drown.

See also
Worst natural disasters: page 47

● During World War II, Lord Mountbatten led a programme to build artificial icebergs to use as aircraft carriers, but the project, codenamed Habbakuk, was abandoned.

● Cruise ship *MS Explorer* struck an iceberg in the Antarctic and sank on 23 November 2007. All 154 passengers and crew were rescued.

www.oceansatlas.org   search

ARCTIC
OCEAN

*Beaufort
Sea*

Greenland

*Baffin
Bay*

*Bering
Sea*

*Gulf of
Alaska*

Rocky Mountains

*Hudson
Bay*

*Labrador
Sea*

NORTH
AMERICA

Climate

Weather and climate are not the
same. Weather is how hot, cold
or wet a place is at a particular time.
Climate is the average weather of an
area over time.

Several things decide the climate of an area, including
how far it is from the Equator, how far from the sea, its
height above sea level and its wind systems. The position
of a place on an area of land and the size of that land
area also affects the climate. Scientists divide the world
into different climate regions: polar and tundra,
temperate, tropical, desert and mountain.

Great
Basin

Mojave
Desert

Sierra Madre

*Gulf of
Mexico*

*Caribbean
Sea*

Warm temperate

These areas have mild winters and
warm to hot summers. There is rain all
year round, but there are plenty of sunny
days. This is an ideal climate for growing
crops such as citrus fruits, grapes and olives.

ATLANTIC
OCEAN

PACIFIC
OCEAN

SOUTH
AMERICA

Andes

Atacama Desert

Patagonian Desert

Climate change

Climates have changed naturally
throughout history. But scientists think
that human activities, such as burning
fossil fuels, are producing greenhouse
gases such as carbon dioxide, and these
are causing global warming. The effects
include ocean currents altering, ice
sheets melting, sea levels rising and
severe weather, such as cyclones
and floods, becoming
more common.

The sea affects
the climate of
coastal regions,
keeping them
warmer than
inland areas in
winter and
cooler in
summer.

Key

- Polar and Tundra
- Cool temperate
- Desert
- Warm temperate
- Tropical
- Mountains

Mountain

The climates of mountain
areas vary according to
altitude. The higher the
mountain, the colder it is. At a
certain point, called the tree
line, trees can no longer grow.
The climate in mountain
areas is usually wetter than in
the lowlands around them.

ARCTIC OCEAN

Barents Sea

Kara Sea

Arctic Circle

Cool temperate

These areas have warm summers and cool winters. In the northern areas the winters can be very cold. Rain falls all year round. Much of this area was once covered with forest.

EUROPE

Kölen

Baltic Sea

Alps

ees

Black Sea

Caucasus

Kirghiz Steppe

Caspian Sea

Kara Kum

Hindu Kush

Zagros Mts

The Gulf

Thar Desert

Tien Shan

Takla Makan

Kunlun Mts

Plateau of Tibet

Himalayas

Altai Mts

Gobi Desert

ASIA

Sea of Okhotsk

Sea of Japan

Polar and tundra

The areas around the North and South Pole are called the Arctic and Antarctic. Both have an average temperature of 0°–10°C (32°–50°F) in summer and as little as -50°C (-58°F) in winter. Few plants can grow. The tundra is land surrounding the Arctic. In summer small plants grow here.

Tropic of Cancer

S a h a r a
D e s e r t

Mediterranean Sea

Red Sea

Arabian Peninsula

Arabian Sea

Bay of Bengal

South China Sea

Philippine Sea

PACIFIC OCEAN

Equator

Ethiopian Highlands

AFRICA

INDIAN OCEAN

Java Sea

Arafura Sea

Coral Sea

Tropic of Capricorn

Namib Desert

Kalahari Desert

Great Sandy Desert

Gibson Desert

Simpson Desert

Great Victoria Desert

AUSTRALIA

Tasman Sea

Southern Alps

Tropical

These areas are hot all year round. In some parts there is heavy rain all year round, too, and that is where rainforests grow. Rainforest plants fruit and flower all year. In other tropical areas, such as savannas and scrubland, there are dry seasons and rainy seasons, when most of the year's rain falls.

Desert

True deserts are very hot – 40°C (104°F) or more – during the day, but cold at night. They are very dry and what little rain there is falls in short sudden bursts and evaporates quickly. Few plants can grow in deserts but some animals manage to survive.

SOUTHERN OCEAN

Antarctic Circle

ANTARCTICA

http://www.wmo.ch   search

The Beaufort scale

The Beaufort scale was introduced in 1806 by British Admiral Sir Francis Beaufort (1774–1857) to describe wind effects on a fully rigged man-of-war ship. It was later extended to describe how winds affect land features such as trees.

The Beaufort scale is divided into values from 0 for calm winds to 12 and above for hurricanes. Forecasters often describe winds by their force number – for example, a force 10 gale. Wind speed can also be measured in knots: 1 knot = 1.85 km/h (1.15 mph).

0 Calm: 0–2 km/h (> 1 mph) Smoke rises vertically; the sea is mirror smooth

1 Light air: 3–6 km/h (1–3 mph) Smoke indicates the direction of the wind

2 Slight breeze: 7–11 km/h (4–7 mph) Wind felt on the face and leaves rustle in trees

3 Gentle breeze: 12–19 km/h (8–12 mph) Wind extends a light flag

4 Moderate breeze: 20–28 km/h (13–18 mph) Loose paper blows around; frequent whitecaps at sea

5 Fresh breeze: 29–38 km/h (19–24 mph) Small trees sway

6 Strong breeze: 39–49 km/h (25–31 mph) Wind whistles in telephone wires; some spray on the sea's surface

7 High wind: 50–61 km/h (32–38 mph) Large trees sway

8 Gale: 62–74 km/h (39–46 mph) Twigs break from trees; long streaks of foam on the sea

9 Strong gale: 75–88 km/h (47–54 mph) Branches break from trees

10 Whole gale: 89–102 km/h (55–63 mph) Trees uprooted; sea takes on a white appearance

11 Storm At a speed of 103–117 km/h (64–72 mph) Widespread damage

12 Hurricane At speeds of more than 118 km/h+ (73 mph+) Structural damage on land; storm waves at sea

A satellite image of Earth shows a hurricane over the Caribbean Sea.

Cloud layers

There are ten types of clouds. Each has a characteristic shape and appears at certain levels in the sky. All types would not appear together as in this diagram.

Altocumulus 2,000–7,000 m (6,562–22,966 ft)

Cirrocumulus 5,000–13,500 m (16,404–44,291 ft)

Cirrus 5,000–13,500 m (16,404–44,291 ft)

Cirrostratus 5,000–13,500 m (16,404–44,291 ft)

Altostratus 2,000–7,000 m (6,562–22,966 ft)

Cumulonimbus 450–2,000 m (1,476–6,562 ft)

Stratus below 450 m (1,476 ft)

Nimbostratus 900–3,000 m (2,953–9,843 ft)

Stratocumulus 450–2,000 m (1,476–6,562 ft)

Cumulus 450–2,000 m (1,476–6,562 ft)

Hottest and coldest

The hottest place where people live is Djibouti, in the Republic of Djibouti, Africa. The average temperature is 30°C (86°F). Next hottest are Timbuktu in Mali and Tirunelevi in India, both 29.3°C (84.7°F). The coldest place where people live is Norilsk, Russia, with an average temperature of -10.9°C (12.38°F). Next coldest is Yakutsk in Russia, at -10.1°C (13.8°F).

World extremes

Windiest place on Earth

Commonwealth Bay, Antarctica, has some consistently high wind speeds, occasionally reaching 320 km/h (200 mph). The highest individual gust of wind measured was 371 km/h (231 mph) at Mt Washington, USA, on 12 April 1934.

Tornado wind speed

Fastest 450 km/h (280 mph) at Wichita Falls, Texas, USA, on 2 April 1958.

Hurricane wind speed

The fastest sustained winds in a hurricane in the USA measured 322 km/h (200 mph), with 338 km/h (210 mph) gusts, on 17–18 August 1969, when Hurricane Camille hit the Mississippi/Alabama coast.

Hottest place on Earth

Dallol in Ethiopia had an average temperature of 34.4°C (94°F) during 1960–66.

Highest shade temperature recorded

Al'Aziziyah, Libyan desert, 57.8°C (136°F) on 13 September 1922. A temperature of 56.6°C (134°F) was recorded at Death Valley, California, USA, on 10 July 1913.

Least sunshine

At the South Pole there is no sunshine for 182 days every year, and at the North Pole the same applies for 176 days.

Driest place

Atacama Desert, Chile, where average annual rainfall is officially nil (also longest drought – 400 years up to 1971). The average rainfall on the Pacific coast of Chile between Arica and Antofagasta is less than 1 mm (0.04 in).

Coldest place

Vostok, Antarctica, -89.2°C (-129°F) on 21 July 1983.

Tornados

Tornadoes, or twisters, are columns of air that spin violently, reaching speeds of over 420 km/h (260 mph). They destroy crops and any houses or vehicles in their path. Tornadoes are rare in the UK, but one struck Kensal Rise, London, on 7 December 2006, damaging houses and cars. In the book and film of *The Wizard of Oz* (1939) Dorothy is carried by a tornado from her Kansas home to the magical land of Oz.

Tools of the trade

Weather forecasters use a range of instruments. Balloons, radar stations and orbiting satellites also provide increasingly accurate weather information, and computer programs are able to make detailed forecasts.

Anemometer

Wind speed is measured by a cup anemometer. This has three or four cups that rotate round a vertical rod. The speed at which the wind spins the cups round is recorded by a counter. A wind vane shows the direction of wind, and an anemograph records the speed on a chart.

Rain gauge

Rain gauges – containers that measure the amount of rain that has fallen – date from ancient China and India. In 1662, British architect Sir Christopher Wren invented a tipping bucket rain gauge, which emptied itself when full.

Thermometer

Galileo invented the thermsocope, a form of thermometer. Later, sealed thermometers using mercury, which expands in a narrow tube as the temperature rises, were developed. Gabriel Fahrenheit's scale dates from 1714, and that of Anders Celsius from 1742. The maximum and minimum thermometer, which records the highest and lowest temperatures reached over a period of time, was invented by James Six at Cambridge in 1780.

A tornado sets down in a field.

www.metoffice.gov.uk   search

Greatest snowfall in 12 months

31,102 mm (1,224 in) at Mt Rainier, Washington, USA, from 19 February 1971 to 18 February 1972. This is an incredible 31 m (102 ft), equivalent to 17 people standing on each other's heads!

Greatest depth of snow

11.46 m (38 ft) at Tamarac, California, USA, in March 1911.

Freak snow storm

In the Sahara Desert, Algeria, 18 February 1979.

Heaviest hailstones

Coffeyville, Kansas, USA, 0.75 kg (1.65 lb), 3 September 1970. The largest hailstone – 17.8 cm (7 in) diameter – fell in Aurora, Nebraska on 22 June 2003.

Most rainfall in 24 hours

Cilaos, La Réunion, 1,870 mm (74 in), 15–16 March, 1952.

Greatest annual rainfall (extreme example)

Cherrapunji, Assam, India, 26,461 mm (1,042 in) between 1 August 1860 and 31 July 1861 – which is close to the length of a tennis court! Also, at the same place, the greatest in one calendar month – 9,300 mm (366 in) – fell in July 1861. That's about the same as five people standing on each other's heads.

Greatest annual rainfall (annual average)

Mawsynram, India, with 11,870 mm (467 in) a year; and Tutunendo, Colombia, 11,770 mm (463 in).

Most rainy days in a year

Mt Waialeale, Kauai, Hawaii, USA, up to 350 days a year. The total rainfall is about 11,684 mm (460 in), which approaches the annual record.

Volcanic eruptions

Santorini
The eruption of the Greek island of Santorini in c1450 BC is believed to have been one of the most powerful ever.

Vesuvius, Italy
On 24 August AD 79 Vesuvius erupted with little warning, engulfing the Roman city of Herculaneum in a mud flow. Nearby Pompeii was buried under a vast layer of pumice and volcanic ash. This preserved the city, including the bodies of many of its inhabitants, until it was excavated by archaeologists in the 19th and 20th centuries. As many as 20,000 people died. Vesuvius erupted again in 1631, killing up to 18,000 people.

Laki, Iceland
Iceland is one of the most volcanically active places on Earth, but the population is small so eruptions seldom cause many deaths. On 11 June 1783 the largest lava flow ever recorded engulfed many villages in a river of lava up to 80 km (50 miles) long and 30 m (98 ft) deep. It released poisonous gases that killed those who managed to escape the lava flow – up to 20,000 people.

Unsen, Japan
On 1 April 1793 the volcanic island of Unsen, or Unzen, completely disappeared, killing all 53,000 inhabitants.

Tambora, Indonesia
On the island of Sumbawa the eruption of Tambora between 5 and 12 April 1815 killed about 10,000 islanders immediately. A further 82,000 died later from disease and famine. This made it the worst-ever eruption for loss of human life.

Krakatoa, Sumatra/Java
The uninhabited island of Krakatoa exploded on 27 August 1883 with what may have been the biggest bang ever heard by humans. People heard it up to 4,800 km (2,980 miles) away!

Mont Pelée, Martinique
Mont Pelée began to erupt in April 1902, after lying dormant for centuries. The 30,000 residents of the main city, St Pierre, were told that they were not in danger, so stayed in their homes. They were there on 8 May when the volcano burst apart and showered the port with molten lava, ash and gas, destroying all buildings and killing as many as 40,000 people.

Nevado del Ruiz, Colombia
In 1985 this Andean volcano gave warning signs that it was about to erupt, but the local people were not evacuated soon enough. On 13 November the hot steam, rocks and ash ejected from Nevado del Ruiz melted its icecap, causing a mudslide. This completely engulfed the town of Armero, killing 22,940 people.

Earthquake detector
Chinese astronomer Chan Heng (AD 78–139) invented an earthquake detector made of a vase adorned with dragons' heads and surrounded by metal frogs. In each of the dragons' jaws was a carefully balanced ball. When the first tremors of an earthquake made the device vibrate, the balls fell into the frogs' mouths, making a noise to warn of the coming danger.

Mount St Helens erupting in 1980

Avalanche!
An avalanche caused by the eruption of the Mount St Helens volcano, Washington, USA, on 18 May 1980, was reckoned to have travelled at 400 km/h (249 mph).

A volcano erupts on Réunion Island in the Indian Ocean. (Inset) Lava pouring from an erupting volcano

www.earthquake.usgs.gov/4kids   **search**

The Richter scale

Seismic waves are vibrations from earthquakes that travel through the Earth. Sensitive instruments called seismographs can record the waves, even at great distances, and calculate their strength and location.

The Richter scale indicates the magnitude or strength of an earthquake based on the size of the seismic waves (the distance the ground moves). The biggest earthquake (9 on the Richter scale) is a billion times greater than the smallest.

0 Detected by sensitive seismographs (some can detect magnitudes of less than zero!)

1 Detected by instruments

2 Lowest felt by humans

3 Slight vibration; more than 100,000 a year around the world

4 Up to 15,000 a year; at 4.5, would be detected by seismographs worldwide, but cause little damage

5 3,000 a year; the 1960 earthquake in Agadir, Morocco was 5.6

6 100 a year worldwide

7 20 a year; the 1995 earthquake in Kobe, Japan was 7.2

8 Major destructive earthquakes; average two a year; the 1904 San Francisco earthquake was probably 8.25

9 No quake higher than 8.9 has been recorded, but 9.0 or even higher is theoretically possible

Earthquake

Earthquakes are movements of the Earth's surface, often as a result of a fault, or fracture, in the crust. They happen more often in some parts of the world than others. In heavily populated areas, they cause great damage to buildings and loss of life.

Worst ever
An earthquake affecting the Middle East and North Africa on 20 May 1202 may have been the worst in human history. Up to 1,000,000 people were killed, 110,000 in Cairo, Egypt alone.

Most powerful
The worst earthquake affecting an inhabited area was in Assam, India on 12 June 1897. It is reckoned to have reached 8.7, killing about 1,500. The Colombia/Ecuador earthquake of 31 January 1906 was 8.9 on the Richter scale. Fortunately, it was 300 km (200 miles) off the coast, and so resulted in fewer than 1,000 deaths on land.

Worst modern earthquakes
An earthquake in Tang-shan, China, on 28 July 1976, killed 242,419. The Kashmir quake of 8 October 2005 officially killed 87,350 people, but it may have been more than 100,000.

Longest-lasting
Most earthquakes last only a minute or two, but the Alaska earthquake of 27 March 1964 continued for at least five minutes and registered 8.6 on the Richter scale. It killed only 131 people but caused more than $450 million (£162 million) worth of damage.

Worst natural disasters

Drought
Serious droughts kill people and livestock and destroy crops. The drought in Australia in 1982 cost £3.5 billion ($6 billion), and one in Spain in 1995 cost £3 billion ($4.7 billion).

Flood
Floods caused by China's Huang He, or Yellow River, were first recorded in 2297 BC. The river has flooded at least 1,500 times since. In 1887 floods killed between 1.5 and 7 million people, making it the worst flood ever.

Tsunami
On 26 December 2004 a tsunami created by an undersea earthquake caused catastrophic floods in Indonesia, Sri Lanka, Myanmar, the Maldives, Malaysia, India and parts of Africa. More than 283,100 people died.

Cyclone
The worst cyclone of the 21st century has been Cyclone Nargis (2008) which killed an estimated 140,000 in Myanmar (Burma), with more than 2.5 million more gravely effected.

Life
Sciences

On the edge

The rare Malagasy rainbow frog, found off Madagascar, is one of the 100 creatures on the 2008 EDGE – Evolutionarily Distinct and Globally Endangered – list. Its striking colours make it popular in the pet trade – a significant threat to this critically endangered species.

Top food plants

Every year the people of the world eat more than 2.2 billion tonnes of cereals, 903 million tonnes of vegetables and 526 million tonnes of fruit. These figures come from the Food and Agriculture Organization of the United Nations, or FAO, which is based in Rome. The aim of the FAO is to help people around the world grow more food and eat a better diet.

Sugar cane 1,392,365,323 tonnes per annum
Maize 695,228,280 tonnes p.a.
Rice 634,605,733 tonnes p.a.
Wheat 605,945,825 tonnes p.a.
Potatoes 315,100,319 tonnes p.a.
Sugar beet 256,406,926 tonnes p.a.
Cassava 226,337,396 tonnes p.a.
Soybeans 221,500,938 tonnes p.a.
Barley 138,642,560 tonnes p.a.
Tomatoes 125,543,475 tonnes p.a.
Sweet potatoes 123,509,771 tonnes p.a.
Watermelons 100,602,392 tonnes p.a.
Bananas 70,756,347 tonnes p.a.
Cabbages 68,991,380 tonnes p.a.
Grapes 68,952,793 tonnes p.a.
Oranges 64,795,383 tonnes p.a.
Apples 63,804,534 tonnes p.a.
Onions 61,636,915 tonnes p.a.
Sorghum 56,485,280 tonnes p.a.
Coconuts 55,324,323 tonnes p.a.

A woman going to work in rice fields in Vietnam

American plants

As many as 30 per cent of the world's most useful plants originally came from North, Central and South America. Early European explorers discovered the plants while on their travels and took them back home to grow.

This was not always easy. Pineapples were so difficult and expensive to cultivate in Europe that they became a symbol of wealth – carved stone pineapples are often seen on the gateposts of many grand houses.

US plants

Here are some of the plants that originally came from America – avocado, beans (kidney, French, etc), cashew nut, cassava, chilli pepper, cocoa, corn, cranberry, loganberry, peanut, pecan, pineapple, potato, pumpkin, quinine, rubber, squash/gourd, sunflower, tobacco, tomato, vanilla

avocado

chilli pepper

peanut

tomato

squash

World forests

Forests cover 29.6 per cent of Earth's land and almost a quarter of these are in Russia. There are three main types of forest which grow in particular climates in different parts of the world.

● Tropical forests or rainforests grow near the Equator where it is always hot and wet. Here, temperatures are about 20–25°C (68–77°F) and there is more than 200 cm (79 in) of rain a year.

● Temperate forests grow in places that have hot summers and cold winters. The summers can be as hot as 30°C (86°F) and winters as cold as -30°C (-22°F). Average rainfall is about 75–150 cm (30–59 in) a year. Many trees are deciduous (drop their leaves in autumn).

● Boreal or taiga forests grow in Russia, Canada and elsewhere in the far north. Winters are long and very cold. There is rainfall of 40–100 cm (16–39 in) a year, but most falls as snow. Most trees are evergreen conifers (cone-producing trees with needle-like leaves).

Important crops

These are the most important crops grown for uses other than food.

Cotton (clothing, household items) 72,008,070 tonnes p.a.
Rubber (tyres, shoes, balls, erasers) 9,918,744 tonnes p.a.
Tobacco (cigarettes, cigars) 6,719,314 tonnes p.a.
Jute (sacks, rope) 3,110,950 tonnes p.a.

Dangerous plants

● Potatoes are safe to eat when cooked, but the stems and leaves of the plants contain a poison called solanine. If potatoes turn green, they may also contain solanine.

● Ricin is extracted from the seeds of the castor oil plant and is more poisonous than cyanide or snake venom. Even minute doses of ricin can be fatal.

● Opium is extracted from the juice of a poppy and contains morphine. Small quantities of both are used legally as painkillers and illegally as drugs. Both can easily cause death.

● The death cap is a highly poisonous mushroom. It is responsible for almost 90 per cent of deaths from eating fungi. The poison causes severe diarrhoea and vomiting.

● Curare is extracted from the bark of certain trees and is used by South American Indian tribes to tip their poison arrows when they go hunting.

● Deadly nightshade is also known as belladonna. It contains a poison called atropine. Less than 10 milligrams (0.0004 oz) could kill a child.

● Nicotine is a yellow oily liquid found in tobacco. About 50 milligrams (0.002 oz) of nicotine would kill an adult within minutes.

● The leaves of the purple foxglove contain digitalis and eating just a few can be fatal. Digitalis is used in tiny doses to treat people suffering from heart disease.

Purple foxglove

Children investigating a Rafflesia flower

Largest and smelliest flower

The flower of the rafflesia, or stinking corpse lily, measures almost 1 m (3.3 ft) across and weighs 11 kg (24 lb). It is one of the world's smelliest flowers, with an odour like rotting flesh. The smell attracts flies, which pollinate the plant.

Record-breaking plants

● **Tallest tree**
The world's tallest tree is called the Stratosphere Giant. It grows in the Rockefeller Forest, Humboldt Redwoods State Park, California. At 112.32 m (369 ft), this redwood is almost three times the height of the Statue of Liberty in New York.

● **Biggest living thing**
The General Sherman giant sequoia in Sequoia National Park, California, USA, is the world's largest living thing. It is 83.8 m (275 ft) tall and measures 2.53 m (8.3 ft) round its mighty trunk. Including its huge root system, the tree weighs about 2,000 tonnes.

● **Oldest trees**
The bristlecone pines in California and Nevada, USA, are almost 5,000 years old and were long believed to be the oldest trees. Latest research suggests that creosote bushes in the USA's Mojave Desert may be even older – some of these plants began life nearly 12,000 years ago.

● **Smallest flowering plant**
Wolffia, a kind of duckweed, is just 0.6 mm (0.024 in) long and weighs about as much as two grains of salt. Its seeds are also the tiniest known – they weigh only 70 micrograms (0.0000025 oz), as much as a single grain of salt.

www.fao.org   search

Grouping living things

Living things are organized by scientists into five groups called kingdoms. These are: Animals (Animalia); Algae and protozoans (Protoctista); Bacteria (Prokaryotae); Mushrooms, moulds and lichens (Fungi); Plants (Plantae).

The animal kingdom alone has thousands of different species. A species is a type of animal, and animals of the same species can breed successfully with each other. Similar species are grouped in a genus. Genera are grouped into families, families into orders, right up to the level of phylum. The phylum chordata contains all vertebrate animals – animals with a backbone. Here's how a human and a giant panda are classified.

	Human	**Giant panda**
Phylum	Chordata	Chordata
Class	Mammalia	Mammalia
Order	Primates	Carnivores
Family	Hominidae	Ursidae
Genus	*Homo*	*Ailuropoda*
Species	*sapiens*	*melanoleuca*

Zoo shopping list

Shopping to feed 650 different species of animals is hard work, but that is the task of keepers at London Zoo. Below is the zoo's basic shopping list for a year.

Hay 47 tonnes
Bananas 29 tonnes
Apples 29 tonnes
Straw 28 tonnes
Clover 26 tonnes
Fish 19 tonnes
Food pellets 18 tonnes
Carrots 13 tonnes
Meat 9 tonnes

Oranges 4.5 tonnes
Grapes 4 tonnes
Potatoes 3.1 tonnes
Tomatoes 2.78 tonnes
Honey 0.25 tonnes
Eggs 38,000 (number)
Lettuces 15,860 (number)
Cabbages 8,320 (number)
Milk 975 litres (2,060 pt)

Animal species

Below is a list of the animals we know about. No one knows exactly how many species there may be altogether. New species are always being found and there may be tens of millions not yet discovered.

Some experts think there may be millions of species of insects and at least a million species of deep-sea fish that no one has ever seen. About half of all known creatures and plants live in tropical rainforests. In a study of just 19 trees in a tropical rainforest, 1,200 beetle species were found. About 80 per cent of these had not been seen before.

- **Arachnids** 75,500 (spiders, scorpions, etc)
- **Molluscs** 70,000 (snails, clams, etc)
- **Crustaceans** 40,000 (shrimps, crabs, etc)
- **Fish** 29,300
- **Nematodes** 20,000 (unsegmented worms)
- **Flatworms** 17,500
- **Segmented worms** 12,000
- **Sponges** 10,000
- **Birds** 9,934
- **Jellyfish, coral, etc** 9,000
- **Reptiles** 8,240
- **Starfish** 6,000
- **Amphibians** 5,918
- **Mammals** 5,416

Insects 950,000

Life on Earth — 3,900 million years ago

The first simple life forms began to appear on Earth almost four billion years ago. More familiar animals appeared about 500 million years ago, and humans only within the past two million. We know a little about extinct creatures and early humans from fossil remains found in rocks from each period.

3,900–2,500 million years ago
Archaean period – the earliest marine life form (blue-green algae)

2,500–540 million years ago
Proterozoic period – the first many-celled organisms evolve

540–490 million years ago
Cambrian period – the first fossils of animals with shells and skeletons

490–443 million years ago
Ordovician period – molluscs, some corals and fishlike vertebrates

443–417 million years ago
Silurian period – fish develop jaws; first sharks

417–354 million years ago
Devonian period – fish dominant; amphibians (the first land animals) evolve

354–290 million years ago
Carboniferous period – insects; first reptiles

290–248 million years ago
Permian period – insects evolve into modern types; reptiles evolve

248–206 million years ago
Triassic period – early dinosaurs; marine reptiles

How fast?

Most of the creatures in this list can keep up these speeds for only a short time – less than an hour. The peregrine falcon achieves its speed as it dives through the air to catch prey, not in level flight.

Peregrine falcon (diving speed) 298 km/h (185 mph)

Spine-tailed swift 171 km/h (106 mph)

Eider duck 113 km/h (70 mph)

Sailfish (fastest fish) 110 km/h (68 mph)

Cheetah (fastest on land) 105 km/h (65 mph)

Pronghorn antelope 89 km/h (55 mph)

Racing pigeon 80 km/h (50 mph)

Lion (charging) 80 km/h (50 mph)

Brown hare 72 km/h (45 mph)

Ostrich (fastest flightless bird) 72 km/h (45 mph)

Blue shark 69 km/h (43 mph)

Horse 69 km/h (43 mph)

Greyhound 68 km/h (42 mph)

Killer whale 56 km/h (35 mph)

Death's head hawkmoth (fastest-flying insect) 53 km/h (33 mph)

Guano bat (fastest-flying mammal) 51 km/h (32 mph)

Skipper butterfly 48 km/h (30 mph)

California sea lion 40 km/h (25 mph)

Dolphin 40 km/h (25 mph)

Fastest man over 100 m (328 ft) 37km/h (23 mph)

Peregrine falcon

Oldest creature?

On 23 March 2006 a giant tortoise called Adwayita died at the Alipore Zoo, Kolkata (Calcutta). He was brought to the zoo in the 1860s from the estate of Lord Robert Clive. He may even have been up to 250 years old when he died.

How long do they live?

Who would have thought that a sea anemone could live for 80 years? All these figures are the longest ever recorded. Most of these animals have much shorter lives.

Marine clam 200
Giant tortoise 150
Human 122
Killer whale 90
Sea anemone 80
Asiatic elephant 78
American alligator 66
Blue macaw 64
Horse 62
Chimpanzee 56

Hippopotamus 54
Slow-worm 54
Beaver 50
Bactrian camel 50
Grizzly bear 50
Blue whale 45
Boa constrictor 40
Domestic cat 34
Lion 30
Pig 27

Common rabbit 18
Queen ant 18
Giant centipede 10
Millipede 7
House mouse 6
Bedbug 6 months
Common housefly (male) 2 weeks

A mouse can live for up to six years

2000s

206–144 million years ago
Jurassic period – reptiles dominate land, sea and air; *Archaeopteryx* (first bird) appears; first mammals

144–65 million years ago
Cretaceous period – dinosaurs become extinct; snakes and lizards appear

65–55 million years ago
Palaeocene period – first large land mammals

55–34 million years ago
Eocene period – modern land mammals and whales appear

34–24 million years ago
Oligocene period – modern mammals dominant

24–5 million years ago
Miocene period – modern mammals eg primates; birds

5–1.8 million years ago
Pliocene period – human-like apes appear

1.8–10,000 million years ago
Pleistocene period – humans appear

10,000 million years ago to present
Holocene period – human civilization

🔍 http://animaldiversity.ummz.umich.edu   search

Types of mammal

A mammal is a warm-blooded vertebrate (animal with a backbone) with some hair on its body. Female mammals feed their young on milk from their mammary glands. Most mammals give birth to live young which develop inside the mother's body, but echidnas and the platypus lay eggs.

Marsupial mammals such as kangaroos give birth to live young, but they are very small and weak. They finish their development in a pouch on the mother's body. There are 21 main groups, or orders, of mammals. Listed below are the names of the main mammal groups, examples of the animals and the approximate number of known species. Common names are given where possible.

Rodents Beavers, squirrels, mice, rats, porcupines, voles, guinea pigs, chinchillas 2,052

Chiroptera Bats 977

Insectivores Shrews, moles, hedgehogs, tenrecs 440

Marsupials Opossums, koalas, bandicoots, kangaroos, wallabies, numbat 292

Primates Lemurs, lorises, tarsiers, marmosets, monkeys, gibbons, apes, humans 270

Carnivores Dogs, foxes, wolves, cats, bears, hyenas, raccoons, civets, mongooses, weasels, pandas 249

Even-toed ungulates Pigs, peccaries, giraffe, okapi, hippopotamuses, deer, camels, llamas, antelopes, cattle 225

Cetacea Whales, dolphins, porpoises 83

Lagomorphia Rabbits, hares, pikas 80

Pinnipedia Seals, sea-lions, walruses 34

Edentates Anteaters, sloths, armadillos 29

Odd-toed ungulates Horses, asses, zebras, rhinos, tapirs 19

Scandentia Tree shrews 19

Macroscelidea Elephant-shrews 15

Monotremes Duck-billed platypus, echidnas 5

Hyracoidea Hyraxes 8

Pholidota Pangolins 7

Sirenia Manatees, dugong 4

Proboscidea Elephants 3

Dermoptera Flying lemurs 2

Tubulidentata Aardvark 1

Big babies

The African elephant has the longest pregnancy of any mammal. She carries her baby for an average of 660 days. When the baby is born it weighs 90–120 kg (198–265 lb). A baby blue whale is even bigger. It weighs 2,000 kg (4,409 lb) and is 7 m (23 ft) long. It puts on weight at the astonishing rate of 90 kg (198 lb) a day.

African elephant

Biggest and smallest

The following are the biggest land mammals according to weight:

African elephant 7,000 kg (14,432 lb)
White rhinoceros 3,600 kg (7,937 lb)
Hippopotamus 2,500 kg (5,512 lb)
Giraffe 1,600 kg (3,527 lb)
American bison 1,000 kg (2,205 lb)
Arabian camel (dromedary) 690 kg (1,521 lb)
Polar bear 600 kg (1,521 lb)

The following are the smallest land mammals, according to length:

Kitti's hog-nosed bat 2.9 cm (1.1 in)
Pygmy shrew 3.6 cm (1.4 in)
Pipistrelle bat 4.0 cm (1.6 in)
Little brown bat 4.0 cm (1.6 in)
Masked shrew 4.5 cm (1.8 in)
Southern blossom bat 5.0 cm (2.0 in)
Harvest mouse 5.8 cm (2.3 in)

Big cats

Big cats like lions are perhaps the most powerful of all mammal predators. These measurements are from the nose to the tip of the tail. The length of tail varies – a leopard's tail can be as long as 110 cm (43 in) and a jaguar's tail as short as 45 cm (18 in).

Tiger (Asia) 330 cm (130 in)
Leopard (Asia, Africa) 320 cm (126 in)
Lion (Africa, Asia) 280 cm (110 in)
Jaguar (North, Central and South America) 271 cm (107 in)
Mountain lion (North, Central and South America) 245 cm (96 in)
Snow leopard (Asia) 240 cm (94 in)
Cheetah (Africa, Asia) 220 cm (87 in)
Clouded leopard (Asia) 197 cm (75 in)

Bears of the world

Scientists have long argued about whether the giant panda should be grouped with the raccoon family or the bears. DNA tests have now proved that it belongs with the bears. The koala, often called koala bear, is actually a marsupial not a bear.

Polar bear (Arctic) Length up to 257cm (101 in); weight 200–800 kg (440–1,760 lb)

Brown (grizzly) bear (North America, Europe, Asia) Length up to 290 cm (114 in); weight 136–390 kg (300–860 lb)

American black bear (North America) Length 127–191 cm (50–75 in); weight 60–300 kg (130–660 lb)

Asiatic black bear (Southern Asia) Length 127–188 cm (50–74 in); weight 100–200 kg (220–440 lb)

Sloth bear (Asia) Length 152–191 cm (60–75 in); weight 80–140 kg (175–310 lb)

Giant panda (China) Length 122–152 cm (48–60 in); weight up to 125 kg (275 lb)

Spectacled bear (South America) Length 152–183 cm (60–72 in); weight 70–113 kg (150–250 lb)

Sun bear (Asia) Length 122–152 cm (48–60 in); weight 27–65 kg (60–145 lb)

Western lowland gorilla

Champion divers

Lots of mammals can dive underwater, including humans, but whales are the champions. All have to hold their breath. These are average dives.

Northern bottlenose whale 120 mins

Sperm whale 112 mins

Greenland whale 60 mins

Seal 22 mins

Beaver 20 mins

Dugong 16 mins

Hippopotamus 15 mins

Porpoise 15 mins

Muskrat 12 mins

Duck-billed platypus 10 mins

Sea otter 5 mins

Human pearl diver 2.5 mins

Human 1 min

Intelligence

Edward O. Wilson, professor of Zoology at Harvard, researched the intelligence of mammals. He defined intelligence on the basis of how fast and how well an animal can learn a wide range of tasks. He also took into account the size of the animal's brain compared with its body. His top ten most intelligent mammals, in order are: human, chimpanzee, gorilla, orang-utan, baboon, gibbon, monkey, small-toothed whale, dolphin and elephant.

Monkeys and apes

Monkeys and apes (and humans) belong to the group of mammals called primates. There are 256 known species of primate. The smallest is the pygmy mouse lemur, which weighs only 30 g (1 oz). The largest is the gorilla, which weighs 220 kg (485 lb). The human comes next at 77 kg (170 lb).

Siberian tiger cubs in the snow

Marine mammals

The biggest creatures in the sea are whales, which are mammals not fish. The blue whale is the largest creature that has ever lived. Whales spend all their lives in the sea, but there are other mammals that spend most of their time in water and some time on land. These include seals, sea lions and otters.

Smallest marine mammals

● The marine otter, which lives off the western coast of South America, is the smallest marine mammal. It weighs up to 4.5 kg (10 lb) and is about 1.15 m (3.77 ft) long. The sea otter of North American coasts is slightly larger.

● Small dolphins include Hector's dolphin, which lives off New Zealand. It is rarely more than 1.5 m (3.77 ft) long and 57.2 kg (126 lb) in weight.

Biggest marine mammals

● The blue whale is 33.5 m (110 ft) long and weighs 130.0 tonnes

● The fin whale is 25.0 m (82 ft) long and weighs 45.0 tonnes

● The right whale is 17.5 m (57.4 ft) long and weighs 40.0 tonnes

● The sperm whale is 18.0 m (59 ft) long and weighs 36.0 tonnes

Blue whales can be as long as three buses

Top food fish

Fish and shellfish are popular foods worldwide. Nowadays, more is specially reared by aquaculture (fish farms) than by capture (using traditional fishing lines and nets).

Type of fish	Total catch in 2005 (tonnes)
Herrings, sardines, anchovies	22,404,769
Carps, barbels, cyprinid	20,190,081
Cod, hake, haddock	8,973,067
Tunas, bonitos, billfish	6,266,037
Shrimps, prawns	6,091,869
Clams, cockles, arkshell	4,881,556
Oysters	4,781,545
Squid, cuttlefish, octopus	3,892,161
Salmon, trouts, smelts	3,017,354
Tilapias, cichlids	2,778,932
Top 10 total	*83,277,371*
Aquaculture	*141,403,138*
Capture	*93,253,346*
World total caught for food	*234,656,484*

The most dangerous fish is the great white shark

Danger in the water

Most creatures living in the world's oceans and rivers are harmless to people, but there are a few that can be very dangerous if you encounter or provoke them.

● The tiny candiru fish lives in South American rivers. It can enter your body and kill you unless it is surgically removed.

● Cone-shells, found in the South Pacific and Indian Oceans, have poisonous barbs that cause paralysis and occasionally death if you touch them. The geographer cone is probably the most dangerous of all.

● Freshwater electric eels live in South America and are the most powerful of all the electric eels. They can release up to 650 volts, which is enough to kill a person. Fortunately, this rarely happens.

● Certain parts of the Japanese puffer fish, also known as the maki-maki or deadly death puffer fish, contain a powerful nerve poison that can kill you if you eat it. There is no known antidote. Despite the danger, puffer fish are eaten in Japan, where they are a very expensive delicacy. People are specially trained to prepare them because eating the wrong part causes death in about 60 per cent of cases. About 50 people a year in Japan die after eating incorrectly prepared puffers.

● Several species of octopus are dangerous. The sting of the

Big fish

Whale sharks are probably the biggest fish in the world. They are usually up to 12 m (39 ft) long – though one caught off Thailand in 1919 was reckoned to be 18 m (59 ft) long.

Whale sharks eat only plankton – tiny plants and animals that float in water. Basking sharks also eat plankton, but most other big fish hunt.

Whale shark 21,000 kg (46,297 lb)
Basking shark 14,515 kg (32,000 lb)
Great white shark 3,314 kg (7,306 lb)
Giant manta 3,000 kg (6,614 lb)
Beluga 2,072 kg (4,568 lb)
Sharptail mola 2,000 kg (4,409 lb)
Ocean sunfish 2,000 kg (4,409 lb)

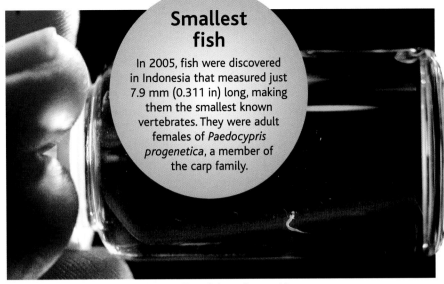

Smallest fish

In 2005, fish were discovered in Indonesia that measured just 7.9 mm (0.311 in) long, making them the smallest known vertebrates. They were adult females of *Paedocypris progenetica*, a member of the carp family.

Paedocypris progenetica is the smallest fish in the world

Giant japanese spider crabs

Deep sea divers

● Emperor penguins sometimes dive to depths of 265 m (870 ft).

● In 1987 a leatherback turtle fitted with a depth-gauge reached a depth of 1,200 m (3,937 ft).

Leatherback turtle

● Sperm whales regularly dive to 1,200 m (3,937 ft) and experts think they may sometimes go down to twice this depth.

● Fish called brotulids are the deepest-living vertebrate animals. They have been found in deep-sea trenches at 8,300 m (27,230 ft) – that is almost as deep as Mount Everest is high.

Amazing sea creatures

Most eggs
The black marlin fish lays as many as 226 million eggs.

Largest crustacean
The giant spider crab's body measures up to 30.5–35.6 cm (12–14 in) across and it has a claw span of 2.4–2.7 m (7.8–8.8 ft).

Smallest crustacean
Pea crabs measure only about 64 mm (2.5 in) across the shell.

Heaviest crustacean
An Atlantic lobster weighing 19.25 kg (42.44 lb) was caught off Virginia, USA in 1934. It was nicknamed Mike.

Heaviest mollusc
A giant squid caught in 1878 had tentacles 10.7 m (35 ft) long and weighed about 1,814 kg (4,000 lb).

Largest clam
A clam known as *Tridacna derasa* measures up to 124 cm (49 in) across and weighs 263 kg (580 lb).

Largest gastropod
The gastropod group includes snails. The largest gastropod is the trumpet or baler conch. It lives off Australian coasts and weighs up to 18 kg (40 lb). Its shell measures 77 cm (30 in) long and 101 cm (40 in) round.

Largest jellyfish
The lion's mane jellyfish (*Cyanea arctica*) is up to 2.3 m (7.5 ft) long, with tentacles that add an extra 37 m (121 ft).

Largest sponge
The barrel sponge of the Caribbean is up to 1.8–2.4 m (6–8 ft) tall.

blue-ringed octopus, which lives in the Australian seas, can cause paralysis and even death.

● Piranha are small but incredibly ferocious fish which live in rivers in parts of South America. They hunt in groups, attacking any creatures in the water – including humans unlucky enough to encounter them. They strip their prey to the bone in minutes.

● Sea wasps, also known as box jellyfish, live off the coast of Australia. They have tentacles up to 9 m (29 ft) long and venom as powerful as that of a cobra. Australian lifeguards often wear nylon tights to protect them against stings, which can cause death within three minutes.

● Most sharks are harmless but a few species have been known to attack people. The great white, tiger and bull shark are the most dangerous. Of 631 attacks on humans recorded from 1580 to 2007, 135 resulted in death.

● Stonefish lie on the seabed where they resemble rocks encrusted with seaweed. Unsuspecting swimmers who tread on the fish receive a very painful sting from their spines. In severe cases, victims may die.

www.fishbase.org   search

Bird fact file

Birds are vertebrate animals with two legs and front limbs that have become adapted to form wings. All birds have feathers and most, but not all, can fly. Birds reproduce by laying eggs from which their young hatch.

Smallest bird
The smallest bird is the bee hummingbird, which is 5.7 cm (2.2 in) long and weighs 1.6 g (0.056 oz).

Longest beak
The bird with the longest beak in relation to its body is the sword-billed hummingbird – its beak is 10.5 cm (4.1 in) long and its body is 13.5 cm (5.3 in) long. The bird with the longest beak of all is the Australian pelican. Its beak is 47 cm (18.5 in) long.

Highest flyer
Ruppell's griffon is the highest-flying bird. In 1973 one was recorded at 11,278 m (37,000 ft) above sea level – 2,427 m (7,963 ft) higher than Mt Everest – after colliding with an airliner.

Longest migration
The Arctic tern migrates further than any other bird. Every year it flies from the Arctic to Antarctica and back again – a round trip of at least 40,000 km (25,000 miles).

Arctic tern

Largest flying birds
- **Great bustard**: wingspan 2.7 m (9 ft); weight 20.9 kg (46 lb)
- **Trumpeter swan**: wingspan 3.4 m (11 ft); weight 16.8 kg (37 lb)
- **Mute swan**: wingspan 3.1 m (10 ft); weight 16.3 kg (36 lb)
- **Albatross**: wingspan 3.7 m (12 ft); weight 15.8 kg (34.8 lb)
- **Whooper swan**: wingspan 3.1 m (10 ft); weight 15.8 kg (34.8 lb)

One and only
The poor-will of North America is the only bird that hibernates. In autumn the bird dozes off in a rock crevice or an old nest and sleeps through the winter. Its heart rate and breathing slow down and its body temperature drops from its normal 41°C (105°F) down to 13°C (55.4°F) so it uses as little energy as possible.

All about feathers

The body of a feather is called its vane, the shaft is known as the rachis and the individual tufts are known as barbs. The barbs have hooks called barbules that cling to the others like Velcro to make a smooth surface.

Peacock feather

- Feathers are made of keratin, the same material as our hair and nails.

- Birds shed their feathers at intervals and grow new ones. This process is called moulting. Feathers fall in a set pattern and in pairs, one from each side, so that the bird's flight is not unbalanced. Birds that do not fly, such as penguins, moult all over.

- A songbird such as a sparrow has about 3,000 feathers in the summer but as many as 3,500 in the winter to keep it warm. A swan may have 25,216 or more – up to 20,000 of them on its head and neck. The bird with the fewest feathers is the ruby-throated hummingbird with only 940.

- Pens for writing were once made from the quills, or feathers, of geese, turkeys and other birds. The word pen comes from the Latin *penna*, a feather.

- Grebes eat their own feathers. They are thought to form pellets that help the birds regurgitate (bring up) the bones and scales of the fish they eat.

- The Japanese phoenix fowl is a domestic bird. It has tail feathers measuring up to 10.6 m (34.8 ft), the longest of any bird. Various types of pheasant have tail feathers of 2 m (6.6 ft) long or more and a peacock's tail feathers can be 1.5 m (5 ft) long.

- Each feather weighs very little, but together they make up a large part of the weight of a bird, especially as flying birds have very light skeletons. The skeleton of the frigate bird, a large bird with a 2.1 m (6.9 ft) wingspan, weighs just 113 g (4 oz), less than the weight of all its feathers.

Largest flightless birds

- **Ostrich**: height 2.74 m (9 ft); weight 156.5 kg (345 lb)
- **Emu**: height 1.52 m (5 ft); weight 40.0 kg (88.2 lb)
- **Cassowary**: height 1.52 m (5 ft); weight 33.5 kg (73.9 lb)
- **Rhea**: height 1.37 m (4.5 ft); weight 25.0 kg (55.1 lb)
- **Emperor penguin**: 1.30 m (4.3 ft); weight 29.4 kg (64.8 lb)

Birds' eggs

The biggest ostrich eggs weigh up to 2.35 kg (5.18 lb), but they are not the largest eggs of all time. The extinct elephant bird (*Aepyornis maximus*) of Madagascar laid eggs that were up to 33 cm (13 in) long.

This is larger than the eggs of any dinosaur, seven times bigger than an ostrich egg, 180 times bigger than a chicken egg and over 20,000 times the size of a hummingbird's egg!

Ostrich 1,600 g (56.44 oz)
Albatross 595 g (20.99 oz)
Kiwi 450 g (15.87 oz)
Emperor penguin 450 g (15.87 oz)
Mute swan 340 g (11.99 oz)
Eagle 145 g (5.11 oz)
Snowy owl 83 g (2.93 oz)
Domestic hen 65 g (2.29 oz)
Mallard 54 g (1.90 oz)
Peregrine falcon 52 g (1.83 oz)
Sparrow 3.0 g (0.106 oz)
Vervain hummingbird 0.375 g (0.013 oz)

Emperor penguins

The Emperor penguin is the largest penguin. It lives in Antarctica, where there are about 200,000 breeding pairs. The female lays one egg, then goes off to feed for about two months. The male keeps the egg warm on his feet, beneath his body. Chicks stay with their mothers for about seven weeks, then gather together in a group to keep warm.

Flying mammals

Bats are the only mammals capable of true flight. They belong to the order Chiroptera, which means hand-wing. Instead of front legs, bats have wings made of skin which are supported by the bones of the arms and hands.

- There are about 977 species of bat. Flying foxes are among the largest. These bats are 45 cm (17.7 in) long, have wings that span 1.7 m (5.6 ft) and weigh up to 1.6 kg (3.5 lb). The Kitti's hog-nosed bat, which lives in Thailand, is the smallest. It weighs 2 g (0.07 oz), which is less than a table tennis ball. It is only 2.9 cm (1.1 in) long, making it the smallest of all mammals.

- Bats sleep during the day and wake up at night, when they go in search of food. Most bats are insect-eaters – a little brown bat can catch 1,200 insects in an hour – but others eat fruit or nectar from plants. Some larger species catch frogs, birds and fish.

- Many bats live in large groups called colonies. Bracken Cave in Texas, USA contains the world's largest bat colony, with about 20 million animals. This is one of the densest populations of any mammal and there can be as many as 5,000 newborn babies per square metre (11 square feet). These bats eat 1,000 tonnes of insects every night.

Emperor penguins and their young

www.bsc-eoc.org/avibase/avibase.jsp   search

Tarantula

Shortest-lived
Male houseflies live for about 17 days and females for about 29 days. Mayflies may live for only a single day as adults, but for two or three years as larvae.

Distance fliers
Butterflies have been tracked flying for 4,828 km (3,000 miles).

Fastest
Dragonflies can fly at speeds of 28.7–32 km/h (18–20 mph).

Spiders

Spiders are not insects. They belong to a separate group called arachnids, which also includes scorpions. A spider's body is divided into two parts linked by a narrow waist. It has four pairs of legs tipped with claws, but no wings. All spiders can make silk but not all spin webs.

There are at least 35,000 species of spider. Most are harmless but a few can be deadly. The banana spider of Central and South America produces enough venom to kill six adults. Other deadly spiders are the funnel-web, which lives in Australia, and the wolf spider of Central and South America. The black widow and various tarantulas are also dangerous and can kill.

Biggest spider
The goliath bird-eating spider, which lives in South American rainforests, has legs up to 25 cm (9.8 in) long.

Smallest spider
A species called *Patu marplesi* from Western Samoa is the smallest known spider. It is only 0.46 mm (0.018 in) long.

Amazing insects

Most abundant
Insects called springtails live in topsoil all over the world. There are probably as many as 600 million per hectare (1.5 billion per acre). Together, they weigh more than the entire human race.

Longest
Stick insects have the longest bodies. Some measure up to 51 cm (20.07 in) long, including their legs.

Heaviest
Goliath beetles can be 11 cm (4.33 in) long and weigh 100 g (3.5 oz).

Largest wingspan
The wings of the female Queen Alexandra birdwing butterfly of Papua New Guinea measure 28 cm (11 in) across.

Smallest
The wings of a battledore wing fairy fly, which is a kind of parasitic wasp, measure only 0.21 mm (0.008 in).

Longest-lived
Jewel beetle larvae, or young, may live inside timber for up to 30 years or more before emerging and turning into adult insects.

Types of insect

The body of most insects has three parts – head, thorax and abdomen. Insects have three pairs of legs and many have two pairs of wings. Listed here are the main groups, or orders, of insects. Numbers are just the species that we know about and have been named. There may be thousands more still to be discovered. Total numbers are huge. Together, all the insects in the world would weigh at least 12 times as much as all the people in the world.

Coleoptera meaning "hard wings": 370,000 species, eg beetles

Hymenoptera "membrane wings": 198,000 species, eg ants, bees, wasps

Lepidoptera "scaly wings": 165,000 species, eg butterflies and moths

Diptera "two-wings": 122,000 species, eg midges, mosquitoes, true flies

Hemiptera "half wings": 82,000 species, eg aphids and cicadas

Orthoptera "straight wings": 20,000 species, eg crickets and locusts

Trichoptera "hairy wings": 8,000 species, eg caddisflies

Collembola "sticky peg": 6,500 species, eg springtails

Phthiraptera "louse wings": 6,000 species, eg biting and sucking lice

Odonata "toothed flies": 5,500 species, eg dragonflies

Bee facts

There are about 20,000 types of bee. The best known is probably the honeybee, but not all bees live in colonies like the honeybee. Many live alone and build their own nests.

● Honeybees are the only insects that make food which humans eat. Bees make honey to feed the inhabitants of their hives during winter. The honey they do not eat is harvested by beekeepers. Bees also make beeswax which is used for making candles and furniture polish.

● Wallace's giant bees are the world's largest at up to 4 cm (1.6 in) long. They were first found in Indonesia in 1858 but were then thought to have become extinct. In 1981 the bees were rediscovered.

www.insectguide.net   search

Honey bee on a flower

Huge colonies of monarch butterflies migrate up to 3,000 km (1,864 miles) every year.

Eating insects

In many countries insects are a popular food. Insect dishes include omelette made from silkworms and fried honeybees in China, fried locusts in Thailand and red ant chutney in India. Many of us may eat insects without realizing it – the red food colouring cochineal is made from the bodies of a Mexican scale insect.

● Honeybees visit up to five million flowers to make 1 kg (2.2 lb) of honey. In doing so, they fly a total distance equal to flying four times round the Earth.

● The smallest bee is the Brazilian *Trigona duckei* at 2–5 mm (0.08–0.20 in) long.

● One beehive may contain 50,000 worker bees – these are the bees which collect nectar from flowers to make honey.

● Honeybees' wings beat 11,400 times a minute. These wing movements make the bees' familiar buzz.

● 1.3 million tonnes of honey are produced worldwide every year. China is the main producer with 276,000 tonnes, followed by the USA with 82,000.

● Some people are allergic to bee stings, which can even be fatal. In 1962 in Rhodesia, Johanne Relleke was stung 2,243 times by wild bees, but survived!

● Queen bees can lay two or three thousand eggs a day – as many as 200,000 eggs a year. They may live as long as five years, so can produce a million eggs.

Thysanoptera "fringed wings": 5,000 species, eg thrips

Neuroptera "net-veined wings": 4,000 species, eg lace-wings

Blattodea "insect avoiding light": 4,000 species, eg cockroaches

Pscoptera "milled wings": 3,500 species, eg hook lice

Isoptera "equal wings": 2,750 species, eg termites

Ephemeroptera "living for a day": 2,500 species, eg mayflies

Phasmatodea "like a ghost": 2,500 species, eg leaf insects

Mantodea "like a prophet": 2,000 species, eg mantids

Plecoptera "Wickerwork wing": 2,000 species, eg stoneflies

Siphonaptera "tube without wings": 2,000 species, eg fleas

Dermaptera "leathery wings": 1,900 species, eg earwigs

Mecoptera "long wings": 550 species, eg hanging flies

Thysanura "fringed tail": 370 species, eg silverfish

Archaeognatha "ancient jaw": 350 species, eg bristletails

Embioptera "lively wings": 300 species, eg web-spinners

Megaloptera "large wings": 250 species, eg alderflies

Raphidioptera "embroidered wings": 150 species, eg snakeflies

Zoraptera "pure + wingless": 30 species, eg angel insects

Grylloblattodea "cricket cockroach": 25 species, eg rock crawlers

REPTILES AND AMPHIBIANS

Reptiles

A reptile is a vertebrate animal with a body covered in tough scales. Most reptiles live on land, but turtles and some kinds of snake live in water.

Crocodiles and their relatives spend time on land and in water. There are more than 8,000 species of reptiles, which are divided into the following groups.

Lizards 4,765 species

Snakes 2,978 species

Turtles and tortoises 307 species

Amphisbaenians (worm lizards) 165 species

Crocodiles, alligators, caimans 23 species

Tuataras 2 species

Deadly snakes

The coastal taipan of Australia injects the most venom per bite with 120 mg (0.004 oz). Just 1 mg (0.00004 oz) would be enough to kill a person. The common krait's venom is even more dangerous – only 0.5 mg (0.00002 oz) can be fatal.

Alligators and crocodiles

The crocodile family contains 23 species, including alligators, caimans and gavials. All are large reptiles with long bodies and short legs. Most crocodiles have narrow V-shaped snouts, but alligators and caimans have wider, U-shaped snouts. The gavial has long slender jaws – just right for catching fish.

In alligators and caimans the teeth of the lower jaw fit into pits in the upper jaw and cannot be seen when the mouth is closed. In crocodiles the fourth tooth on each side of the lower jaw fits into a notch on the upper jaw, so they are always visible. Crocodiles are generally bigger and more aggressive than alligators.

Alligators

American alligator (southern USA) 4–4.5 m (13.1–14.8 ft)

Chinese alligator (China) 2 m (6.6 ft)

Spectacled caiman (South America) 2–2.5 m (6.6–8.2 ft)

Broad-snouted caiman (South America) 2 m (6.6 ft)

Yacaré caiman (South America) 2.5–3 m (8.2–9.8 ft)

Black caiman (South America) 4–6 m (13.1–19.7 ft)

Cuvier's dwarf caiman (South America) 1.5–1.6 m (4.9–5.2 ft)

Schneider's or Smooth-fronted caiman (South America) 1.7–2.3 m (5.6–7.5 ft)

Crocodiles

American crocodile (southern USA, Mexico, Central and South America) 5 m (16.4 ft)

Slender-snouted crocodile (West Africa) 2.5 m (8.2 ft)

Orinoco crocodile (northern South America) 6 m (19.7 ft)

Australian freshwater crocodile (Australia) 2.5–3 m (8.2–9.8 ft)

Philippine crocodile (Philippines) 3 m (9.8 ft)

Morelet's crocodile (Central America) 3 m (9.8 ft)

Nile crocodile (Africa) 5 m (16.4 ft)

New Guinea crocodile (New Guinea) 3.5 m (11.5 ft)

Mugger or marsh crocodile (India, Sri Lanka) 4–5 m (13.1–16.4 ft)

Estuarine or saltwater crocodile (Southeast Asia, Australia) 6–7 m (19.7–23 ft)

Cuban crocodile (Cuba) 3.5 m (11.5 ft)

Siamese crocodile (Southeast Asia, very rare) 3–4 m (9.8–13.1 ft)

African dwarf crocodile (Central and West Africa) 1.9 m (6.2 ft)

False gharial or gavial (Southeast Asia) 5 m (16.4 ft)

Gavials

Indian gavial or gharial (India, Pakistan, Bangladesh, Nepal) 5–6 m (16.4–19.7 ft)

Estuarine or saltwater crocodile

Amphibians

An amphibian is a vertebrate animal that spends at least some of its life in water. Its skin is not scaly. There are about 5,578 species of amphibian, divided into:

Frogs and toads 4,896 species
Newts and salamanders 517 species
Caecilians (legless amphibians) 165 species

Caecilian   Salamander

Snake facts

Largest snakes
Many people believe that the South American anaconda is the longest snake. There are reports of anacondas up to 36.5 m (120 ft) long, but this has never been proved. The reticulated or royal python is probably the longest snake at up to 10.7 m (35 ft), but the anaconda may be the heaviest at up to 230 kg (500 lb).

Smallest snake
The thread snake is rarely longer than 108 mm (4.3 in). The spotted dwarf adder is the smallest venomous snake at 22.8 cm (9 in) long.

Turtles and tortoises

These reptiles all have a hard shell that protects the body. There are about 250 species, some of which live in the sea, others in fresh water and the rest on land.

Biggest
● Fossils of the extinct turtle *Stupendemys geographicus* have been found with shells up to 3 m (10 ft) long. They would have weighed more than 2,040 kg (4,497 lb).

● The largest living turtle is the leatherback. A male washed up on the coast of Wales in 1988 holds the record – he was 291 cm (113.5 in) long and weighed 916 kg (2,019 lb).

● The Aldabra giant tortoise, which lives on an island in the Seychelles, weighs up to 304 kg (670 lb) and is the largest land-living tortoise. It is also one of the slowest tortoises. It moves at an average speed of 0.27 km/h (0.17 mph).

Smallest
The smallest turtle or tortoise is the common musk turtle which is 7.62 cm (3 in) long and weighs 227 g (8 oz).

Blue poison arrow frog

Fantastic frogs and toads

Largest frogs and toads
● The world's largest known frog is the goliath frog, which lives in central Africa. It measures up to 87.63 cm (34.5 in) long and weighs as much as 3.66 kg (8.1 lb).

● The largest tree frog is *Hyla vasta*, which lives only on the island of Hispaniola. It is more than 12 cm (4.7 in) long and has huge round finger and toe disks which grip like superglue.

● The world's largest toad is the South American marine toad. It can have a body length of over 23 cm (9.1 in) and weigh up to 1.2 kg (2.6 lb).

Smallest frog
The smallest frog and the world's smallest amphibian is the *Eleutherodactylus limbatus* frog, which measures only 8.5–12 mm (0.3–0.5 in).

Newest frogs
In 2006, 20 previously unknown frog species were discovered in an expedition to Indonesia (see page 69) including a tiny microhylid frog that measures less than 14 mm (0.6 in).

Egg laying
The marine toad lays 35,000 eggs a year, but the Cuban arrow-poison frog lays only one egg.

Highest and lowest homes
The green toad has been seen at 8,000 m (26,247 ft) in the Himalayas and toads have been discovered more than 3,048 m (10,000 ft) down a coal mine.

Most poisonous
The poison-arrow frogs of Central and South America are the most deadly. The world's most poisonous amphibian is the golden poison-arrow frog of western Colombia. One adult contains enough highly toxic poison in its skin to kill 1,000 people.

Smelliest
The smelliest frog is the Venezuela skunk frog, which was discovered in 1991. It warns off its enemies by releasing a bad-smelling chemical identical to the one produced by skunks.

Longest jumps
● On 21 May 1977, a female sharp-nosed frog leaped 10.2 m (33.5 ft) in three consecutive jumps at a frog derby at Larula Natal Spa, Paulpietersburg in South Africa.

● The cricket frog is only 3.5 cm (1.4 in) and can jump 36 times its own length. If an adult human jumped 36 times his own length, the long-jump record could stand at 65.8 m (216 ft)!

Life on man

As many as 100 trillion viruses and bacteria live on each of us. However much we wash, there are always ten million or so bacteria on every square centimetre of our skin. There are also many tiny creatures called parasites, which can live inside or on the human body, feeding on our blood.

● Parasites such as roundworms, hookworms, flukes and tapeworms – which can grow as long as 9.75 m (32 ft) – can live inside our bodies. They may cause such diseases as elephantiasis, in which the patient's limbs swell to gigantic sizes. Head lice live on human heads and feed on blood. The lice lay little white eggs, called nits, which cling to individual hairs.

● Follicle mites are in everyone's hair, even among our eyelashes. They were first described by 19th-century scientist Richard Owen (the man who first named dinosaurs), but are so tiny that few people have ever seen them or are even aware that they are there.

● Some of the tiny creatures that feed on us may also transmit diseases. Tsetse flies carry African sleeping sickness. Mosquitoes can infect humans with diseases such as malaria, dengue fever and yellow fever when they bite. Malaria has killed more people in human history than any other disease.

● Ticks can carry diseases such as encephalitis and Lyme disease. Mites and chiggers (baby mites) cause skin diseases and may transmit typhus.

See also
Black Death: page 104

Head louse with egg

The first teddy bear

Teddy bears are named after US President Theodore (Teddy) Roosevelt. The story began when the president refused to shoot a young bear while on a hunting trip. This incident appeared in a cartoon by Clifford K. Berryman, published in the Washington Post on 16 November 1902. Soon after, Morris Michtom, a New York shopkeeper, started making stuffed bears and advertising them as "Teddy's Bears" with Roosevelt's permission.

At about the same time, Margarete Steiff, a German toymaker, started making her first toy bears and exported them to the USA to meet the demand created by Teddy's Bears. In 1903 Steiff's factory produced 12,000 bears.

By 1907, the figure had risen to 974,000. Steiff teddy bears, with a distinctive tag on their ear, are still made and are sold internationally. Early examples are prized by collectors.

Counting sheep

There are about 1,101,639,064 sheep in the world – an average of one sheep for every six people. In some countries there are more sheep than humans.

Falkland Islands 690,000 sheep, 3,060 people = 225 sheep per person
New Zealand 40,106,800 sheep, 4,121,662 people = 10 sheep per person
Australia 100,100,000 sheep, 20,245,629 people = 5 sheep per person
Mongolia 12,884,500 sheep, 2,644,595 people = 5 sheep per person
Uruguay 9,712,000 sheep, 3,383,284 people = 3 sheep per person
Mauritania 8,850,000 sheep, 3,022,150 people = 3 sheep per person

Plague carriers

Fleas are perhaps the most dangerous creatures of all – they were the carriers of the deadly bubonic plague that killed millions of people in medieval times.

Humans and animals

Since ancient times humans have used many types of animals for a vast range of different purposes.

Meat, milk and honey

Humans have always hunted and eaten wild animals. Milk from such animals as cows, goats, sheep, camels, buffalo, reindeer, llamas and yaks is drunk, used in cooking and made into butter and cheese. The eggs from birds such as hens, ducks, geese and quail are another important food. Honey has long been taken from the hives of wild bees, and now from domesticated bees kept in artificial hives.

Wool, fur and skin

Wool is shorn from live sheep, which then regrow their coats. The fur and leather of many other animals can be taken only after the animal has been killed. Cattle, goats, rabbits, mink, seals, wolves, foxes, kangaroos, big cats such as leopards, and alligators and snakes are among the many animals that have been used in this way. There are some very special uses for animal skin: for example, medieval manuscripts were written on vellum, made from calfskin.

Silk

Silk comes from the silkworm, the caterpillar of the silkmoth. Silkworms eat a tonne of mulberry leaves to make 5 kg (11 lb) of silk.

Beasts of burden and transport

Strong animals such as horses, donkeys, camels, reindeer and buffalo are used to pull agricultural equipment and carts, and to carry people. Elephants drag heavy logs, pit ponies once drew trucks in coal mines, and dogs – usually huskies – pull sledges.

Security

Guard dogs (and even guard geese), police dogs and sniffer dogs (to detect drugs) are widely used.

Helpers

Sheepdogs, hunting hounds, retrievers and guide dogs for the blind are among the best known, but other animals, such as monkeys, can be trained to aid the disabled. Search and rescue dogs help to find missing people, lost walkers and climbers, and earthquake victims. Less well-known human helpers include pigs used to find truffles (edible fungi) and cats kept by the British Post Office to prevent mice from eating the mail! Animals kept as pets also provide millions of people with companionship.

Military

The warhorse is one of the most familiar of all military animals, but elephants have also been successfully used in battles. Many military organizations use dogs, goats and other animals as regimental mascots. Message-carrying dogs and carrier pigeons have been used by armies. During the Iraq war in 2004, dolphins were trained to find mines.

Maneater

A tigress known as the Champawat maneater, after the part of India in which she lived, killed a record 436 people over five years. She was shot in 1907 by British big-game hunter Colonel Jim Corbett (1875–1955).

Indian elephant carrying a log at a logging camp

Top farm animals

These are the most popular farm animals worldwide (2006). They are kept for their meat, eggs and milk. The total number of these types of animal alone is three times that of the world's human population.

Bird flu

Avian or bird flu is a disease that affects domesticated and wild birds. In recent years, a type known as H5N1 has killed many birds, and a small number of people who have been in contact with them. Experts fear that if the virus mutates it could start to pass from human to human.

Chickens 16,887,556,000
Cattle 1,383,157,265
Sheep 1,101,639,064
Ducks 1,057,677,000
Pigs 989,763,628
Goats 837,235,801
Rabbits and hares 661,821,000

PET POWER

Countries with most pets

These totals include cats, dogs, birds, fish, small mammals (hamsters, guinea pigs, etc) and reptiles.

USA 363,268,690		**Italy** 59,850,000	
China 274,103,310		**UK** 49,281,000	
Germany 77,495,000		**Turkey** 41,001,580	
Brazil 72,026,640		**Philippines** 31,604,030	
France 67,150,000		**Netherlands** 29,713,000	
Japan 66,451,000		**Mexico** 26,978,440	
Russia 60,075,000		**Canada** 25,463,000	

Playful kitten

Top UK pets

Just over half (52.3 per cent) of the households in the UK own a pet, ranging from dogs, cats and rabbits to the more exotic snakes and spiders.

Cat 6,100,800 households (hh)
Dog 5,232,800 hh
Goldfish 2,033,600 hh
Fish in ponds 1,711,200 hh
Tropical fish 967,200 hh
Budgerigar 694,400 hh
Hamster 620,000 hh
Bird* 520,800 hh
Guinea pig 464,400 hh
Fish in aquariums 372,000 hh
Other rodent (rats, mice) 372,000 hh
Reptile 258,000 hh
Parrot 248,000 hh
Horse or pony 223,200 hh
Canary 198,400 hh
* other than budgerigars and canaries

Racing greyhounds

Homeward bound

There are amazing stories of cats and dogs that travel great distances home after getting separated from their owners. Bobbie, a collie dog, made one of the longest journeys. He was lost on a family holiday in Indiana, USA, on 15 August 1923. Six months later, he arrived home in Silverton, Oregon, 4,828 km (3,000 miles) away. He became known as Silverton Bobbie, the Wonder Dog of Oregon.

Cat-alogue

Heaviest
Himmy, owned by Thomas Vyse of Queensland, Australia, weighed 21.3 kg (47 lb). He had a 38.1 cm (15 in) neck and an 84 cm (33 in) waist – similar to that of an adult human! He died in 1986 at the age of ten.

Smallest
Tinker Toy, a male Blue Point Himalayan owned by Katrina and Scott Forbes of Illinois, USA, is 7 cm (2.8 in) tall, 19cm long and weighs 625 g (1.4 lb).

Biggest breed
Maine Coons are a North American breed of muscular, big-boned cats. Males often reach 6–8 kg (13–17.5 lb) in weight.

Oldest
There are several contenders for this title. The most reliable record is that of the French-born cat Grandpa Rex's Allen. This was a Sphynx cat owned by Jake Perry of Austin, Texas, USA. The cat died in 1998 at the age of 34.

Largest litter
In 1970 Tarawood Antigone, a female Burmese owned by Valerie Gane of Kingham, Oxfordshire, gave birth to 19 kittens. Fifteen of the litter survived.

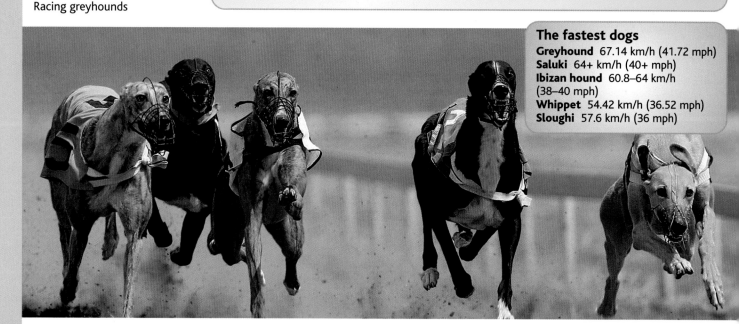

The fastest dogs
Greyhound 67.14 km/h (41.72 mph)
Saluki 64+ km/h (40+ mph)
Ibizan hound 60.8–64 km/h (38–40 mph)
Whippet 54.42 km/h (36.52 mph)
Sloughi 57.6 km/h (36 mph)

Famous cat-lovers

Edward Lear and Foss
Foss was the subject of a number of Lear's nonsense poems and comic drawings. When Foss died in 1887, Lear said he was 31 years old.

Winston Churchill and Margate
A black kitten turned up at 10 Downing Street on 10 October 1953 and Churchill adopted it. It was named Margate to commemorate an important speech Churchill was to make in the town that day. Later cats in Number 10 have included Harold Wilson's Nemo and Margaret Thatcher's Wilberforce. Humphrey, a stray cat, moved in with Mrs Thatcher and stayed on with John Major and then Tony Blair.

Charles Dickens and Williamina
Williamina was called William until she had a litter of kittens. One of these, known as The Master's Cat, used to put out Dickens's candle with its paw.

Domenico Scarlatti and Pulcinella
The Italian composer's cat used to jump on to his harpsichord keyboard and stroll along the keys. This inspired Scarlatti to compose *The Cat's Fugue*.

Abraham Lincoln and Tabby
Tabby was one of the first White House cats. More recent examples include J.F. Kennedy's Tom Kitten, Ronald Reagan's Cleo and Sara, and Bill Clinton's Socks.

Dog-alogue

Largest dog
In 1989 Aicama Zorba of La-Susa, an Old English mastiff owned by Chris Eraclides of London, weighed 155.58 kg (343 lb) and measured 2.5 m (8.25 ft) from nose to tail.

Smallest dog
A Yorkshire terrier owned by Arthur Marples of Blackburn in the 1940s was just 6.3 cm (2.5 in) tall and weighed 113 g (4 oz).

Oldest dog
Bluey, an Australian cattle-dog owned by Les Hall of Victoria, Australia, died in 1938 at the age of 29 years 5 months.

Largest litter
In 1944, Lena, an American foxhound, produced 23 puppies, all of which survived. Other dogs have equalled this record, but not all the pups have survived.

Longest jumper
Bang, a greyhound, jumped 9.14 m (30 ft) while chasing a hare at Brecon Lodge in Gloucestershire.

Greatest climber
Tschingel, a beagle, climbed more than 50 peaks in the Alps, including the 4,165 m (13,664 ft) Jungfrau and the 3,974 m (13,038 ft) Eiger.

Famous dog-lovers

Francis Barraud and Nipper
British artist Francis Barraud sold a painting called *His Master's Voice* to the Gramophone Company. It showed his dog Nipper listening to a gramophone. The company adopted it as its trademark and later changed its company name to His Master's Voice or HMV.

J.M. Barrie and Luath
Luath, a Newfoundland dog, was the model for Nana in Barrie's book *Peter Pan*.

George Bush and Millie
Millie, the springer spaniel belonging to US President George Bush (Snr) had a bestselling "autobiography" *Millie's Book*, written by First Lady Barbara Bush.

Elizabeth Barrett Browning and Flush
The English poet's cocker spaniel became famous from Virginia Woolf's book *Flush: A Biography* (1933), which looks at the world from the dog's point of view.

John Gray and Greyfriars Bobby
Bobby was a Skye terrier who faithfully guarded his master's grave at Greyfriars, Edinburgh, for 14 years from 1858. The true story of the devoted dog has been the subject of books and films.

Charles Schulz and Spike
American cartoonist Charles Schulz based his comic character Snoopy on his family's Basset hound Spike. In later strips a dog called Spike appears as Snoopy's brother.

Intelligent dogs
American psychology professor and pet trainer Stanley Coren ranked 133 breeds of dogs for intelligence. He studied their responses to a range of IQ tests, as well as the opinions of dog obedience judges. The five top breeds were the border collie, poodle, German shepherd, golden retriever and Doberman pinscher.

Tyrannosaurus rex skull and reconstruction (below)

Dinosaurs

Dinosaurs first appeared about 230 million years ago. These amazing reptiles then dominated life on Earth until they became extinct 65 million years ago. The first dinosaurs to be described were *Megalosaurus* (great lizard) by William Buckland in 1824 and *Iguanodon* (iguana tooth) by Gideon Mantell in 1825.

They were named before the word "dinosaur" had been invented. The name *dinosauria* (terrible lizards) was suggested by British scientist Richard Owen in July 1841. Since then 700 species have been identified. Not all dinosaurs were enormous – some measured less than 60 cm (24 in) long, about the size of a chicken. Sizes of dinosaurs are mostly estimates worked out from the size of bones. The largest known complete skeleton is of a *Brachiosaurus* and is 22.3 m (73.2 ft) long. The skeleton is in the Humboldt Museum, Berlin, Germany.

Biggest dinosaurs

Seismosaurus weight 99,792 kg (220,000 lb); length 45.7 m (150 ft)

Argentinasaurus weight 90,720 kg (200,000 lb); length 36.6 m (120 ft)

Supersaurus weight 54,432 kg (120,000 lb); length 36.6 m (120 ft)

Ultrasaurus weight 63,504 kg (140,000 lb); length 30.5 m (100 ft)

Brachiosaurus weight 54,432 kg (120,000 lb); length 30.5 m (100 ft)

Dinosaur facts

● The biggest dinosaurs were all herbivores. *Tyrannosaurus rex*, one of the largest carnivorous dinosaurs, measured up to 15 m (49.2 ft) long and weighed 60,000 kg (132,277 lb) or more. Its huge jaws were packed with 60 teeth, the biggest of which were 23 cm (9 in) long!

● A new type of tyrannosaur called *Guanlong wucaii* has recently been discovered in China. It lived 160 million years ago, measured about 3 m (10 ft) long, and looked like a miniature version of *Tyrannosaurus rex*.

● The largest flying prehistoric creatures were pterosaurs. The wings of the biggest pterosaur, *Quetzalcoatlus*, measured 10.96 m (36 ft) from tip to tip.

● The largest known dinosaur egg belonged to *Hypselosaurus*. The 100 million-year-old egg measures 30 by 25.5 cm (12 by 10 in), about three times the volume of an ostrich egg.

● The fastest dinosaur, *Ornithomimus*, could probably run at a speed of up to 70 km/h (43.5 mph). The ostrich runs at a similar speed today.

● Dinosaurs have been in space! Fragments of bone and an eggshell of *Maiasaura peeblesorum* were taken into space by astronaut Loren Acton in 1985. A *Coelophysis* skull was taken into space by astronaut Bonnie Dunbar in 1998.

Coelacanth: a living fossil

Palaeontologists discovered a large fish known as the coelacanth from fossil remains. They thought it had become extinct about 65 million years ago. But on 22 December 1938 one was caught alive off East London in South Africa. This strange-looking creature, about 1.7 m (5.6 ft) long, snapped at the hand of Captain Henrik Goosen, but died soon afterwards. Captain Goosen realized that he had found something unusual so took the fish to a local museum where scientists identified it as a "living fossil". Since then, more than 200 coelacanths, some measuring up to 1.9 m (6.2 ft) long, have been caught, mostly off the Comoros islands.

Animals in danger

In the past 500 years, hundreds of species of animals have become extinct – they have disappeared from Earth for ever. In many cases this is because of human actions. The animals have been hunted, or the areas where they lived have been destroyed.

Some creatures become extinct in the wild but have survived in artificial settings, such as zoos. If they can be successfully bred, they may be taken back to the wild. Przewalski's horse, for example, became extinct in the wild but has since been bred in captivity. Now there are herds of these wild horses in their old home around the Gobi Desert. Other species are defined as "threatened", or in danger of becoming extinct. According to the degree of threat they may be considered "critically endangered", "endangered" or "vulnerable".

Amphibians 6,199 known species; 1,808 threatened

Birds 9,956 known species; 1,217 threatened

Fishes 30,000 known species; 1,201 threatened

Mammals 5,416 known species; 1,094 threatened

Molluscs 81,000 known species; 978 threatened

Insects 950,000 known species; 623 threatened

Crustaceans 40,000 known species; 460 threatened

Reptiles 8,240 known species; 422 threatened

Corals 2,175 known species; 5 threatened

Others 130,200 known species; 42 threatened

Dodo

Last seen alive

Sabre-toothed tiger 12,000 years ago

Woolly mammoth 10,000 years ago

Moa 1,000 years ago

Aurochs (giant wild ox) 1627

Aepyornis (elephant bird) 1649

Dodo 1681

Steller's sea cow 1768

Great auk 1844

Tarpan (wild horse) 1851

Labrador duck 1875

Quagga (zebra-like creature) 1883

Pilori muskrat 1902

Badlands bighorn sheep 1905

Japanese grey wolf 1905

Passenger pigeon 1914

Carolina parakeet 1918

California grizzly bear 1922

Schomburgk's deer 1938

Arabian ostrich 1941

Euler's flycatcher 1955

Eskimo curlew 1963

Guam flying fox 1968

Pyrenean ibex 2000

Yangtze River dolphin 2006

Western black rhinoceros 2006

Madeiran large white butterfly 2007

www.bbc.co.uk/dinosaurs   search

Lost world

In 2006 a team of 12 scientists returned from an area of rainforest in Indonesia where no humans had ever set foot before. It lies in the Foja Mountains on the island of New Guinea and it is so difficult to reach that the explorers had to be dropped in by helicopter. They discovered dozens of new animals and plants, including an orange-faced honeyeater, a golden-mantled tree kangaroo, 20 new species of frog, 4 new species of butterfly, a giant rhododendron flower (about 15 cm [6 in] across), and a species of bird that had been considered extinct for over 100 years.

The end of the tiger?

Some very familiar animals are under threat of extinction. They include the gorilla, African and Asian elephants, the black rhino, the giant panda and many species of whale, such as the blue, right and fin whale.

Tigers are also in serious danger. A century ago there were more than 100,000 tigers. Of the eight known subspecies of tiger, three – the Bali, Caspian and Javan – became extinct. There are now fewer than 5,000–7,500 tigers left in the wild because their habitats have been destroyed and they have been illegally hunted for their bones and other parts used in traditional Chinese medicines.

Numbers of the Amur or Siberian, the largest tiger, have recovered slightly to 600 in the wild, with fewer than 501 in wildlife parks and zoos. The Sumatran tiger is down to about 400–500, with 232 in captivity. The Bengal, including the rare white tiger, ranges from 3,176–4,556, with about 200 in zoos, and there are only an estimated 1,227–1,785 of the Indochinese, with 60 in zoos.

The rarest tiger of all is the South China tiger. Its population is down to only 20–30 individuals in the wild and 48 in zoos.

Siberian tiger

Pollution fact file

Pollution happens when unwanted gases and other materials escape into the environment. It causes waste, financial losses and damage to human, animal and plant health. Huge growth in industry and in the world's population in the last 100 years have led to more and more industrial processes and pollution. Deliberate dumping and accidents such as oil spillages have seriously affected the Earth's air, land and water.

Loggers cutting down rainforest in Borneo

Air pollution

Most air pollution comes from burning fossil fuels (coal, oil and gas) and solid waste, or from gases released into the air. Carbon monoxide from vehicle exhausts is poisonous because it prevents the absorption of oxygen. Nitrogen oxide reacts with sunlight to produce smog (a combination of smoke and fog).

Acid rain

Acid rain is caused when nitrogen oxide, sulphur dioxide and other chemicals from volcanic eruptions and human sources combine with rain and fall as acid. It can damage buildings, kill fish and harm trees and other plants.

Land pollution

Soil can be damaged by the dumping of chemicals, toxic (poisonous), radioactive and other waste as well as the overuse of pesticides and fertilizers. Polluted land is unsafe for anything to live on.

Global warming

Greenhouse gases in Earth's atmosphere, such as carbon dioxide, nitrous oxide, water vapour and methane, help to trap heat and stop too much of it escaping into space. Without these gases, the Earth would not be warm enough for us to live on. But more and more greenhouse gases are being released into the atmosphere from human activities, and too much heat is being trapped. The Earth became 0.5°C (0.9°F) warmer during the 20th century and a further rise of even a couple of degrees will damage its natural balance.

Reversing pollution

Many countries have become more aware of pollution and the damage it causes and are taking action to reduce it. For example, laws have been passed in Britain and other countries to reduce lead in petrol and paint. Clean air laws have reduced pollution in cities, and scientists are making vehicles that do not burn fossil fuels. People and businesses are heavily fined for dumping waste and chemicals. However, pollution is still a huge problem.

Destroying forests

About 90,000 sq km (34,749 sq miles) of forest are cut down every year worldwide to obtain timber or to clear land so it can be used for farming. This is about the same area as Portugal.

Cutting down forests increases the amount of carbon dioxide in the atmosphere, which can affect climate and destroy the homes of many animals and plants.

Country	Average annual forest loss 2000–2005
Brazil	34,660 sq km (13,382 sq miles)
Indonesia	14,448 sq km (5,578 sq miles)
Sudan	11,780 sq km (4,548 sq miles)
Zambia	5,322 sq km (2,055 sq miles)
Mexico	3,950 sq km (1,525 sq miles)

How much water?

People worldwide use 3,802,300,000,000,000 litres (8,035,600,000,000,000 pt) of water every year. On average everybody in the world uses 633,000 litres (1,337,767 pt) a year, or 1,734 litres (3,665 pt) a day. Of this, 9 per cent (156 litres [330 pt]) a day is used in homes, 20 per cent (347 litres [733 pt]) by industry and 71 per cent (1,231 litres [2,602 pt]) by agriculture.

In the UK we use 163,000 litres (344,480 pt) per head a year – 9,500,000,000,000 litres (20,100,000,000,000 pt) in total.

Household water usage
Brushing teeth (tap off) 2.5 litres (5.3 pt)
Brushing teeth (tap on) 5 litres (10.6 pt)
Toilet flush 5–20 litres (10.6–42.3 pt)
Shower (per minute) 22 litres (46.5 pt)
Washing machine 120 litres (253.6 pt)
Bath (full) 170 litres (359.3 pt)
Washing car 200 litres (422.7 pt)
Watering garden (1 hour) 600–1,500 litres (1,268–3,170 pt)

Worst polluters

Carbon dioxide (CO_2) pollution enters the atmosphere from three main sources – burning fossil fuel (coal and oil), cement manufacturing and gas burning.

These figures show the total amounts produced by some of the leading industrial countries in 2004 measured in tonnes of carbon, one of the components of carbon dioxide, rather than the weight of CO_2. CO_2 is produced naturally by animals, forest fires and other sources. But natural production has been overtaken by the amount produced by human activities. More carbon dioxide in the atmosphere increases the amount of heat absorbed, and this leads to global warming (see Pollution fact file).

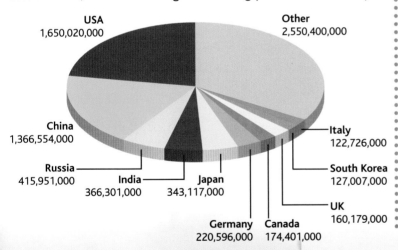

USA 1,650,020,000
Other 2,550,400,000
China 1,366,554,000
Russia 415,951,000
India 366,301,000
Japan 343,117,000
Germany 220,596,000
Canada 174,401,000
UK 160,179,000
South Korea 127,007,000
Italy 122,726,000

Worst oil tanker spills

About two million tonnes of oil are spilled into the sea every year from oil tankers, mostly during collisions or other accidents. Most spills are small (7 tonnes or less), but some are much more serious. When huge quantities of oil are discharged into the sea and washed up on shorelines they harm many birds and other creatures.

The 1989 grounding of the *Exxon Valdez* in Prince William Sound, Alaska, caused the USA's worst oil spill. The quantity spilled was smaller than the spills listed (35,000 tonnes), but thousands of birds, fish, otters, seals and whales were killed.

Atlantic Empress and ***Aegean Captain***, off Tobago, 1979, 287,000 tonnes
ABT Summer, off Angola, 1991, 260,000 tonnes
Castillio de Bellver, off Saldanha Bay, South Africa, 1983, 252,000 tonnes
Olympic Bravery, off Ushant, France, 1976, 250,000 tonnes
Amoco Cadiz, off Finistère, France, 1978, 223,000 tonnes

Water pollution

Increasing quantities of heavy metals such as mercury and lead, chemicals, sewage and oil spills are polluting lakes, rivers and oceans. Water in some places is now unsafe to drink or bathe in and animals are harmed or killed.

www.environment-agency.gov.uk **search**

A brief history of rubbish

The ancient world

In ancient times, nomadic peoples simply left their rubbish and moved on. Once people settled in villages, they were faced with the problem of having to dispose of rubbish where they lived. Often they just covered it with earth. This caused the ground level in ancient cities, such as Troy, to increase by over 1 metre (3.3 ft) a century. The first anti-dumping law was issued in Athens, Greece in 320 BC, when citizens were compelled to bury their rubbish or put it in pits outside the city.

The Middle Ages

In medieval cities, people often threw their rubbish into the street, causing the spread of rats, mice – and disease. Free-roaming pigs ate some of it, except in Paris where they were banned after King Louis VI's son was killed when his horse tripped over a pig in 1131. In London, kites and ravens scavenged among the rubbish tips. The birds were so important that killing one was punishable by death.

The 19th century

Rag-and-bone men were a common sight in 19th-century streets. They went from house to house with a horse and cart, gathering anything that could be re-sold. Dustmen collected cinders from home fires to be used in brickmaking; human waste and horse manure were taken to farms for fertilizer; and dog droppings were used in the leather tanning trade. The first rubbish-burning incinerator, called The Destructor, was built in Nottingham in 1874. The first dustbin appeared in Paris, France in 1883. It was introduced by Eugène Poubelle, the Prefect of Police. To this day, the French call a dustbin a *poubelle*.

The 20th century

During the 20th century, thousands of new, disposable goods were invented and fewer people had open fires so more rubbish was thrown away. Disused electronic equipment including TVs, computers, mobile phones and fax machines began to join the growing rubbish dumps.

Household waste

per person per year (OECD countries only)

Ireland	**Denmark**
760 kg (1,675 lb)	670 kg (1,477 lb)
USA	**Switzerland**
740 kg (1,631 lb)	660 kg (1,455 lb)
Iceland	**Germany, Luxembourg, Spain**
730 kg (1,609 lb)	650 kg (1,433 lb)
Norway	**UK**
700 kg (1,543 lb)	610 kg (1,345 lb)
Australia	**The Netherlands**
690 kg (1,521 lb)	600 kg (1,323 lb)

How much rubbish is that?

Every person in the UK produces approximately half a tonne of household rubbish every year, which means that the UK as a whole produces 30 million tonnes. That's enough to fill dustbins stretching from the Earth to the Moon.

But that's not all. Household rubbish makes up only 7 per cent of the yearly total. The rest comes from mining and quarrying (114 million tonnes), agriculture (86 million), demolition and construction – bricks, soil, etc (80 million), industrial waste (55 million), dredged spoils from rivers and harbours (34 million), commercial waste (25 million) and sewage (4 million).

How long to rot

Cotton rags 1–5 months
Paper 2–5 months
Orange peel up to 6 months
Wool socks 1–5 years
Cigarette ends 1–12 years
Plastic-coated drink cartons 5 years
Plastic bags 10–20 years
Photo film 20–30 years
Leather shoes 25–50 years
Artificial fibre clothes (nylon, etc) 30–40 years
Tin cans 50–100 years

Paper and card 32%

Kitchen/food waste 21%

Plastics 11%

Glass 9%

Metals 8%

Miscellaneous combustible 8%

Fines (ash, dust) 7%

Miscellaneous non-combustible 2%

Textiles 2%

Where does it go?

Landfills

Most waste ends up underground – in giant municipal pits, or landfill sites, where it can rot out of sight. These are usually lined to prevent dangerous chemicals seeping into the ground. However, many discarded objects take decades, even centuries to break down, and we are running out of suitable places to bury waste.

Incineration

Burning rubbish is another solution. Burning gets rid of most kinds of waste and the heat can be converted into energy for other uses. The problem is that incineration releases harmful gases, some of which may contribute to global warming.

🔍 www.wasteonline.org.uk   **search**

Compost is recycled organic waste

Recycling

Recycling uses old waste to make new products. It cuts down the amount of rubbish and saves natural resources by reducing the need for new raw materials. Items most suitable for recycling are organic matter (plant and animal) which can be composted and used as fertilizer, metals (such as aluminium cans), glass and paper.

Reduce and reuse

The most sustainable solution is to reduce the amount of waste we create. Compared with 50 years ago, food cans are 50 per cent lighter, yoghurt pots are 60 per cent lighter, glass bottles are 50 per cent lighter and plastic carrier bags are half as thick. Shoppers can help by choosing not to buy goods with lots of packaging or disposable containers, as these make up 10–20 per cent of all domestic rubbish.

Aluminium cans that could be recycled

Ways to reduce waste

1 Use a shopping bag and refuse unnecessary carrier bags

2 Buy refills

3 Buy fruits and vegetables loose, not pre-packed

4 Buy recycled goods

5 Buy reusable nappies

6 Buy soft drinks in large bottles and pour into smaller bottles for daily use

7 Reuse wrapping paper, packing materials and envelopes

8 Pack your lunch in a reusable box rather than foil or clingfilm

9 Choose durable products over disposable ones, eg rechargeable batteries

10 Donate unwanted clothes to charity shops or jumble sales

11 Donate unwanted furniture to a furniture recycling project

12 Buy drinks in glass bottles – they can be reused 20 times

13 If it's broken, mend it – don't throw it away!

14 Return clothes hangers to dry cleaners

15 Take glass, cans, paper and cardboard to recycling banks

16 Compost leftover food, garden waste, paper (in small amounts) and vacuum cleaner dust

A mountain of junk

More than 1,000 people have climbed Mt Everest since it was conquered in 1953. They, and their support teams, have dropped more than 50 tonnes of rubbish, making Everest the world's highest rubbish dump. In 2007, climbers recovered 500 kg (about 1,000 lbs) of discarded tents, ladders, oxygen cylinders, food containers and other equipment left on the slopes. A garbage deposit of £2,000 ($4,000) is paid by each expedition, in addition to climbing fees of $10,000–$25,000 per climber.

Science & Technology

Collision course

Completed in 2008, ATLAS – the large particle detector at the CERN laboratory, Switzerland – lies 100 metres underground. It will research the atomic particles created when proton beams collide. Scientists hope that this will help them understand the 'God particle' – one of the remaining mysteries of science.

How dense?

A cubic metre (m³) (35.31 ft³) of pure water weighs 1,000 kg (2,204.62 lb) or one tonne. Materials that have a density greater than water sink, and those that are less dense float.

Lightweight metals such as aluminium and titanium are important to engineers – for example, for building aircraft that need to be strong but light enough to fly. These are the average densities of some of the substances around us.

	kg/m³	(lb/ft³)		kg/m³	(lb/ft³)
Air at 0°C	1.29	(0.08)	Chalk	2,300	(143.58)
Styrofoam	100	(6.24)	China	2,300	(143.58)
Balsa wood	150	(9.36)	Concrete	2,300	(143.58)
Cork	240	(14.98)	Sand	2,500	(156.07)
Steam	600	(37.46)	Glass	2,600	(162.31)
Petrol	730	(45.57)	Aluminium	2,700	(168.56)
Oak	750	(46.82)	Marble	2,700	(168.56)
Butter	900	(56.19)	Human tooth		
Paper	900	(56.19)	enamel	2,900	(181.04)
Ice	920	(57.43)	Diamonds	3,500	(218.50)
Olive oil	920	(57.43)	Titanium	4,507	(281.36)
Rubber	940	(58.68)	The Earth		
Wax	950	(59.31)	(average for		
Pure water			whole planet)	5,520	(344.60)
at 0°C	1,000	(62.43)	Iron	7,874	(491.56)
Milk	1,030	(64.30)	Copper	8,920	(556.86)
Sea water	1,030	(64.30)	Silver	10,490	(654.86)
Ebony	1,200	(74.91)	Lead	11,340	(707.93)
Spider silk	1,260	(78.66)	Mercury	13,570	(847.15)
Coal	1,400	(87.40)	Tungsten	19,250	(1,201.74)
Bone	1,800	(112.37)	Gold	19,300	(1,204.86)
Brick	2,100	(131.10)	Platinum	21,090	(1,316.61)
Salt	2,165	(135.16)	Osmium	22,610	(1,411.5)
Carbon	2,267	(141.52)			

Strange studies

Angelology Angels
Aphnology Wealth
Biometrology The effect of weather on people
Cereology Crop circles
Cryology Snow, ice and frozen ground
Cryptology Codes and ciphers
Draconology Dragons
Enigmatology Puzzles
Eremology Deserts
Fromology Cheese
Garbology Rubbish
Gelotology Laughter
Googlology The Google search engine
Googology Large numbers
Hypnology Sleep
Kalology Beauty
Limacology Slugs
Loimology Plagues
Momilogy Mummies
Nanotechnology Very small objects
Nephology Clouds
Osmology Smells
Pharology Lighthouses
Polemology Wars
Pomology Fruit-growing
Rhinology Noses
Siphonapterology Fleas
Teratology Monsters
Toxicology Poisons
Tsiology Tea
Ufology Unidentified flying objects
Vermeology Worms
Xylology Wood

Cryology is the study of snow, ice and frozen ground

An iceberg is made of almost pure water. This is less dense than sea water, so the iceberg floats.

See also
Conversions: page 84

www.exploratorium.edu   search

Acids and alkalis

The pH (potential Hydrogen) system was invented in 1909 by Danish chemist Søren Sørensen (1868–1939). In this, pH is a measure of the concentration of hydrogen ions, which shows whether something is acid or base (also known as alkali).

Pure water has a pH of 7.0. Substances that have a pH of less are acid. Substances with a pH of more than 7.0 are base (alkali). Acids make lemon juice and vinegar taste sharp, and acid rain harms trees and other plants. The traditional way of testing pH is by using litmus paper – acidic substances turn blue litmus red, while alkalis turn red litmus blue.

Substance	pH	Substance	pH
Hydrochloric acid	0	Orange juice	3.7
Car battery acid	1.0	Wine/beer	4.0
Gastric (digestive) juices	1–3	Tomato juice	4.3
Lime juice	2.3	Normal rainfall	5.6
Lemon juice	2.4	Saliva	6.4–6.9
Acid rain	2.4–3.6	Milk	6.6
Apple	3.0	Pure water	7.0
Vinegar	3.0	Human blood	7.4
Grapefruit	3.2	Sea water	7.8–8.3

A rainbow is created when sunlight passes through water droplets.

Spectrum colours

The electromagnetic spectrum includes all forms of light, from radio waves and microwaves at one end of the scale to X-rays and gamma rays at the other. In between is visible or white light, which is made up of a range of colours.

We can see the individual colours when they are split up by water droplets and form a rainbow, or by passing white light through a prism. The colours of the spectrum are red, orange, yellow, green, blue, indigo and violet.

Sound levels

The decibel (dB) is a way of measuring sound. Sounds of 80–90 dB or more can damage hearing and it is dangerous for people to work in sound levels of more than 90 dB.

Sounds above 130 dB become painful, and people should wear hearing protectors with sounds of more than 140 dB. A decibel level of more than 150 dB can cause permanent deafness.

Silence	0 dB
Rustle of leaves	10 dB
Quiet whisper at 5 m (16.25 ft); library	20–30 dB
Normal conversation; soft music	30 dB
Sailing boat	35 dB
Quiet countryside; ticking watch	40 dB
Inside average home	45–50 dB
Restaurant; office; loud conversation	50–60 dB
Background music; motorboat	60 dB

Hairdryer	60–80 dB
Workshop	65 dB
Radio; telephone ring; busy traffic; orchestra; loud TV	70 dB
Inside car; underground train	80 dB
Pneumatic drill at 15 m (48.75 ft); Niagara Falls; top level of comfort	85 dB
Very loud snore	88 dB
Heavy traffic at 15 m (48.75 ft); roaring lion	90 dB
Loud shout at 15 m (48.75 ft); lawnmower; chainsaw; blender	100 dB
Heavy truck 1 m (3.25 ft) away; orchestra playing Beethoven's Ninth Symphony	105 dB

Circular saw at 1 m (3.25 ft); car horn at 5 m (16.25 ft)	110 dB
Shouting in someone's ear	114 dB
Personal stereo	115 dB
Loud scream; thunder; explosion; submarine engine room	120 dB
Loud rock music	120–130 dB
Racing car	125 dB
Motorbike (without silencer)	130 dB
Banger; jumbo jet takeoff at 30 m (98.4 ft)	140 dB
Rock music (peak at 5 m [16.25 ft] from speaker)	150 dB
Level at ear of person firing powerful rifle	160 dB
Launch of *Saturn V* space rocket	172 dB
Blue whale call	188 dB
Volcanic eruption	272 dB

A flash of lightning gives out 80,000,000 candelas

Brightness scale

A candela is a unit of light intensity. It was originally equivalent to the amount given out by a candle, but is now more precise.

Candelas per m² (ft²)

Overcast sky	2,000 (186)
Moon	2,500 (232)
Clear sky (average)	8,000 (743)
Candle (brightest spot)	10,000 (929)
Domestic light bulb	100,000 (9,290)
Sun at Equator	1,600,000 (148,645)
Flash of lightning	80,000,000 (7,432,243)
Atom bomb	2,000,000,000 (185,806,087)

What is an element?

The elements are sometimes called the building blocks of the Universe because everything in the Universe – including ourselves – is made of them. The nucleus of each element consists of atoms with the same number of protons. Each element is unique, although elements can exist in different forms – for example, carbon may be soft graphite or hard diamond. Elements cannot usually be broken down into any other substance.

There are about 118 elements altogether, and 91 occur naturally on Earth. Others can be created in laboratories, but in minute quantities and they have very short lifespans of only thousandths of a second. Each element is also known by a one- or two-letter symbol as well as its name; for example, Fe is iron.

A chemical compound is a combination of two or more elements linked together, which can be broken down again into their constituent parts but no further. Water, for example, is made up of two hydrogen atoms linked to one oxygen atom. Salt, or sodium chloride, is a compound of sodium and chlorine.

One and only

Element 98 was given the name Californium by the four scientists who discovered it in 1950. They were working at the University of California at Berkeley, and named the element for both the state and their university. One of them, Glen Theodore Seaborg (1912–99), received the Nobel Prize for Chemistry in 1951. The 106th element, Seaborgium, was named after him in 1994. It was the first to be named in honour of a living person.

Highest melting points

1 Carbon 3,527°C (6,381°F)
2 Tungsten 3,422°C (6,192°F)
3 Rhenium 3,186°C (5,767°F)
4 Osmium 3,033°C (5,491°F)
5 Tantalum 3,017°C (5,463°F)

The surface of the Sun reaches 5,605°C (10,121°F), so no element could approach it and remain solid.

See also

Air transport: pages 216–17

Various weights of gold in a gold refinery

The heaviest elements

● **Osmium**

Osmium is the heaviest element (22.61 g/cm³ [13.07 oz/in³]). It was discovered in 1803. It was named after the Greek word for smell because it smelt bad. Osmium is very hard, and is used to make hard-wearing points, such as the nibs of fountain pens.

● **Platinum**

Platinum was used before anyone realized that it was an element. It weighs almost as much as osmium (21.45 g/cm³ [12.39 oz/in³])

and is used to make jewellery. It is also used in catalytic converters in cars to reduce the pollution from exhaust gases.

● **Plutonium**

Plutonium was discovered in 1941 and is a heavy and highly radioactive metal. It is used as a nuclear fuel and in nuclear weapons – a kilogram of plutonium produces an explosion equivalent to 20,000 tonnes of TNT.

● **Gold**

Gold is the best-known of all heavy metals – though at 19.29 g/cm³ (11.15 oz/in³) it is less heavy than the others here. Gold has been prized since ancient times and has many uses beyond coins and jewellery.

The lightest elements

● Hydrogen

Hydrogen is the simplest and lightest element, and the most common – 93 per cent of all atoms in the universe are hydrogen atoms. On Earth, it is relatively rare in the atmosphere – only 5 of every 100 million litres (8.8 of 176 million pints) of air are hydrogen, but hydrogen combined with oxygen forms all the water in the world. Hydrogen is very light. This is why it was used in balloons carrying human passengers: the second-ever flight, in Paris on 1 December 1783, was in a hydrogen balloon. Hydrogen was also used in giant airships until 6 May 1937, when the giant German airship *Hindenburg* exploded, killing 36 people, at Lakehurst, New Jersey, USA. Today, hydrogen fuel cells are used to power clean-energy cars.

● Helium

Helium is twice as heavy as hydrogen, but it is still only one-seventh the weight of air. Unlike hydrogen, helium does not burn, so it is used in modern airships.

● Lithium

Lithium was discovered in 1817 and takes its name from the Latin word for rock, although it is actually a metal. Lithium is so light and so soft that it can be easily cut with a knife. It floats because it is half as heavy as water and lighter than some types of wood. It is used to make lithium batteries.

● Potassium and sodium

Both were discovered in 1807. Both are metals that are lighter than water. In a laboratory, potassium and sodium are usually kept in paraffin because if they come into contact with water they will catch fire. Potassium is vital for plant growth and human well-being – our bodies contain about 140 g (5 oz) of it. Sodium is relatively common as part of a compound: in combination with chlorine it is ordinary table salt.

Elements in sea water

Sea water is a treasure chest of elements, but sodium and chlorine, combined as sodium chloride, are the only two that are taken from it in large amounts. Other elements, such as gold, are too expensive to extract – even though there may be as much as 500 kg of gold in a cubic kilometre of sea water (4,595 lb/ml^3).

Elements in the sea

1 Oxygen* 857,000 mg/l (114.43 oz/gall)
2 Hydrogen* 107,800 mg/l (14.39 oz/gall)
3 Chlorine 19,870 mg/l (2.65 oz/gall)
4 Sodium 11,050 mg/l (1.48 oz/gall)
5 Magnesium 1,326 mg/l (0.18 oz/gall)
* Combined as water

Elements on Earth

There is calcium in the Earth and sea in the form of calcium carbonate. Sodium exists in the form of sodium chloride, the salt in the sea and on our tables.

The quantities of both calcium and sodium are so vast that these elements are considered unlimited.

There are quite small amounts of some precious metals on Earth, which is why they are so valuable. For example, there are about one million tonnes of silver and 15,000 tonnes of gold. Elements are constantly being taken from Earth, but new discoveries are being made.

The *Hindenburg*, a giant airship filled with hydrogen, bursts into flames.

www.webelements.com   search

Cowboy inventions

All these items, beloved of cowboys, are named after their inventors.

Levi jeans

Levi Strauss (1829–1902) was a Bavarian immigrant who arrived in San Francisco in 1850 at the height of the California gold rush. Strauss noticed that the gold miners needed strong trousers and began making them, first from tent canvas and later from denim. The company is now one of the world's largest clothing manufacturers.

Bowie knife

The large knife was supposedly invented by James Bowie (1799–1836), a Texan adventurer who died during the siege of the Alamo fortress by Mexican soldiers. In fact, his older brother, Rezin Pleasant Bowie (1793–1841), may have invented the knife. It had a blade 25–38 cm (10–15 in) long, with a guard between the blade and the handle.

Colt revolver

The Colt was invented by Samuel Colt (1814–62). Colts were used during the American Civil War, and the six-gun, the six-shot, single-action .45-calibre Peacemaker model introduced in 1873, made Samuel Colt a wealthy man.

Stetson hat

John Stetson (1830–1906) was a hat maker from New Jersey. He started the John B. Stetson Manufacturing Company of Philadelphia, which made the famous ten-gallon hat worn by cowboys.

Leonardo da Vinci

Italian Leonardo da Vinci (1452–1519) is best known as a painter, anatomist, sculptor and architect. *The Last Supper* and *Mona Lisa* are among the most famous paintings of all time.

But he is also hailed as one of the greatest inventors. Among his notebooks he left plans for countless advanced machines, often with descriptions written in secret mirror writing. Many of them were never built, but they anticipated modern inventions, often by hundreds of years. They include the following:

Air conditioner	Magnetic compass
Alarm clock	Mileometer
Crane	Multi-barrelled machine gun
Diving suit and diving bell	Parachute
Double-hull ship	Revolving stage
Flying machine	Shrapnel bomb
Gas mask	Spectacles
Gears	Steam engine
Giant catapults and crossbows	Tank-like armoured vehicle
Helicopter	Telescope
Lifebelt	Water turbine

Crazy inventions

There are many odd items dreamed up by inventors – a self-raising hat (1896) for the polite man with his arms full; spectacles for chickens to protect their eyes from other fowl that might attempt to peck them (1903); a motorized ice cream cone (1998) which rotates against the tongue. Here are some other examples.

Parachute fire escape

This invention was patented in 1879 by Benjamin B. Oppenheimer of Trenton, Tennessee, USA. It was made up of a parachute attached to a helmet and padded shoes that would allow a person to leap out of a blazing building and land safely – if he was lucky enough not to break his neck.

Spider ladder

This invention was perhaps not so crazy for people who are scared of spiders. British inventor Edward Doughney's 1994 patent helps spiders to climb out of a bath.

100 years of everyday inventions 1903

1903 the safety razor was invented by King Camp Gillette

1904 the ice cream cone was invented by Italo Marcioni

1906 the electric washing machine was invented by Alva J. Fisher

1907 vacuum cleaners with bags were invented by J. Murray Spangler

1913 the crossword puzzle was invented by Arthur Wynne

1913 the zip fastener was invented by Gideon Sundback

1920 the tea bag was invented by Joseph Krieger

1924 frozen food was invented by Clarence Birdseye

1926 the aerosol spray was invented by Erik Rotheim

1927 the pop-up toaster was invented by Charles Strite

1928 elastoplast was invented by Horatio Nelson Smith

1928 sliced bread was invented by Otto Rohwedder

1931 the electric razor was invented by Col. Jacob Schick

1934 the trampoline was invented by George Nissen and Larry Griswold

1938 the ballpoint pen was invented by László Biro

1938 instant coffee was invented by the Nestlé company

1945 the microwave oven was invented by Percy LeBaron Spencer

1945 Tupperware (food containers) was invented by Earl W. Tupper

1947 the long-playing record was invented by Goldmark

1950 the credit card was invented by Frank X. McNamara

Peter Chilvers

Chilvers was 12 when he invented boardsailing (windsurfing) in 1958 off Hayling Island, UK.

What is a patent?

A patent is granted by a government to an inventor. It gives him or her the right for a limited period – usually 20 years – to stop others from making, using or selling the invention without the inventor's permission. The invention is territorial and protected only in the country in which it is patented. The first patent was granted to Filippo Brunelleschi in Florence in 1421, for a barge crane to transport marble.

Brainchildren: young inventors

Horatio Adams
Adams was only 16 when he assisted his father, Thomas, in his experiments with chicle, the dried sap of a Mexican jungle tree. This led to the invention of chewing gum.

Charles Babbage
Babbage was 19 when he first thought of the idea of the mechanical computer.

Louis Braille
He invented Braille, the raised-dot writing used by blind people, at the age of 15. Louis himself was blind.

Frank Epperson
The Popsicle or ice lolly was invented by 11-year-old Frank Epperson of San Francisco, California, in 1905. He had the idea when he left a fruit drink out during a freezing winter night and originally called it the Epsicle. He did not apply for a patent until 1923, by which time his son had renamed it Popsicle.

Chester Greenwood
Greenwood of Farmington, Maine, USA, was aged 15 in 1873 when he invented earmuffs. He started Greenwood's Ear Protector Factory and made a fortune by supplying his product to US soldiers in World War I.

Walter Lines
British schoolboy Lines invented the scooter at the age of 15. He later founded Triang Toys, once Britain's leading toy manufacturer.

John J. Stone-Parker
In 1989, when he was only four years old, John and his sister, Elaine W. Stone-Parker, invented a star-shaped gadget to prevent ice from slipping out of a drinking-glass. He is the youngest-ever holder of a patent.

Austin Meggitt
American schoolboy Meggitt was nine when he invented a device for carrying a baseball bat, ball and glove safely on the handlebars of a bicycle. In 2000 he received US Patent No. 6,029,874.

See also
Computer timeline: page 86

2005

1955 Lego was invented by Gotfried Kirk Christiansen

1956 Velcro was invented by Georges de Mestral

1958 videotape was invented by A.M. Poniatoff

1963 the ring-pull can was invented by Alcoa

1971 the digital watch was invented by George Theiss and Willy Crabtree

1971 E-mail was invented by Ray Tomlinson

1971 the pocket calculator was invented by the Sharp company

1974 the personal computer was invented by MITS

1975 the digital camera was invented by Steven Sasson and Kodak

1979 Post-it notes were invented by Spencer Silver and 3M

1979 the mobile phone was invented by NTT

1979 the Walkman was invented by Akio Morita

1981 the compact disc was invented by Philips

1982 the camcorder was invented by Sony

1989 the World Wide Web was invented by Tim Berners-Lee

1994 the GPS (completed) was invented by I. Getting and B. Parkinson

2000 the iPod digital music player was invented by Apple Computer, Inc

2001 Self-cleaning glass was invented by Kevin Sanderson

2008 MyVu launches personal media viewer (video glasses)

Roman numerals

Roman numerals use seven letters (I, V, X, L, C, M and D). A small numeral in front of a larger one is subtracted from it, so 90 is written as X (10) subtracted from C (100) – XC. A small number after a larger one is usually added to it – for example, XI (11).

Roman numerals are still in use today. You can find them in the introduction pages of books (i, ii, iii, iv, etc), on traditional clock and watch faces, in film and TV credits (2007 will appear as MMVII), in serial film titles (such as *Star Wars: Episode III – Revenge of the Sith*). They are also used in the names of sporting events – the Beijing 2008 Olympics will be the XXIX (29th) Games.

Roman	Arabic	Roman	Arabic	Roman	Arabic
I	1	XX	20	CCC	300
II	2	XXX	30	CCCC	400
III	3	XL	40	D	500
IV	4	L	50	DC	600
V	5	LX	60	DCC	700
VI	6	LXX	70	DCCC	800
VII	7	LXXX	80	CM	900
VIII	8	XC	90	M	1,000
IX	9	C	100	MM	2,000
X	10	CC	200		

Mega multiples

Certain prefixes are used in the metric system. The prefixes are the same whether describing weight, such as a kilogram, distance, such as a kilometre, or other measurements.

Prefix	Name	Value
exa-	quintillion	1,000,000,000,000,000,000
peta-	quadrillion	1,000,000,000,000,000
tera-	trillion	1,000,000,000,000
giga-	billion	1,000,000,000
mega-	million	1,000,000
kilo-	thousand	1,000
hecto-	hundred	100
deca-	ten	10
	one	1
deci-	tenth	0.1
centi-	hundredth	0.01
milli-	thousandth	0.001
micro-	millionth	0.000,001
nano-	billionth	0.000,000,001
pico-	trillionth	0.000,000,000,001
femto-	quadrillionth	0.000,000,000,000,001
atto-	quintillionth	0.000,000,000,000,000,001

Useful mathematical formulae

Area of a rectangle	length x height
Area of a triangle	½ length x height
Area of a circle	$\pi \times radius^2$
Diameter of a circle	radius x 2
Circumference of a circle	$\pi \times diameter$
Volume of a sphere	$\frac{1}{3}\pi \times radius^3$
Surface of a sphere	$4 \times \pi^2$
Volume of a cylinder	$\pi \times radius^2 \times height$
Curved area of cylinder	$2 \times \pi \times radius \times height$
Area of a cone	$\pi \times radius \times length$
Volume of a cone	$\frac{1}{3}\pi \times radius^2 \times height$

π = pi, pi = 3.14159265

"Big Ben", London, uses Roman numerals.

Mathematical symbols

Symbol	Meaning	Symbol	Meaning
+	Plus or positive	%	Per cent
–	Minus or negative	>	Greater than
±	Plus or minus, positive or negative	<	Less than
		√	Square root
x	Multiplied by	Σ	Sum of
÷ or /	Divided by	π	Pi
=	Equal to	°	Degree
≠	Not equal to	∞	Infinity
~	Of the order of, similar to		

Big numbers

The terms used for big numbers differ between the UK and the USA and other parts of the world. A billion used to be a million million in the UK, but a thousand million elsewhere. The UK has changed this definition to match the rest of the world, but other numbers are still different.

Number	Equivalent to	Zeros US	Zeros UK
Trillion	1,000 billion	12	18
Quadrillion	1,000 trillion	15	24
Quintillion	1,000 quadrillion	18	30
Sextillion	1,000 quintillion	21	36
Septillion	1,000 sextillion	24	42
Octillion	1,000 septillion	27	48
Nonillion	1,000 octillion	30	54
Decillion	1,000 nonillion	33	60
Undecillion	1,000 decillion	36	66
Duodecillion	1,000 undecillion	39	72
Tredecillion	1,000 duodecillion	42	78
Quattuordecillion	1,000 tredecillion	45	84
Quindecillion	1,000 quattuordecillion	48	90
Sexdecillion	1,000 quindecillion	51	96

● There are names for even bigger numbers, including a centillion (303 zeros in the USA and 600 zeros in the UK), a trigent-billillion (60,000,003 zeros) and sextent-billillion (1,800,000,003 zeros).

● In 1938, nine-year-old Milton Sirotta came up with the word googol, which means a one followed by 100 zeros. Milton was the nine-year-old nephew of an American mathematician called Edward Kasner (1878–1955).

● A googolplex is an even bigger number – a one with a googol of zeros, or 10 to the googol power. This number is so vast that, as Kasner explained, "... there would not be enough room to write it, if one went to the furthest stars, touring all the nebulae in the Universe and putting down zeros every inch of the way."

● There is no such number as a zillion – the word just means a really huge amount.

www.factmonster.com/mathmoney.html search

Prime numbers

A prime number is a whole number that can be divided only by one and itself, and not by any other number. Examples include 2, 3, 5, 7, 11 and 13. All prime numbers, except for 2, are also odd numbers. There are 168 prime numbers under 1,000.

Regular polygons

A polygon is a shape enclosed by straight lines. Regular polygons have sides of equal length and the angles inside are all the same. A regular polygon fits inside a circle with all its points touching the circumference. An irregular polygon does not.

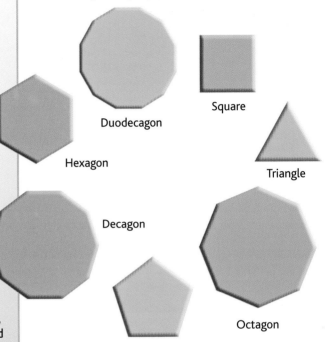

Duodecagon

Square

Hexagon

Triangle

Decagon

Octagon

Pentagon

Polygon	Number of sides	Each internal angle	Sum of internal angles
Triangle	3	60°	180°
Square (or quadrilateral)	4	90°	360°
Pentagon	5	108°	540°
Hexagon	6	120°	720°
Heptagon	7	128.57°	900°
Octagon	8	135°	1,080°
Nonagon	9	140°	1,260°
Decagon	10	144°	1,440°
Undecagon	11	147.27°	1,620°
Duodecagon (or dodecagon)	12	150°	1,800°
Quindecagon	15	156°	2,340°
Icosagon	20	162°	3,240°

Dodecahedron (12 sides)

Octahedron (8 sides)

Cube (6 sides)

Tetrahedron (4 sides)

Isosahedron (20 sides)

Regular solids

There are five types of regular solid. All faces on a regular solid are exactly the same shape. If you put a regular solid inside a sphere, all its points will touch the surface of the sphere.

Conversions

There are two systems of measuring length, area, weight, volume and so on – metric and imperial. Here's how to convert between the two different systems.

From Area	To	Multiply by
Square centimetres (cm²)	Square inches (in²)	0.1550
Square inches (in²)	Square centimetres (cm²)	6.4516
Square metres (m²)	Square feet (ft²)	10.7639
Square feet (ft²)	Square metres (m²)	0.0929
Square metres (m²)	Square yards (yd²)	1.1960
Square yards (yd²)	Square metres (m²)	0.8361
Square kilometres (km²)	Square miles (ml²)	0.3861
Square miles (ml²)	Square kilometres (km²)	2.5900
Hectares (ha)	Acres	2.4711
Acres	Hectares (ha)	0.4047

From Speed	To	Multiply by
Metres per second (m/s)	Feet per second (ft/s)	3.2808
Feet per second (ft/s)	Metres per second (m/s)	0.3048
Kilometres per hour (km/h)	Miles per hour (mph)	0.6214
Miles per hour (mph)	Kilometres per hour (km/h)	1.6093

From Weight	To	Multiply by
Grams (g)	Ounces (oz)	0.0353
Ounces (oz)	Grams (g)	28.3495
Kilograms (kg)	Pounds (lb)	2.2046
Pounds (lb)	Kilograms (kg)	0.4536
Stones	Kilograms (kg)	6.3503
Kilograms (kg)	Stones	0.1575
Hundredweight (cwt)	Kilograms (kg)	50.8024
Kilograms (kg)	Hundredweight (cwt)	0.0197
Tonnes	Tons (long)	0.9842
Tons (long)	Tonnes	1.0160
Tonnes	US short tons	1.1023
US short tons	Tonnes	0.9072

From Length	To	Multiply by
Centimetres (cm)	Inches (in)	0.3937
Inches (in)	Centimetres (cm)	2.5400
Metres (m)	Feet (ft)	3.2808
Feet (ft)	Metres (m)	0.3048
Metres (m)	Yards (yd)	1.0936
Yards (yd)	Metres (m)	0.9144
Kilometres (km)	Miles (ml)	0.6214
Miles (ml)	Kilometres (km)	1.6093

Namesakes

These measurements were named after the people who discovered them.

Ampere is a measure of electrical current. It was named after André-Marie Ampère (French, 1775–1836).

Beaufort scale measures wind speed and was named after Sir Francis Beaufort (British, 1774–1857).

Marie Curie in her laboratory

Bel/decibel is a measure of sound named after Alexander Graham Bell (Scots/USA, 1847–1922).

Celsius is a temperature measure. It was named for Anders Celsius (Swedish, 1701–44).

Curie is a measure of radiation named after Marie Curie (Polish/French, 1867–1934).

Fahrenheit is a measure of temperature named after Gabriel Fahrenheit (German, 1686–1736).

Joule is a measure of energy named after James Prescott Joule (British, 1818–89).

Kelvin is a temperature measure. It was named after William Thomson, Lord Kelvin (British, 1824–1907).

Mercalli scale measures earthquakes. It was named after Giuseppe Mercalli (Italian, 1850–1914).

Mohs' scale measures hardness and was named after Friedrich Mohs (German, 1773–1839).

Ohm/Mho measures electrical resistance. It was named after Georg Simon Ohm (German, 1787–1854).

Richter scale measures earthquakes and was named after Charles Richter (USA, 1900–85).

Volt is a measure of electromagnetic force. It was named after Alessandro Volta (Italian, 1745–1827).

Watt is a measure of power and was named after James Watt (British, 1736–1819).

Volume conversions

From	To	Multiply by
Cubic centimetres (cc)	Cubic inches (in³)	0.0610
Cubic inches (in³)	Cubic centimetres (cc)	16.3871
Cubic feet (ft³)	Cubic metres (m³)	0.0283
Cubic metres (m³)	Cubic feet (ft³)	35.3147
Cubic yards (yd³)	Cubic metres (m³)	1.3080
Cubic metres (m³)	Cubic yards (yd³)	0.7646
Cubic kilometres (km³)	Cubic miles (ml³)	0.2399
Cubic miles (ml³)	Cubic kilometres (km³)	4.1682
Litres (l)	Pints	1.7598
Pints	Litres (l)	0.5683
Litres (l)	UK gallons (gal)	0.2200
UK gallons (gal)	Litres (l)	4.5461
Litres (l)	US gallons (gal)	0.2642
US gallons (gal)	Litres (l)	3.78532

Temperature conversions

Celsius (°C) to Fahrenheit (°F)
$\times 9 \div 5 + 32$

Fahrenheit (°F) to Celsius (°C)
$- 32 \times 5 \div 9$

The world's smallest

Atomic clock The smallest clock in the world was made in 2004 by the National Institute for Standards in Technology (USA). It measures 1.5 mm (0.06 in) by 4 mm (0.16 in) and it is accurate to one second in 300 years.

Robot In 2005 Donald Laboratory (USA) built a micro-robot that measured 250 micrometres (0.0098 in) by 60 micrometres (0.0024 in), which is the thickness of a single hair.

Car The French Ligier Be Up is the smallest car that is still in production and can be driven on public roads. It has two seats and measures 268 cm (106 in) long, 141 cm (55.5 in) wide and 156 cm (61.4 in) high. It weighs 330 kg (727.5 lb) and has a top speed of 100 km/h (62.2 mph).

The Ligier Be Up has a 505 cc engine.

Weighty words

Acre
An acre describes an area of land and comes from the Old English word *aecer*, meaning a ploughed field. It was the area a team of oxen could plough in one day. In the UK in 1824, an acre was set as 4,840 square yards.

Celsius
A temperature scale invented in 1742 by Swedish astronomer Anders Celsius. A Celsius degree is 1/100th of the difference between the freezing and boiling points of water (0° and 100°).

Fahrenheit
This temperature scale was devised by German physicist Gabriel Fahrenheit. On this scale the freezing point of water is 32°.

Foot
Foot originally meant the average length of an adult foot, and has been used since ancient times. Before France invented the metric system, the French foot was based on the length of the Emperor Charlemagne's foot.

Metre
The metre was introduced in France in June 1799. It was first set as one ten-millionth of a quarter of the circumference of the Earth. It was later set as the distance between two lines on a metal bar which was kept in Sèvres, France. The distance is now more precise. It is the distance light travels in a vacuum in 1/299792458th of a second. A centimetre is 1/100th of a metre. A millimetre is 1/1,000th of a metre and a kilometre is 1,000 metres.

Gram/kilogram
Gram comes from the same ancient Greek word that gave us grammar, and means a marked-off division. A kilogram is 1,000 grams. Kilo comes from the Greek chilioi, meaning one thousand.

Hectare
This is used for measuring land areas and comes from the ancient Greek hekaton, meaning one hundred. One hectare is equivalent to 10,000 square metres or 2.4711 acres.

Hundredweight/ton
A hundredweight is 1/20th of a ton. A British or long hundredweight is 112 pounds, and a long ton is 2,240 pounds. An American or short hundredweight is 100 pounds. A short ton is 2,000 pounds.

Special measurements

Carat
The weight of diamonds and other valuable gems is measured in carats. The word comes from the carob bean, which has a consistent weight of 0.2 of a gram (0.007 oz).

Hand
The height of horses is measured in hands. The measurement is taken from the ground to the highest point on the animal's shoulder. One hand is 10.16 cm (4 in).

Knot
Speed at sea is measured in knots, which is the time it took a ship to travel the length of a knotted rope. A knot is now the same as a nautical mile, which is 1,852 m (6,076 ft).

Point
This is used by typographers and printers and refers to the size of a letter such as an x. One point is equal to 0.3528 mm (0.0139 in), so 6-point type is 2.116 mm (0.083 in) high.

Troy ounce
This name comes from the city of Troyes, France, where dealers in precious stones and metals gathered in medieval times. Gold and other rare metals are still measured in troy ounces (31.1035 g/1.1677 oz).

Computer use worldwide

In 1943 Thomas Watson, the chairman of IBM, made one of the least accurate predictions ever. He said, "I think there is a world market for maybe five computers."

There are now over one billion personal computers around the world. It is forecast that by 2010 there will be 1.35 billion computers, one for every person on the planet. One in five (290 million) of them will be in the USA.

Computer speak

Storage

1 bit equals 0.125 (0 or 1/on or off) bytes

1 nibble equals 0.5 bytes

8 bits equals 1 bytes

1 kilobyte equals 1,024 bytes

1 megabyte equals 1,018,576 bytes

1 gigabyte equals 1,073,741,824 (over 1 billion) bytes

1 terabyte equals 1,099,511,627,776 (over 1 trillion) bytes

1 petabyte equals 1,125,899,906,842,624 (over 1 quadrillion) bytes

1 exabyte equals 1,152,921,504,606,846,976 bytes

1 zettabyte equals 1,180,591,620,717,411,303,424 bytes

1 yottabyte equals 1,208,925,819,614,629,174,706,176 bytes

What that means in data

Storage

10 bytes equals one word

2 kilobytes equals one page of typewritten text

10 kilobytes equals one page of a reference book

1 megabyte equals a short novel

5 megabytes equals the complete works of Shakespeare

100 megabytes equals 1 metre (3.25 ft) of books on a shelf

250 megabytes equals the total output of data per year for every person on Earth

500 megabytes equals a CD-ROM

20 gigabytes equals the complete works of Beethoven on CD

10 terabytes equals All the printed works in the USA Library of Congress (the world's largest library)

200 petabytes equals everything ever printed

5 exabytes equals every word ever spoken

Computer timeline   1800s   1900s

1642 Blaise Pascal, France, makes a numerical wheel calculator, an early mechanical adding machine

1694 Gottfried von Leibniz, Germany, makes a machine that can multiply numbers

1820 Charles Xavier de Colmar, France, makes an "Arithometer" that can add, subtract, multiply and divide

1822 Charles Babbage, England, devises his Difference Engine

1829 Wheatstone uses punched paper tape to store data

1834 Babbage conceives the Analytical Engine

1889 Hollerith's punch card machine used in US Census

1928 IBM adopts 80-column punched card

1944 Harvard's Mark I, first digital computer

1952 Univac computer accurately predicts the US presidential election winner

1953 First IBM electronic digital computer (IBM 701)

1956 First hard disk drive (IBM). Term "artificial intelligence" devised

1958 First chess game between computer and human

1960 USA has 6,000 computers

1963 ASCII (American Standard Code for Information Interchange) introduced

1967 IBM releases floppy disk

1970 Douglas Engelbart patents first computer mouse

1971 Intel builds the microprocessor, "computer on a chip". Wang 1200, first word processor

1972 E-mail invented by Ray Tomlinson. First electronic video game, *Pong*

1975 Microsoft founded by William Gates, later to become the world's richest person

1976 First Apple computer. Cray-1, first supercomputer

1979 Compuserve launches first commercial Bulletin Board (BBN) service

Computers then and now

Computers have come a long way since Charles Babbage (1791–1871) invented his Difference Engine No. 2. His early computer could make complicated calculations and print the results.

However, it had over 4,000 parts, measured 3.4 m (11.2 ft) wide and 2.1 m (7 ft) high, weighed 2.6 tonnes and was operated by cranking a handle hundreds of times. By comparison, some of the latest personal computers measure less than 3 cm (1.2 in) thick and weigh as little as 2.54 kg (5.6 lb), with processing speeds of up to 2.16 GHz.

Babbage's Difference Engine, 1822

Apple's MacBook Air, 2008

Internet milestones

In little over 10 years, the Internet has become a global phenomenon. In 1995 it was used by about 45 million people around the world. By 2006 the figure had more than doubled to 1,018,057,389. By the time you read this, the figures will have increased again.

1960s
During the 1960s scientists in the USA began trying to work out how organizations could keep in touch with one another after a nuclear attack. In 1965 ARPA (Advanced Research Projects Agency) suggested linking computers. In 1969 computers at four US universities were connected and could "talk" to each other for the first time.

1970s
The network was extended and in 1973 computers were connected between London and Norway. At the same time, electronic mail (e-mail) was being used more and more to send messages between computers. In 1979 the first Usenet newsgroups (online discussion groups) began.

1980s
By 1981 the ARPA network had 213 hosts (sites to which users could connect). A new host was added approximately every 20 days. In 1982 a language called TCP/IP was invented which allowed all Internet computers to communicate with each other and the network was first called an Internet. The Internet began to be used commercially and by governments and universities.

Google
Google is the most-used Internet search engine in the world. In 2007, the company employed 16,805 people and had total revenue of $16.6 billion (£8.3 billion). In 2008, software giant Microsoft attempted to buy Yahoo to turn it into a rival to Google.

1990s
In 1991 the World Wide Web (www) was created. By 1994 about 40 million people were connected to the Internet. They could exchange information, sell goods and work from any computer with a phone line. Schools started using it as an electronic library. By 1996 users in almost 150 countries around the world were connected to the Internet.

2000s
High-speed broadband and wireless access is now widespread and more and more businesses are using the Internet. The number of people using the Internet more than doubled from 2000 to 2007, with the number in China increasing nearly six times. More than one billion people use the Internet worldwide.

2000s

1980 USA has more than one million computers. First laptop computers

1981 First Nintendo home video game. Commercial introduction of the computer mouse. Microsoft introduces software for IBM personal computers

1982 Worldwide, 200 computers connected to the Internet

1984 Apple Macintosh computers launched

1985 Microsoft ships Windows 1.0

1986 USA has more than 30 million computers

1988 4.7 million microcomputers, 120,000 minicomputers and 11,500 mainframe computers sold in USA

1989 100,000 hosts on the net

1990 World Wide Web described by Tim Berners-Lee. First palmtop computers

1991 First use of the phrase "surfing the net", by Jean Armour Polly

1993 Mosaic, the first graphical Internet browser, launched

1994 135 million PCs worldwide. First ads on the World Wide Web (ad for *Wired* magazine claimed as first)

1995 Amazon.com Internet bookseller founded. Microsoft's Internet Explorer browser launched

1999 150 million people use Internet worldwide (more than half in USA)

2002 iPod digital music players launched

2007 Sales of iPods top 100 million

2008 Over 330 million broadband lines in use worldwide

 www.computer.howstuffworks.com　search

The first telegraph message was sent by Morse code using a hand-operated key.

TELECOMMUNICATIONS

From fixed cables to satellites

In the early years of telecommunications, the only way of linking one telephone with another was by fixed cables. Links between continents relied on cables under the sea. The invention of radio brought the first wireless communications, but because the surface of the Earth is curved these signals could not travel far.

Satellites changed everything. They sit at an exact height above the Earth's equator (usually around 35,000 km/22,000 miles) and they rotate at the same speed as the Earth spins. This means that they stay in a fixed position. Telephone signals can be sent to the satellites and bounced back to Earth. Everywhere on the planet can be covered by only five or six satellites, except for the poles and surrounding areas, which are out of their range.

Cables under the sea

Soon after telegraph cables came into use in the 1840s, attempts were made to lay them across rivers and between islands and mainlands. Most didn't work. In 1850 the first cable was laid across the English Channel. It had to resist attack by salt water, ocean currents and water pressure, so had a thick, water-resistant, steel cover. Inside were copper wires that carried the power and signal.

Technical improvements and the demand for faster communications led to cables being laid over ever greater distances. Several attempts to lay them across the Atlantic failed when the cables snapped, but one was completed in 1858. To mark the occasion, Queen Victoria sent a telegraph message to President Buchanan in the USA. It took almost 18 hours. Attempts were made to increase the pace by raising the voltage, but this burned out the cable. In 1865 the world's largest ship at the time, the *Great Eastern*, laid the first continuous cable across the Atlantic.

During the 20th century, telegraph cables, which transmitted Morse code were steadily replaced by telephone cables, which could transmit voices. Hundreds of thousands of kilometres of underwater cables were laid across the world's oceans and seas. These have been replaced by fibre-optic cables, which offer faster transmission and many more connections.

Telecom timeline

1850s

1870s

1793 Word "telegraph" first used (in France)

1837 Charles Wheatstone and William Cooke set up first electric telegraph in London

1843 Morse code inventor Samuel Morse (USA) sends first telegraph message between Washington and Baltimore

1850 Telegraph cable laid between England and France across English Channel, but fails; 19,312 km (12,000 miles) of telegraph line in USA

1851 Thomas Crampton lays successful Dover-Calais cable

1852 First telegraph line in India; there are now 37,015 km (23,000 miles) of telegraph line in USA

1854 First Australian telegraph line (Melbourne to Williamstown)

1858 First transatlantic telegraph cable laid, but fails

1861 First USA transcontinental telegraph

1862 51,500 km (32,000 miles) of telegraph line and more than 5 million messages sent in USA

1867 First theory suggests using radio waves for telecommunication

1876 Alexander Graham Bell patents the telephone – beating his rival Elisha Gray by a matter of hours. He makes his historic first call to his assistant, Thomas Watson, who is in the next room: "Mr Watson, come here, I want to see you." The invention is demonstrated at the Centennial Exposition, Philadelphia, USA where Emperor Don Pedro of Brazil hears Bell recite the "To be or not to be" speech from *Hamlet* over the phone.

1877 Bell makes the first long-distance call between Boston and Salem, Massachusetts, 22.5 km (14 miles) away

1878 Bell demonstrates his telephone to Queen Victoria at Osborne House on the Isle of Wight. She becomes the first European monarch to use a phone

1884 First telephone handset is launched

1889 First coin-in-the-slot public phone, USA

1891 France and England are connected by telephone cable

Alexander Graham Bell making the first telephone call between New York and Chicago

Telephone Bell

Alexander Graham Bell (1847–1922) is often called the father of the telephone. He was born in Edinburgh, Scotland, moved to Canada in 1870, and later to the USA. He became an expert on the science of speech and his first inventions helped deaf people to hear sounds. During his research, Bell developed a method of transmitting voice messages along a wire. In 1876 he patented the device, which he called the harmonic telegraph. This was the first telephone.

Countries with most mobile phones

China	534,000,000
India	242,400,000
USA	233,000,000
Russia	150,000,000
Japan	100,700,000
UK	69,675,000
World total	3,300,000,000

In 2006, India joined the list of countries with more than 100 million mobile phones, and has since risen rapidly to take second place on the world list.

2000s

1894 Guglielmo Marconi invents wireless telegraphy

1897 There are seven phones per 1,000 people in the USA

1901 Marconi sends a radio signal across the Atlantic

1902 The trans-Pacific telephone cable connects Canada, New Zealand and Australia

1907 There are an estimated 1,653,356 km (1,027,348 miles) of land telecommunications lines and 376,302 km (233,823 miles) of submarine cable worldwide

1914 The first radio message is sent to an aircraft; the first transcontinental telephone call is made in the USA

1919 Rotary dial telephones are invented

1945 British writer Arthur C. Clarke proposes putting communications satellites in orbit above the Earth, which move at the same speed as the Earth spins; this means they stay in a fixed position, and communication with the ground is not interrupted.

1956 The first transatlantic telephone cable is laid

1965 Intelsat I (*Early Bird*), the first commercial telecommunications satellite, is launched

1967 The first cordless telephones go on sale

1975 The first handheld mobile phones are sold

1988 The first transatlantic fibre optic cable is laid

2004 There are 1.2 billion telephone lines around the world: 538,981,500 in Asia,

327,657,500 in Europe, 295,292,700 in North and South America, 25,929,800 in Africa and 13,773,000 in Oceania

2005 Mobile phone users now number more than 2 billion worldwide

2006 US company Western Union ends its telegraph service after 150 years, as e-mails replace telegrams

2007 The iPhone has sold 5 million worldwide and expects to hit 10 million in 2008.

Human Body

Brain waves

In 2008, the 'Babylab' research centre in Uppsala, Sweden, received widespread media attention for its projects which monitor a baby's brain activity. The study will help scientists understand how the brain develops and to better understand conditions such as autism.

Your amazing body

Blood

An adult man's body contains about 5 l (10.5 pt) of blood. A woman's contains about 4.3 l (9.1 pt). The blood travels along 100,000 km (62,137 miles) of blood vessels. It contains 25,000,000,000 to 30,000,000,000 red cells. The life span of red cells is only about 120 days, and 1,200,000 to 2,000,0000 of them are made every second.

Brain power

You lose 100,000 brain cells every day! Luckily you have 100 billion altogether. If the surface area of your brain could be ironed out it would measure 2,090 sq cm (324 sq in).

Breathing

The average person inhales 6 l (12.6 pt) of air per minute, or 8,640 l (18,260 pt) a day. You take 13–17 breaths a minute when sitting still and up to 80 during vigorous exercise.

Cells

There are 50 trillion cells in your body and 3 billion of them die every minute (4,320,000,000,000 a day). Most of these are replaced. You make 10 billion new white blood cells each day. You have a total of 1,000,000,000,000 white cells, which help fight germs and infections.

Chemicals

There is enough carbon in your body to fill 900 pencils, enough fat to make 75 candles, enough phosphorus to make 220 match heads and enough iron to make a 7.5 cm (3 in) nail.

Digestive system

Your stomach produces up to 2 l (4.2 pt) of hydrochloric acid a day. It does not damage the stomach walls because 500,000 cells in your stomach lining are replaced every minute. The small intestine is about 5 m (16.4 ft) long. The large intestine is thicker, but only about 1.5 m (4.9 ft) long.

Eyes

You blink about 20,000 times a day.

Gas

On average, you release 2 l (4.2 pt) of gases from your intestines as burps or farts.

Hair

Hair grows about 0.5 mm (0.02 in) a day.

Heartbeats

Your heart pumps 13,640 l (28,800 pt) of blood around your body in a day. An average heartbeat rate of 70 beats a minute adds up to more than 100,000 beats a day.

Mouth

You will produce 37,800 l (79,900 pt) of saliva in your life.

Nerves

Your body has about 13,000,000,000,000 nerve cells, transmitting messages at speeds of 290 km/h (180 mph).

Sweat

You lose about 0.5 l (1.1 pt) of water a day through 3,000,000 sweat glands. In hot climates you may lose as much as 13.5 l (28.5 pt) a day.

Urine

You will pass 400 to 2,000 ml (0.8 to 4.2 pt) of urine every day, depending on your age, your size and outside conditions, especially temperature.

Highly magnified image of red blood cells

Largest human organs

The weights listed below are all averages, but sometimes organs are much larger. Some brains have weighed more than 2,000 g (4.4 lb), but that doesn't mean the owners were super-intelligent!

Skin 10,886 g (384 oz)
Liver 1,560 g (55 oz)
Brain male 1,408 g (49.7 oz)
Brain female 1,263 g (44.6 oz)
Lungs right 580 g (20.5 oz)
Lungs left 510 g (18 oz)
Heart male 315 g (11.1 oz)
Heart female 265 g (9.3 oz)
Kidney left 150 g (5.3 oz)
Kidney right 140 g (4.9 oz)

Spleen 170 g (6 oz)
Pancreas 98 g (3.5 oz)
Thyroid 35 g (1.2 oz)
Prostate (male only) 20 g (0.7 oz)
Adrenals left 6 g (0.2 oz)
Adrenals right 6 g (0.2 oz)

One and only

The only bone in the human body that is not connected to another bone is the hyoid bone, a U-shaped bone at the base of the tongue. It is supported by the muscles in the neck, but it is not connected to any other bone.

What's your body made of?

Most of the human body is made up of water, or H_2O, which is a combination of hydrogen and oxygen. As much as 99 per cent of the body is made up of oxygen, carbon, hydrogen, nitrogen, calcium and phosphorus. There are also small amounts of other elements.

Element	Avg. in 70 kg (154 lb) person g (oz)	Element	Avg. in 70 kg (154 lb) person g (oz)
Oxygen	43,000 (1,1517)	Potassium	110–140 (4–5)
Carbon	16,000 (564)	Sodium	100 (3.5)
Hydrogen	7,000 (247)	Chlorine	95 (3.35)
Nitrogen	1,800 (64)	Magnesium	25 (0.8)
Calcium	1,200 (42)	Iron	4 (0.1)
Phosphorus	780 (28)	Zinc	2.3 (0.08)
Sulphur	140 (5)	Silicon	1 (0.03)

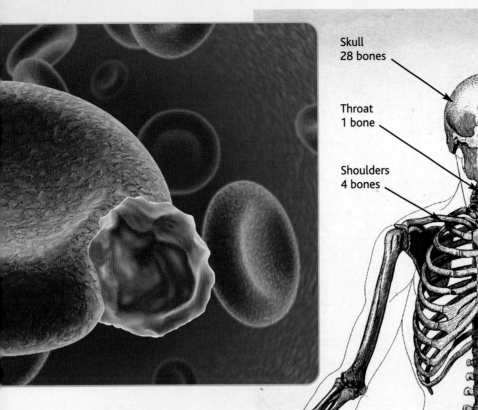

Skull
28 bones

Throat
1 bone

Shoulders
4 bones

The ear bones
are the smallest
in the body.

Sternum
(breastbone)
3 bones

Ribs
24 bones

Vertebrae
(backbone)
26 bones

Pelvis
2 bones

Arms and
hands
60 bones

Legs and feet
58 bones

Human skeleton

The skeleton is the body's framework. The bones of the skeleton support the body, protect the internal organs such as the heart and lungs, and allow you to move.

Longest bones in the body

These are the average measurements of the longest bones of an adult male. The same bones in the female skeleton are usually 6–13 per cent smaller, except the breastbone which is almost the same.

Femur (thighbone, upper leg)
50.50 cm (19.88 in)
Tibia (shinbone, inner lower leg) 43.03 cm
(16.94 in)
Fibula (outer lower leg) 40.50 cm
(15.94 in)
Humerus (upper arm)
36.46 cm (14.35 in)
Ulna (inner lower arm) 28.20 cm
(11.10 in)
Radius (outer lower arm) 26.42 cm (10.40 in)
7th rib 24.00 cm (9.45 in)
8th rib 23.00 cm (9.06 in)
Hipbone (one half of pelvis)
18.50 cm (7.28 in)
Sternum (breastbone) 17.00 cm (6.69 in)

Nails

Your fingernails grow 0.05 cm (0.02 in) a week, four times faster than your toenails.

Skin

Your skin weighs up to 4 kg (8.8 lb) and covers up to 1.3–1.7 sq m (14–18.3 sq ft). Getting dressed and undressed, rubbing body parts together and even breathing cause microscopic flakes of skin to fall off at the rate of 50,000 flakes a minute. In a lifetime you will shed 18 kg (39.7 lb) of skin.

How heavy?

The human skeleton makes up about one-fifth of a person's entire weight. An average adult weighing 70 kg (154 lb) will have a skeleton that weighs 14 kg (31 lb).

Q www.innerbody.com   search

Weighty wonder

Daniel Lambert (1770–1809) was one of the heaviest British people of all time. At his largest, he weighed 330 kg (727.5 lb) and measured 2.8 m (9.2 ft) round his body and 94 cm (37 in) round his leg. Lambert used to charge visitors to his house a shilling (five pence) just to look at him.

When he died in 1809, it took 34 m (111.5 ft) of elm planking to make his coffin, which looked like a gigantic packing case. A window and part of the wall of his house had to be removed to get the coffin out, and it had to be mounted on wheels to trundle it to the cemetery.

Daniel Lambert

Body records

Longest beard
Hans Langseth (1846–1927) had a beard that measured 5.33 m (17 ft 6 in). It has been in the Smithsonian Institution, Washington DC, USA, since 1967.

Longest nails
Shridhar Chillal of Pune, India (1937–) has not cut the nails on his left hand since 1952. By 2000 the total length of his nails on that hand was over 600 cm (236 in).

Longest moustache
Kalyan Ramji Sain of Sundargath, India, holds the record. His moustache is 3.29 m (11 ft 11.5 in) from tip to tip.

Longest hair
Swami Pandarasannadhi was the head of a monastery in Madras, India. When his hair was measured in 1949 it was 7.9 m (26 ft) long.

Longest sneezing bout
Donna Griffiths of Pershore, Worcestershire, started sneezing on 13 January 1981 and continued for 978 days.

Maths genius
When he was only eight years old, American Zerah Colburn (1804–40) worked out how many seconds had elapsed since the birth of Christ. He did this in his head

Hans Langseth

within seconds. When Zerah was asked whether 4,294,967,297 was a prime number (one that cannot be divided evenly by another number), he instantly replied that it was not – it is equal to 641 times 6,700,417.

Longest hiccuping
Charles Osborne of Anthon, Iowa, USA, hiccuped from 1922 to 1990.

Infant prodigy
By the age of four, Kim Ung-Yong of Korea (1963–) could speak fluent Korean, English, Japanese and German, and could solve calculus problems.

Memory
Gon Yang-ling of Harbin, China, has memorized more than 15,000 telephone numbers.

World's oldest people

Below is a list of the world's longest-living people, or supercentenarians. It includes only those for whom there are accurate records of their birth and death dates.

Although Christian Mortensen is ninth in the list, he is the world's oldest man. The others in the list are women.

Jeanne Calment (1875–1997), France: 122 years and 164 days
Sarah DeRemer Knauss (1880–1999), USA: 119 years and 97 days
Lucy Hannah (1875–1993), USA: 117 years and 248 days
Marie-Louise Meilleur (1880–1998), Canada: 117 years and 229 days
Maria Capovilla (1889–2006) Ecuador: 116 years and 347 days
Tane Ikai (1879–1995), Japan: 116 years and 175 days
Elizabeth Bolden (1890–2006) USA: 116 years and 118 days
Maggie Barnes (1882–1998), USA: 115 years and 319 days
Christian Mortensen (1882–1998), Denmark/USA: 115 years and 252 days
Charlotte Hughes (1877–1993), UK: 115 years and 228 days

Oldest living person
Edna (Scott) Parker was born in Indiana, USA, on 20 April 1893, and celebrated her 115th birthday in 2008, making her the oldest person alive in the world.

Tom Thumb and friends
American showman Phineas T. Barnum first met Charles Sherwood Stratton (USA, 1838–83) when he was four years old. He was 61cm (24 in) tall and weighed 6.8 kg (15 lb). Barnum persuaded Charles's parents to allow him to exhibit their son for a fee of $3 a week. He was advertised as "General Tom Thumb, a dwarf eleven years of age, just arrived from England". By the time he died, he had grown to 1 m (3 ft 3 in) and weighed 32 kg (70 lb). Lavinia Warren (USA, 1841–1919) was 79 cm (31 in) tall. Her first husband was Tom Thumb.

"Commodore" Nutt (USA, 1844–81) was 74 cm (29 in) tall. Like Tom Thumb he was exhibited by Phineas T. Barnum.

Amazing feats

● In 1997, at Sydney Airport, Australia, David Huxley pulled a 187-tonne Boeing 747-400 a distance of 91 m (298.5 ft). He had previously hauled a Boeing 737 and a Concorde.

● In 2005, US arm-wrestler Ed Shelton ripped up 55 telephone directories, each 1,044 pages thick. It took him three minutes.

● Sri-Lankan born Arulanantham Suresh Joachim currently holds 30 endurance records, including a drumming marathon (84 hours), the longest time standing still (76 hours 40 minutes), running 100 miles/161 km on a treadmill (42 minutes 33 seconds) and crawling one mile/1.6 km (37 minutes 17 seconds). In 2006 he announced his intention to run a mega-marathon through 54 countries in 181 days – over 6,000 km (3,729 miles).

Run-up records

In the annual Empire State Building Run-Up, runners race up the famous skyscraper's 1,576 steps. In 2006 Andrea Mayr of Austria set a new women's record of 11 minutes 23 seconds. The overall record-holder is Australian athlete Paul Crake. In 2003, he got to the top in 9 minutes 33 seconds. In 2008, Thomas Dodd (Germany) won the race for the third consecutive year.

Robert Wadlow

Tallest real giants

These are the most reliable records. All are men, except Trijntje Keever and Jeng Jinlian.

Robert Pershing Wadlow (1918–40), USA: 2.72 m (8 ft 11.1 in)

John William Rogan (1868–1905), USA: 2.68 m (8 ft 9.8 in)

John Aasen (1887–1938), USA: 2.67m (8 ft 9.8 in)

John F. Carroll (1932–69), USA: 2.64 m (8 ft 7.6 in)

Al Tomaini (1918–62), USA: 2.55 m (8 ft 4.4 in)

Trijntje Keever (1616–33), Netherlands: 2.54 m (8 ft 3.3 in)

Edouard Beaupre (1881–1904), Canada: 2.50 m (8 ft 2.5 in)

Bernard Coyne (1897–1921), USA: 2.49 m (8 ft 1.2 in)

Don Koehler (1925–81), USA: 2.49 m (8 ft 1.2 in)

Jeng Jinlian (1964–82), China: 2.48 m (8 ft 1.1 in)

Väinö Myllyrinne (1909–63), Finland: 2.48 m (8 ft 1.1 in)

Louis Moilanen (1885–1913), Finland/USA: 2.46 m (8 ft 1 in)

Gabriel Estavo Monjane (1944–90), Mozambique: 2.46 m (8 ft 0.75 in)

Life expectancy

Life expectancy is the average number of years people in different countries are likely to live. Conditions can improve or sometimes get worse, so life expectancy can get higher or lower.

The country with the highest life expectancy is Andorra at 83.54 years. The country with the lowest life expectancy is Swaziland with 31.88 years. People who live in the UK and the USA have an average life expectancy of 76.52 years and 75.42 years respectively.

Commodore Nutt, Miss Warren, normal-sized man and Tom Thumb

A fear of snakes is called ophidiophobia.

Common phobias

A phobia is a strong fear of a particular animal, object, situation or activity. The fear is often out of proportion to the reality and may make people vomit, sweat, tremble and even faint. People may go to great lengths to avoid the subjects of their phobias.

Most common phobias

Fear of snakes is called ophidiophobia

Fear of flying is called aerophobia or aviatophobia

Fear of open spaces is called agoraphobia, cenophobia or kenophobia

Fear of confined spaces is called claustrophobia, cleisiophobia, cleithrophobia or clithrophobia

Fear of spiders is called arachnephobia or arachnophobia

Fear of heights is called acrophobia, altophobia, hypsophobia or hypsiphobia

Unusual phobias

Fear of beards is called pogonophobia

Fear of chickens is called alektorophobia

Fear of dancing is called chorophobia

Fear of dolls is called pediophobia

Fear of fish is called ichthyophobia

Fear of frogs is called batrachophobia

Fear of hair is called chaetophobia

Fear of mirrors is called eisoptrophobia

Fear of the number 13 is called triskaidekaphobia

Fear of string is called linonophobia

Fear of teeth is called odontophobia

Calorie counts

A Calorie (with a capital C) is a unit that measures the amount of energy in foods. It is also known as a kilocalorie and is equal to 1,000 calories (with a small c). A calorie is the amount of heat needed to raise the temperature of 1 gram (0.035 oz) of water by 1°C (1.8°F).

An adult might eat up to 3,000 Calories a day. Eating too many Calories that the body does not use for energy may make you fat. The figures below are based on the average number of Calories a 70 kg (155 lb) adult burns when doing an activity for one hour. A lighter person uses fewer Calories; a heavier person more.

Squash 844 Calories

Rugby, skipping, swimming 704 Calories

Basketball, cycling, running, walking upstairs 563 Calories

Canoeing or rowing 493 Calories

Football, ice skating, roller skating, skiing, tennis 493 Calories

Aerobics 422 Calories

Mowing lawn 387 Calories

Cricket (batting or bowling), gardening, skateboarding 352 Calories

Dancing 317 Calories

Golf, table tennis 281 Calories

Housework, walking dog 246 Calories

Frisbee, surfing 211 Calories

Playing piano 176 calories

Standing 120 calories

Sitting 90 calories

Sleeping 65 calories

Causes of death worldwide

There are big differences between the causes of death in developing countries and in developed countries. In developing countries, many more deaths are caused by infectious diseases and illnesses spread by insects such as malaria.

In developed countries more people become ill from being overweight and eating rich diets. There are about 57,029,000 deaths a year worldwide.

Heart diseases 16,733,000 per year

Cancers 7,121,000 per year

Respiratory infections 3,963,000 per year

Lung diseases 3,702,000 per year

HIV/AIDS 2,777,000 per year

Digestive diseases 1,968,000 per year

Diarrhoeal diseases 1,798,000 per year

Tuberculosis 1,566,000 per year

Malaria 1,272,000 per year

Road traffic injuries 1,192,000 per year

Neuropsychiatric disorders 1,112,000 per year

Medical milestones   1800s

c. 460 BC The first medical studies were carried out by Hippocrates (Greece)

AD 1543 Accurate anatomical drawings were made by Andreas Vesalius (Belgium)

1628 Blood circulation was discovered by William Harvey (UK)

1683 Bacteria were first described by Antonie van Leeuwenhoek (the Netherlands)

1796 The first smallpox vaccination was carried out by Edward Jenner (UK)

1805 Morphine was used as a painkiller by Friedrich Sertürner (Germany)

1810 Homeopathy was used by Samuel Hahnemann (Germany)

1816 The stethoscope was invented by René Laënnec (France)

1818 The first blood transfusion was carried out by Thomas Blundell (UK)

1842 Ether was administered as an anaesthetic by Crawford Long (USA)

1844 Nitrous oxide (laughing gas) was used as an anaesthetic by Horace Wells (USA)

1846 Ether vapour was used as an anaesthetic by William Morton (USA)

1847 Chloroform was used as an anaesthetic by John Bell/James Simpson (UK)

1864 The Red Cross was founded by Henri Dunant (Switzerland)

1867 Antiseptic was used before surgery by Joseph Lister (UK)

1885 Rabies vaccine was developed by Louis Pasteur (France)

1895 X-rays were discovered by William von Röntgen (Germany)

1895 Psychoanalysis was used by Sigmund Freud (Austria)

1898 Aspirin was made by Felix Hoffman (Germany)

1901 Blood groups were identified by Karl Landsteiner (Austria)

Sleep fact file

● About one-third of our lives are spent sleeping, but very little is really known about it.

● We sleep in different stages. These range from light sleep to deep sleep, with periods of REM (Rapid Eye Movement) in between, during which we dream.

● The connection between REM and dreaming was discovered in 1953. It usually begins about 90 minutes after falling asleep and occurs in bursts, totalling about two hours a night, or 20 per cent of total sleep time.

● At least 30 per cent of adults snore. Many inventors have come up with anti-snoring gadgets to solve the problem. These include mouth or nose devices that alter breathing by blasting the snorers with sound, giving them electric shocks or shaking their beds.

● Trains have a "dead man's handle", which must be held at all times. If the driver falls asleep and loses his grip, the train stops.

● The scientific word for stretching and yawning is pandiculaton.

● Newborn babies can sleep for up to 21 hours out of 24. Children and teenagers need about 10 hours of sleep a night, while most adults need only 7–9 hours. Those over 65 need the least of all – about six hours. Older people also have less deep sleep and less REM sleep than young people.

Sir Winston Churchill

First face transplant

The world's first face transplant was carried out in 2005 on Isabelle Dinoire (born 1967) of Valenciennes, France. Her nose, lips and chin had been seriously injured when she was attacked by her dog. In an operation that lasted 15 hours, she was successfully given the face of a brain-dead donor.

● It is claimed that several famous people have existed on polyphasic sleep – short naps of a few minutes – instead of one long period of sleep. These include Leonardo da Vinci and Winston Churchill.

2000s

1906 Vitamins were discovered by Frederick Hopkins (UK)

1922 Insulin was used to treat diabetes by Frederick Banting and John Macleod (Canada) and Charles Best (USA)

1927 Iron lung was invented by Philip Drinker (USA)

1928 Penicillin was discovered by Alexander Fleming (UK)

1940 Penicillin was first used by Howard Florey (Australia) and Ernest Chain (UK)

1952 The first artificial heart valve was used by Charles Hufnagel (USA)

1953 DNA structure was identified by Francis Crick (UK) and James Watson (USA)

1955 Kidney dialysis machine was invented by Willem J. Kolff (the Netherlands/USA)

1957 First heart pacemaker was used by Clarence Lillehie (USA)

1967 The first human heart transplant was performed by Christiaan Barnard (S. Africa)

1970 First artificial heart was used by Robert Jarvik (USA)

1971 CAT scanner was first used by Godfrey Hounsfield (UK)

1978 First test-tube baby (Louise Brown) was born after procedure perfomed by Patrick Steptoe (UK)

1980 Smallpox was eradicated by World Health Organization

1984 Genetic fingerprinting was invented by Alec Jeffreys (UK)

1984 AIDS virus was first identified by Centers for Disease Control (USA)

1996 First mammal was cloned (Dolly, a sheep) by Ian Wilmut, Roslin Institute (UK)

2000 Human DNA genome sequence was completed

2006 Robot heart surgery was performed by Carlo Pappone (Italy)

2007 DNA testing enables people to check for genetic disorders

1928 poster advertising milk chocolate sweets

F.L. Cailler

CHOCOLAT AU LAIT

The birth of the burger

The name hamburger is nothing to do with ham, but comes from the German city of Hamburg. A burger was originally called a Hamburg steak. In 1889, the word hamburger first appeared in a restaurant review in the US newspaper *Walla Walla Union*. It was in a phrase that was itself a mouthful: "You are asked if you will have porkchopbeefsteakhamandegg hamburgersteakorliver andbacon."

Burger with all the trimmings

What we eat

A family food survey is carried out in the UK every year. The latest figures for what we eat in the home (not including takeaways and eating out) show that the average person will consume more than 50 tonnes of food and drink in an 80-year lifespan. These are some of the main items in the survey, and the amounts each of us can expect to eat in our lives:

Milk and cream 8,599 kg (18,957 lb)
Soft drinks 7,147 kg (15,756 lb)
Fresh fruit 3,561 kg (7,850 lb)
Bread 2,916 kg (6,428 lb)
Alcoholic drinks 2,484 kg (5,476 lb)
Fresh potatoes 2,442 kg (5,383 lb)
Poultry 1,082 kg (2,385 lb)
Mineral water 1,052 kg (2,319 lb)
Fats 761 kg (1,677 lb)
Ice cream 724 kg (1,596 lb)
Fish 695 kg (1,532 lb)
Biscuits 686 kg (1,512 lb)
Breakfast cereals 562 kg (1,238 lb)
Cakes and pastries 541 kg (1,192 lb)
Sugar and preserves (jam, etc) 537 kg (1,183 lb)

Sweets 512 kg (1,128 lb)
Beef and veal 499 kg (1,100 lb)
Cheese 483 kg (1,064 lb)
Bacon and ham 466 kg (1,027 lb)
Eggs 402 kg (886 lb)
Rice 374 kg (824 lb)
Pasta 370 kg (815 lb)
Pizza 308 kg (679 lb)
Beverages 237 kg (522 lb)
Mutton and lamb 220 kg (485 lb)

Extraordinary feasts

● Philip, Duke of Burgundy, gave a four-day banquet in 1454. The highlight came when a huge pie was brought into the room. The lid was raised to reveal 28 musicians playing inside the pie.

● On 23 October 1843, the statue of Lord Nelson was due to be hauled to the top of Nelson's Column in Trafalgar Square, London. Before this was done, 14 men sat down to a dinner of rump steak on the plinth on top of the column, 51 m (167 ft) above the ground.

● Businessman C.K.G. Billings had a dinner at Sherry's restaurant in New York on 28 March 1903 to celebrate the completion of his new stables. All the guests were on horseback. Their horses were brought by lift and the floor was laid with turf. The main course was served in nosebags, and the champagne in buckets.

● American millionaire George A. Kessler held his birthday party at the Savoy Hotel in London on 30 June 1905. He had the courtyard flooded and decorated Venetian style. His guests sat in a gondola and were served by waiters dressed as gondoliers.

Lunch in a dinosaur

On New Year's Eve 1853, dinosaur expert Professor Richard Owen held a banquet inside the framework of a model of a gigantic iguanodon dinosaur.

Richard Owen's banquet was held inside a model of a dinosaur.

Bottles and barrels

The first bottles were made in sizes that were easy to carry. The 750 ml (1.9 pt) bottle became the standard size for most types of wine in the 19th century. In the USA this has been the legal size since 1979, even though metric measurements are not widely used there.

Some wine and champagne bottle sizes have Biblical names – the name Jeroboam was used for the four-bottle size as early as 1725 in Bordeaux, and others were soon named in the same way.

The origins of the names used for bottles
● Jeroboam (4 bottles), first king of Israel
● Rehoboam (6 bottles), son of Solomon, the first king of Judah
● Methuselah (8 bottles), Biblical leader said to have lived 969 years
● Salmanazar (12 bottles), an Assyrian king
● Balthazar (16 bottles), served wine at a great feast
● Nebuchadnezzar (20 bottles), king of Babylon
● Melchior (24 bottles), one of the Three Wise Men

Barrels were invented during the Iron Age. They gradually replaced the pottery containers or amphorae the ancient Greeks and Romans used for their wine, oil and other liquids. Barrels come in a range of different sizes.

Pin is 4.5 gallons (20.5 litres)
Firkin is 9 gallons (40.9 litres)
Kilderkin is 18 gallons (81.8 litres)
Barrel is 36 gallons (163.7 litres)
Hogshead is 54 gallons (245.5 litres)
Puncheon is 72 gallons (327.3 litres)
Butt is 108 gallons (491.0 litres)
Tun is 216 gallons (981.9 litres)

Bottled water

Then...
● In the 19th century contaminated water from taps and pumps spread the killer disease cholera. Bottled water became popular as a safe alternative.

● In 1741 the English scientist Dr William Brownrigg created the first artificial mineral water. He added health-giving minerals and carbon dioxide for fizziness. He was also the first scientist to extract the element platinum.

● In 1792 Joseph Schweppe moved from Vienna to London and began to produce his own brand of artificial mineral water. His company grew to become one of the world's most famous manufacturers of soft drinks.

● French doctor Louis Perrier gave his name to Perrier water, which became the best-known mineral water in the world. In the 1960 James Bond novel *For Your Eyes Only*, Bond insists on drinking only this brand of water.

...and now
● Over 164 billion litres (43,297,400,000 gall) of bottled water are drunk in the world every year. That's enough to fill 65,600 Olympic-size swimming pools. In the UK the average adult drinks 36 litres (9.5 gall) each year, but Italians drink the most – 191 litres (50.5 gall) per adult every year.

● Many people choose bottled water over tap water because it lacks substances, such as chlorine, which affect the flavour of tap water and bottles are portable. Bottled water is also produced to strict safety standards, so in some places it may be safer.

● Bottled water removes billions of litres of underground water, while making and transporting the bottles uses huge amounts of energy. Over 2.5 million tonnes of plastic go into the bottles every year and this has to be disposed of. Bottled water may also lack fluoride and other useful minerals found in tap water so may be less healthy than the water in our homes.

Types of bottled water

Bottled or table water can come from underground springs and wells, or taps. It is purified before it is bottled. Natural mineral water and spring water are types of underground water that contain naturally-occurring minerals. Sparkling water has carbon dioxide added to make it fizzy. If this occurs naturally, it is often removed and replaced to ensure that it is always at the same level.

World History

Castro bows out

In 2008, after almost 50 years as President of Cuba, Fidel Castro announced his retirement. His younger brother Raúl has taken power in the country, which remains governed as a communist dictatorship.

Prehistoric ages

Prehistory is the time before events were written down and recorded. Human prehistory is usually divided into three periods.

Stone Age
The period when stone was used for tools. It is divided into two parts: Palaeolithic (Old Stone) from about 2 million to 10,000 BC and Neolithic (New Stone) from about 10,000 to 3300 BC.

Bronze Age (c. 3300–c. 2500 BC)
The period when people began to make things with bronze, which was more reliable and hardwearing than stone.

Iron Age (c. 1200 BC–c. AD 50–1000)
The period when iron was used for making tools. Bronze is a better material, but iron was more widely available, so cheaper.

Neolithic burial place, called a dolmen, in Portugal

Historical periods

History is usually divided into different periods to make it easier to study and talk about. The following are the main periods in the history of the Western world since the fall of the Roman empire.

The early Middle Ages (Dark Ages)
This period came after the fall of the Roman empire in AD 476, when so-called barbarians (Germanic tribes) took over areas that had been under Roman control. It became known as the Dark Ages because there was very little writing, science or culture during this time. The lack of writing also means that we do not know much about what happened. The early Middle Ages came to an end after the Norman Conquest when there was a revival in learning.

The Middle (Medieval) Ages
This was a very religious time. Most people believed in an all-powerful God, responsible for bringing order and prosperity. The Church was very influential and wealthy, and many great cathedrals and monasteries were built during this period. It was a great age of learning, and the first universities were founded in Parma and Bologna, then Paris and Oxford. Chartres Cathedral in France was built and the writings of Dante and Chaucer were published.

The Renaissance
The Renaissance began in Italy during the 14th century, and spread to northern Europe in the 16th century. The name Renaissance comes from the French word for rebirth; people looked back to Greek and Roman ideals in arts such as architecture and sculpture at this time. These ideas spread with the help of printing, which was invented by German Johannes Gutenberg in the mid-15th century. The Renaissance was marked by people's belief in progress and personal achievement. The playwright William Shakespeare and the artist Leonardo da Vinci lived and worked during this time.

The Reformation
In 16th-century Europe most people belonged to the Roman Catholic Church, which was headed by the Pope. Some were concerned that the Church was too involved with power and money. Leaders such as Erasmus and Martin Luther wanted people to reject the priests and return to the roots of Christianity and the Bible. This led to the start of Protestantism and its split from the Roman Catholic Church.

The age of colonialism
In 1492 Christopher Columbus discovered the Americas. This encouraged many European countries to invade and conquer other smaller or weaker countries so they could use their resources, trade with them or use them as stopping points for their ships. Portugal gained control of what is now Brazil, and Spain took most of Latin America, as well as large parts of what is now the USA. The Dutch gained the Indonesian islands and the French took Canada. Britain was the most powerful colonizing power. It gained 13 colonies in North America, plus Australasia, some Caribbean islands and vast tracts of Africa and Asia, including India. European colonization continued throughout the 19th century and up to the First World War (1914–18). After the War, the victors divided many of the territories of the losers.

See also
Inventions:
pages 80–81

Extent of European colonialism 1815–1914

Belgian

British

Dutch

French

German

Italian

Portuguese

Russian

Spanish

NORTH AMERICA

SOUTH AMERICA

The Industrial Revolution

The Industrial Revolution began with the invention of steam power and steam-driven machinery (mainly used in the textile industry) in 18th-century Britain. During the following century inventions such as steam-powered ships and railways spread throughout the world. This revolution led thousands of people to leave the countryside and move to crowded slum towns where there were large factories employing huge numbers of workers. The new industries needed better transport to bring supplies and deliver finished goods, so a huge network of roads and canals was built during the 18th century, followed by railways in the 19th. The Industrial Revolution also led to a growth in child labour and a widening divide between rich and poor people.

The modern age

During the 20th century advances in technology led to great changes in society and global politics. New weapons and military techniques changed the way wars were fought. Huge numbers of people died during World Wars I and II. During the Cold War between the USA and the USSR there was no fighting, but both sides were afraid of the nuclear weapons they were developing.

Air travel, television and, most recently, the Internet have all enabled more people to experience the world beyond their own country. At the same time, cheap domestic appliances such as washing machines and dishwashers allow people more time to spend on activities such as entertainment and shopping.

Modern living

In the 20th century, factories began to mass-produce cars that ordinary people could afford. This allowed them to live further from their work places and led to the building of suburbs all over the Western world.

Working on a car production line

ASIA

EUROPE

AFRICA

AUSTRALIA

View down an elevator inside a shopping centre

www.schoolshistory.org.uk   search

HISTORICAL EVENTS

Romulus and Remus, the founders of Rome, nursed by a she-wolf

753 BC Rome founded

According to legend, Rome was founded by Romulus and Remus, the twin sons of the god Mars and priestess Rhea Silvia. The city is named after Romulus, who killed his brother and ruled as Rome's first king. Rome was the capital of the Roman empire, which controlled the entire Mediterranean region and far beyond by 44 BC.

1789 French Revolution

The French people had many complaints against their system of government, especially the power of the monarchy and the land-owning aristocracy. These erupted in a revolution in which the Bastille prison was seized. The violent period that followed became known as the Reign of Terror, and King Louis XVI and many other members of the ruling class were executed.

The Statue of Liberty in New York has a tablet in her left hand which reads July 4 1776.

Black Death

This epidemic was probably caused by bacteria that were passed on by fleabites and by contact with infected sufferers. It was known as the Black Death because victims suffered from black blotches on their skin before dying. The plague swept across Asia and Europe in the 14th century, killing as many as a third of the people.

1776 US Independence

The Declaration of Independence was prepared after years of tension between Britain and the American colonies over matters such as taxation. It listed the colonies' complaints and expressed the determination of the people of America to separate themselves from their British rulers. The declaration was signed on 4 July 1776. The armed conflict that followed ended with America's victory in 1781. In 1783 the Treaty of Paris recognized the country's independence.

History timeline   1000s   1600s

753 BC Rome founded

221 BC Qin Shihuangdi becomes first Emperor of China

about AD 33 Jesus crucified

43 Emperor Claudius invades Britain

79 Pompeii in Italy destroyed by the eruption of Vesuvius volcano

476 Roman empire ends when Goths invade

632 Death of Muhammad, founder of Islam

1066 Battle of Hastings; William the Conqueror becomes king of England

1086–7 Domesday Book records all land in England

1096–99 First Crusade – European Christians attempt to recover Jerusalem and the Holy Land from Muslim control

1215 King John signs Magna Carta, granting rights to English citizens

1347–80s Black Death kills 75 million in Asia and Europe

1337–1453 100 Years War between England and France; France eventually wins

1415 Henry V of England defeats the French at Agincourt and goes on to conquer Normandy

1431 17-year-old French patriot Joan of Arc leads an army and defeats the English (1429), but is burned at the stake

1455–85 Wars of the Roses (civil war in England)

1476 Caxton begins printing in London

1478 Spanish Inquisition begins the persecution of non-Catholics

1492 Columbus sails from Palos, Spain, to Americas

1517 Reformation starts when Martin Luther publishes protests against Catholic Church

1519-22 Ferdinand Magellan's expedition circumnavigates the globe

1588 Spanish Armada defeated by the English fleet, fireships and storms

1618–48 Thirty Years War (Catholic v Protestant) in Europe

1620 The Pilgrim Fathers sail from Plymouth for America and found a new colony

1642–49 English Civil War

1649 King Charles I executed

1660 Restoration of the monarchy; Charles II becomes king

1664–65 The Great Plague kills 70,000 in London

1666 Great Fire of London

1707 Act of Union – Scotland and England unite

1776 US Declaration of Independence

Lenin addressing a crowd of workers

1917 Russian Revolution

The rule of the Russian royal family led by the tsar ended with the February Revolution in 1917. The revolution was triggered by problems such as food shortages and Russia's involvement in World War I. The October Revolution followed later that year, when Soviet forces seized control. They murdered the tsar and his family and attempted to create a Communist state under the leadership of Lenin. A civil war followed from 1918 to 1922. Soviet rule lasted until 1991.

1989 Fall of Berlin Wall

After World War II, control of the East German city of Berlin was split between West Germany (with American, British and French troops) and Soviet East Germany. In 1961 the East Germans built the Berlin Wall to stop its inhabitants fleeing to the West, and 192 people were shot while trying to defect. The wall was a symbol of the divide between the Soviet Union and the West. When the Soviet Union collapsed, the wall was torn down and East and West Germany were reunited, with Berlin as the new capital city.

2009 Centenaries

1509
Henry VIII became king of England. His reign saw the Reformation in England and progress in art, architecture and literature.

1609
The Italian scientist Galileo Galilei demonstrated his first astronomical telescope.

The colony of Virginia was granted a royal charter.

1709
Iron smelting using coke, in place of charcoal, was started in England by Abraham Darby.

Daniel Fahrenheit (Germany) invented the thermometer.

1809
US soldier John Stevens's first ocean-going steamship *Phoenix* sailed from New York to Philadelphia.

1909
Ernest Shackleton (Anglo-Irish) explored Antarctica, discovered the Beardmore glacier and was the first to climb Mt Eberus.

Robert Peary (USA) claimed to have reached the North Pole, but his achievement has been disputed.

In his monoplane *Blériot XI*, Louis Blériot (France) became the first to fly across the English Channel.

See also

First telescopes: page 27
Famous artists: pages 242–243

2000s

1776–83 American War of Independence

1783 First balloon flight (Montgolfier brothers, France)

1788 First European settlers arrive in Australia

1789 French Revolution

1793 Louis XVI of France executed

1815 Battle of Waterloo; Wellington defeats Napoleon

1825 World's first public railway, Stockton to Darlington

1833 Slavery abolished in the British empire

1853–56 Crimean War

1860–65 American Civil War

1863 First underground railway, London

1869 Suez Canal opens

1869 US transcontinental railway completed

1876 Alexander Graham Bell invents telephone

1901–10 Peak decade for immigration into USA (8.8 million immigrants)

1903 First aeroplane flights (Wright brothers, USA)

1903 Henry Ford begins mass production of cars

1914–18 World War I – 8,545,800 military deaths

1917 Russian Revolution establishes Soviet Union

1929–33 Great Depression (world economic crisis)

1939–45 World War II – 15,843,000 military deaths

1945 Atom bombs dropped on Hiroshima and Nagasaki, Japan

1945–90 Cold War between USSR and the West

1950–53 Korean War

1959–75 Vietnam War (USA involved 1961–73)

1961 First man in space (Yuri Gagarin, USSR)

1961 Berlin Wall built, separating East and West Germany

1963 US President John F. Kennedy assassinated

1969 Neil Armstrong becomes first man on the Moon

1989 Fall of the Berlin Wall triggers the end of the Soviet Union

1994 Nelson Mandela becomes president of South Africa

2001 World Trade Center, New York, destroyed by terrorists; USA retaliates by invading Afghanistan

2003 Iraq War and Saddam Hussein overthrown; elections later held but violence continues

2006 Saddam Hussein executed

2008 United States elects its 44th President.

Mesopotamia/Sumeria

Mesopotamia was a region around the Tigris and Euphrates rivers, which is now part of Turkey, Syria and Iraq. The area was controlled by several different peoples, beginning with the Sumerians in around 3500 BC. They set up a number of city-states that constantly battled to control land and trade routes until they were united under one ruler in 2350 BC. The Sumerians are said to have invented the wheel and cuneiform script, which many people claim is the earliest form of writing. They finally became absorbed into other races around 2000 BC.

Ancient Egypt

Egypt is an area in the Nile valley which was ruled as a single state from about 3200 BC. There were 30 dynasties, led by pharaohs who were both kings and gods. The pyramids were built during the fourth dynasty (2575–2467 BC) as tombs for the pharaohs of that time. The Great Pyramid of Giza was the world's tallest building for 4000 years, and it is the only wonder of the world that still stands. The Egyptians are also famous for their hieroglyphic writing and sea-going ships. Like other powerful empires, ancient Egypt was weakened by invasions, until it was taken over by Alexander the Great in 332 BC.

Ancient Greece

Ancient Greece was called Hellas. The civilization was at its strongest in 500–400 BC, after Greece colonized Cyprus, parts of Italy, Ukraine and the South of France. This era was known as the Golden Age. Some city-states, such as Athens and Sparta, became great centres of art, learning and politics. Many famous thinkers lived in Athens during this period, including Aristotle, Plato, Socrates and Aristophanes. The ancient Greeks also created the idea of democracy: its citizens were encouraged to debate and then vote on issues. The Golden Age ended in wars between the city-states, which paved the way for King Philip of Macedonia to invade Greece, followed later by his son Alexander.

Alexander the Great's empire

Alexander III of Macedonia lived for only 33 years, from 356 to 323 BC. In that short time he built an empire covering Persia (modern Iraq, Iran, Syria and Turkey), Egypt, Greece and Babylon. It was difficult to keep this huge empire together, and it collapsed soon after his death.

Chinese empire

China was one of the first places where people are known to have lived. From 1600 BC it was made up of many small kingdoms which all united in 221 BC under one leader or emperor. Various dynasties ruled the empire, starting with the Qin dynasty. During this time, the Great Wall of China was built to keep invaders out. China was an extremely learned civilization, ahead of Europe in the arts and sciences by up to 200 years. The empire finally fell apart under the Han dynasty in AD 220 as a result of corruption and poverty.

Roman empire

The Roman empire was formed in 31 BC under the leadership of Caesar Augustus, who ruled over every aspect of Roman life. Caesar Augustus brought peace, prosperity and culture. The empire expanded so much that by the 2nd century AD Rome had colonies which stretched from the Middle East to Spain, and from Great Britain to North Africa. The sheer size of the empire brought problems. There was not enough money to pay for an army spread across the world, which made the empire vulnerable to enemies. Constant attacks by German barbarians eventually defeated the army, and the empire fell in AD 476. The influence of ancient Rome is staggering: Roman roads still cross Europe, the Roman legal system is still the model for countries in Europe and Latin America, and its language, Latin, is the basis of many languages spoken today.

Greek empires

- Colonies of the Ancient Greeks
- Empire of Alexander the Great

The Great pyramid of Giza (seen here in the centre), also called the Pyramid of Khufu, stands near the smaller pyramids of Khafre and Menkaure.

Mayan pyramid in Tikal, once the capital of the Mayan empire

The Taj Mahal in Agra, India

Mayan empire

The Mayan empire was made up of city-states that stretched across southern Mexico and northern Central America. There have been Mayan people since 2000 BC but their greatest period was from AD 300 to 900, when architectural wonders such as Palenque and Uxmal were built. These structures and many others show that the Mayans had an advanced knowledge of mathematics. The Mayan empire gradually declined after 900, and the Spanish invaded the area in the 15th century.

Inca empire

The Incas had a great empire that stretched 900,000 sq km (350,000 sq miles) across South America, including Colombia, Bolivia and Argentina, with a capital, Cuzco, in Peru. It lasted from around 1200 until 1533. Inca society was very organized: every person was told which job they had to do and where to do it. In return, they were looked after by the state. Like the Aztecs, the Incas were brutally repressed by Spanish conquistadors in the 15th century.

Aztec empire

The Aztecs arrived in Mexico in 1325 and founded the city of Tenochtitlán, home to about 90,000 people. It showed the Aztecs' skill in engineering and included a system of drainage that was far ahead of any in Europe. The Aztecs conquered neighbouring city-states and extended their empire until it stretched from the Pacific to the Gulf of Mexico into Guatemala. The empire ended when the Spanish, led by Hernán Cortés, invaded between 1519 and 1522.

Ottoman empire

The Ottoman empire was an Islamic state from the 13th to 20th centuries and the most powerful empire in the world during the 1500s and 1600s. It covered Turkey, parts of southwest Asia, southeast Europe and North Africa. The capital was Constantinople (now Istanbul). The empire began to decline because its rulers refused to modernize and they lost lands in several wars. It allied with Germany in World War I. Defeated, its remaining lands were divided among the victors.

Mogul empire

The Mogul empire was founded in 1526 in northern India by a descendent of Genghis Khan. This was a hugely wealthy civilization and the Moguls greatly valued education, culture and art. The Taj Mahal was built by Moguls from 1632–53. This beautiful mausoleum was made for Emperor Shah Jahan's favourite wife, Mumtaz Mahal, and is built of marble with exquisite inlaid decoration. The empire's Muslim leaders wanted the people to keep Muslim ways, but many of its subjects were Hindu. In 1691 the empire was torn apart by bloody battles between Muslims and Hindus. The Mogul empire was finally overthrown by the British in 1857.

British empire

At the beginning of the 20th century, about a quarter of the world's people lived under British rule. The British had been expanding their empire since the 15th century, and by 1900 its lands included South Africa, Kenya, Egypt, Hong Kong, India, Iraq, Nepal, Singapore, Malta, Australia, New Zealand and Canada. Most of Britain's former colonies have now won or been granted independence. Many belong to the Commonwealth, which is a voluntary association of independent states founded in 1931 (see map on pages 102–103).

Ottoman empire

Extent of the Ottoman empire 1600

US presidents

US presidents are elected for a term of four years. George Washington was the first president of the USA and he served two terms. Only Franklin Delano Roosevelt served three terms. He died shortly after he was elected for a fourth term.

In 1951 the 22nd Amendment to the US Constitution ruled that two terms are the most any president may serve. The two main political parties in the USA today are the Democratic Party and the Republican Party.

1 George Washington (Federalist party) first elected 1789

2 John Adams (Federalist party) first elected 1797

3 Thomas Jefferson (Dem-Rep party) first elected 1801

4 James Madison (Dem-Rep party) first elected 1809

The heads of presidents Washington, Jefferson, Lincoln and Roosevelt are carved into the face of Mt Rushmore in South Dakota, USA.

Abraham Lincoln on a US 1-cent coin

5 James Monroe (Dem-Rep party) first elected 1817

6 John Quincy Adams (Dem-Rep party) first elected 1825

7 Andrew Jackson (Democratic party) first elected 1829

8 Martin Van Buren (Democratic party) first elected 1837

9 William Henry Harrison (Whig party) first elected 1841

10 John Tyler (Whig party) first elected 1841

11 James Knox Polk (Democratic party) first elected 1845

12 Zachary Taylor (Whig party) first elected 1849

13 Millard Fillmore (Whig party) first elected 1850

14 Franklin Pierce (Democratic party) first elected 1853

15 James Buchanan (Democratic party) first elected 1857

16 Abraham Lincoln (Republican party) first elected 1861

17 Andrew Johnson (Democratic party) first elected 1865

18 Ulysses Simpson Grant (Republican party) first elected 1869

19 Rutherford Birchard Hayes (Republican party) first elected 1877

20 James Abram Garfield (Republican party) first elected 1881

21 Chester Alan Arthur (Republican party) first elected 1881

22 Grover Cleveland (Democratic party) first elected 1885

23 Benjamin Harrison (Republican party) first elected 1889

24 Grover Cleveland (Democratic party) first elected 1893

25 William McKinley (Republican party) first elected 1897

26 Theodore Roosevelt (Republican party) first elected 1901

27 William Howard Taft (Republican party) first elected 1909

28 Woodrow Wilson (Democratic party) first elected 1913

29 Warren Gamaliel Harding (Republican party) first elected 1921

30 Calvin Coolidge (Republican party) first elected 1923

31 Herbert Clark Hoover (Republican party) first elected 1929

32 Franklin Delano Roosevelt (Democratic party) first elected 1933

33 Harry S. Truman (Democratic party) first elected 1945

34 Dwight David Eisenhower (Republican party) first elected 1953

35 John Fitzgerald Kennedy (Democratic party) first elected 1961

36 Lyndon Baines Johnson (Democratic party) first elected 1963

37 Richard Milhous Nixon (Republican party) first elected 1969

38 Gerald Rudolph Ford (Republican party) first elected 1974

39 Jimmy Carter (Democratic party) first elected 1977

40 Ronald Reagan (Republican party) first elected 1981

41 George Bush (Republican party) first elected 1989

42 Bill Clinton (Democratic party) first elected 1993

43 George W. Bush (Republican party) first elected 2001

World monarchies

A monarchy is a country where the head of state is a king, queen or other hereditary ruler – someone who inherits the throne from a family member. In some countries, such as Malaysia, the monarch is elected.

Bahrain Shaikh Hamad bin Isa al-Khalifa succeeded to the throne in 1999

Belgium King Albert II succeeded to the throne in 1993

Bhutan King Jigme Singye Wangchuck succeeded to the throne in 1972

Brunei Sultan Haji Hassanal Bolkiah succeeded to the throne in 1967

Cambodia King Norodom Sihamoni succeeded to the throne in 2004

Denmark Queen Margrethe II succeeded to the throne in 1972

Japan Emperor Akihito succeeded to the throne in 1989

Jordan King Abdullah II succeeded to the throne in 1999

Kuwait Shaikh Sabah al-Ahmad al-Sabah succeeded to the throne in 2006

Lesotho King Letsie III succeeded to the throne in 1996

Liechtenstein Prince Hans Adam II succeeded to the throne in 1989

Luxembourg Grand Duke Henri succeeded to the throne in 2000

Amazing monarchs

Oldest monarch to ascend the British throne
William IV (ruled 1830–37) was 64 when he was crowned.

British monarchs with the most children
Edward I had 16 children (6 sons and 10 daughters). Both George III and James II had 15.

Most-married British monarch
Henry VIII had six wives who suffered various fates. They were: Catherine of Aragon (divorced), Anne Boleyn (beheaded), Jane Seymour (died 1537), Anne of Cleves (divorced), Catherine Howard (beheaded) and Catherine Parr, who survived Henry.

Henry VIII

Youngest British monarchs
Henry VI was just eight months old when he became king on 1 September 1422 after the death of his father, Henry V. When his grandfather, Charles VI, died 50 days later on 21 October 1422, Henry also became king of France.

Shortest-reigning British monarchs
Queen Jane (Lady Jane Grey), ruled for only nine days in 1553, before being sent to the Tower of London. She was executed the following year. Edward V ruled for 75 days. He was one of the Princes in the Tower, who were allegedly murdered on the orders of their uncle, Richard III. Edward VIII abdicated (gave up the throne) on 11 December 1936, before his coronation. He had ruled for just 325 days.

Longest-reigning world monarch
King Louis XIV of France became king at the age of five. He ruled for 72 years, from 1643–1715.

Longest-reigning British monarch
Queen Victoria was 18 years old when she became queen in 1837 and she ruled for 63 years.

Richest world ruler
Although no longer the richest man in the world, the Sultan of Brunei is estimated to have a fortune of $28 million.

Monarchies with the most rulers
Japan's monarchy dates from 40 BC. Since then, it has had 125 rulers.

Oldest king to be crowned
The crown usually passes to the next in line when the king or queen dies. Charles, Prince of Wales, is Queen Elizabeth II's oldest son and heir. If he becomes king on or after 20 September 2013, he will have overtaken William IV, who was crowned in 1830 at the age of 64 years 10 months and 5 days and currently holds the record as the oldest monarch to ascend the British throne. Queen Elizabeth II celebrated her 82nd birthday on 21 April 2008.

Henry VII was the first Tudor. He devised the Tudor Rose to symbolize unity between the House of York (white rose) and the House of Lancaster (red rose).

See also
Types of government: pages 110–111

Malaysia Sultan Mizan Zainal Abidin succeeded to the throne in 2006

Monaco Prince Albert II succeeded to the throne in 2005

Morocco King Mohammed VI succeeded to the throne in 1999

Nepal King Gyanendra Bir Bikram Shah Dev succeeded to the throne in 2001

Netherlands Queen Beatrix succeeded to the throne in 1980

Norway King Harald V succeeded to the throne in 1991

Oman Sultan Qaboos Bin Said al-Said succeeded to the throne in 1970

Qatar Shaikh Hamad bin Kaalifa al-Thani succeeded to the throne in 1995

Samoa Tuiatua Tupua Tamasese Efi, a member of one of the country's ruling families, was elected head of state in 2007

Saudi Arabia King Abdullah ibn Abdul Aziz al-Saud succeeded to the throne in 2005

Spain King Juan Carlos I succeeded to the throne in 1975

Swaziland King Mswati III succeeded to the throne in 1986

Sweden King Carl XVI Gustaf succeeded to the throne, 1973

Thailand King Bhumibol Adulyadej succeeded to the throne in 1946

Tonga George Tupou V succeeded to the throne in 2006

United Kingdom Queen Elizabeth II succeeded to the throne in 1952

WORLD POLITICS

Votes for women

The Isle of Man was the first place to give women the vote, in 1880, but the island is part of the UK and not a separate country. Until 1920 the only European countries that allowed women to vote were Sweden (1919) and Czechoslovakia (1920).

In the USA women were granted the vote in 1920, although some states allowed it earlier. Women could not vote in France or Italy until 1945, in Switzerland until 1971 or in Liechtenstein until 1984. Women were granted the right to vote in Kuwait for the first time in 2005, but they are still not allowed to vote in Brunei, Saudi Arabia and the United Arab Emirates. There are other countries where women have no vote – but neither do men.

1 The first country to give women the vote was New Zealand in 1893.

2 Australia followed suit in 1902 although women had the vote in South Australia in 1894 and in Western Australia in 1898 before the separate states were united in 1901.

3 Finland (then a Grand Duchy under the Russian Crown) granted women the vote in 1906.

4 Norway gave some women the vote in 1907. It was not until 1913 that all women over 25 could vote.

5 Denmark and Iceland (a Danish dependency until 1918) allowed women to vote in 1915.

6 The Netherlands and the USSR both gave women the vote in 1917.

8 Austria, Canada, Germany, Poland, Great Britain and Ireland all gave women the vote in 1918. (In Ireland, part of the UK until 1921, only women over 30 got the vote in 1918. This was lowered to 21 in 1928.)

www.rulers.org   search

British poster demanding votes for women

Types of government

There have been many different types of government around the world throughout history. Many of the names for them end in the term -cracy, from a Greek word meaning power.

Aristocracy
Rule by a small group of members of a privileged class.

Autocracy
Government by one person with unrestricted power; also known as despotism and dictatorship.

Fidel Castro was President of Cuba for almost 50 years before handing power to his brother Raúl.

Communist
Government of a classless state in which private ownership is abolished and the state controls all means of production, as in China and Cuba.

Democracy
Government by the people directly or through elected representatives, as in the UK and USA.

Roosevelt's Four Freedoms

On 6 January 1941 during World War II, US President Roosevelt made a famous speech to the US Congress. He proclaimed that four freedoms are essential to a democracy: freedom of speech, freedom of worship, freedom from want, and freedom from fear. He looked forward to these freedoms being possible after the defeat of Hitler and the Axis powers. In 1997 a memorial park was opened in Washington DC, honouring Roosevelt. It contains The Four Freedoms fountain as a symbol of his ideas.

Major international organizations

A number of international organizations have been set up to deal with issues that concern the world in general, rather than the interests of individual countries. These organizations are not linked to political parties but often become involved in political matters.

Flags flying outside the United Nations, New York

Women in parliament

There are 50 countries with at least 20 per cent of their parliament made up of women – but a number of countries still do not have any women representatives at all.

Based on the most recent general election results, these countries have the highest percentages of women in parliament: Rwanda 48.8 per cent, Sweden 47.0 per cent, Finland 41.5 per cent, Argentina 40.0 per cent, Netherlands 33.3 per cent.

Meritocracy
Government by leaders selected according to their ability.

Monarchy
Government in which power is held by a king (or queen, emperor or empress) who can pass power on to their heirs.

Oligarchy
Government by a small group of people.

Plutocracy
A government or state in which wealthy people rule.

Theocracy
Government ruled by or subject to religious authority.

United Nations

The UN was founded in 1945. Most countries of the world – a total of 192 – are members. The General Assembly of the UN makes decisions about peacekeeping and human rights.

Amnesty International (AI)
Amnesty International is a charitable organization set up in 1961. It campaigns for human rights throughout the world and against the detention of political prisoners.

International Monetary Fund (IMF)
The IMF was established in 1944 and promotes world trade. It has 185 member countries.

International Red Cross and Red Crescent Movement
These organizations help the victims of such events as warfare and natural disasters.

Organization for Economic Co-operation and Development (OECD)
The OECD was formed in 1961. It aims to encourage economic and social development in industrialized countries and provide aid to developing countries.

United Nations Children's Fund (UNICEF)
UNICEF was set up in 1947. It works to improve the health and welfare of children and mothers in developing countries.

United Nations Educational, Scientific and Cultural Organization (UNESCO)
UNESCO was set up in 1946. It encourages countries to get together on matters such as education, culture and science.

World Bank
The World Bank was founded in 1944 and has 185 member countries. It helps developing countries by giving loans.

World Health Organization
The WHO is part of the UN. It promotes health matters worldwide and aims to raise medical standards and monitor diseases.

World Trade Organization (WTO)
The Swiss-based WTO has 151 member countries. It establishes trade agreements between countries.

World Wildlife Fund (WWF)
The WWF was set up in 1961 and is the world's largest conservation organization. Its main aims are to protect endangered animals and the places where they live.

NATO
The North Atlantic Treaty Organization (NATO) was founded in 1949. Ten countries signed a defence treaty that committed them to helping each other in the event of attack. There are now 26 country members, and the NATO headquarters are based in Belgium.

G8

The Group of 8 (G8) is made up of the world's leading industrial countries (Canada, France, Germany, Italy, Japan, the UK, the USA and Russian Federation). The heads of the G8 countries meet each year to discuss global issues such as world poverty and security.

Countries
of the
World

A new country is born

The world's newest country, Kosovo, declared its independence from Serbia in 2008. It is the latest development following the years of conflict that led to the break-up of Yugoslavia.

ARCTIC OCEAN

Beaufort Sea

Greenland
(DENMARK)

*Baffin
Bay*

Arctic Circle

Alaska
(USA)

ICELAND

*Bering
Sea*

*Hudson
Bay*

*Labrador
Sea*

UNITED
KINGDOM

*Gulf of
Alaska*

CANADA

IRELAND

PACIFIC
OCEAN

UNITED STATES

ATLANTIC
OCEAN

PORTUGAL

MEXICO

*Gulf of
Mexico*

Canary Islands
(SPAIN)

MOR

Tropic of Cancer

Hawaii
(USA)

BAHAMAS

Western
Sahara
(MOROCCO)

CUBA

DOMINICAN
REPUBLIC

MAURITANIA

CAPE
VERDE

JAMAICA HAITI

Puerto Rico (USA)

ANTIGUA & BARBUDA

BELIZE

ST CHRISTOPHER
& NEVIS

DOMINICA

MAL

SENE

GAMBIA

GUATEMALA HONDURAS

Caribbean Sea

ST VINCENT & THE
GRENADINES

ST LUCIA
BARBADOS

GUINEA-BISSAU

BU

EL SALVADOR NICARAGUA

GRENADA

TRINIDAD &
TOBAGO

GUINEA

CC

COSTA RICA PANAMA

VENEZUELA

SIERRA
LEONE

D'IV

COLOMBIA

GUYANA

French Guiana
(FRANCE)

LIBERIA

SURINAME

Equator

Galapagos Islands
(ECUADOR)

ECUADOR

BRAZIL

PERU

BOLIVIA

PACIFIC
OCEAN

PARAGUAY

Easter Island
(CHILE)

CHILE

ARGENTINA

URUGUAY

ATLANTIC
OCEAN

Falkland Islands
(UNITED KINGDOM)

Antarctica

Key to numbered countries

Europe
1 Netherlands
2 Luxembourg
3 Andorra
4 Monaco
5 Lichtenstein
6 Vatican City State
7 San Marino
8 Slovenia
9 Boznia-Herzegovina
10 Serbia
11 Macedonia
12 Montenegro

Africa
13 Republic of Congo

Asia
14 Singapore

ARCTIC OCEAN

Svalbard
(NORWAY)

Barents Sea

Kara
Sea

Arctic Circle

NORWAY

SWEDEN

FINLAND

Baltic Sea

ESTONIA

LATVIA

LITHUANIA

NMARK

Russia

POLAND

BELARUS

GERMANY

1

CZECH
REP.

SLOVAKIA

UKRAINE

AUSTRIA

8

HUNGARY

ROMANIA

MOLDOVA

9

10

CROATIA

7

6

Black Sea

BULGARIA

ITALY

12

ALBANIA

11

GEORGIA

Corsica
(FRANCE)

Sardinia
(ITALY)

GREECE

ARMENIA

AZERBAIJAN

Ilorca
AIN)

MALTA

TURKEY

CYPRUS

LEBANON

SYRIA

Tunisia

Mediterranean Sea

ISRAEL

IRAQ

IRAN

LIBYA

EGYPT

SAUDI
ARABIA

KUWAIT

BAHRAIN

QATAR

UNITED ARAB
EMIRATES

RUSSIA

KAZAKHSTAN

MONGOLIA

Aral
Sea

Caspian Sea

UZBEKISTAN

KYRGYZSTAN

TURKMENISTAN

TAJIKISTAN

AFGHANISTAN

PAKISTAN

CHINA

Sea of
Okhotsk

NORTH
KOREA

Sea of
Japan

SOUTH
KOREA

JAPAN

NEPAL

BHUTAN

INDIA

PACIFIC
OCEAN

Tropic of Cancer

TAIWAN

NIGER

CHAD

SUDAN

NIGERIA

YEMEN

OMAN

ERITREA

DJIBOUTI

Red Sea

Arabian
Sea

Bay of
Bengal

BANGLADESH

MYANMAR

LAOS

Philippine
Sea

South
China
Sea

THAILAND

CAMBODIA

VIETNAM

PHILIPPINES

MARSHALL
ISLANDS

MICRONESIA

PALAU

GIA

AlGERIA

CAMEROON

CENTRAL
AFRICAN
REPUBLIC

ETHIOPIA

SOMALIA

SRI LANKA

MALDIVES

MALAYSIA

BRUNEI

14

Equator

UATORIAL

OMÉ &
NCIPE

13

DEMOCRATIC
REPUBLIC OF
CONGO

UGANDA

KENYA

RWANDA

BURUNDI

TANZANIA

SEYCHELLES

INDONESIA

PAPUA
NEW
GUINEA

EAST TIMOR

NAURU

KIRIBATI

SOLOMON
ISLANDS

TUVALU

SAMOA

Angola

ANGOLA

ZAMBIA

MALAWI

COMOROS

MADAGASCAR

Coral Sea

VANUATU

New Caledonia
(FRANCE)

FIJI

TONGA

ZIMBABWE

MOZAMBIQUE

NAMIBIA

BOTSWANA

SWAZILAND

LESOTHO

SOUTH
AFRICA

MAURITIUS

INDIAN
OCEAN

Tropic of Capricorn

AUSTRALIA

Tasman Sea

NEW
ZEALAND

SOUTHERN OCEAN

Antarctic Circle

Antarctica

St Peter's, Vatican City

Largest countries

These figures are based on total land area, including inland water, such as rivers and lakes. If the water area was not taken into account, China would be second largest, at 9,326,410 sq km (3,600,947 sq miles), the USA third with 9,161,923 sq km (3,537,439 sq miles) and Canada fourth at 9,093,507 sq km (3,511,023 sq miles).

Largest countries

Country	Area sq km (sq miles)
Russia	17,075,200 (6,592,772)
Canada	9,984,670 (3,855,103)
USA	9,826,630 (3,794,083)
China	9,596,960 (3,705,407)
Brazil	8,511,965 (3,286,488)
Australia	7,686,850 (2,967,910)

Smallest countries

Country	Area sq km (sq miles)
Vatican City	0.44 (0.17)
Monaco	2 (0.77)
Nauru	21 (8)
Tuvalu	26 (10)
Bermuda	53 (20)
San Marino	61 (24)
Liechtenstein	160 (62)

Biggest landlocked countries

A landlocked country has no coastline. This means that it has no direct access to the sea and fishing. Also, people and goods travelling to and from the country must go through another country. This may be difficult or expensive.

There are more than 40 landlocked countries in the world. The largest, Kazakhstan, has a coast on the Caspian Sea – which is a landlocked sea. The largest landlocked European country is Hungary (92,300 sq km [35,637 sq miles]). Europe also contains the world's smallest landlocked countries – Andorra, Liechtenstein, San Marino and Vatican City. All are less than 500 sq km (193 sq miles) in size. Liechtenstein and Uzbekistan are both double-landlocked. This means that they are surrounded by other landlocked countries.

Kazakhstan 2,717,300 sq km (1,049,155 sq miles)
Mongolia 1,564,116 sq km (603,908 sq miles)
Chad 1,284,000 sq km (495,755 sq miles)
Niger 1,267,000 sq km (489,191 sq miles)
Mali 1,240,000 sq km (478,766 sq miles)
Ethiopia 1,127,127 sq km (435,186 sq miles)
Bolivia 1,098,580 sq km (424,164 sq miles)

Longest and shortest frontiers

A country's frontier is made up of the combined length of all its land borders.

Longest
China 22,117 km (13,743 miles)
Russia 20,097 km (12,488 miles)
Brazil 16,885 km (10,488 miles)
India 14,103 km (8,763 miles)
USA 12,034 km (7,478 miles)

Shortest
Vatican City 3.2 km (2.0 miles)
Monaco 4.4 km (2.7 miles)
Cuba 29.0 km (18 miles)
San Marino 39.0 km (24 miles)
Qatar 60 km (37 miles)

Biggest and smallest populations

In most countries, more people are born every day than die, so population figures are going up all the time. China has the biggest population, but India is catching up fast.

Biggest population

Country	Population
China	1,313,552,038
India	1,152,342,278
USA	305,072,714
Indonesia	227,070,492
Brazil	192,047,523
Pakistan	155,360,000
Nigeria	147,357,690
Bangladesh	143,481,419
Russia	141,833,475
Japan	127,939,307

Smallest population

Country	Population
Vatican City	549
Tuvalu	9,916
Nauru	10,147
Palau	20,548
San Marino	30,684
Monaco	33,639
Liechtenstein	35,406
St Christopher and Nevis	48,925
Marshall Islands	53,236
Dominica	70,581

Population density

In densely populated countries, lots of people live on a small amount of land, usually in cities. The least densely populated countries are usually difficult for people to live in. The climate may be very cold or very hot, or there may be large areas of mountain, desert or forest.

Most densely populated countries
Monaco 17,251 people per sq km (44,680 per sq mile)
Singapore 7,286 people per sq km (18,871 per sq mile)
Malta 1,280 people per sq km (3,315 per sq mile)
Vatican City 1,248 people per sq km (3,232 per sq mile)
[**UK** 251 people per sq km (650 per sq mile)]

Least densely populated countries
Mongolia 1.69 people per sq km (4.37 per sq mile)
Namibia 2.58 people per sq km (6.68 per sq mile)
Australia 2.64 people per sq km (6.83 per sq mile)
Mauritania 2.92 people per sq km (7.56 per sq mile)
Iceland 3.06 people per sq km (7.92 per sq mile)

Crowded shopping street in Shanghai, China

Country development

These rankings from the United Nations are based on a range of factors, including how long people can expect to live, how much money they earn, education level and quality of life.

Most developed	Least developed
1 Iceland	**1** Sierra Leone
2 Norway	**2** Burkina Faso
3 Australia	**3** Niger
4 Canada	**4** Guinea-Bissau
5 Ireland	**5** Mali
12 USA	**6** Central African Republic
16 UK	

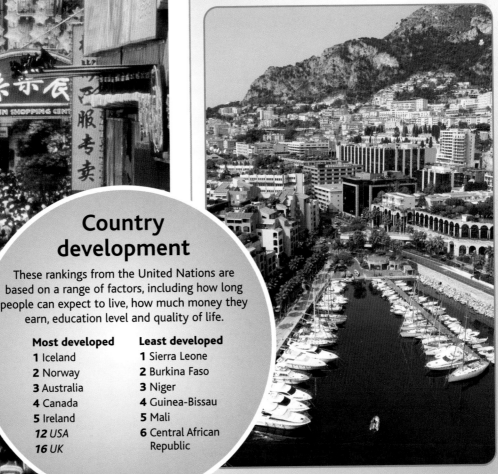

Monaco

www.census.gov/main/www/popclock.html   search

Changing names

Many cities change their names after the countries they are in become independent. Others are renamed after political changes, such as those ending the former Soviet Union. Some changes come from variations in the way in which foreign languages are translated from one alphabet to another.

Was called/country	Now called (since)
Batavia, Indonesia	Jakarta (1949)
Bombay, India	Mumbai (1995)
Christiana, Norway	Oslo (1924)
Byzantium/Constantinople, Turkey	Istanbul (1930)
Danzig, Poland	Gdansk (1945)
Leningrad, USSR	St Petersburg, Russia (1991)
Léopoldville, Belgian Congo	Kinshasa, Zaire (1960)
New Amsterdam, America	New York, USA (1664)
Pretoria, South Africa	Tshwane (2005)
Rangoon, Burma	Yangon, Myanmar (1989)
Saigon, Vietnam	Ho Chi Minh City (1975)
Salisbury, Rhodesia	Harare, Zimbabwe (1980)
Santa Isabel, Equatorial Guinea	Malabo (1973)
Tsaritsyn/Stalingrad, USSR	Volgograd, Russia (1961)

Cities with the most people*

1 Tokyo, Japan	37,203,122
2 New York, USA	22,981,510
3 Mexico City, Mexico	22,968,205
4 Seoul, South Korea	22,254,620
5 Mumbai (Bombay), India	20,870,764
6 São Paulo, Brazil	20,218,868
7 Manila, Philippines	19,195,048
8 Jakarta, Indonesia	18,588,548
9 Delhi, India	18,362,625
10 Los Angeles, USA	18,215,539

*Estimated figures for city and adjoining populated areas 2008. This calculation applies throughout this section. Source: World Gazetteer.

www.citypopulation.de/cities.html   search

Highest towns and cities

Some towns and cities are in surprisingly high places. The Chinese city of Wenchuan, founded in 1955, is at more than half the height of Everest. Even the towns and cities at the bottom of this list are at more than a third the height of Everest.

1 Wenchuan, China – 5,099 m (16,729 ft)
2 Potosí, Bolivia – 3,976 m (13,045 ft)
3 Oruro, Bolivia – 3,702 m (12,146 ft)
4 Lhasa, China – 3,684 m (12,087 ft)
5 La Paz, Bolivia – 3,632 m (11,916 ft)
6 Cuzco, Peru – 3,399 m (11,152 ft)
7 Huancayo, Peru – 3,249 m (10,659 ft)
8 Sucre, Bolivia – 2,835 m (9,301 ft)
9 Tunja, Colombia – 2,820 m (9,252 ft)
10 Quito, Ecuador – 2,819 m (9,249 ft)

La Paz, the world's highest capital city

What is a city?

A city is a large town. In some countries, a city has a special status. In the UK it may have been given a royal charter. In the USA it is an urban area with its own government.

A town is a densely populated area with a defined boundary and its own government. A town is smaller than a city and larger than a village.

A village is a small group of houses and other buildings in a country area.

A hamlet is a small village or a cluster of houses in a country area. In the UK a village is a hamlet if it does not have a church.

A settlement is a small group of inhabited buildings, or a small countryside community, such as a ranch or farm with a few dwellings.

The rediscovered city of Troy

Lost cities

There are some cities that were very famous in the past but have since been destroyed or abandoned.

Angkor, Cambodia
Angkor was once the largest city in the world and more than a million people lived there. The city had an area of more than 78 sq km (30 sq miles) and was surrounded by a water-filled moat. It was abandoned in about AD 1100. Frenchman Henri Mouhot was the first westerner to discover the city, in 1861.

One and only

The only city in two continents: Istanbul, Turkey, is partly in Europe and partly in Asia.

The only city centre with no cars: Venice. Its only traffic is boats on the canals.

The only non-US capital city named after a US president: Monrovia, the capital of Liberia, in Africa, was named after US president James Monroe.

Atlantis
Some people believe that there was a city and island of Atlantis, perhaps in the Mediterranean, that was destroyed by an earthquake and flooding almost 12,000 years ago. No one knows exactly where it was or even whether it really existed.

Chichén Itzá, Mexico
Chichén Itzá was once the centre of the Mayan empire. It was built in about AD 400 and had many buildings used in Mayan rituals. The city was abandoned in AD 1200.

Cliff Palace (Mesa Verde), Colorado, USA
This Native American Indian city was built on a cliff side, but was abandoned during a long drought in the late 13th century. It lay unknown until 18 December 1888, when Richard Wetherill, a local farmer, spotted it while looking for stray cattle.

Machu Picchu, Peru
The fortified Inca city on top of a mountain was stumbled on in 1911 by American explorer Hiram Bingham. He was searching for Vilcabamba, another lost Inca city.

Pompeii, Italy
The entire city was buried by volcanic ash when Mount Vesuvius erupted in AD 79. Nearby Herculaneum was buried at the same time. Excavations began in 1748, and many treasures have been uncovered, including beautifully preserved murals (wall paintings). Plaster casts have been made of the bodies of inhabitants who were buried beneath the debris.

Troy, Turkey
Troy was once thought to have existed only in legends, but its site was discovered in the 1870s.

Ur, Iraq
Ur was once one of the greatest cities in the world, but was abandoned in the 4th century BC. Its magnificent royal tombs and other sites were excavated by archaeologists in 1922–34 and many treasures discovered.

See also
World civilizations and empires: pages 106–107

Grand Canal, Venice

Banff National Park, Alberta, Canada

Canada

Canada is the second largest country in the world, after Russia. Almost half of Canada's land area is covered by forest and it exports more timber, pulp and newsprint than any other country. Canada also has a successful fishing industry and lots of natural resources, such as minerals and metals. Its varied landscape attracts millions of tourists each year. Famous Canadian landmarks include Niagara Falls and the Rocky Mountains.

Area 9,984,670 sq km (3,855,103 sq miles)
Country population 32,213,280
Capital city (pop) Ottawa (1,152,721)
Official languages French/English
Currency Canadian dollar

 # United States

The USA is made up of 50 states (including Alaska and Hawaii) and the District of Columbia, which contains the capital city, Washington. It includes a huge variety of landscapes, from hot deserts to snow-covered mountains. The country was once a colony under British rule but has been independent since 1776. It is now the world's wealthiest country and a great economic and military superpower.

Area 9,826,630 sq km (3,794,083 sq miles)
Country population 305,072,714
Capital city (pop) Washington DC (8,281,142)
Official language English
Currency US dollar

 # Mexico

Some of the world's oldest civilizations have lived in Mexico, such as the Aztecs and Mayans. Nowadays, many tourists visit and it has plenty of natural resources. However, almost half the people are very poor and many try to cross the border into the USA every year. Some of them are arrested by border patrols.

Area 1,972,550 sq km (761,606 sq miles)
Country population 107,236,677
Capital city (pop) Mexico City (22,968,205)
Official language Spanish
Currency Peso

 # Guatemala

Guatemala is one of Central America's most beautiful countries, with a dramatic landscape of forests, lakes and volcanoes. It is also one of the poorest and most violent. The country is still suffering from the after-effects of a long civil war (1960–96). Two-thirds of Guatemalan children live in poverty.

Area 108,890 sq km (42,043 sq miles)
Country population 13,994,079
Capital city (pop) Guatemala City (3,293,168)
Official language Spanish
Currency Quetzal

 # Honduras

Honduras lies in Central America between the Caribbean Sea and the Atlantic Ocean. It is one of the world's poorest countries, although it has valuable stocks of timber. In 1998 Hurricane Mitch caused four billion dollars' worth of damage.

Area 112,090 sq km (43,278 sq miles)
Country population 7,761,830
Capital city (pop) Tegucigalpa (2,063,368)
Official language Spanish
Currency Lempira

 # El Salvador

The tiny country of El Salvador is on Central America's Pacific coast. It often suffers hurricanes and earthquakes. Coffee is a major crop, but El Salvador relies heavily on aid money from other countries.

Area 21,040 sq km (8,124 sq miles)
Country population 7,218,048
Capital city (pop) San Salvador (1,912,758)
Official language Spanish
Currency US dollar

Nicaragua

Nicaragua is the largest country in Central America. It is one of the poorest countries in the Western world and half its people are very poor indeed. In 1998, Hurricane Mitch caused great damage and left 20 per cent of Nicaraguans homeless.

Area 129,494 sq km (49,998 sq m)
Country population 5,353,272
Capital city (pop) Managua (1,752,912)
Official language Spanish
Currency Córdoba

 # Panama

Panama is a narrow strip of land stretching between North and South America. It has coastlines on the Atlantic Ocean and the Pacific Ocean and has a canal, which connects the two oceans. Panama receives money from the many ships that use the canal each year and has other successful industries, but nearly 40 per cent of the people are poor.

Area 78,200 sq km (30,193 sq miles)
Country population 3,426,464
Capital city (pop) Panama City (1,242,192)
Official language Spanish
Currency Balboa

Costa Rica

Costa Rica is one of the most successful Central American countries and has a good standard of living. Its landscape is beautiful, with many mountains and tropical forests, and tourism is increasing. However, the country is also becoming more and more involved in the illegal drugs trade.

Area 51,100 sq km (19,730 sq miles)
Country population 4,572,364
Capital city (pop) San José (1,666,585)
Official language Spanish
Currency Costa Rican colón

 # St Christopher and Nevis

The Caribbean islands of St Christopher (also known as St Kitts) and Nevis became independent of the UK in 1983. Most of the people are descended from slaves brought from West Africa to work on the islands. Sugar has always been the islands' main crop, but tourism and financial services are now important industries.

Area 261 sq km (101 sq miles)
Country population 39,129
Capital city (pop) Basseterre (12,849)
Official language English
Currency East Caribbean dollar

 # The Bahamas

The Bahamas is made up of more than 700 islands, which lie southeast of Florida in the Atlantic Ocean. The islands were ruled by the British, but became independent in 1973. Queen Elizabeth II is still the head of state. About 40 per cent of people work in tourism, but banking and finance are also important.

Area 13,940 sq km (5,382 sq miles)
Country population 335,187
Capital city (pop) Nassau (235,102)
Official language English
Currency Bahamian dollar

 # Jamaica

The Caribbean island of Jamaica became independent of the UK in 1962, but has remained in the Commonwealth. Tourism is its main industry, but many visitors are put off by the island's poverty and violence. Jamaica has one of the world's highest murder rates.

Area 10,991 sq km (4,244 sq miles)
Country population 2,687,852
Capital city (pop) Kingston (941,433)
Official language English
Currency Jamaican dollar

 # Dominican Republic

The Dominican Republic makes up the eastern two-thirds of the island of Hispaniola, sharing it with Haïti. It is the oldest European settlement in America. The Dominican Republic is one of the Caribbean's poorest countries, but it is now very popular with tourists.

Area 48,730 sq km (18,815 sq miles)
Country population 9,679,893
Capital city (pop) Santo Domingo (3,338,850)
Official language Spanish
Currency Dominican Republic peso

 # Belize

Belize was a British colony called British Honduras, but became independent in 1981. Queen Elizabeth II is still the head of state. The coral reef off the coast is the world's second largest after Australia's Great Barrier Reef. Belize is now popular with tourists.

Area 22,966 sq km (8,867 sq miles)
Country population 321,243
Capital city (pop) Belmopan (17,570)
Official language English
Currency Belize dollar

 # Antigua and Barbuda

The Caribbean islands of Antigua and Barbuda were settled by the Spanish, the French and the British before becoming independent in 1981. They are still part of the Commonwealth and Queen Elizabeth II is the head of state. The islands are popular with tourists.

Area 443 sq km (171 sq miles)
Country population 85,420
Capital city (pop) St John's (22,077)
Official language English
Currency East Caribbean dollar

 # Haïti

Haïti shares the island of Hispaniola with the Dominican Republic. In 1804, Haïti was the first Caribbean state to become independent. Now Haïti is the poorest country in the Americas, after years of dictatorship and violence. Financial help from the EU and US was stopped in 2000 after unfair elections, and drug-trafficking is a big problem.

Area 27,750 sq km (10,714 sq miles)
Country population 8,558,135
Capital city (pop) Port-au-Prince (1,720,655)
Official languages Haïtian Creole/French
Currency Gourde

Cuba

Cuba is 150 km (93 miles) south of Florida and is the largest island in the Caribbean. It has a Communist government, which has been led by Fidel Castro since 1959. Cuba attracts more and more tourists, but the collapse of the Soviet Union and trade restrictions put on Cuba by the USA have caused financial problems.

Area 110,860 sq km (42,803 sq miles)
Country population 11,237,171
Capital city (pop) Havana (2,599,655)
Official language Spanish
Currency Cuban peso

A street in Havana, Cuba

St Vincent and the Grenadines

This Caribbean nation includes 33 small islands. It became independent from Britain in 1979, but it is still a member of the Commonwealth. Bananas are the main crop. Many tourists visit the islands.

Area 389 sq km
(150 sq miles)
Country population 102,133
Capital city (pop) Kingstown (16,610)
Official language English
Currency East Caribbean
dollar

Boats moored near the island of St Vincent

 ## Dominica

This tropical, mountainous Caribbean island was once under British rule. It became independent in 1978. Dominica's main exports are bananas and fruit juices, but the crops are often destroyed by hurricanes.

Area 750 sq km (291 sq miles)
Country population 70,581
Capital city (pop) Roseau (13,803)
Official language English
Currency East Caribbean dollar

 ## Barbados

This Caribbean island became an independent state in 1966, but it remains part of the Commonwealth. Queen Elizabeth II is the head of state. The main industries are tourism and sugar manufacturing.

Area 431 sq km (166 sq miles)
Country population 276,965
Capital city (pop)
Bridgetown (92,467)
Official language English
Currency Barbados dollar

 ## Grenada

Grenada lies between the Caribbean Sea and the Atlantic Ocean, north of Trinidad and Tobago. Nearly 400,000 tourists visit Grenada every year. The island exports spices, and about a quarter of the world's nutmegs come from there.

Area 344 sq km (133 sq miles)
Country population 106,478
Capital city (pop) St George's (5,159)
Official language English
Currency East Caribbean dollar

 ## Trinidad and Tobago

The Caribbean islands of Trinidad and Tobago lie northwest of Venezuela. They have large reserves of oil and natural gas and are among the richest of all Caribbean nations. Tobago is quieter than Trinidad. Both islands are popular with tourists.

Area 5,128 sq km (1,980 sq miles)
Country population 1,339,932
Capital city (pop) Port of Spain (49,959)
Official language English
Currency Trinidad and Tobago dollar

South America

 ## Argentina

Argentina was once ruled by Spain, but it became independent in 1816. This South American country is famous for its beef and has large mineral deposits.

Area 2,766,890 sq km (1,068,302 sq miles)
Country population 39,792,277
Capital city (pop) Buenos Aires (14,197,085)
Official language Spanish
Currency Peso

 ## Venezuela

Venezuela is a land of great natural beauty in northern South America. Angel Falls is the world's highest waterfall, and Maracaibo is the largest lake in South America. Venezuela has large reserves of oil, coal and gold, but almost half of Venezuelans live in poverty.

Area 912,050 sq km (352,145 sq miles)
Country population 28,522,297
Capital city (pop) Caracas (4,259,737)
Official language Spanish
Currency Bolívar

 ## Suriname

This is the smallest independent nation in South America. It was governed by the Netherlands but became independent in 1975. Suriname has large amounts of timber as well as bauxite and gold, but 70 per cent of the people are still very poor.

Area 163,270 sq km (63,039 sq miles)
Country population 518,285
Capital city (pop) Paramaribo (233,795)
Official language Dutch
Currency Suriname dollar

St Lucia

This mountainous island lies between the Atlantic Ocean and the Caribbean Sea. It is famous for its two large, cone-shaped peaks known as the Pitons. Bananas are the island's main crop, but banking and tourism are also important.

Area 616 sq km
(238 sq miles)
Country population 170,718
Capital city (pop)
Castries (9,914)
Official language English
Currency East Caribbean dollar

Colombia

Colombia is in the northwest of South America. The main crops are coffee, bananas and sugar, and the country has oil and mineral reserves. Colombia is also the world's leading producer of cocaine.

Area 1,138,910 sq km (439,736 sq miles)
Country population 44,459,803
Capital city (pop) Bogotá (8,148,808)
Official language Spanish
Currency Colombian peso

 # Ecuador

Ecuador lies on the Equator and stretches across the Andes Mountains. The country's main exports are fish, bananas, cocoa and coffee. Oil was discovered there in 1972.

Area 283,560 sq km (109,483 sq miles)
Country population 13,835,076
Capital city (pop) Quito (1,594,883)
Official language Spanish
Currency US dollar

 # Paraguay

The Republic of Paraguay is landlocked. It has one of the smallest populations in South America. Alfredo Stroessner, the region's longest-ruling dictator, was overthrown in 1989, but Paraguay is still struggling with political and financial problems.

Area 406,750 sq km (157,047 sq miles)
Country population 6,243,757
Capital city (pop) Asunción (2,014,725)
Official languages Spanish/Guaraní
Currency Guaraní

Uruguay

Uruguay is the second smallest country in South America. It is wealthier than most South American nations because of its livestock, tourism and banking industries. It has a good welfare system and its people are well educated.

Area 176,220 sq km (68,039 sq miles)
Country population 3,383,284
Capital city (pop) Montevideo (1,843,196)
Official language Spanish
Currency Uruguayan peso

 # Bolivia

The Andes mountain range crosses Bolivia. The Bolivian capital La Paz is in the Andes and is the highest capital city in the world. Bolivia is one of only two landlocked countries in South America.

Area 1,098,580 sq km (424,164 sq miles)
Country population 10,300,696
Capital city (pop) La Paz (2,175,731)
Official language Spanish
Currency Boliviano

 # Peru

Peru lies on South America's Pacific coast. It has been home to famous ancient civilizations, including the Inca Empire. Peru has important natural resources, including gold and oil, but they have not yet been developed.

Area 1,285,220 sq km (496,226 sq miles)
Country population 26,901,638
Capital city (pop) Lima (8,057,397)
Official languages Spanish/Quechua
Currency New sol

 # Guyana

Guyana is the only country in South America where English is the official language. Its natural resources include gold and diamonds, but it is very poor and has political problems. The country has many fascinating animals and plants and is popular with tourists interested in nature.

Area 214,970 sq km (83,000 sq miles)
Country population 742,165
Capital city (pop) Georgetown (247,588)
Official language English
Currency Guyana dollar

Statue of Christ, Rio de Janeiro, Brazil

 # Brazil

Area 8,511,965 sq km (3,286,488 sq miles)
Country population 192,047,523
Capital city (pop) Brasília (2,492,188)
Official language Portuguese
Currency Real

Brazil covers nearly half of South America. It contains the world's second longest river, the Amazon, and vast tropical rainforests. About 82 per cent of Brazil's population lives in cities, which are mostly on the coast in the south and southeast of the country. Brazil is the leading nation in South America but there are wide divisions between rich and poor.

 # Chile

Chile is an extremely long, narrow country, which lies between the Andes Mountains and the Pacific Ocean. It is one of the most successful nations in South America and has many natural resources, including minerals and timber, as well as thriving agriculture and fishing industries.

Area 756,950 sq km (292,260 sq miles)
Country population 16,998,021
Capital city (pop) Santiago (5,099,129)
Official language Spanish
Currency Chilean peso

Norway

Norway is famous for its fjords. The population is small and has a very good standard of living, thanks to the country's plentiful natural resources. Only Russia and Saudi Arabia export more oil than Norway, and it is the world's biggest exporter of seafood.

Area 323,802 sq km (125,021 sq miles)
Country population 4,714,633
Capital city (pop) Oslo (846,584)
Official language Norwegian
Currency Krone

Oil rig supply boat in Bergen harbour, Norway

Ireland

Ireland was divided in the 1920s, when 26 counties in the south gained independence from the United Kingdom. Since then there has been conflict in Northern Ireland between those who want to remain part of the United Kingdom and those who want a united, independent Ireland. Since Ireland joined the European Community in 1973 it has become a modern, high-tech nation with successful industry. It began using the Euro in January 1999, along with ten other nations.

Area 70,200 sq km (27,135 sq miles)
Country population 4,364,523
Capital city (pop) Dublin (1,058,265)
Official languages Irish/English
Currency Euro

Denmark

Denmark shares a border with Germany and is the smallest, most southerly Scandinavian nation. It is a wealthy, high-tech country and has all the oil and natural gas it needs. The standard of living is high. Denmark is a monarchy and the kingdom includes the Faeroe Islands and Greenland.

Area 43,094 sq km (16,639 sq miles)
Country population 5,466,444
Capital city (pop) Copenhagen (1,082,884)
Official language Danish
Currency Danish krone

Finland

Since the end of World War II, Finland has changed from being a rural country covered with dense forest into a modern nation. It has very successful industries and an excellent welfare system. Finland joined the European Union in 1995 and adopted the Euro as its currency in 2002.

Area 338,145 sq km (130,559 sq miles)
Country population 5,291,078
Capital city (pop) Helsinki (1,262,805)
Official languages Finnish/Swedish
Currency Euro

Luxembourg

Luxembourg is landlocked by Belgium, Germany and France. Its inhabitants have an amazingly high standard of living. Steel was once the main industry, but financial services have now become more important.

Area 2,586 sq km (999 sq miles)
Country population 463,129
Capital city (pop) Luxembourg (75,552)
Official languages French/German
Currency Euro

Window in Heidelberg Castle, Germany

Sweden

Sweden is a rich country with a high standard of living. Swedes have one of the world's longest life expectancies. The country has many natural resources including iron ore, lead, granite, zinc and forests. Forests cover about half the land and there are important timber and paper industries.

Area 449,964 sq km (173,732 sq miles)
Country population 9,146,262
Capital city (pop) Stockholm (1,737,995)
Official language Swedish
Currency Swedish krona

Germany

Germany was divided after World War II. The Soviet Union and Poland claimed the East, and the USA, UK and France controlled the West. The East became a Communist state and the West became a democracy. Thousands of East Germans fled to the West. The Berlin Wall was built in 1961 to close the border and stop the flow of people. The decline of the USSR led to the fall of the Berlin Wall in 1989 and Germany was reunited in 1990. Today, 80 per cent of Germany's people live in the West, and the effects of Communism are still felt in the East.

Area 357,021 sq km (137,847 sq miles)
Country population 82,191,106
Capital city (pop) Berlin (4,040,690)
Official language German
Currency Euro

People bathing in the Blue Lagoon, Iceland

Iceland

Iceland is a volcanic island and is the most westerly country in Europe. Its capital city is the furthest north in the world. Iceland is a wealthy country with low unemployment and a good welfare system. Fishing provides 70 per cent of its exports, which could cause problems as fish stocks decline.

Area 103,000 sq km (39,769 sq miles)
Country population 315,450
Capital city (pop) Reykjavík (201,008)
Official language Icelandic
Currency Icelandic króna

The Netherlands

The Netherlands is a low-lying country and much of it has been reclaimed from the sea. Nearly a quarter of the land lies below sea level, which makes it vulnerable to flooding, despite coastal defences and a network of dykes and canals. Banking, shipping and fishing all are important industries. The Netherlands is the sixth largest exporter in the world.

Area 41,526 sq km (16,033 sq miles)
Country population 16,409,082
Capital city (pop) Amsterdam (749,372)
Official language Dutch
Currency Euro

Belgium

Belgium is divided into Flanders (in the northwest), and Wallonia (in the southeast). Brussels is the headquarters of the European Union. This has brought wealth to the country as multinational companies have settled in the city. Belgium is well known for its fine chocolates and beer – and Tintin!

Area 30,528 sq km (11,787 sq miles)
Country population 10,629,899
Capital city (pop) Brussels (2,175,008)
Official languages Flemish/French/German
Currency Euro

France

France is the largest country in Western Europe and a key member of the European Union. It has a varied landscape ranging from coastal plains to the Alps in the southeast. Farms and forests cover a large proportion of the country, and agricultural products – particularly wine and liqueurs – are major exports. France once had one of the world's largest empires. Most of its former colonies are now independent, but French Guiana, Guadeloupe, Martinique, Réunion, Mayotte, St Pierre and Miquelon, French Polynesia, New Caledonia, Wallis and Futuna and the Southern and Antarctic Territories all still have links with France.

Area 643,427 sq km (248,428 sq miles)
Country population 62,015,826
Capital city (pop) Paris (11,818,503)
Official language French
Currency Euro

United Kingdom

The United Kingdom is made up of Great Britain (England, Scotland and Wales) and Northern Ireland. Although it is a small country, the UK has had a huge influence on the world because of its cultural, military and industrial strengths. At one time, it controlled a vast empire of lands across the globe and was the world's leading industrial nation. Traditional manufacturing industries are now less important. In the 21st century the UK's main industries are technology, tourism and services such as banking, and it is still an important economic power.

Area 244,820 sq km (94,526 sq miles)
Country population 61,264,416
Capital city (pop) London (12,577,225)
Language English
Currency British pound

Monaco

Monaco is a principality – it is ruled by a prince. It is surrounded by France and is the second smallest independent state in the world. It has no income tax and low business taxes so rich people flock there to escape taxes.

Area 2 sq km (0.77 sq miles)
Country population 33,639
Capital city (pop) Monaco (955)
Official language French
Currency Euro

Plaza de España in Seville, Spain

Spain

Spain covers most of the Iberian peninsula. The country has many cultures. Basque, Catalan, Galician and Valencian are spoken in different regions, but Castilian Spanish is the official language. There are 19 regions with their own elected authorities. There is a campaign for independence by the Basque country in the north, which has caused ongoing problems for the government. Spain is the world's second most popular tourist destination (after France) and has more than 50 million visitors every year. The fishing industry is one of the biggest in Europe, but unemployment is high.

Area 504,782 sq km (194,897 sq miles)
Country population 46,113,018
Capital city (pop) Madrid (6,270,551)
Official language Castilian Spanish
Currency Euro

Portugal

Portugal lies to the west of Spain on the Iberian peninsula. It is one of the European Union's least developed countries and has the highest number of people working on the land. Portugal's economy has grown rapidly since it joined the European Union in 1986. Tourism is one of its fastest growing industries. Portugal once had a vast empire, stretching across the Americas, Africa and Asia. Over 177 million people worldwide speak Portuguese.

Area 92,391 sq km (35,672 sq miles)
Country population 10,634,138
Capital city (pop) Lisbon (2,634,878)
Official language Portuguese
Currency Euro

Malta

Malta, which includes the neighbouring island of Gozo, used to be under British rule. It became independent in 1964, but remains a part of the Commonwealth. Malta became the European Union's smallest new member in 2004. Tourism is the island's most important industry and Malta has more than a million visitors every year.

Area 316 sq km (122 sq miles)
Country population 403,266
Capital city (pop) Valletta (255,377)
Official languages Maltese/English
Currency Maltese lira

Vatican City State

The Vatican City is the smallest country in the world, both in area and population. It is surrounded by the city of Rome. The Vatican is home to the Pope and it is the spiritual centre of the Roman Catholic Church. It depends on contributions from Roman Catholics all over the world for its income, and the sale of souvenirs and publications.

Area 0.44 sq km (0.17 sq miles)
Country population 549
Capital city (pop) Vatican City (549)
Official languages Latin/Italian
Currency Euro

San Marino

San Marino is entirely surrounded by Italy and it is the third smallest state in Europe. The tiny republic attracts about three million tourists every year. San Marino's inhabitants (known as Sammarinese) enjoy the world's sixth highest income per person.

Area 61 sq km (24 sq miles)
Country population 30,684
Capital city (pop) San Marino (4,638)
Official language Italian
Currency Euro

Andorra

Andorra is a small principality (a state ruled by a prince), which dates from 1278. It lies in the mountains between France and Spain. Tourism is its main industry, but financial services are also becoming important.

Area 468 sq km (181 sq miles)
Country population 86,417
Capital city (pop) Andorra la Vella (25,204)
Official language Catalan
Currency Euro

Estonia

The small Baltic state of Estonia regained its independence in 1991 when the Soviet Union collapsed. It was one of the Eastern European nations that joined the European Union in 2004.

Area 45,226 sq km (17,462 sq miles)
Country population 1,339,330
Capital city (pop) Tallinn (394,898)
Official language Estonian
Currency Kroon

Italy

Italy is a long, narrow country reaching into the Mediterranean Sea. It includes the islands of Sicily and Sardinia among others. Italy can be divided into two: the wealthy, industrial north, and the poorer south, where most people work on the land and around 20 per cent of the population is unemployed. About 40 million foreign tourists visit Italy every year, many of them to see its beautiful cities, which include Rome, Venice and Florence.

Area 301,230 sq km (116,306 sq miles)
Country population 59,279,992
Capital city (pop) Rome (3,858,111)
Official language Italian
Currency Euro

Austria

Austria is a small mountainous country. It is landlocked by the Czech Republic, Slovakia, Italy, Slovenia, Hungary, Germany, Switzerland and Liechtenstein. It was once the centre of the powerful Austro-Hungarian empire, until its defeat in World War I. It was occupied by Nazi Germany and then by the Allies after World War II. Since the war Austria has flourished, and it is now a popular holiday spot.

Area 83,870 sq km (32,382 sq miles)
Country population 8,370,759
Capital city (pop) Vienna (2,123,722)
Official language German
Currency Euro

Switzerland

Switzerland is the most mountainous country in Europe. The Alps occupy 60 per cent of its land area. It has a very high income per person, low unemployment and its people have a long life expectancy. Switzerland was not involved in either World War and has not joined the European Union.

Area 41,290 sq km (15,942 sq miles)
Country population 7,555,082
Capital city (pop) Bern (121,837)
Official languages German/French/Italian/Romansch
Currency Swiss franc

Belarus

Belarus became independent when the Soviet Union collapsed in 1991. It continues to have close ties with Russia. The country still suffers from the effects of nuclear fallout from the 1986 Chernobyl accident, which took place in neighbouring Ukraine.

Area 207,600 sq km (80,155 sq miles)
Country population 9,615,624
Capital city (pop) Minsk (1,753,547)
Official languages Belarusian/Russian
Currency Belarusian rouble

Poland

Poland is the largest nation in Central Europe and has the highest population. It was devastated by World War II, when more than six million people died – more than in any other country. In 1989 Poland was the first Eastern European nation to topple its Communist leaders. In May 2004 it joined the European Union.

Area 312,685 sq km (120,729 sq miles)
Country population 38,077,421
Capital city (pop) Warsaw (2,251,474)
Official language Polish
Currency Zloty

Czech Republic

The Czech Republic was part of Czechoslovakia until it split from Slovakia in 1993. It now attracts investment from other countries and has a thriving tourism industry. The country joined the European Union in 2004.

Area 78,866 sq km (30,450 sq miles)
Country population 10,310,957
Capital city (pop) Prague (1,406,142)
Official language Czech
Currency Koruna

Astronomical clock in Prague, Czech Republic

Latvia

Latvia is bounded by the Baltic Sea, Estonia, Lithuania, Belarus and Russia. It became independent of the Soviet Union in 1991 and in 2004 it was accepted into the European Union.

Area 64,589 sq km (24,938 sq miles)
Country population 2,268,001
Capital city (pop) Riga (808,248)
Official language Latvian
Currency Lats

Lithuania

Lithuania became independent of the Soviet Union in 1991. It used to depend on Russia, but more recently it has developed trade links with the West. It joined the European Union in 2004.

Area 65,200 sq km (25,174 sq miles)
Country population 3,366,913
Capital city (pop) Vilnius (543,642)
Official language Lithuanian
Currency Litas

Liechtenstein

Liechtenstein is the sixth smallest country in the world. Its low taxes have encouraged extraordinary economic growth, and thousands of foreign companies have bank accounts there.

Area 160 sq km (62 sq miles)
Country population 35,406
Capital city (pop) Vaduz (5,088)
Official language German
Currency Swiss franc

Panoramic view of Florence, Italy

View of Rovinj, Croatia

 # Croatia

Croatia was one of Yugoslavia's most advanced and prosperous areas, and declared its independence in 1991. The country borders the Adriatic Sea and its coast was popular with tourists. The Yugoslavian conflict of 1991–95 threw the country into turmoil, but visitors are now returning.

Area 55,542 sq km (21,831 sq miles)
Country population 4,447,495
Capital city (pop) Zagreb (703,185)
Official language Croatian
Currency Kuna

 # Bulgaria

Bulgaria was Communist until 1990, when it became a democracy. It has now joined the European Union, despite organized crime, corruption, inflation and unemployment. Bulgaria is becoming popular with tourists, especially the historic capital city of Sofia.

Area 110,910 sq km (42,823 sq miles)
Country population 7,535,211
Capital city (pop) Sofia (1,205,048)
Official language Bulgarian
Currency Lev

 # Bosnia and Herzegovina

Bosnia and Herzegovina was recognized as an independent state in 1992 after Yugoslavia collapsed in 1991. Since then clashes between Bosnia's Croats, Serbs and Muslims have caused civil war, which is still not resolved. Despite this, more tourists are beginning to visit the country again.

Area 51,129 sq km (19,741 sq miles)
Country population 3,827,694
Capital city (pop) Sarajevo (424,354)
Official languages Bosnian/Croatian/Serbian
Currency Convertible marka

 # Slovakia

Slovakia is landlocked and mountainous. It became independent in 1993, when Czechoslovakia divided into the Czech Republic and Slovakia. It joined the European Union in 2004.

Area 48,845 sq km (18,859 sq miles)
Country population 5,395,346
Capital city (pop) Bratislava (419,211)
Official language Slovak
Currency Koruna

 # Moldova

Moldova is Europe's poorest country. It has no natural resources and imports all its energy supplies from Russia, from which it became independent in 1991.

Area 33,843 sq km (13,067 sq miles)
Country population 3,640,569
Capital city (pop) Chisinau (697,475)
Official language Moldovan
Currency Moldovan leu

 # Ukraine

Ukraine is a vast area between Poland and Russia. It became independent after the collapse of the Soviet Union. In 1986 it was the scene of the world's worst nuclear disaster, when a reactor at the Chernobyl nuclear plant exploded.

Area 603,700 sq km (233,090 sq miles)
Country population 46,396,212
Capital city (pop) Kiev (3,000,198)
Official language Ukrainian
Currency Hryvna

 # Albania

Albania depends mostly on farming, and its main crops are wheat, maize, sugar beet, potatoes and fruit. It has borders with Serbia, Montenegro, Kosovo, Macedonia and Greece.

Area 28,748 sq km (11,100 sq miles)
Country population 3,175,119
Capital city (pop) Tirana (399,999)
Official language Albanian
Currency Lek

Georgia

Georgia lies in a key position east of the Black Sea between Russia and Turkey. It has coal deposits, but they have not yet been exploited. The country relies on farming – particularly grapes from which wine is made.

Area 69,700 sq km (26,911 sq miles)
Country population 4,658,143
Capital city (pop) Tbilisi (1,310,819)
Official language Georgian
Currency Lari

The Millennium Monument in Budapest, Hungary

 # Hungary

Hungary became Communist after World War II. In the 1990s, it defied the Soviet Union and began some free trade with the West. This central European country has flourished since the Soviet Union's collapse and it entered the European Union in 2004.

Area 93,030 sq km (35,919 sq miles)
Country population 10,071,943
Capital city (pop) Budapest (2,578,731)
Official language Hungarian
Currency Forint

Slovenia

About half of Slovenia is covered in forest, making it the third most forested country in Europe. Slovenia became independent from Yugoslavia in 1991 and joined the European Union in 2004. Its people now have a reasonably good standard of living.

Area 20,273 sq km (7,827 sq miles)
Country population 2,018,689
Capital city (pop) Ljubljana (258,810)
Official language Slovene
Currency Euro

Azerbaijan

Azerbaijan regained its independence from the Soviet Union in 1991. The country has rich mineral resources as well as oil and natural gas. However, conflict and corruption have kept it from developing a healthy economy.

Area 86,600 sq km (33,436 sq miles)
Country population 8,770,714
Capital city (pop) Baki/Baku (2,176,777)
Official language Azerbaijani
Currency Manat

Greece

The ancient country of Greece lies in an important position between Europe, Asia and Africa. It includes about 2,000 islands as well as the mainland. About 14 million tourists visit Greece every year. However, it has few natural resources and relies on money from the European Union.

Area 131,940 sq km (50,942 sq miles)
Country population 11,205,946
Capital city (pop) Athens (3,829,018)
Official language Greek
Currency Euro

Windmill on the Greek island of Santorini

Macedonia

Macedonia's full name is the Former Yugoslav Republic of Macedonia (FYROM), not to be confused with the Greek region of Macedonia. Macedonia became independent in 1991. Since then there have been clashes between the country's large Albanian minority and its Macedonian majority.

Area 25,333 sq km (9,781 sq miles)
Country population 2,047,846
Capital city (pop) Skopje (589,307)
Official languages Macedonian/Albanian
Currency Denar

Armenia

Armenia was the first country formally to adopt Christianity in AD 301. This mountainous country is bordered by Azerbaijan, Georgia, Iran and Turkey. Its key position between Europe and Asia led to invasions by the Persian, Ottoman, Roman and Byzantine empires, among others.

Area 29,800 sq km (11,506 sq miles)
Country population 3,237,660
Capital city (pop) Yerevan (1,414,740)
Official language Armenian
Currency Dram

Romania

The mountainous Republic of Romania is the largest Balkan nation. The Communist regime was overthrown in 1989 when the dictator Nicolae Ceausescu was executed. The country is still very poor, with almost half of Romanians living in poverty. It is now a member of the European Union.

Area 237,500 sq km (91,699 sq miles)
Country population 21,503,193
Capital city (pop) Bucharest (2,192,372)
Official language Romanian
Currency Leu

Cyprus

The Mediterranean island of Cyprus has been divided since Turkey invaded the north of the island in 1974. The Turkish Republic of Northern Cyprus is recognized only by Turkey. Greek Cyprus attracts many tourists and was accepted into the European Union in 2004. The Turkish part depends heavily on loans from Turkey.

Area 9,250 sq km (3,571 sq miles)
Country population 1,099,421
Capital city (pop) Nicosia (213, 027)
Official languages Greek/Turkish
Currency Cyprus pound

Serbia

This landlocked country was formerly part of Yugoslavia but is now independent.

Area 88,361 sq km (34,116 sq miles)
Country population 9,567,484
Capital city (pop) Belgrade (1,818,237)
Official language Serbian
Currency Serbian dinar

Kosovo

Kosovo declared its independence from Serbia in 2008 and has received partial recognition from United Nations member states.

Montenegro

Montenegro was a former part of Yugoslavia and became independent from Serbia in 2006. It is now a full member of the United Nations and, although not a member of the European Union, it has adopted the Euro as its national currency.

Area 14,026 sq km (5,415 sq miles)
Country population 625,536
Capital city (pop) Podgorica (143,718)
Official language Serbian
Currency Euro

Morocco

Morocco is in northwestern Africa. The country was divided between Spanish and French rule, but gained independence in 1956. It has rich mineral deposits and nearly three-quarters of the world's phosphate. Tourism is becoming increasingly important, but almost half the population work on the land.

Area 446,550 sq km (172,414 sq miles)
Country population 30,886,980
Capital city (pop) Rabat (1,754,425)
Official language Arabic
Currency Dirham

Algeria

Algeria became independent from France in 1962. Throughout the 1990s the country was torn apart by civil war, in which 100,000 people are thought to have died. Algeria is still struggling to control its religious militants.

Area 2,381,740 sq km (919,595 sq miles)
Country population 34,498,821
Capital city (pop) Algiers (6,253,265)
Official languages Arabic/Berber
Currency Algerian dinar

Tunisia

The North African country of Tunisia shares borders with Algeria and Libya and has a Mediterranean coastline. About one-fifth of the people live by farming and fishing.

Area 163,610 sq km (63,170 sq miles)
Country population 10,326,500
Capital city (pop) Tunis (2,050,434)
Official language Arabic
Currency Tunisian dinar

Cape Verde

Cape Verde is made up of the Windward Islands and the Leeward Islands in the Atlantic Ocean off the west coast of Africa. Their main exports are bananas and coffee.

Area 4,033 sq km (1,557 sq miles)
Country population 499,362
Capital city (pop) Praia (124,661)
Official language Portuguese
Currency Cape Verdean escudo

Ethiopia

Ethiopia is Africa's oldest independent country. It has suffered many droughts and famines. These, combined with civil war and a border dispute with Eritrea, have made Ethiopia one of Africa's poorest nations. Its natural resources are underdeveloped, and 85 per cent of the people still depend upon the land for a living.

Area 1,127,127 sq km (435,186 sq miles)
Country population 79,183,659
Capital city (pop) Addis Ababa (3,144,918)
Official language There is no official language, but Amharic is the most widely used of the 70 languages
Currency Ethiopian birr

Eritrea

Eritrea is in eastern Africa and has had violent border disputes with Ethiopia since 1998. The conflict has affected Eritrea's economy, but the government continues to improve the country's roads, schools and transport systems. Its Red Sea ports are an important source of income.

Area 121,320 sq km (46,842 sq miles)
Country population 4,936,403
Capital city (pop) Asmara (1,146,822)
Official languages No official language; Arabic, Tigrinya and English are the main working languages. Italian is also spoken.
Currency Nakfa

Libya

Libya has large oil reserves, but its economy has suffered from sanctions imposed by the United Nations. These were in response to the bombing of an airliner over Lockerbie in Scotland in 1988. Sanctions have now been lifted and Libya's leader, Colonel Gaddafi, has promised to bring his country back into the international community.

Area 1,759,540 sq km (679,362 sq miles)
Country population 6,455,346
Capital city (pop) Tripoli (1,943,454)
Official language Arabic
Currency Libyan dinar

Camel and rider near the Great Pyramid in Egypt

Egypt

Egypt lies in a key position. It has a coastline on both the Mediterranean and Red Seas, and borders with the Sudan, Libya, Israel and the Gaza Strip. Egypt also controls the vital Suez Canal. This allows about 15,000 ships each year to travel between the Mediterranean and the Indian Ocean without sailing around Africa. Famous landmarks include the pyramids.

Area 1,001,450 sq km (386,662 sq miles)
Country population 75,099,806
Capital city (pop) Cairo (16,078,877)
Official language Arabic
Currency Egyptian pound

Fortified town of Aït Benhaddou in the High Atlas mountains, Morocco

 Senegal

Senegal is almost divided into two by The Gambia. It became independent from France in 1960. It is now popular with tourists, but has few natural resources, high unemployment and more than half its people live in poverty.

Area 196,190 sq km (75,749 sq miles)
Country population 11,291,344
Capital city (pop) Dakar (2,485,851)
Official language French
Currency CFA franc

 Guinea

Guinea has been placed under great strain by thousands of refugees from its war-torn neighbours, Liberia and Sierra Leone. Guinea has natural resources, including iron ore, gold and diamonds.

Area 245,857 sq km (94,926 sq miles)
Country population 10,174,655
Capital city (pop) Conakry (1,857,153)
Official language French
Currency Guinean franc

 Somalia

Somalia is one of the world's poorest countries and there has been conflict between different groups. The north declared independence under the name Somaliland, but is not recognized by any foreign government.

Area 637,657 sq km (246,201 sq miles)
Country population 12,692,376
Capital city (pop) Mogadishu (1,609,050)
Official languages Somali/Arabic
Currency Somali shilling

 Mauritania

Mauritania is mainly desert. It became independent from France in 1960. There is conflict between the country's African and Arab peoples. Mauritania has rich mineral deposits, but these have not yet been exploited.

Area 1,030,700 sq km (397,955 sq miles)
Country population 3,022,150
Capital city (pop) Nouakchott (775,758)
Official language Arabic
Currency Ouguiya

 Niger

Niger is the largest nation in West Africa. It is also one of the hottest and poorest countries in the world. Niger borders the Sahara Desert and droughts often kill much of the country's vital livestock. It has one of the world's lowest literacy rates.

Area 1,267,000 sq km (489,191 sq miles)
Country population 13,949,837
Capital city (pop) Niamey (931,928)
Official language French
Currency CFA franc

 Gambia

The Gambia is a sliver of land and the smallest country in mainland Africa. About 80 per cent of Gambians work on the land. It is becoming increasingly popular as a tourist destination.

Area 11,300 sq km (4,363 sq miles)
Country population 1,546,400
Capital city (pop) Banjul (33,820)
Official language English
Currency Dalasi

 Sudan

Sudan is the biggest country in Africa. It has large oil reserves, which have been exploited since 1999. However, the country has suffered from civil war since its independence in 1956. This war has been going on longer than any other war in Africa. Since 2003 fighting has been particularly severe in the western region of Darfur, which is one of the poorest parts of the country. The United Nations has described this as the world's worst humanitarian crisis.

Area 2,505,810 sq km (967,499 sq miles)
Country population 37,423,543
Capital city (pop) Khartoum (8,873,889)
Official language Arabic
Currency Sudanese dinar

 Djibouti

Djibouti lies in a key position between Ethiopia and the Red Sea. The country provides refuelling facilities for ships and operates a free port, which bring money into Djibouti.

Area 23,000 sq km (8,880 sq miles)
Country population 496,375
Capital city (pop) Djibouti (c. 400,000)
Official languages Arabic/French
Currency Djibouti franc

Dogon people from Mali dancing on stilts

 Mali

Mali's first democratically elected government came to power in 1992 after more than 20 years of dictatorship. This West African nation is one of the world's poorest countries. About 80 per cent of the people depend on farming for a living.

Area 1,240,000 sq km (478,766 sq miles)
Country population 12,781,404
Capital city (pop) Bamako (2,111,790)
Official language French
Currency CFA franc

Nigeria

Nigeria has the biggest population of any African country. It is the leading oil producer south of the Sahara. However, about 60 per cent of Nigerians live in poverty because of corruption, unequal distribution of money and a rapidly growing population.

Area 923,768 sq km (356,668 sq miles)
Country population 147,357,690
Capital city (pop) Abuja (781,199)
Official language English
Currency Naira

Guinea-Bissau

Guinea-Bissau is one of the poorest countries in the world. A civil war in 1998 destroyed many of its roads, schools and hospitals, and ruined its economy. Most people live by fishing and farming. Cashew nuts are the main crop.

Area 36,120 sq km (13,946 sq miles)
Country population 1,403,569
Capital city (pop) Bissau (408,627)
Official language Portuguese
Currency CFA franc

Burkina Faso

Burkina Faso is an inland country in West Africa that was called Upper Volta. About 90 per cent of people work on the land. It has the lowest literacy rate in the world.

Area 274,200 sq km (105,869 sq miles)
Country population 14,337,906

Capital city (pop) Ouagadougou (1,286,529)
Official language French
Currency CFA Franc

Ghana

Ghana was a British colony, but in 1957 it became the first African country to become independent. It contains Lake Volta, the world's largest artificial lake, and it is one of the world's top ten gold producers.

Area 239,460 sq km (92,456 sq miles)
Country population 23,428,820

Capital city (pop) Accra (3,905,009)
Official language English
Currency Cedi

Liberia

The West African country of Liberia was founded by freed American slaves. It has been independent since 1847. Its president is Africa's first elected female head of state.

Area 111,370 sq km (43,000 sq miles)
Country population 3,283,000

Capital city (pop) Monrovia (1,690,270)
Official language English
Currency Liberian dollar

Benin

The African country of Benin became fully independent from France in 1960. It now has a thriving tourist industry, which provides much-needed money.

Area 112,620 sq km (43,483 sq miles)
Country population 8,052,780
Capital city (pop) Porto Novo (250,262)
Official language French
Currency CFA Franc

Transporting dried grasses by river in Chad

Chad

The Sahara desert covers much of Chad. Since gaining independence from France in 1960, it has suffered conflict with its neighbour Libya. Oil has been found in Chad and is now being exported. Most of its people work on the land.

Area 1,284,000 sq km (495,755 sq miles)
Country population 8,988,735
Capital city (pop) N'Djaména (1,518,988)
Official languages Arabic/French
Currency CFA Franc

Republic of Congo

The region of Middle Congo became independent from France in 1960 and was renamed the Republic of Congo. The country has large oil deposits and is one of Africa's largest producers of petroleum. It also produces zinc, lead, gold and diamonds.

Area 342,000 sq km (132,047 sq miles)
Country population 3,702,311
Capital city (pop) Brazzaville (1,180,176)
Official language French
Currency CFA franc

Cameroon

Cameroon in West Africa became an independent republic in 1972. It has good natural resources, including bauxite and aluminium, and grows crops such as cocoa, coffee and rubber.

Area 475,440 sq km (183,568 sq miles)
Country population 19,018,638
Capital city (pop) Yaoundé (2,075,562)
Official languages French/English
Currency CFA Franc

Côte d'Ivoire

Côte d'Ivoire became independent from France in 1960. It was a peaceful, prosperous African country until its first military coup in 1999. Trouble then began between rebels and the government which is still going on.

Area 322,460 sq km (124,502 sq miles)
Country population 20,794,345
Capital city (pop) Yamoussoukro (226,994)
Official language French
Currency CFA Franc

Sierra Leone

Sierra Leone became independent from Britain in 1971. Between 1991–2002 the country was in a state of civil war. Many thousands of people were killed and thousands more were forced to move from their homes. Sierra Leone has diamond and gold deposits, but its political problems have made it one of the world's poorest countries, along with Somalia and East Timor. Unemployment is high and about three-quarters of its people live on less than US $2 a day.

Area 71,740 sq km (27,698 sq miles)
Country population 5,226,221
Capital city (pop) Freetown (819,634)
Official language English
Currency Leone

Traditional woven baskets from the Republic of Congo

 # São Tomé and Príncipe

The islands of São Tomé and Príncipe lie on the Equator in the Gulf of Guinea and make up Africa's smallest country. Cocoa is the main crop, but São Tomé and Príncipe has other potential sources of income, such as newly discovered oil.

Area 1,001 sq km (387 sq miles)
Country population 157,847
Capital city (pop) São Tomé (62,531)
Official language Portuguese
Currency Dobra

Gabon

Gabon has a small population and good oil and mineral reserves. It is one of Africa's richest nations. However, many of its people are very poor because its wealth has been mismanaged and is unequally distributed.

Area 267,667 sq km (103,346 sq miles)
Country population 1,725,105
Capital city (pop) Libreville (713,167)
Official language French
Currency CFA franc

 # Central African Republic

The Central African Republic is a landlocked country in central Africa. It became independent from France in 1960. Since then there have been almost constant political problems and it is now a very poor country. It exports some timber and diamonds, but most people work on the land.

Area 622,984 sq km (240,536 sq miles)
Country population 3,347,188
Capital city (pop) Bangui (752,914)
Official language French
Currency CFA Franc

Rare mountain gorilla in the Democratic Republic of Congo

Democratic Republic of Congo

The Democratic Republic of Congo, which was called Zaïre, is Africa's third largest country. In 2003 a five-year struggle between government forces and rebels ended and since then it has been fairly peaceful. The country has good natural resources but has been very poor since the war.

Area 2,345,410 sq km (905,567 sq miles)
Country population 64,105,984
Capital city (pop) Kinshasa (9,166,685)
Official language French
Currency Congolese franc

 # Togo

Togo was the French territory of Togoland until it became independent in 1960. More than half the people work on the land. Cotton, coffee and cocoa are the main exports. Nearly a third of the people are very poor.

Area 56,785 sq km (21,924 sq miles)
Country population 5,582,583
Capital city (pop) Lomé (828,228)
Official language French
Currency CFA franc

 # Equatorial Guinea

Equatorial Guinea is made up of five islands and part of the African mainland. It became independent from Spain in 1968 and is one of the smallest countries in Africa. Many people work on the land, but gas and oil have been found and so the country is becoming wealthier.

Area 28,051 sq km (10,831 sq miles)
Country population 540,109
Capital city (pop) Malabo (170,964)
Official languages Spanish/French
Currency CFA franc

Sand dune in the Namib desert

Namibia

Namibia became independent from South Africa in 1990. The country often suffers from drought so much of its food has to be imported from other countries. Namibia is an important producer of diamonds, but the wealth from this is unevenly distributed. Half of all Namibians are living in poverty.

Area 825,418 sq km (318,696 sq miles)
Country population 2,128,560
Capital city (pop) Windhoek (296,366)
Official language English
Currency Namibian dollar

Rwanda

Rwanda is a densely populated country in Central Africa. It is still suffering the effects of a civil war that began in 1990 and lasted for four years. At least 60 per cent of the people live in poverty.

Area 26,338 sq km (10,169 sq miles)
Country population 8,995,038
Capital city (pop) Kigali (904,779)
Official languages Kinyarwanda/French/English
Currency Rwanda franc

Angola

Angola became independent from Portugal in 1975. Since then, there has been a civil war almost all the time. The country has valuable oil and diamond deposits, but has many financial problems.

Area 1,246,700 sq km (481,354 sq miles)
Country population 16,853,679
Capital city (pop) Luanda (2,524,459)
Official language Portuguese
Currency Kwanza

Uganda

Uganda is a landlocked West African nation on the shores of Lake Victoria. It is now a fairly peaceful country, after a devastating civil war and a military dictatorship. The land is fertile and it has natural resources, but Uganda is still being held back by a large international debt.

Area 236,040 sq km (91,136 sq miles)
Country population 29,395,836
Capital city (pop) Kampala (1,805,077)
Official language English
Currency Uganda shilling

Burundi

Burundi gained independence in the 1960s. Since then it has been devastated by fighting between the two main tribes, the Hutus and the Tutsis. Burundi lies between the politically troubled countries of Rwanda and the Democratic Republic of Congo, and is being held back by uncertainty over its future.

Area 27,830 sq km (10,745 sq miles)
Country population 8,731,814
Capital city (pop) Bujumbura (360,278)
Official languages Kirundi/French
Currency Burundi franc

Malawi

In 1964, the British territory of Nyasaland in southeastern Africa became Malawi, which is an independent republic. The country has had many natural disasters and depends on aid from other countries. About 15 per cent of the adult population has HIV or AIDS, and Malawi now has one of the world's lowest life expectancies.

Area 118,480 sq km (45,745 sq miles)
Country population 13,444,359
Capital city (pop) Lilongwe (866,272)
Official languages Chichewa/English
Currency Kwacha

Zambia

The landlocked country of Zambia in Central Africa has a small population. Copper is its chief export, but demand for copper has fallen and Zambia is now one of the world's poorest countries. Almost 90 per cent of its people live on less than US $1 dollar a day.

Area 752,614 sq km (290,586 sq miles)
Country population 12,450,229
Capital city (pop) Lusaka (2,679,083)
Official language English
Currency Kwacha

Swaziland

Swaziland is one of the world's few absolute monarchies – political parties were banned by the king in 1973. The country relies on South Africa for trade. About 40 per cent of the people live on less than US $1 a day. It has one of the highest levels of HIV/AIDS in the world and the world's lowest life expectancy.

Area 17,363 sq km (6,704 sq miles)
Country population 1,194,882
Capital city (pop) Mbabane (82,887)
Official languages English/Swazi
Currency Lilangeni

Lesotho

The Kingdom of Lesotho was once called Basutoland and became independent from the UK in 1966. It is entirely surrounded by South Africa. Lesotho has diamond mines but few other resources. Most people work on the land or in South African mines.

Area 30,355 sq km (11,720 sq miles)
Country population 1,884,897
Capital city (pop) Maseru (240,663)
Official languages Sotho/English
Currency Loti

Tanzania

Tanzania is made up of the country that used to be called Tanganyika on the eastern African mainland, and the island of Zanzibar, which is in the Indian Ocean just off the coast of Tanganyika. The two nations joined in 1964 after becoming independent. The country contains Lake Victoria, Mount Kilimanjaro and Serengeti National Park.

Area 945,087 sq km (364,900 sq miles)
Country population 40,120,715
Capital city (pop) Dodoma (203,999)
Official languages Swahili/English
Currency Tanzanian shilling

Botswana

Botswana used to be called the British Protectorate of Bechuanaland, but in 1966 it became an independent Commonwealth republic. It is now one of the wealthiest countries in Africa. Botswana has many natural resources and is one of the world's largest producers of diamonds. However, around one-third of the population has HIV/AIDS.

Area 600,370 sq km
(231,804 sq miles)
Country population
1,914,815

Capital city (pop) Gaborone
(224,990)
Official language English
Currency Pula

Zimbabwe

Zimbabwe was previously the British colony of Rhodesia. It used to be a fairly well-off country, but since 2000 has suffered a series of political problems and upsets. Zimbabweans now have an extremely low standard of living: one-third have HIV/AIDS and 70 per cent live in poverty.

Area 390,580 sq km
(150,804 sq miles)
Country population
12,352,402

Capital city (pop) Harare
(2,999,481)
Official language English
Currency Zimbabwe dollar

Madagascar

Madagascar is in the Indian Ocean off the coast of Africa. It is the fourth largest island in the world. More than 80 per cent of people work on the land. The country has often suffered natural disasters. In 2000 most of its rice crop was destroyed by cyclones.

Area 587,040 sq km
(226,657 sq miles)
Country population
18,622,208

Capital city (pop)
Antananarivo (1,699,114)
Official languages
Malagasy/French
Currency Malagasy franc

Mauritius

Mauritius is a group of islands in the Indian Ocean. It has a stable government, and Mauritians have high incomes. The country exports sugar cane and has a thriving tourist industry. It is home to some of the world's rarest plants and animals.

Area 2,040 sq km
(788 sq miles)
Country population
1,261,926
Capital city (pop)
Port Louis
(637,324)

Official languages
English/French
Currency Mauritius rupee

Women of the Samburu tribe in Kenya performing a traditional dance

Kenya

Kenya lies on the Equator on the east coast of Africa. It has some of the most fertile land in Africa, and 75 per cent of the people work in farming. It is also one of Africa's most popular tourist destinations.

Area 582,650 sq km (224,962 sq miles)
Country population 35,527,559
Capital city (pop) Nairobi (3,988,257)
Official languages Swahili/English
Currency Kenya shilling

Mozambique

Mozambique used to be a Portuguese colony. It gained independence in 1975, became a republic in 1990, and held its first free elections in 1994. About 70 per cent of its people live in poverty. But since the beginning of the 21st century, things have begun to improve and other countries have started to invest in Mozambique.

Area 801,590 sq km
(309,496 sq miles)
Country population 21,000,335
Capital city (pop) Maputo
(1,994,900)
Official language Portuguese
Currency Metical

South Africa

South Africa lies on the southern tip of the continent. Until 1994 the country was ruled by its white minority and had an apartheid policy. This segregated the races – kept black and white apart – and denied black citizens the vote. Because of this many other countries refused to trade with South Africa. The African National Congress won South Africa's first inclusive elections in 1994, and it has been in power ever since.

Mount Kilimanjaro, Tanzania, is the highest mountain in Africa.

Area 1,219,912 sq km
(471,011 sq miles)
Country population
48,394,880
Capital city (pop) The seat of government is Tshwane (Pretoria) (2,253,260); the seat of the legislature is Cape Town (4,715,046); the seat of the judiciary is Bloemfontein (495,006)
Official languages
11 official languages:
Afrikaans, English, Ndebele, Pedi, Sotho, Swazi, Tsonga, Tswana, Venda, Xhosa, Zulu
Currency Rand

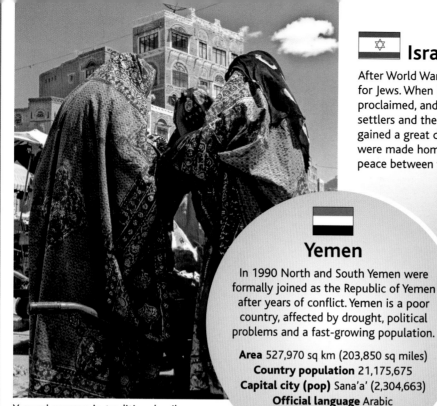

Yemeni women in traditional veils

Israel

After World War II, Israel was created in Palestine as a homeland for Jews. When Britain left the area in 1948 the State of Israel was proclaimed, and there was immediate conflict between the Jewish settlers and the Arabs who were living there. The State of Israel gained a great deal of land in the conflict, and many Palestinians were made homeless. There have been many attempts to make peace between the two sides, but the conflict continues.

Area 20,770 sq km (8,019 sq miles)
Country population 7,325,999
Capital city (pop) Jerusalem (750,892)
Jerusalem is the seat of government but is not recognized as the capital by the UN because East Jerusalem is part of the Occupied Territories captured in 1967. The UN considers Tel Aviv (1,117,842) to be the capital.
Official languages Hebrew/Arabic
Currency Shekel

Yemen

In 1990 North and South Yemen were formally joined as the Republic of Yemen after years of conflict. Yemen is a poor country, affected by drought, political problems and a fast-growing population.

Area 527,970 sq km (203,850 sq miles)
Country population 21,175,675
Capital city (pop) Sana'a' (2,304,663)
Official language Arabic
Currency Riyal

Turkey

Turkey is in a key position between Europe and Asia. The territory west of the Bosphorus strait is in Europe, while the much larger area to the east is in Asia. Turkey is popular with tourists, and between seven and ten million people every year visit its coastline and the historic city of Istanbul.

Area 780,580 sq km (301,384 sq miles)
Country population 76,375,182
Capital city (pop) Ankara (3,714,056)
Official language Turkish
Currency Turkish lir

Syria

Syria has been home to some of the world's oldest civilizations, and Damascus is probably the oldest city in the world. Syria became independent from France in 1946. Its people come from many different ethnic groups and religions, including Arabs, Kurds, Assyrians and Armenians, and Muslims, Christians and Jews.

Area 185,180 sq km (71,498 sq miles)
Country population 19,989,814
Capital city (pop) Damascus (2,688,278)
Official language Arabic
Currency Syrian pound

Kazakhstan

Kazakhstan is an enormous, landlocked nation almost four times the size of Texas. It was part of the former Soviet Union. Kazakhstan is rich in minerals and fossil fuels, including oil, coal, natural gas, gold, silver and lead.

Area 2,717,300 sq km (1,049,155 sq miles)
Country population 15,663,189
Capital city (pop) Astana (389,189)
Official language Kazakh
Currency Tenge

United Arab Emirates

The UAE is a group of seven Middle Eastern states and is one of the wealthiest countries in the region. It used to be a very poor country where most people lived by fishing, but is now the Gulf's third largest oil producer.

Area 83,600 sq km (32,278 sq miles)
Country population 5,402,375
Capital city (pop) Abu Dhabi (859,749)
Official language Arabic
Currency UAE dirham

The Burj Al Arab hotel in Dubai, United Arab Emirates

Kuwait

Kuwait has large oil reserves that make up more than eight per cent of the world's total. The country's economy was almost destroyed when Iraqi forces invaded in 1990 and burned oil wells as they retreated. The Kuwaiti government has spent billions of dollars on repairs, and oil production is now higher than it was before the invasion.

Area 17,820 sq km (6,880 sq miles)
Country population 2,906,764
Capital city (pop) Kuwait City (2,394,046)
Official language Arabic
Currency Kuwaiti dinar

 # Jordan

Jordan shares borders with Syria, Israel, the West Bank, Saudi Arabia and Iraq. Despite the problems of its neighbours the country is relatively peaceful. It doesn't have many natural resources, and its vital supplies of Iraqi oil were halted by the Iraq war of 2003.

Area 92,300 sq km (35,637 sq miles)
Country population 5,913,809
Capital city (pop) Amman (1,135,733)
Official language Arabic
Currency Jordanian dina

 # Saudi Arabia

Saudi Arabia is a monarchy. It is ruled by the sons and grandsons of Abdul Aziz ibn Saud, who founded the kingdom. Saudi Arabia is one of the richest countries in the Middle East. It has the largest reserves of petroleum in the world and exports more than any other country. It is about the same size as Western Europe and includes an area called the Empty Quarter, the world's largest sand desert. Saudi Arabia is a Muslim country and includes the city of Makkah (or Mecca). This was the birthplace of the Prophet Muhammad and millions of Muslims make a pilgrimage there every year.

Area 2,149,690 sq km (830,000 sq miles)
Country population 24,686,696
Capital city (pop) Riyadh (4,606,888)
Official language Arabic
Currency Saudi riyal

 # Iran

Iran is a mountainous Middle Eastern country. Until 1935 it was known as Persia. It shares borders with several of the world's most troubled nations, including Iraq, Afghanistan and Pakistan. This discourages investment from other countries and tourism, and Iran's economy depends on oil.

Area 1,648,000 sq km (636,297 sq miles)
Country population 71,028,973
Capital city (pop) Tehran (12,664,286)
Official language Farsi
Currency Rial

 # Iraq

Iraq has had a violent recent history. From 1979 to 2003, Iraq was controlled by the dictator President Saddam Hussein. The USA, supported by countries including the UK, Spain, Australia, Poland and Denmark, removed Hussein from power in 2003. Hussein was executed in 2006, but conflict continues in Iraq.

Area 437,072 sq km (168,754 sq miles)
Country population 27,141,340
Capital city (pop) Baghdad (10,634,225)
Official language Arabic
Currency New Iraqi dinar

 # Lebanon

Lebanon is a small country bordering the Mediterranean Sea. It became independent from France in 1943. Since Lebanon's civil war of 1975–91 huge sums have been spent on rebuilding the country and it is heavily in debt.

Area 10,400 sq km (4,015 sq miles)
Country population 4,602,431
Capital city (pop) Beirut (1,987,173)
Official language Arabic
Currency Lebanese pound

The GUM department store, Moscow, Russia

 # Russia

The Russian Federation is the largest country in the world, almost twice the size of the United States. It stretches from Europe to Asia and covers 13 per cent of the world's total land area. Russia was the chief republic of the former Soviet Union, which in 1991 was split into 15 separate republics. Oil, natural gas, timber and metals make up more than 80 per cent of its exports. The country is still held back by poor transport and other systems. It also suffers from violent conflict in the Chechnya region.

Area 17,075,200 sq km (6,592,772 sq miles)
Country population 141,833,475
Capital city (pop) Moscow (14,744,150)
Official language Russian
Currency Rouble

Bahrain

The island state of Bahrain is 32 km (19.9 miles) off the east coast of Saudi Arabia. Oil is its main source of income, but the country is also a centre for offshore banking.

Area 665 sq km (257 sq miles)
Country population 788,873
Capital city (pop) Manama (668,089)
Official language Arabic
Currency Bahraini dinar

Qatar

Qatar became independent from Britain in 1971 and has changed from being a poor country dependent on pearl fishing to one of the Gulf's richest states. It has large reserves of oil and gas, which have brought great wealth.

Area 11,437 sq km (4,416 sq miles)
Country population 928,404
Capital city (pop) Doha (761,019)
Official language Arabic
Currency Qatar riyal

 # Oman

Oman borders Yemen, Saudi Arabia and the United Arab Emirates so is in a key position for the transportation of oil. Oil makes up more than 80 per cent of Oman's exports, but the government wants to encourage tourism and information technology.

Area 212,460 sq km (82,031 sq miles)
Country population 2,721,576
Capital city (pop) Muscat (1,090,797)
Official language Arabic
Currency Omani rial

Kyrgyzstan

Kyrgyzstan is a picturesque country of mountains, glaciers and lakes. It became independent from the former Soviet Union in 1991. Since then it has seen many political changes.

Area 198,500 sq km (76,641 sq miles)
Country population 5,285,799
Capital city (pop) Bishkek (914,932)
Official languages Kyrgyz/Russian
Currency Som

Tajikistan

Tajikistan lies west of China in Central Asia. It was part of the former Soviet Union. About 50,000 people died in the civil war of 1992–97 and the country is still violent and unsettled.

Area 143,100 sq km (55,251 sq miles)
Country population 7,350,401
Capital city (pop) Dushanbe (937,445)
Official language Tajik
Currency Somoni

Bhutan

The mountainous kingdom of Bhutan lies between Tibet (China) and India in the eastern Himalayas. Its main exports are rice, machinery and diesel oil, but tourism is also important.

Area 47,000 sq km (18,147 sq miles)
Country population 671,887
Capital city (pop) Thimphu (79,185)
Official language Dzongkha
Currency Ngultrum

Afghanistan

Afghanistan is a mountainous country in Central Asia. It has been through more than 20 years of political upheaval. The country was controlled by the Taliban from 1996 until 2001, when the Taliban was overthrown by an alliance led by the US military. At present many people are involved in the drugs trade and over one million of the population may be close to starvation.

Area 647,500 sq km (250,001 sq miles)
Country population 23,725,835
Capital city (pop) Kabul (2,436,111)
Official languages Dari (Persian)/Pashto
Currency Afghani

Mongolia

Mongolia is a landlocked nation between Russia and China. It is three times the size of France and is a land of deserts, grasslands, forests and mountains. Temperatures range from summer highs of 40°C (104°F) in the Gobi Desert to -40°C (-40°F) during the winter. More than half the population are nomads – they move from place to place with their livestock. Gers (moveable tent-like huts) are the most common form of shelter, even in cities.

Area 1,564,116 sq km (603,908 sq miles)
Country population 2,644,595
Capital city (pop) Ulaanbaatar (903,273)
Official language Khalkha Mongolian
Currency Tugrik

India

India is the largest democratic country in the world. It became independent from the UK in 1947 when it was divided into India and Pakistan. This division has led to three wars. India has the world's largest population, after China. In 1999 its population passed the one billion mark. Most people still live by farming and around 70 per cent of the population live in rural areas. India has a booming information technology industry and one of the most successful film industries in the world.

Area 3,287,590 sq km (1,269,346 sq miles)
Country population 1,152,342,278
Capital city (pop) New Delhi (18,362,625)
Official languages Hindi/English
Currency Indian rupee

Turkmenistan

Turkmenistan borders the Caspian Sea in Central Asia. About 90 per cent of its land is desert. It has the fifth largest oil and natural gas reserves in the world, but is crippled by debt to other countries.

Area 488,100 sq km (188,456 sq miles)
Country population 7,193,046
Capital city (pop) Ashgabat (891,879)
Official languages Turkmen
Currency Manat

Pakistan

Pakistan was created in 1947 as a home for Indian Muslims. It was divided into Pakistan and Bangladesh in 1971. The country is in dispute with India over ownership of the state of Kashmir. This has led to fears of an arms race, as both countries are believed to have nuclear weapons.

Area 803,940 sq km (310,403 sq miles)
Country population 155,360,000
Capital city (pop) Islamabad (657,788)
Official language Urdu
(Punjabi is the most commonly used language, and English is used in business, government and higher education)
Currency Pakistan rupee

Sri Lanka

Sri Lanka was called Ceylon until 1948, when it became independent from the UK. It is a tropical island in the Indian Ocean, only 20 km (12 miles) from the south coast of India. The country has textile, food processing and telecommunications industries. It is held back, however, by nearly 20 years of conflict between some of its people, the Tamils, who want independence, and the government.

Area 65,610 sq km (25,332 sq miles)
Country population 20,293,592
Capital city (pop) Colombo (2,588,148)
Official language Sinhala
Currency Sri Lankan rupee

Nepal

Nepal is home to Everest, the world's highest mountain, and tourism brings vital money into the country. In 2001, Nepal's Crown Prince murdered ten members of the royal family before taking his own life.

Area 147,181 sq km (56,827 sq miles)
Country population 26,942,600
Capital city (pop) Kathmandu (1,611,647)
Official language Nepali
Currency Nepalese rupee

Yak train making its way over the Khumbu glacier, Nepal

China

China is one of the oldest civilizations in the world and has the oldest continuously used language system. It also is home to the world's largest population. The economy of China is growing rapidly and it is now the world's fifth largest exporter of goods. Tourism has also become a major industry.

Area 9,596,960 sq km (3,705,407 sq miles)
Country population 1,313,552,038
Capital city (pop) Beijing (11,941,418)
Official language Mandarin Chinese
Currency Renminbi (also known as the yuan)

Taiwan

The island of Taiwan lies 150 km (93 miles) from mainland China. Taiwan has a thriving electronics industry. It is one of the world's leading producers of computer technology. Taiwan is home to the world's tallest building, the Taipei 101.

Area 35,980 sq km (13,892 sq miles)
Country population 23,195,487
Capital city (pop) Taipei (8,366,945)
Official language Chinese
Currency New Taiwan dollar

Uzbekistan

Uzbekistan has the largest population in Central Asia. It has been independent of the Soviet Union since 1991. It is the second largest exporter of cotton in the world and has mineral deposits. However, its people are poor because the wealth is distributed unequally.

Area 447,400 sq km (172,742 sq miles)
Country population 27,363,389
Capital city (pop) Tashkent (3,247,012)
Official language Uzbek
Currency Som

Bangladesh

Bangladesh won independence from Pakistan in 1971. About 70 per cent of the people work in farming and the country produces all its own food. The main industries include cotton, tea, leather, sugar and natural gas, and its leading export is clothing.

Area 144,000 sq km (55,599 sq miles)
Country population 143,481,419
Capital city (pop) Dhaka (13,240,743)
Official language Bengali
Currency Taka

North Korea

North Korea is one of the world's few remaining Communist states. As many as three million North Koreans have probably died of starvation because of famine and financial mishandling, while the regime spends money on military equipment. North Korea's nuclear programme threatens the international food aid that keeps the population going at present.

Area 120,540 sq km (46,541 sq miles)
Country population 23,708,186
Capital city (pop) Pyongyang (3,128,617)
Official language Korean
Currency Won

South Korea

During the three-year Korean War in 1953 north Korea attacked the South with Chinese support. The Korean Peninsula was then divided into two. South Korea is a democratic country and has a thriving, high-tech economy and a growing tourism industry.

Area 98,480 sq km (38,023 sq miles)
Country population 48,426,195
Capital city (pop) Seoul (22,254,620)
Official language Korean
Currency Won

Dochu La pass in the Himalayas, Bhutan

ASIA

Typical capsule hotel in Japan

Japan

Japan is made up of four large islands and many smaller islands. This mountainous and volcanic country is one of the world's most densely populated places, and there are more people in Tokyo than any other city in the world. Japan is a wealthy country and a world leader in the electronics, robotics and car production industries.

Area 377,835 sq km (145,882 sq miles)
Country population 127,939,307
Capital city (pop) Tokyo (37,203,122)
Official language Japanese
Currency Yen

The Philippines

The Philippines is made up of more than 7,000 islands in Southeast Asia. More than 80 per cent of the population is Roman Catholic – the Philippines is the only Asian nation that is mainly Christian. It suffers from natural disasters, such as volcanic eruptions and typhoons, as well as a very high birth rate. Many Filipinos go to work abroad and their country depends on the US $6–7 billion they send home each year.

Area 300,000 sq km (115,831 sq miles)
Country population 90,317,981
Capital city (pop) Manila (19,195,048)
Official languages Filipino/English
Currency Philippine peso

Myanmar

Myanmar used to be called Burma. The country is ruled by an undemocratic military government and has been accused by foreign governments of severe human rights abuses. It may also be a major producer of heroin. These things have led the European Union and the USA to limit trade with the country.

Area 678,500 sq km (261,970 sq miles)
Country population 56,950,062
Capital city (pop) Rangoon (4,886,305)
Official language Burmese
Currency Kyat

Malaysia

Malaysia is made up of two regions, separated by about 1,030 km (640 miles) of the South China Sea. The country used to rely on farming and exports of raw materials, but it is now a leading producer and exporter of high-tech, electronic merchandise.

Area 329,750 sq km (127,317 sq miles)
Country population 27,737,693
Capital city (pop) Kuala Lumpur (7,239,871)
Official language Bahasa Malaysia (Malay)
Currency Malaysian dollar (Ringgit)

Vietnam

North and South Vietnam were rejoined in 1976 after 30 years of war. At first the war was between the Communists and the French colonialists, and later between the Communist North Vietnam and the South, which was supported by the USA. Nearly four million people died and much of Vietnam's landscape was destroyed. There is now a Communist socialist government. Vietnam is now one of the world's leading rice exporters, and the country's oil production has increased.

Area 329,560 sq km (127,243 sq miles)
Country population 86,240,477
Capital city (pop) Hanoi (2,686,290)
Official language Vietnamese
Currency Dông

Thailand

Until 1939, Thailand was called Siam. It is the only country in Southeast Asia never to have been under the control of a European power. About ten million tourists visit Bangkok and the country's beautiful coasts each year. Farming is important and about half the people still work on the land.

Area 514,000 sq km (198,456 sq miles)
Country population 63,629,485
Capital city (pop) Bangkok (9,791,333)
Official language Thai
Currency Baht

Singapore

The city state of Singapore in Southeast Asia is one of the richest nations in the world. Its people have one of the world's highest standards of living. Singapore's thriving manufacturing industry includes shipbuilding and electronics.

Area 693 sq km (267 sq miles)
Country population 4,974,232
Official languages Malay/Mandarin/Tamil/English
Currency Singapore dollar

Laos

Laos is a landlocked, mountainous country bordered by China, Vietnam, Cambodia, Thailand and Myanmar. It is one of the world's last remaining Communist states. Laos is popular with adventurous tourists, but it is extremely primitive. There are few paved roads and no railways.

Area 236,800 sq km (91,429 sq miles)
Country population 5,931,809
Capital city (pop) Vientiane (206,211)
Official language Lao
Currency Kip

Villamendhoo Island in the Maldives

East Timor

East Timor became independent from Indonesia in 2002. It is Southeast Asia's youngest nation and the world's newest democracy. East Timor is a very poor country and often suffers floods.

Area 15,007 sq km (5,794 sq miles)
Country population 969,816
Capital city (pop) Dili (170,490)
Official languages Portuguese/Tetum
Currency US dollar

Brunei

Brunei gained full independence from Britain in 1984. It is ruled by the Sultan, whose family have reigned for six centuries. Brunei is enormously wealthy because of its natural gas and oil fields.

Area 5,770 sq km (2,228 sq miles)
Country population 406,849
Capital city (pop) Bandar Seri Begawan (32,331)
Official language Malay
Currency Brunei dollar

The Comoros

The Comoros is a group of volcanic islands between Madagascar and Mozambique. It is one of the world's poorest countries. The Comoros has few natural resources. It exports vanilla, cloves and essential oils, but depends on aid from other countries.

Area 2,170 sq km (838 sq miles)
Country population 626,930
Capital city (pop) Moroni (47,040)
Official languages Arabic/French
Currency Comorian franc

Seychelles

The Seychelles is made up of 155 islands in the Indian Ocean, east of mainland Africa. It became independent from Britain in 1976. About 90 per cent of the islands' people live on the main island of Mahé and are reasonably well off, thanks to successful tourism and tuna fishing industries.

Area 455 sq km (176 sq miles)
Country population 86,200
Capital city (pop) Victoria (22,198)
Official languages English/French/Creole
Currency Seychelles rupee

Traditional wayang golek wooden puppets from Indonesia

Indonesia

Indonesia includes more than 17,000 islands. The world's largest Muslim population lives on about 6,000 of these. Indonesia is rich in minerals, and it exports petroleum, textiles, timber, natural gas and rubber. There are frequent natural disasters.

Area 1,919,440 sq km (741,100 sq miles)
Country population 227,070,492
Capital city (pop) Jakarta (18,588,548)
Official languages Indonesian/Bahasa
Currency Rupiah

Maldives

The Maldives are a chain of 1,190 coral islands, which are threatened by rising sea levels. The chief industries are fishing and tourism. Few crops can be grown there and almost all food must be imported.

Area 300 sq km (116 sq miles)
Country population 308,797
Capital city (pop) Malé (113,172)
Official language Dhivehi
Currency Rufiyaa

Cambodia

1999 was Cambodia's first full year of peace after more than 20 years of conflict. In 1975 Phnom Penh was captured by Communist Khmer Rouge forces, who executed millions of Cambodians. The country is still very poor. Farming and fishing are the main occupations, but tourism has become more important.

Area 181,040 sq km (69,900 sq miles)
Country population 14,103,096
Capital city (pop) Phnom Penh (1,398,449)
Official language Khmer
Currency Riel

Papua New Guinea

Papua New Guinea is made up of many small islands and one half of New Guinea, the world's second largest island. It has mineral deposits such as gold and copper, as well as oil and natural gas. It has been difficult to use these to the full because the country lacks good roads and transport, and there are large areas of rainforest.

Area 462,840 sq km (178,704 sq miles)
Country population 6,315,896
Capital city (pop) Port Moresby (301,817)
Official language English
Currency Kina

Kiribati

Kiribati is made up of 33 islands in the Pacific Ocean, halfway between Hawaii and Australia. Kiribati's main exports are coconuts and fish.

Solomon Islands

The Solomon Islands include several densely forested volcanic islands in the South Pacific. People live by farming, forestry and fishing, but since 1998 there has been conflict between different groups in the population. Law and order has broken down, and the islanders' average income has been halved. A peacekeeping force led by Australia arrived in 2003.

Area 28,450 sq km (10,985 sq miles)
Country population 506,992
Capital city (pop) Honiara (57,456)
Official language English
Currency Solomon Islands dollar

Area 811 sq km (313 sq miles)
Country population 97,031
Capital city (pop) Tarawa (45,754)
Official language English
Currency Australian dollar

The Olgas, natural rock formations in Australia

Palau

The Republic of Palau is made up of 340 islands in the Pacific Ocean, southeast of the Philippines. It became independent in 1994 and is one of the world's youngest nations. The islands rely mainly on tourism. The waters around Palau are rich in marine life, and visitors come to snorkel and scuba-dive. The islands also export fish, shellfish and coconuts.

Area 458 sq km (177 sq miles)
Country population 20,548
Capital city (pop) Koror (10,650)
Official languages Palauan/English
Currency US dollar

Micronesia

The Federated States of Micronesia is a group of more than 600 islands in the North Pacific Ocean. It gained independence from the USA in 1986, but the USA has kept the right to have military bases on the islands. This agreement brings Micronesia billions of dollars of financial aid.

Area 702 sq km (271 sq miles)
Country population 108,287
Capital city (pop) Palikir (7,321)
Official language English
Currency US dollar

A view of the city of Auckland in New Zealand

New Zealand

New Zealand lies in the Pacific Ocean, about 1,600 km (994 miles) east of Australia. It is made up of two main islands and several smaller ones. The capital, Wellington, lies further south than any other capital city. New Zealand is mountainous and relatively unspoilt, and is becoming more and more popular with tourists from all over the world.

Area 268,680 sq km (103,738 sq miles)
Country population 4,121,662
Capital city (pop) Wellington (364,586)
Official languages English/Maori
Currency New Zealand dollar

Australia

Australia was discovered by Captain James Cook in 1770. It became independent in 1931, but it is part of the British Commonwealth and Queen Elizabeth II is the head of state. Australia is the world's sixth largest country. It has important mineral resources and vast areas are given over to sheep and cattle farming. Some famous landmarks include the Great Barrier Reef and Uluru.

Area 7,686,850 sq km (2,967,910 sq miles)
Country population 20,245,629
Capital city (pop) Canberra (329,200)
Official language English
Currency Australian dollar

Tonga

Tonga is a group of 169 islands in the southern Pacific Ocean. It is the only country in the Pacific ruled by a monarchy. The islands have no natural resources and people rely on farming. Tonga exports products such as coconuts, vanilla and yams. Around half of the Tongan people live abroad, particularly in the USA and Australasia.

Area 748 sq km
(289 sq miles)
Country population
114,689
Capital city (pop)
Nuku'alofa (23,854)
Official languages
Tongan/English
Currency Pa'anga

Traditional Polynesian canoe on a beach in Tonga

Vanuatu

Vanuatu is a chain of 83 volcanic islands in the South Pacific Ocean, between Hawaii and Australia. About 65 per cent of the people work on the land, but offshore banking and tourism are growing industries. However, the islands sometimes suffer earthquakes, tsunamis and cyclones, which may limit the growth of tourism.

Area 12,200 sq km
(4,710 sq miles)
Country population 208,869
Capital city (pop) Port Vila
(38,438)
Official languages
Bislama/English/French
Currency Vatu

Fiji

Fiji is made up of more than 300 volcanic islands in the South Pacific Ocean, about 1,770 km (1,100 miles) north of New Zealand. Fiji's main export is sugar cane, and it has a flourishing tourism industry. However, political problems from time to time have discouraged other countries from investing in the islands.

Area 18,270 sq km
(7,054 sq miles)
Country population 905,949
Capital city (pop) Suva
(206,631)
Official languages There is no official language, but the main languages are Fijian and Hindi
Currency Fiji dollar

Nauru

The island of Nauru lies 53 km (33 miles) south of the Equator in the Pacific Ocean. It is the smallest independent republic in the world. At present, the people have one of the highest incomes per head in the world, thanks to the export of phosphates (fertilizer). However, Nauru's phosphate reserves are running low, and it has few other resources.

Area 21 sq km
(8 sq miles)
Country population 13,287
Capital city (pop) no official capital
Official languages
Nauruan/English
Currency Australian dollar

Samoa

Samoa is a group of islands in the South Pacific Ocean. Samoa's beaches and rainforests have led to a booming tourism industry. This now brings in a quarter of the islands' income.

Area 2,944 sq km (1,137 sq miles)
Country population 176,908
Capital city (pop) Apia (41,204)
Official languages Samoan/English
Currency Tala

Tuvalu

Tuvalu was a British colony until 1975. It is a group of nine coral atolls in the South Pacific Ocean. It is the second lowest country in the world and is under threat from rising sea levels. Tuvalu has the world's second smallest population. The country has no known natural resources, and has fewer than 1,000 tourists a year. The islanders rely on exporting fish, stamps and handicrafts, as well as the money sent home from Tuvaluans working abroad.

Area 26 sq km (10 sq miles)
Country population 11,992
Capital city (pop) Funafuti (4,921)
Official languages Tuvaluan/English
Currency Australian dollar

Marshall Islands

The Marshall Islands lie in the central Pacific. The islands were occupied by the USA after World War II until 1986, and were used for nuclear weapons testing. About half the people work in farming. Coconut oil is the main export.

Area 11,854 sq km (4,576 sq miles)
Country population 60,422
Capital city (pop) Dalap-Uliga-Darrit (21,512)
Official languages Marshallese/English
Currency US dollar

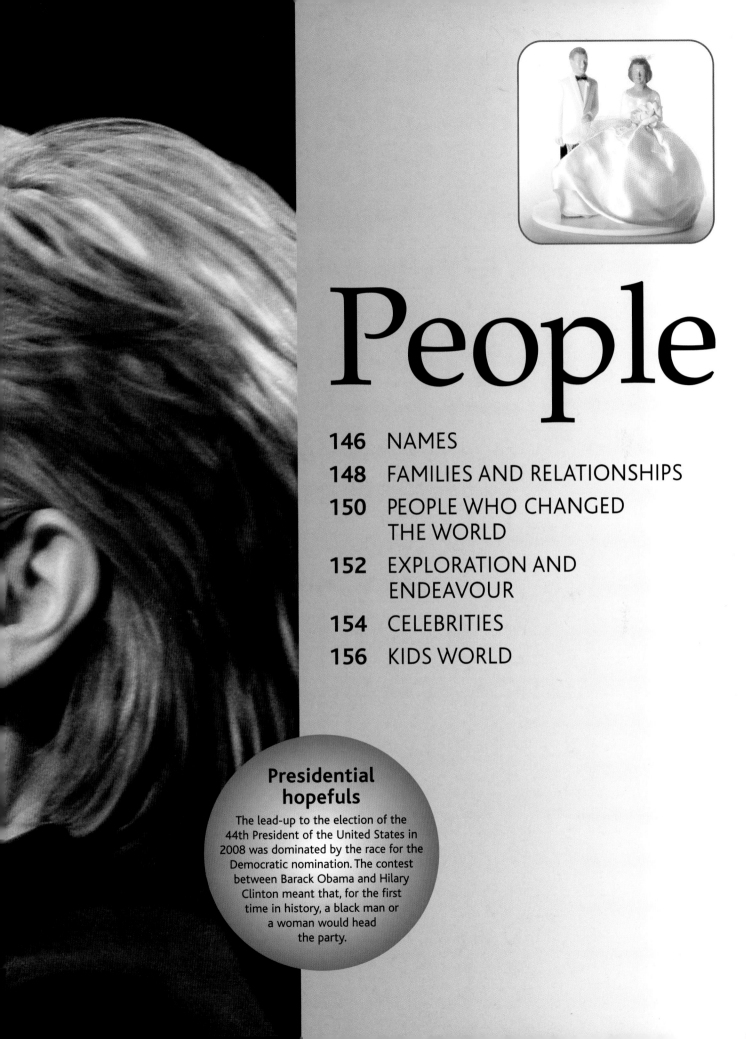

People

Presidential hopefuls

The lead-up to the election of the 44th President of the United States in 2008 was dominated by the race for the Democratic nomination. The contest between Barack Obama and Hilary Clinton meant that, for the first time in history, a black man or a woman would head the party.

http://www.behindthename.com **search**

Popular first names

First name fashions change – especially those for girls. Some traditional names remain popular but new names come into use. Olivia was not in the Top 10 in the UK until 1999 or in the USA until 2001, but has kept its popularity. These are the most popular names now and 100 years ago in England and Wales and USA.

Princes Harry and William: Their names are now two of the favourite boys' names in England and Wales.

Surnames around the world

Surnames were not used in Britain until after the Norman Conquest in 1066. Until then, most people were known only by their first name. People started to add extra names in order to be able to tell one William from another.

Some surnames came from where a person lived or the person's father's name – so the son of someone called John was known as Johnson. Others were based on a person's occupation (a blacksmith would be called Smith) or their appearance (a brown-haired person might be called Brown). The origins of some surnames have been forgotten.

A very long name

Anna Pepper was born in Derby, England, on 19 December 1882. She was given 26 first names, one for each letter of the alphabet, in alphabetical order: Anna Bertha Cecilia Diana Emily Fanny Gertrude Hypatia Inez Jane Kate Louisa Maud Nora Ophelia Prudence Quince Rebecca Starkey Teresa Ulysis Venus Winifred Xenophon Yetty Zeus Pepper.

England & Wales Girls/Boys	USA Girls/Boys	England & Wales (1904) Girls/Boys	USA (1908) Girls/Boys
1 Grace/Jack	1 Emily/Jacob	1 Mary/William	1 Mary/John
2 Ruby/Thomas	2 Emma/Michael	2 Florence/John	2 Helen/William
3 Olivia/Oliver	3 Madison/Joshua	3 Doris/George	3 Margaret/James
4 Emily/Joshua	4 Isabella/Ethan	4 Edith/Thomas	4 Ruth/George
5 Jessica/Harry	5 Ava/Matthew	5 Dorothy/Arthur	5 Anna/Robert
6 Sophie/Charlie	6 Abigail/Daniel	6 Annie/James	6 Dorothy/Joseph
7 Chloe/Daniel	7 Olivia/Christopher	7 Margaret/Charles	7 Elizabeth/Charles
8 Lily/William	8 Hannah/Andrew	8 Alice/Frederick	8 Mildred/Frank
9 Ella/James	9 Sophia/Anthony	9 Elizabeth/Albert	9 Alice/Edward
10 Amelia/Alfie	10 Samantha/William	10 Elsie/Ernest	10 Marie/Thomas

Most common surnames

Eng. & Wales	USA	China	Denmark	France	Germany	India	Ireland
1 Smith	1 Smith	1 Lo	1 Jensen	1 Martin	1 Müller	1 Singh	1 Murphy
2 Jones	2 Johnson	2 Wáng	2 Nielsen	2 Bernard	2 Schmidt	2 Kumar	2 Kelly
3 Williams	3 Williams	3 Zhang	3 Hansen	3 Dubois	3 Schneider	3 Sharma/Sarma	3 O'Sullivan
4 Taylor	4 Jones	4 Liú	4 Pedersen	4 Thomas	4 Fischer	4 Patel	4 Walsh
5 Brown	5 Brown	5 Chén	5 Andersen	5 Robert	5 Meyer	5 Shah	5 Smith
6 Davies	6 Davis	6 Yáng	6 Christensen	6 Richard	6 Weber	6 Lal	6 O'Brien
7 Evans	7 Miller	7 Huáng	7 Larsen	7 Petit	7 Schulz	7 Gupta	7 Byrne
8 Wilson	8 Wilson	8 Zhào	8 Sørensen	8 Durand	8 Wagner	8 Bhat	8 Ryan
9 Thomas	9 Moore	9 Zou	9 Rasmussen	9 Leroy	9 Becker	9 Rao	9 O'Connor
10 Johnson	10 Taylor	10 Wú	10 Jørgensen	10 Moreau	10 Hoffmann	10 Reddy	10 O'Neill

Known by one name

Some people are so famous they are instantly recognizable by just one name.

Another long name!

In the late 19th century, the Reverend Ralph William Lyonel Tollemache of Grantham, Lincolnshire gave his 15 children very long names. These included Lyulph Ydwallo Odin Nestor Egbert Lyonel Toedmag Hugh Erchenwyne Saxon Esa Cromwell Orma Nevill Dysart Plantagenet Tollemache-Tollemache (1876–1961). The initial letters of his first names spell 'Lyonel the Second'.

Aaliyah US singer/actress Aaliyah Haughton, 1979–2001

Barbie US doll Barbara Millicent Roberts, 1959–

Beyoncé US singer Beyoncé Knowles, 1981–

Björk Icelandic singer/actress Björk Gudmundsdóttir, 1965–

Bono Irish rock band U2 singer Paul Hewson, 1960–

Canaletto Italian painter Giovanni Antonio Canale, 1697–1768

Cher US singer Cherilyn Sarkasian, 1946–

Colette French writer Sidonie-Gabrielle Colette, 1873–1954

Dido UK singer Dido Armstrong, 1971–

Eminem US rap singer Marshall Mathers, 1972–

Enya Irish singer Eithne ní Bhraonáin, 1961–

Evita Argentinean politician Eva Peron, 1919–52

Flea US Red Hot Chili Peppers bass guitarist Michael Peter Balzary, 1962–

Hergé Belgian Tintin cartoonist Georges Rémi, 1907–83

Houdini US magician Erich Weiss, 1874–1926

Jewel US singer Jewel Kilcher, 1974–

Lulu UK singer Marie McDonald McLaughlin, 1948–

Madonna US singer Madonna Louise Ciccone, 1958–

Meatloaf US singer Marvin/Michael Lee Aday, 1947–

Michelangelo Italian painter Michelangelo Buonarroti, 1475–1564

Moby US musician Richard Melville Hall, 1965–

Pelé Brazilian footballer Edson Arantes Nascimento, 1940–

Pink US singer Alecia Moore, 1979–

Ronaldo Brazilian footballer Ronaldo Luiz Nazario de Lima, 1976–

Shaggy Jamaican singer Orville Richard Burrell, 1968–

Sting UK singer Gordon Matthew Sumner, 1951–

Initial impressions

These famous people are known by their initials and surnames, rather than their full first names.

Early Heinz wagon from about 1900

W.H. (Wystan Hugh) Auden was a poet

Rev. W. (Wilbert) Awdry wrote *Thomas the Tank Engine*

P.T. (Phineas Taylor) Barnum was a circus proprietor

J.M. (James Matthew) Barrie was the author of *Peter Pan*

T.S. (Thomas Stearns) Eliot wrote the book on which the musical *Cats* was based

W.C. (William Claude) Fields was a film actor

W.G. (William Gilbert) Grace played cricket

H.J. (Henry John) Heinz manufactured food

k.d. (Kathryn Dawn) Lang is a singer

D.H. (David Herbert) Lawrence was a writer

T.E. (Thomas Edward) Lawrence was a soldier/writer (Lawrence of Arabia)

C.S. (Clive Staples) Lewis wrote *The Lion, the Witch and the Wardrobe*

A.A. (Alan Alexander) Milne wrote *Winnie the Pooh*

E. (Edith) Nesbit wrote *The Phoenix and the Carpet*

J.K. (Joanne Kathleen) Rowling is the author of *Harry Potter*

O.J. (Orenthal James) Simpson was a footballer

R.L. (Robert Lawrence) Stine wrote the *Goosebumps* series

J.R.R. (John Roland Ruel) Tolkien wrote *Lord of the Rings*

J.M.W. (Joseph Mallord William) Turner was a painter

H.G. (Herbert George) Wells was a science-fiction author

E.B. (Elwyn Brooks) White wrote *Charlotte's Web* and *Stuart Little*

F. W. (Frank Winfield) Woolworth was a retailer

Japan	Norway	Russia	Scotland	Spain	Sweden
1 Sato	1 Hansen	1 Ivanov	1 Smith	1 García	1 Johansson
2 Suzuki	2 Olsen	2 Smirnov	2 Brown	2 Fernández	2 Andersson
3 Takahashi	3 Johansen	3 Vasilev	3 Wilson	3 González	3 Karlsson
4 Tanaka	4 Larsen	4 Petrov	4 Campbell	4 Rodríguez	4 Nilsson
5 Watanabe	5 Andersen	5 Kyznetsov	5 Stewart	5 López	5 Eriksson
6 Ito	6 Nilsen	6 Fedorov	6 Thomson	6 Martínez	6 Larsson
7 Yamamoto	7 Pedersen	7 Mikhailov	7 Robertson	7 Sánchez	7 Olsson
8 Nakamura	8 Kristiansen	8 Sokolov	8 Anderson	8 Pérez	8 Persson
9 Kobayashi	9 Jensen	9 Pavlov	9 Macdonald	9 Martín	9 Svensson
10 Saito	10 Karlsen	10 Semenov	10 Scott	10 Gómez	10 Gustafsson

Even longer!

Louis Jullien (1812–1860) was a French conductor and composer, born in Sisteron, France. His parents were persuaded by the 36 members of the local Philharmonic Society that they should all be godfathers, and Louis received all their names.

Who's who in the family?

We all know who's who in our immediate family – our mothers, fathers, grandparents, aunts and uncles, sisters and brothers. But who is a second cousin or a cousin once removed?

Nephew
Son of your sister or brother

Niece
Daughter of your sister or brother

Cousin, or first cousin
Child of your aunt and uncle

Second cousin
Child of your first cousin. Second cousins have the same great-grandparents as you, but not the same grandparents. Third cousins have the same great-great-grandparents, and so on.

Removed
A child of your first cousin is called "once removed". Removed means a different generation. Once removed is one generation, twice removed is two generations, and so on.

Step
Stepmother, stepfather, stepsister, stepbrother, stepson or stepdaughter is a person who is related to you only by the remarriage of someone in your immediate family after death or divorce. For example, if a woman marries again, her new husband will be her children's stepfather but he has no blood relationship with them.

Half
A half-sister or half-brother has either the same mother or father as you, but not both.

In-law
A relative by marriage – so the wife of your son is your daughter-in-law or the wife of your brother is your sister-in-law. It refers only to immediate members of your family (your own marriage, that of your brothers and sisters, and your children).

Weddings and divorces around the world

The number of people marrying every year varies from country to country. Some are tropical islands and countries that are popular with tourists who travel there for a romantic wedding.

Others have cultures that place a specially high value on marriage. The number of divorces varies greatly from country to country, according to the legal system and religion.

Number of marriages per 1000 per year*	Number of divorces per 1000 per year*
High rates	**High rates**
China 35.9	Russia 5.30
Cook Islands 32.8	Aruba 5.27
Barbados 13.1	USA 4.19
Cyprus 12.9	Ukraine 3.79
Medium rates	**Medium rates**
USA 7.8	Australia 2.85
Australia 5.4	UK 2.58
UK 5.1	Canada 2.24
Canada 4.7	
	Low rates
Low rates	Guatemala 0.12
Venezuela 3.3	Belize 0.17
Argentina 3.2	Mongolia 0.28
Armenia 3.2	
Saudi Arabia 3.2	* In those countries for which data available

Wedding on a Pacific island beach

Till death do us part...

Longest marriages
● Sir Temulji Bhicaji Nariman and Lady Nariman of Mumbai (Bombay), India were married in 1853 at five years old. They stayed married for 86 years until Sir Temulji's death in 1940.

● Lazarus Rowe and Molly Weber were allegedly married in Greenland, New Hampshire, USA, in 1743. They remained married for 86 years until 1829 when Lazarus died.

According to the Bible, King Solomon had 700 wives as well as 300 concubines.

Most marriages
● King Mongkut of Siam (1804–68) had 39 wives and 82 children. His life inspired the musical *The King and I* and the film *Anna and the King* (1999).

● American Glynn "Scotty" de Moss Wolfe (1908–97) was married 29 times, which is a US record. His 29th and last wedding was on 20 June 1996 to Linda Essex. It was her 23rd wedding – another US record.

● US asbestos millionaire Tommy Manville (1894–1967) was married 13 times.

Seventh time lucky
In the UK, Sir Francis Ferdinand Maurice Cook (1907–78) was married seven times.

crest
coronet
mantling
supporter
helm
arms
charge
motto scroll
compartment
DILIGENT · SECRET · AND

Coat of arms

A coat of arms is the symbol or badge of a family, person or even organization. The idea started in Europe in the Middle Ages, when knights began to add decoration to their armour. This helped soldiers tell the difference between their own army and the enemy on a battlefield. It also helped people to tell knights apart in jousting contests.

The designs on a coat of arms symbolized the achievements of the family, and were passed on from generation to generation. A coat of arms is still put together by people called heralds, and the process is known as heraldry.

Parts of a coat of arms
Each coat of arms has a unique combination of colours and symbols. The positions of the different features are described in special terms, such as sinister (left) and dexter (right).

Ordinaries
The geometric designs in a coat of arms are called ordinaries.

Colours
The background or field uses one of two metals: Gold (known as or in the language of heraldry), represented by yellow, and Silver (argent), shown as white. There are five basic colours: Gules (red), Azure (blue), Sable (black), Vert (green) and Purpure (purple). Patterns called furs, such as ermine, are also used. Each colour or pattern symbolizes a special feature, such as red for bravery. Special rules dictate how these devices are used: a metal may not be placed on metal, and so on.

Charge, supporters and other features
An object on the body of a shield is called a charge. It may include real and imaginary animals, often lions, eagles or dragons. At each side of the shield are the supporters, which may be animals, birds, or people. There may also be other features such as a family motto in a banner above the shield and a crest or helmet, which may feature the same animals used as the charge or supporters.

Anniversary gifts

There is a very old tradition of celebrating wedding anniversaries by presenting special types of gift. For example, for a 25th anniversary people give gifts made of silver. In the UK and USA most people celebrate only the milestone anniversaries: the 25th, 30th, 40th, 50th and 60th.

The 75th anniversary was traditionally the diamond but few married couples live long enough to celebrate it. Since Queen Victoria's Diamond Jubilee was held to mark her 60 years on the throne, the 60th wedding anniversary has become the diamond celebration.

1st Cotton (UK); paper (US)
2nd Paper (UK); cotton, calico (US)
3rd Leather
4th Fruit, flowers (UK); linen, silk (US)
5th Wood
6th Sugar, sweets, iron
7th Wool, copper
8th Bronze
9th Pottery, willow
10th Tin, aluminium
11th Steel
12th Silk, linen
13th Lace
14th Ivory
15th Crystal, glass
20th China
25th Silver
30th Pearls
35th Coral, jade
40th Rubies
45th Sapphires
50th Gold
55th Emeralds
60th Diamonds
70th Platinum
75th Diamonds (again)

Christopher Columbus landing in the New World

Karl Marx
(1818–83) German
Karl Marx's ideas on economic history and sociology changed the world. Marx was a social philosopher who attacked the state and predicted a future in which everyone was equal. He explained his theories in the *Communist Manifesto* (compiled with Friedrich Engels and published in 1848) and *Das Kapital* (1867–94). His ideas eventually led to the Russian Revolution and communism. By 1950 almost half of the world's people lived under communist regimes.

Christopher Columbus
(1451–1506) Italian
Christopher Columbus is one of the most famous of all explorers. He believed he could reach Asia by sailing west across the Atlantic Ocean and in 1492 he set sail in the *Santa Maria* to prove his theory. Instead, he landed on the islands now known as the West Indies. His discoveries led to the European exploration and settlement of the Americas.

William Shakespeare
(1564–1616) English
William Shakespeare is generally agreed to be the greatest playwright in the English language. He began as an actor and wrote at least 154 love poems and 37 plays, including *King Lear*, *Hamlet*, *Romeo and Juliet* and *Macbeth*. Shakespeare also probably introduced more than 1,700 new words to the English language.

A US stamp commemorating the 400th anniversary of Shakespeare's birth in 1964

Charles Darwin
(1809–82) English
Naturalist Charles Darwin established the theory of evolution. He began forming his ideas when he served as official naturalist on a world voyage on *HMS Beagle* (1831–36) and spent the rest of his life back in England developing them. When his famous book *The Origin of Species by Means of Natural Selection* was published in 1859 there were violent reactions against it. Darwin challenged the Bible's account of creation, and explained that human beings are descended from an ape-like ancestor. Another English naturalist, Alfred Russel Wallace, independently developed very similar ideas at the same time as Darwin.

Emmeline Pankhurst
(1858–1928) English
Emmeline Pankhurst was the most famous of the women who campaigned for the right to vote in the UK. From 1905 she fought for the vote by any means possible and was frequently arrested and imprisoned. She died in 1928 shortly before her aims were realized and every woman over 21 years old was granted the vote.

Emmeline Pankhurst, 1914

Mahatma Gandhi
(1869–1948) Indian
Gandhi began his career as a lawyer but became a great political and spiritual leader. He led the peaceful civil disobedience of Indians against British rule in India and negotiated with the British government until 1947, when India was granted independence. Gandhi became the first icon of a people's struggle against oppression. His simple lifestyle and his belief in religious tolerance have made him a symbol of decency and peace ever since.

Albert Einstein
(1879–1955) German/American
Einstein was one of the greatest of all physicists and his name has become a symbol of genius. When his most famous work, *The General Theory of Relativity*, was proven in 1919, Einstein became the most celebrated scientist in the world, and he won the Nobel Prize for Physics in 1921. Einstein was a firm believer in pacifism, but his scientific theories helped his adopted country, the USA, to develop the atomic bomb. A week before he died Einstein wrote to Bertrand Russell, a British philosopher and leading anti-nuclear campaigner, asking to put his name to a manifesto urging all countries to give up their nuclear weapons.

Adolf Hitler

(1889–1945) Austrian

Adolf Hitler was Germany's leader from 1933 to 1945, during which time he led the world into the most devastating war in history. Hitler's hatred of Jewish people and his desire for a blue-eyed, blond-haired master race led to the murder of six million people during World War II; most died in concentration camps in Eastern Europe.

Nelson Mandela

(1918–) South African

Nelson Mandela dedicated his life to the fight against apartheid – a policy which kept black and white South Africans apart and denied black citizens the vote. He was imprisoned in 1964 for his aggressive opposition to South Africa's racist government and was held for 26 years. In 1990, after his release, Mandela was elected president of the African National Congress. In 1993 he won the Nobel Peace Prize for his work to end apartheid.

See also

History timeline: page 104

Mao Zedong/ Mao Tse-tung/ Chairman Mao

(1893–1976) Chinese

Mao Zedong was one of the founders of the Chinese Communist Party and the first chairman of the People's Republic of China in 1949. He had an enormous influence on his country and was greatly admired for founding the Chinese republic and for changes in the early years of his rule. During his rule, Mao's image was displayed everywhere – in every school, home, factory and workplace.

James Watson (1928–) American and Francis Crick

(1916–2004) English

American biologist James Watson and English scientist Francis Crick discovered the molecular structure of DNA, using theories already written by Maurice Wilkins. Their theory helps to explain how DNA carries hereditary information and their discoveries have revolutionized our understanding of genetics and the study of disease.

Martin Luther King, Jr

(1929–68) American

Martin Luther King was a Baptist minister who campaigned against the segregation of blacks in the southern states of the USA. He was influenced by Gandhi and believed in peaceful protest. He won the Nobel Peace Prize in 1964. King was assassinated in 1968, but will always be remembered for his dignified, passive resistance to an unjust society.

Bill Gates

(1955–) American

Bill Gates created his first computer program while still at high school, co-founded Microsoft in 1977, and by 1993 was the richest man on Earth. In 2000 Gates and his wife formed the Bill & Melinda Gates Foundation, which is the largest charity in the world. One of its aims is to rid the Third World of polio and other deadly diseases.

Vintage Chinese Chairman Mao lapel badges

Women adventurers

These are just some of the intrepid women who went where no other woman – in some cases, no man – had gone before.

● French novelist Jules Verne's novel *Around the World in 80 Days* inspired American journalist Nellie Bly (real name Elizabeth Cochrane, 1864–1922) to beat this time. She set out in 1889, and returned to New York on 25 January 1890 – a record round-the-world trip of 72 days, 6 hours, 11 minutes and 14 seconds.

● Amelia Earhart (USA, 1898–1937) became the first woman to fly solo across the Atlantic in 1932.

● Cosmonaut Valentina Tereshkova (USSR, 1937–) was the first woman in space. She went into orbit on 16 June 1963.

● Sheila Scott (UK, 1927–88) was the first woman to fly round the world solo, in 1971. She was also the first woman to pilot a plane over the North Pole.

● Clare Francis (UK, 1946–) became the first woman to sail solo across the Atlantic in 1973.

● Ellen MacArthur (UK, 1978–) set a world record for the fastest single-handed, round-the-world voyage of 71 days 14 hours 18 minutes 33 seconds, on 7 February 2005.

Polar exploration firsts

The North and South Poles are two of the most difficult places on Earth to reach and so have been great challenges for explorers. These are some of the people who reached the poles by one means or another.

First to reach the North Pole
American adventurer Frederick Albert Cook (1865–1940) claimed he and two Eskimo companions reached the North Pole on 21 April 1908, but he probably faked his journey. Another American, Robert Edwin Peary (1856–1920), his companion Matthew Alexander Henson (1866–1955) and four Eskimos were first at the pole on 6 April 1909.

First to reach the South Pole
Norwegian explorer Roald Amundsen (1872–1928) and four companions reached the South Pole on 14 December 1911. They just beat British explorer Robert Falcon Scott and his team, who got there on 17 January 1912 but died on their return journey.

First pole-to-pole journey
British explorer Sir Ranulph Fiennes and his partner Charles Burton were the first people to walk from pole to pole. They crossed the South Pole on 15 December 1980 and reached the North Pole on 10 April 1982.

First solo overland journey to the North Pole
Japanese explorer Naomi Uemura reached the North Pole on 1 May 1978. He travelled by dog sled, but was then picked up by an aircraft. Frenchman Jean-Louis Etienne made the first solo journey without dogs. He reached the pole on 11 May 1986.

First woman to reach the South Pole solo
Norwegian Liv Arnesen trekked to the South Pole unaided in 50 days, arriving at the pole on 25 December 1994.

First swim at the North Pole
British swimmer Lewis Gordon Pugh swam 1 km in gaps between ice at the North Pole, 15 July 2007.

First manned descent to North Pole seabed
On 2 August 2007, two Russian *MIR* submarines placed a Russian flag on the seabed beneath the North Pole.

First cat to sail round the world

Trim the cat was born on board *HMS Reliance* in 1799 on the way to Australia. The following year he sailed to England and back to Australia.

First round the world

Since the first voyage round the world, almost 500 years ago, people have been looking for different ways of circumnavigating (travelling right round) the planet by land, sea or air.

First circumnavigation
Juan Sebastian de Elcano and his crew of 17 on *Vittoria* sailed from Spain in 1519 and returned 1,079 days later. The expedition was led by Ferdinand Magellan, but he was murdered in the Philippines on 27 April 1521.

First British circumnavigation
Sir Francis Drake and a crew of 50 left Plymouth, England in 1577 on the *Golden Hind* and returned on 26 September 1580.

First solo sailing
Canadian-born sailor Captain Joshua Slocum (1844–1910) sailed round the world alone in *Spray*, an oyster boat he built himself. He left the USA on 24 April 1895 and returned on 27 June 1898.

First walk
George Matthew Schilling (USA) claimed to have walked round the world between 1897 and 1904, but his journey has not been verified. David Kunst (USA) made the first confirmed journey from 20 June 1970 to 5 October 1974. He wore out 21 pairs of shoes during his 23,250 km (14,446 miles) walk.

Explorers and travellers

Today there are few places that have not been explored, but this was not always the case. America was unknown to Europeans until little over 500 years ago, and Australia was scarcely known by the rest of the world until the late 18th century. These are some of the people who made Europeans aware of the rest of the world.

Marco Polo (c. 1254–1324)
Italian traveller Marco Polo was one of the first Europeans to visit China and other Far Eastern territories. His reports were not believed, but he encouraged the idea of trading with the East.

John Cabot (1450–98)
Italian-born explorer John and his son Sebastian Cabot were employed by British merchants to seek a western route to Asia. During their travels they discovered parts of the northeast coast of America.

Christopher Columbus (1451–1506)
Italian explorer Christopher Columbus discovered North, Central and South America and the islands of the West Indies.

Vasco da Gama (c. 1460–1524)
Portuguese explorer Vasco da Gama travelled round the Cape of Good Hope and up the East coast of Africa. He discovered a trade route to India.

Ferdinand Magellan (1480–1521)
Magellan was a Portuguese explorer who led the first voyage round the world. He discovered the Strait of Magellan, near the tip of South America.

Abel Tasman (1603–59)
Abel Tasman, a Dutchman, explored Australia. In 1642 he discovered Van Diemans Land (later called Tasmania) and New Zealand.

Henry Hudson (c. 1550–1611)
Henry Hudson was an English navigator who searched for a Northwest Passage (a route to the East by travelling north of America). He discovered Hudson Bay.

James Cook (1728–79)
British Captain James Cook led several major expeditions. He explored the coasts of Australia, New Zealand and North America.

David Livingstone (1813–73)
Livingstone was a Scottish missionary and explorer of Africa. He discovered and named the Victoria Falls after Queen Victoria.

Sir Richard Burton (1821–90)
Burton was one of the first Europeans to travel to Arabia. With John Hanning Speke he discovered Lake Tanganyika in Africa.

John Hanning Speke (1827–64)
Speke discoverered Lake Tanganyika with Burton. He also discovered Lake Victoria, believed to be the source of the River Nile.

Sir Henry Morton Stanley (1841–1904)
Stanley was a British explorer of Africa and was involved in the search for Livingstone.

Top of the world

The first people to succeed in climbing Everest, the world's highest mountain, were Edmund Hillary from New Zealand and Tenzing Norgay from Nepal. They reached the summit on 29 May 1953.

Steve Fossett in *Virgin Atlantic Global Flyer*

First non-stop flight
USAF B-50A bomber *Lucky Lady II* piloted by Capt. James Gallagher flew from Fort Worth, Texas on 26 February 1949. The journey took 94 hours 1 minute and the plane was refuelled four times in mid-air.

First underwater
US Navy nuclear submarine *Triton* travelled round the world underwater between 16 February and 25 April 1960.

First non-stop solo voyage
British yachtsman Robin Knox-Johnston sailed from and returned to Falmouth, UK, in *Suhali* between 14 June 1968 and 22 April 1969.

First in a wheelchair
Rick Hansen (Canada) went round the world in a wheelchair between 21 March 1985 and 22 May 1987. He travelled through 34 countries.

First balloon flight
Brian Jones (UK) and Bertrand Piccard (Switzerland) made a round-the-world voyage in the *Breitling Orbiter 3*. They left on 1 March 1999 and their journey took three weeks.

First solo flight
On 7 March 2005 Steve Fossett (USA) achieved the first solo round-the-world flight without refuelling in *Virgin Atlantic Global Flyer*. He covered

36,818 km (22,878 miles) in a flight time of 67 hours, 2 minutes and 38 seconds. On 1 February 2006 he once again took off from the USA to fly around the world. This time he carried on to Bournemouth, UK, making this voyage the longest ever solo, non-stop, round-the-world flight. He travelled a distance of 36,912.68 km (22,936.5 miles) in 76 hours, 42 minutes and 55 seconds.

Apollo 8 astronauts James Lovell, William Anders and Frank Borman, 1968 "people of the year"

Late success

As people live longer, many continue to work well into what was once thought of as extreme old age. These are all people who made great achievements in their eighties and beyond.

Alice Porlock, British writer, published her first book at 102 years old.

Ichijirou Araya, Japanese climber, climbed Mount Fuji aged 100 years.

George Burns, US actor, appeared in *Radioland Murders* (1994) at 98.

Dimitrion Yornanidis, Greek athlete, ran a marathon at 98.

Pablo Casals, Spanish musician, conducted the Israel Festival Youth Orchestra when he was 96.

Michelangelo, Italian artist, produced his Rondandini *Pietà* sculpture at the age of 88.

Claude Monet, French painter, completed his water-lily paintings when he was 84 years old.

Against the odds

All these people triumphed over disability or illness to achieve fame.

Lance Armstrong (1971–) US cyclist, contracted cancer that affected his brain and lungs. He recovered and went on to win the gruelling Tour de France cycle race a record seven times in a row, 1999–2005.

Douglas Bader (1910–82) became a British war hero and flying ace, despite losing both his legs in a plane crash.

Lord Horatio Nelson

(1758–1805) was a British admiral. He lost an arm and an eye in battle, but won many naval victories, including the Battle of Trafalgar in 1805.

Stephen Hawking

(1942–) a British physicist and celebrated author of *A Brief History of Time*, suffers from motor neurone disease. He is confined to a wheelchair and speaks with the aid of a voice synthesizer.

In the news

Every year the editors of *Time* magazine nominate a person of the year – the individual or group who has most influenced world events during the year. The winner may not always have had a good influence – Adolf Hitler was nominated in 1938.

Nominees may be a man, a couple (Chinese leaders General and Madame Chiang Kai-shek in 1937), a woman (Queen Elizabeth II in 1952), a group of people (three astronauts in 1968), even a machine (a computer in 1982). Here are just some of the winners.

2007 Vladimir Putin (Russian president)
2006 You
2005 Bill and Melinda Gates/Bono
2003 The American Soldier
2000/04 George W. Bush (US president)
1999 Jeff Bezos (founder of Amazon.com)
1994 Pope John Paul II
1992/98 Bill Clinton (US president)
1987/89 Mikhail Gorbachev (Soviet leader)
1966 Young people
1963 Martin Luther King, Jr (civil rights campaigner)
1961 John F. Kennedy (US president)
1949 Winston Churchill (British prime minister)
1935 Haile Selassie (Ethiopian ruler)
1930 Mohandas Gandhi (Indian leader)

Stephen Hawking

http://s9.com   search

William Gladstone, British politician, became prime minister for the fourth time when he was 82 years old.

Benjamin Franklin, American statesman, helped write the US Constitution when he was 81 years old.

George Cukor, US film director, directed *Rich and Famous* (1981) at 81 years old.

One and only

At the age of 82, Irish playwright George Bernard Shaw won an Oscar® for Best Screenplay for *Pygmalion* (1938). He had already won the Nobel Prize for Literature in 1925, so became the only person ever to win both a Nobel and an Oscar®.

Ludwig van Beethoven
(1770–1827) was one of the world's greatest composers. He continued to compose music even after he became totally deaf in 1817.

Sarah Bernhardt
(1844–1923) French actress, lost a leg in 1914 but continued acting.

Andrea Bocelli
(1958–) an Italian opera singer who was blinded at the age of 12. He went on to achieve international singing success.

Louis Braille
(1809–1852) was blind and invented the Braille system of printing with raised dots to enable blind people to read.

Terry Fox
(1958–81) Canadian athlete, lost a leg to cancer. He took up long-distance running, and through this he raised money for a cancer charity.

Frank Gardner
(1952–) British television reporter, was paralysed in 2004 from a gun attack while working in Saudi Arabia. He later resumed work with the BBC.

Evelyn Glennie
(1965–) Scottish percussionist, overcame profound deafness to become a world-class musician.

Mark Inglis
(1959–) In 2006, the New Zealander became the first double amputee to reach the top of Everest.

Helen Keller
(1880–1968) was a famed author and lecturer despite being blind and deaf.

Awards

Awards are presented in almost every area of achievement. The ones that receive the most attention in newspapers and on television are those given to famous film stars, writers, artists and singers. Among the best known are the following.

Academy Awards (Oscars®)
These are the most famous of all film awards. The Oscar® presentations are now watched on television by more than a billion people worldwide. The Academy Awards – also called the Oscars® after the statuette that winners receive – were first presented in 1929. Walt Disney has won the most, a total of 20.

BAFTA Awards
The British Academy of Film and Television Arts awards began in 1947. British actress Judi Dench has won nine awards for her television and film roles.

Booker Prize
This British book prize was set up in 1968 and is awarded each year for a novel published in the previous 12 months. It is now known as the Man Booker Prize.

BRIT Awards
The BRITs are popular music awards, which started in 1977. Robbie Williams has been the most successful act by far, with 15 wins (including four as a member of Take That).

Cannes Film Festival
This annual international film festival is held in Cannes in the South of France. Its most important award is the Palme d'Or (Golden Palm), which dates back to 1955.

Golden Globe Awards
These US film awards began in 1943. Julia Roberts has been nominated six times and won three awards, and Tom Hanks has won four of the six awards for which he was nominated.

Grammy Awards
The US music awards have been presented since 1959. The classical awards have been dominated by conductor Sir Georg Solti, who won 38 Grammys. U2 has won more awards than any other band, a total of 22, while Amy Winehouse won in five categories in 2008.

MTV Video Music Awards
The music television channel MTV established its awards in 1984. Madonna is the most successful MTV artist, with 70 nominations and 21 awards.

Nobel Prize
These international awards are named after Alfred Nobel, the inventor of dynamite, and were first presented in 1901. There are now six categories – Physics, Chemistry, Medicine, Literature, Peace and Economics. Famous winners include Winston Churchill (Literature, 1953) and Mother Theresa (Peace, 1979).

Pulitzer Prizes
These US awards are given for achievements in journalism, writing (fiction, non fiction and poetry) and music. They are named after publisher Joseph Pulitzer and began in 1917.

Turner Prize
This British art prize is named after landscape painter J.M.W. Turner and was established in 1984. The winning works are often controversial, and usually not conventional paintings. Damien Hirst is a notorious winner.

Golden Raspberry awards

The Golden Raspberries, founded in 1980, are joke awards presented to the worst films and actors! Madonna was a notable winner. She also received the Razzies award for worst actress of the 20th century. In 2008 Lindsay Lohan won the worst actress award for both her roles in worst film award-winner *I Know Who Killed Me*.

"Oscar®"

Where are the children?

In countries such as India, where people have large families and relatively short lives, there are more children than older people. In the USA and UK there are more middle-aged and older people than children. Most people have smaller families so there are fewer young people. In the UK there are 10,219,887 children.

No. of children aged 0–14 yrs*

India	362,874,979
China	265,167,835
Indonesia	67,499,548
USA	61,482,447
Pakistan	60,993,354
Nigeria	59,666,293
Bangladesh	52,594,517
Brazil	47,463,314
Ethiopia	34,269,058

* Estimated for 2009

Schoolchildren in India taking part in a physical education class

Early success

Wolfgang Amadeus Mozart
(Austria, 1756–91)
began composing music at the age of five, and a year later began a concert tour across Europe.
William James Sidis (USA, 1898–1944) went to Harvard University to study mathematics at the age of 11.
Balamurali Ambati (USA, 1977–) graduated from university at 13 and from medical school at the age of 17, becoming the world's youngest qualified doctor.

Young populations

Countries with a lot of people under 15 usually have high birth rates and high death rates. In countries where families have many children who are too young to work and adults die relatively young, there are not enough people of working age to earn money to feed and take care of the families. As a result, these countries tend to be among the world's poorest.

Population under 15 years old*

1 Uganda 50.0 per cent
2 Mali 48.3 per cent
3 Democratic Republic of Congo 47.3 per cent
4 Niger 46.9 per cent
5 São Tomé and Príncipe 46.8 per cent
6 Chad 46.7 per cent
7 Republic of Congo 46.0 per cent
World average 26.9 per cent

The USA, UK and Canada have a lower than average proportion of children.
USA 20.1 per cent
UK 16.7 per cent
Canada 16.9 per cent

* Estimated for 2009

Harry Potter fame

Daniel Jacob Radcliffe (born 23 July 1989) was 11 years old when he won the role of Harry Potter in the film *Harry Potter and the Philosopher's Stone* (2001).

He was reported to have earned £7.1 million ($14 million) for his appearance in *Harry Potter and Order of the Phoenix* (2007). With the 2008 release of *Harry Potter and the Half-Blood Prince*, he will have earned over £20 million ($39 million) from the Harry Potter films alone.

Hollywood star Angelina Jolie visiting a refugee camp in her role as Goodwill Ambassador for the United Nations High Commissioner for Refugees

The UN Convention on the Rights of the Child

The United Nations issued its Declaration on the Rights of the Child in 1959 to try to relieve the suffering of children in poor and war-torn countries. It came into force as a convention in 1990. 193 countries are parties to the Convention: Somalia and the USA are not.

All the signaturies agree to make sure that children under 18 have certain basic rights, such as housing and medical care. Recent optional additions include one that children will not have to serve in military action.

The Convention on the Rights of the Child states that all children have the right to:

● a name and nationality

● affection, love, understanding and material security

● adequate nutrition, housing and medical services

● special care if disabled – physically, mentally or socially

● be among the first to receive protection and relief in all circumstances

● be protected against all forms of neglect, cruelty and exploitation

● full opportunity for play and recreation and equal opportunity

to free and compulsory education, to enable the child to develop his/her individual abilities and to become a useful member of society

● develop his/her full potential in conditions of freedom and dignity

● be brought up in a spirit of understanding, tolerance, friendship among peoples, peace and universal brotherhood

● enjoy these rights regardless of race, colour, sex, religion, political or other opinion, national or social origin and property, birth or other status.

International youth organizations

Scouts and Cub Scouts

Sir Robert Baden-Powell (1857–1941), a former general in the British army, launched the scouting movement in 1907. Today there are scouts in almost every country in the world – a total of 28 million. More than six million are in the USA and half a million in the UK, but the leading scouting country is Indonesia, with almost nine million members. Scouting is forbidden in some countries, including Cuba and North Korea. The junior division for boys under 11 is called the Cub Scouts (formerly Wolf Cubs in the UK) and was founded in 1930.

Girl Guides/Girl Scouts and Brownies

The Girl Guide Movement was started in 1910 by Sir Robert Baden-Powell and his sister Agnes (1858–1945). Today the World Association of Girl Guides and Girl Scouts (WAGGGS) has 144 member organizations with a total membership of ten million. It is the largest international organization for girls and young women. The junior division, for girls under 11, is called the Brownies.

YMCA and YWCA

The YMCA (Young Men's Christian Association) was founded by George Williams in the UK in 1844 and in the USA in 1851. Its aim was to provide shelter and other support for young men who came into cities to find work. The YMCA now has branches in 122 countries. The YWCA (Young Women's Christian Association), was founded in the UK in 1855 and in the USA in 1858.

www.unicef.org/crc/crc.htm   search

Beliefs & Ideas

Religious movement

The key role played by Buddhist monks in mass protests against the military government of Myanmar (Burma) highlighted the ruling regime's violence to the rest of the world in 2007. The monks are highly revered by the country's predominantly Buddhist population and their involvement drew the attention of the world's press.

Gods and goddesses

In most of the world's major religions today only one god is worshipped. But in many ancient religions, followers worshipped a group of gods. Each god had special characteristics and responsibilities, and some could appear in a variety of forms.

The myths and legends of ancient cultures and the range of gods worshipped often changed over thousands of years as different gods and goddesses rose or fell in importance. Those listed on these pages are a selection of the most revered and long-standing gods of some of the world's ancient cultures.

Chinese gods

The Chinese worshipped a large range of gods for more than 4,000 years, up to the coming of Chinese communism in the 20th century. Some Chinese people continue to worship these gods – often in secret – today.

Dragon Kings Ao-shin (North), Ao-chin (South), Ao-kuang (East) and Ao-jun (West), the gods of rain, rivers and seas
Fu-xi god of arts and creativity
Guan-yin god and goddess of compassion
Guan-yu god of war
Meng-po goddess of the underworld
Nu-guawas serpent goddess of creation
Pan-gu giant creator god
Qi-yu god of the rain (half bull, half giant)
Three Pure Ones supreme trinity of Yuan-shi-tian-zong, Ling-bao-tian-song and Lao-jun
Xi-he goddess of light
Xi-wangmu goddess of immortality
Yi-di god of wine
Zao-jun god of the household

Ancient Egyptian gods

Egyptian religion dates back about 5,000 years and lasted until the coming of Christianity and Islam. Its huge range of gods and goddesses were believed to control almost every aspect of people's lives.

Amun-Ra king of the gods
Anubis jackal god of death and Egyptian mummies
Aten god of the sun-disc
Bast/Bastet cat goddess of fertility
Bes lion-like domestic god
Hathor cow-headed goddess of happiness
Horus falcon-headed sky god
Isis wife of Osiris, mother of Horus, goddess of motherhood and royalty
Month falcon-headed god of war

Nefertum god of the sacred blue lotus and the rising sun
Osiris god of the underworld and agriculture
Ptah creator god and patron of craftsmen
Ra Sun-god, ancient Egypt's most important god
Reshef god of war and thunder
Sekhmet/Sakhmet lion-headed goddess of war and destruction
Seth god of storms and violence
Thoth ibis-headed god of the Moon, arts and sciences

See also
World civilizations and empires: pages 106–107
Time: pages 14–16

Ancient Egyptian falcon-headed god Horus depicted on a mummy mask

Greek and Roman gods

The ancient Greeks had 12 major gods and goddesses. They believed the gods all lived on Mount Olympus and influenced the well-being of all humans. As the Greek civilization declined and the Roman empire grew, the Romans renamed the Greek gods and took them as their own.

Greek/Roman
Hera/Juno chief goddess – marriage
Aphrodite/Venus goddess of beauty
Artemis/Diana goddess of hunting
Athena/Minerva goddess of wisdom

Demeter/Ceres goddess of the harvest, nature
Hestia/Vesta goddess of the hearth
Zeus/Jupiter chief god – sky and air
Apollon/Apollo god of poetry, music, Sun

Ares/Mars god of war
Hephaistos/Vulcan god of blacksmiths
Hermes/Mercury messenger of the gods
Poseidon/Neptune god of the sea

Aztec gods

The Aztecs were based in central Mexico. They flourished from the 14th century until their conquest by Spanish invaders in 1522. They sacrificed humans to the gods, who were believed to control daily life and agriculture.

Chalchiuhtlicue goddess of lakes and streams, youth and beauty
Cinteotl god of maize
Coyolxauhqui goddess of the Moon
Ehecatl god of the wind and weather
Huehueteotl god of the hearth, the fire of life
Huitzilopochtli war god
Ilamatecuhtli goddess of the Earth, death and the Milky Way
Itztlacoliuhqui god of stone and the Morning Star
Mayahuel goddess of alcohol and the maguey plant (from which alcoholic drinks were made)
Mictlantecuhtli god of death
Quetzalcoatl creator god – and bringer of chocolate!
Tepeyollotl god of caves and earthquakes
Tezcatlipoca god of night and death
Tlahuizcalpantecuhtli god of dawn
Tonacatecuhtli god of food
Xipe-totec god of spring and agriculture, patron of goldsmiths
Xochipilli god of love, flowers, singing and dancing
Xochiquetzal goddess of love

Statue of the Aztec god Xochipilli, made between the 14th and 16th centuries

The 12 Norse gods

The Norse people lived in ancient and medieval Scandinavia (modern Norway, Sweden, Finland, Iceland and Denmark).

The 12 Norse, or Scandinavian, gods were together called the Aesir, and their homeland was Asgard. There was also a second group of gods called the Vanir, who fought the Aesir. Later some Vanir gods, including Frey and his sister Freya, became Aesir.

● Odin, or Woden, chief god in Norse mythology

● Thor, red-haired and bearded son of Odin and Jord, god of war (his name gave us Thursday – Thor's day)

● Tyr, Tiu or Tiw, another son of Odin, god of warfare and battle (his name is commemorated in Tuesday)

● Balder or Baldur, god of sunlight

● Brag or Bragi, god of poetry

● Vidar, god of silence, stealth and revenge

● Hoder the blind

● Hermód or Hermoder the Brave, Odin's son and his messenger

● Hönir or Hoenir, a minor god

● Odnir, husband of Freya

● Loki, god of strife or mischief, capable of changing shape and performing tricks

● Vali, Odin's youngest son by Rind, a giantess. He slew Hod, who had murdered his brother Balder

Inca gods

The Inca people lived in the part of South America that is now Peru from about 1200 to 1533. Inca gods were thought to influence natural events.

Apocatequil god of lightning
Apu Illapu god of thunder
Ilyap'a weather god
Inti Sun god
Kon god of rain and the southern wind
Mama Oello mother goddess, daughter of Inti and Mama Quilla

Mama Quilla Moon goddess, daughter of Viracocha and wife of Inti
Manco Capac creator god, Sun and fire
Pachacamac Earth god
Punchau Sun god
Vichaama god of death
Viracocha god of creation

Mayan gods

The Mayan civilization and neighbouring Olmec culture date back 3,000 years. Descendants of the Mayans still live in southern Mexico, Belize and Guatemala.

Bacabs gods of the four directions – Mulac (north), Cauac (south), Kan (east) and Ix (west)
Balu-chabtan god of war and sacrifice
Chak god of rain, fertility and agriculture
Hunahau god of death

Itzamna reptile creator god
Ix-chel Moon goddess
Kinichi-ahau Sun god
Kukulcan feathered serpent god
Xbalanque god of the jaguar
Yum-kaax corn god

The five pillars of Islam

The following are the five most important aspects of the Muslim faith.

1 ash-Shahada – profession of faith in Allah and his prophet Muhammad

2 salat – prayer five times a day, facing Makkah

3 zakat – giving alms to the poor and needy

4 sawm – fasting between dawn and dusk during Ramadan

5 hajj – pilgrimage to Makkah, at least once in one's lifetime

Jihad, meaning holy war, is sometimes added as an extra pillar.

Religious buildings

- Abbey – a building occupied by monks or nuns and run by an abbot or abbess
- Basilica – a type of early Christian church
- Cathedral – the main church in an area and the seat of the bishop
- Chapel – a place of worship within a larger building, or a nonconformist Christian religious building
- Church – a building used for public worship by Christians
- Convent or nunnery – the home of a community of nuns
- Dagoba – a Buddhist shrine
- Friary – home to friars, members of a religious order
- Meeting house – a place where certain religious groups, such as Quakers, gather
- Monastery – the home to a religious community of monks
- Mosque – a Muslim place of worship
- Pagoda – an Eastern temple
- Priory – a religious house run by a prior; it may be under the control of an abbey

Major religions

Christianity 2,159,141,594*
Islam 1,345,175,832*
Hinduism 859,893,462*
Buddhism 380,567,154*
Chinese folk-religions 380,486,297*
Sikkhism 22,199,953*
Judaism 14,678791*

* followers worldwide

The Golden Temple, Amritsar, India

Holy places

A holy place is somewhere that is especially revered by the followers of a religion. Examples include the birthplace of the founder of a religion, shrines and places of pilgrimage. There has been conflict in some of these holy places when members of other religions have claimed or attacked the sites.

Amritsar, India
This city is the Sikh religion's spiritual centre. The Golden Temple is the main shrine.

Athos, Greece
This is a holy mountain for the Greek Orthodox Church where there are many monasteries. Women are forbidden to go on to the mountain.

Benares, India
This Hindu holy city is dedicated to the god Shiva.

Bethlehem, Israel
The birthplace of Jesus

Canterbury, UK
The city was once England's most important pilgrimage centre.

Ganges, India
The Ganges river is sacred to Hindus, who bathe here and scatter the ashes of their dead in its waters.

Jerusalem, Israel
A holy city for Christians, Muslims and Jews. Sites include the Western Wall, Dome of the Rock and Church of the Holy Sepulchre.

Karbala, Iraq
This city is the centre of Shi'a Islam and contains the shrine of the prophet Muhammad's grandson al-Husain.

● Shrine – a place of worship connected with a sacred person or saint. It may contain sacred objects or relics
● Synagogue – a building for Jewish religious services
● Tabernacle – a house or tent used for worship, named after the tent used by the Israelites to cover the Ark of the Covenant
● Temple – a place of worship dedicated to a particular god or gods. Also sometimes used instead of synagogue

Gate of a Shinto shrine in Miyajima, Japan

Hindu gods and goddesses

About 80 per cent of the people of India are Hindus. Most believe that God takes many different forms, so the Hindu religion has a range of gods and goddesses. Brahma, Vishnu and Shiva are the most important.

Gods of the Vedas (sacred books)

Indra is the thunder god of battle.
Varuna is the guardian of order.
Agni is the god of fire.
Surya is the sun deity.
Other Hindu gods
Brahma is the creator.
Vishnu is the preserver, who has ten incarnations:
  Matsya, the fish
  Kurma, the tortoise
  Varah, the boar
  Nrisinha, half-man, half-lion
  Vamana, the dwarf
  Parasurama, Rama with the axe
  Ramachandra, Rama with bow and arrows
  Krishna, god of the Bhagavadgita
  Buddha, teacher
  Kalki, "the one to come".

Shiva is the god of destruction.
Ganesh is the elephant-headed god.
Hanuman is the monkey warrior god.
Hindu goddesses
Durga or Amba is the warrior god.
Parvati is the wife of Shiva.
Kali is the goddess of destruction.
Lakshmi is the wife of Vishnu, goddess of beauty, wealth and fortune.
Saraswati is the goddess of learning, arts and music.

Figure of the Hindu god Krishna

Lhasa, Tibet (China)
The centre of Tibetan Buddhism. The monastery here was once the home of the Dalai Lama.
Lourdes, France
In 1858 Bernadette Soubirous (later St Bernadette) saw visions of the Virgin Mary in a grotto at Lourdes. Since then Catholics have made pilgrimages there, seeking cures for their illnesses.

Makkah (Mecca), Saudi Arabia
Every year, millions of Muslims go on pilgrimage to this city. They also turn to face Makkah when they pray.
Medina, Saudi Arabia
This is the site of the tomb of the prophet Muhammad.
Olympus, Greece
The ancient Greeks believed the mountain to be the home of Zeus and other gods.

Salt Lake City, Utah, USA
The headquarters of the Church of Latter-Day Saints (Mormons)
Santiago de Compostela, Spain
In the 9th century a tomb believed to belong to the apostle James the Greater was discovered here. Christians make pilgrimages to a shrine made on the site.

Mount Shasta, California, USA
A dormant volcano and a sacred site for Native Americans
Vatican City
The city-state in Rome, Italy, is the centre of the Roman Catholic faith.

 www.adherents.com   search

The Koran

Allah is the Islamic name for God. Muslims believe that He revealed His wishes for the world to a man called Muhammad. These messages were later collected together as the Koran (also written Qur'an). Muslims believe that the words of the Koran are the exact words of Allah. It is said that it has not been altered since it first appeared in AD 632. The Koran is written in Arabic, the language which Muhammad spoke, and it contains the main teachings of Islam.

The Cairo Koran, made for the Sultan of Morocco in the 18th century

Boy reading from the Torah at a bar mitzvah ceremony

The Torah

The Torah is Judaism's most sacred text. It includes the first five books of the Bible, also known as the Pentateuch. These include the laws that God revealed to Moses on Mount Sinai. The Jewish scriptures also include the books of the prophets, historical writings and the Talmud. The Talmud contains instructions for following a Jewish way of life and understanding Jewish laws.

Sacred books

The Vedas

The four books of the Vedas contain the earliest Hindu beliefs and they have also influenced Buddhism, Sikhism and Jainism. The *Rig Veda* is the oldest of the Vedas. It was composed about 1500 BC, although it was not written down until around 300 BC. The Vedas include rituals and hymns that give us a glimpse of life in ancient India. Another important Hindu text is the *Bhagavad Gita*, or Song of the Lord. This is one section of a very long epic poem called the *Mahabharata*. The *Bhagavad Gita* is about 700 verses long and sets out Hindu philosophy, explaining the importance of selflessness, duty, devotion and meditation.

The Pali Canon

The Pali Canon is a collection of sacred texts followed by the Theravada school of Buddhism. The teachings of the Buddha were first passed on through the spoken word and were not written down until the 1st century BC. The Pali Canon is written in the Pali language, and is also known as the Tripitaka, meaning three baskets. The texts are divided into three sections which were originally written on palm leaf scrolls and kept in three different baskets. They include rules for Buddhist monks and nuns, tales of the Buddha's life and teachings, stories and philosophical arguments.

Guru Granth Sahib

Sikhs believe that the Guru Granth Sahib is the supreme spiritual authority and head of the Sikh religion, rather than any living person. The original version was compiled by Guru Arjan Dev, the fifth Sikh guru, in 1604. He collected the compositions of previous gurus over a number of years. The text includes almost 6,000 hymns and poems composed at different times and in different languages, which makes it very difficult to translate. It also includes Hindu and Muslim writings, reflecting the religious tolerance of the gurus.

The Bible

The Christian sacred book is called the Bible. It is made up of two parts – the Old Testament and the New Testament. The Old Testament describes the history of the Israelites and contains books of history, law, poetry and wisdom. It was written by different people, probably between 1100 and 200 BC. The New Testament describes the story of Jesus's life and his importance for Christians, and also contains writings by some important early Christians. It was probably written between AD 50 and 150. Passages from the Bible are read at Christian church services, and Christians also see the Bible as containing a code to live by and guidance in following their faith.

The original 12 disciples

1 Andrew: a fisherman and brother of Simon Peter; crucifed in Achaia, Greece; the patron saint of Scotland and Russia (30 November)

2 Bartholomew (24 August)

3 James the Great: son of Zebedee and brother of John; martyred by Herod Agrippa (25 July)

4 James the Less (3 May)

5 John: son of Zebedee and younger brother of James the Great; also known as John the Evangelist; said to have written the Gospel that bears his name (27 December)

6 Judas Iscariot: the disciple who betrayed Jesus in return for 30 pieces of sliver; he later hung himself

7 Jude: known as Judas, son of James; said to have been martyred in Persia with Simon (28 October)

8 Matthew: originally a tax collector before he became a disciple; author of the first Gospel (21 September)

9 Peter: a fisherman from Capernaeum; according to tradition he was crucified upside-down; usually depicted holding the keys to heaven; considered to have been the first pope (29 June)

10 Philip (3 May)

11 Simon: also called Peter; a Galilee fisherman (28 October)

12 Thomas: known as Didymus, "the twin"; the patron saint of Portugal (21 December)

See also

Bestsellers: page 230

The Last Supper, painted by Pomponio Amalteo in 1574

The Last Supper

The Last Supper is an event described in the New Testament, which took place the day before Jesus was crucified. Jesus's 12 followers, called disciples, were all there. Following his crucifixion, they elected Matthias and Paul of Tarsus to join them, making a total of 14. Together they are known as the apostles and are regarded as the original Christians who acted as missionaries, spreading Jesus's teachings. All except Judas Iscariot later became saints in the Catholic church and have feast days devoted to them, listed above (some dates differ in other church traditions). The historical accounts of their lives contain many conflicting legends and details of their martyrdoms.

The Ten Commandments

The commandments are the divine law handed down to Moses by God on Mount Sinai.

They are key to both Christian and Jewish religions. The commandments appear in the books of Exodus and Deuteronomy in the Old Testament of the Bible, but are also described by Jesus in Matthew's Gospel in the New Testament, where he shortens them to just two – Love God, Love your neighbour.

1 Thou shalt have no other gods before me
2 Thou shalt not make unto thee any graven image
3 Thou shalt not take the name of the Lord thy God in vain
4 Remember the sabbath day, to keep it holy
5 Honour thy father and thy mother
6 Thou shalt not kill
7 Thou shalt not commit adultery
8 Thou shalt not steal
9 Thou shalt not bear false witness against thy neighbour
10 Thou shalt not covet thy neighbour's house, thou shalt not covet thy neighbour's wife, nor his manservant, nor his maidservant, nor his ox, nor his ass, nor any thing that is thy neighbour's (Exodus xx.3)

Animals in the Bible

There are many animals mentioned in the Bible. Sheep and lambs are referred to most often, probably because they were important for their meat and wool.

The lion appears because it is a symbol of power, strength and wisdom.

Animal	OT*	NT*	Total
1 Sheep	155	45	200
2 Lamb	153	35	188
3 Lion	167	9	176
4 Ox	156	10	166
5 Ram	165	0	165
6 Horse	137	27	164

* Occurrences in verses in the King James Bible
OT: Old Testament, NT: New Testament

CHRISTIANITY

Longest-serving popes

Popes are usually chosen from among senior cardinals. They rarely live long enough to serve more than about 20 years. However, Pope Benedict IX is said to have been only 12 years old when he was elected in 1033!

Pius IX was the longest-serving pope. He was 85 years old when he died. Leo XIII was even older at 93. The shortest-serving pope was Urban VII, who died of malaria 12 days after his election in 1590.

Pius IX was in office for 31 years (16 June 1846 to 7 February 1878).
John Paul II was in office for 26 years (16 October 1978 to 2 April 2005).
Leo XIII was in office for 25 years (20 February 1878 to 20 July 1903).
Pius VI was in office for 24 years (15 February 1775 to 29 August 1799).
Adrian I was in office for 23 years (1 February 772 to 25 December 795).
Pius VII was in office for 23 years (14 March 1800 to 20 August 1823).
Alexander III was in office for 21 years (7 September 1159 to 30 August 1181).

The Holy Grail

The Holy Grail was the cup that Jesus used at the Last Supper. According to legend, it was taken to England by Joseph of Arimathea but was lost, and King Arthur and his Knights of the Round Table went on a quest to find it. The cup was said to have magical powers – but only for those with a pure heart. The legend featured in many 19th-century paintings, as well as modern films, including *Monty Python and the Holy Grail* (1975), *Indiana Jones and the Last Crusade* (1989) and *The Da Vinci Code* (2006), based on the novel by Dan Brown.

Knights of the Round Table, a painting in the church of Trehorenteuc, France

Largest Christian populations

1 **USA** 245,859,613
2 **Brazil** 170,597,790
3 **Russia** 113,863,473
4 **China** 109,576,362
5 **Mexico** 99,945,687
6 **Philippines** 75,520,618
7 **India** 65,962,801

Christianity timeline

300s

1000s

c. 6-4 BC Birth of Jesus Christ, Bethlehem
AD c. 33 Christ crucified
c. 60-100 Gospels written
c. 64 Persecution of Christians by Roman Emperor Nero
312 Emperor Constantine converts to Christianity, leading to it becoming sole religion in the Roman Empire

324 Building of St Peter's Basilica, Vatican, Rome, begun on site of Circus of Nero
c. 380 Final agreement on which books should be in the Christian Bible
635 Jerusalem and most of Middle East conquered by Muslims
999 Most of Europe converted to Christianity

1054 Christian church splits into Western (Catholic) and Eastern (Orthodox)
1095–1272 Crusades (series of wars by Christians to take holy sites in Middle East away from Muslim control)
1187 Jerusalem captured by Saladin
1209 Franciscan order of monks started

1382 John Wycliffe translates Bible into English
1456 First printed Bible (Johannes Gutenberg, Germany)
1479 Spanish Inquisition begins to persecute heretics
1517 Martin Luther begins Protestant Reformation, Germany

Patron saints

A patron saint is a saint chosen to be the protector of a particular person or group of people, or associated with a particular problem or situation.

Many more saints are called upon for help with problems than are linked with pleasant events. For example, at least 26 saints are connected with difficult marriages, but only one (Saint Valentine) with happy marriages.

Patron saints for special problems

Appendicitis Erasmus
Arthritis/rheumatism James the Greater
Broken bones Drogo+
Cold weather Sebaldus
Coughs Blaise+
Dog bites Vitus

Earache Cornelius+
Famine Walburga
Floods Christopher+
Headaches Acacius+
Insect bites Felix+
Knee problems Roch+
Lost articles Anne+
Natural disasters Agatha

Poisoning Benedict+
Shipwreck Anthony of Padua
Snake bites Hilary of Poitiers+
Storms Scholastica+
Toothache Apollonia+
+ More than one saint

Patron saints of professions and groups

Accountants Matthew the Apostle
Actors Genesius of Rome+
Air travellers Joseph of Cupertino
Ambulance drivers Michael the Archangel
Architects Barbara+
Artists Luke the Apostle+
Astronauts Joseph of Cupertino
Athletes Sebastian
Authors Francis de Sales
Bakers Elizabeth of Hungary+
Beekeepers Ambrose of Milan+
Booksellers John of God+
Boys John Bosco+
Bricklayers Stephen of Hungary
Broadcasters Gabriel the Archangel
Cab drivers Christopher+
Carpenters Joseph+
Children Nicholas of Myra+
Comedians Vitus+
Cooks Martha+
Dentists Apollonia
Doctors Cosmas+
Farmers Isidore the Farmer+
Fathers Joseph

Firefighters Florian+
Fishermen Andrew the Apostle+
Gardeners Adelard
Girls Agnes of Rome+
Hairdressers Cosmas+
Librarians Jerome+
Mathematicians Barbara
Mothers Monica+
Motorcyclists Our Lady of Grace
Musicians Cecilia+
Nurses Agatha+
Plumbers Vincent Ferrer
Poets David+
Police officers Michael the Archangel+
Postal workers Gabriel the Archangel
Printers Augustine of Hippo+
Prisoners Dismas
Sailors Francis of Paola+
Scientists Albertus Magnus+
Sculptors Claude de la Columbiere+
Soldiers George+
Teachers Catherine of Alexandria+
+ More than one saint

Stained glass window of Christ with Matthew, Mark, Luke and John

One and only

According to legend, the only female saint to have grown a beard is Wilgefortis. Wilgefortis was the daughter of a king of Spain. She converted to Christianity, vowing to serve God and to remain unmarried. So when her father arranged for her to marry the king of Sicily, she prayed for a way to escape. She promptly grew a huge beard, which made her so unattractive that the wedding was called off. In a rage, her father crucified her. She became a popular saint in the Middle Ages. In Britain, she was known as Uncumber and women with troublesome husbands often prayed to her!

1800s 1900s

1534 Henry VIII breaks with Rome; leads to the founding of the Church of England
1610–1795 Baptist, Congregationalist, Presbyterian, Quaker (Society of Friends) and Methodist Churches founded
1611 King James Bible published

1800–1900 The Age of the Mission. Western Churches send missionaries to every country in the world. Number of Christians doubles by the end of the century
1830 Church of the Latter-Day Saints (Mormons) founded, Fayette, New York, USA
1872 Jehovah's Witnesses founded by Charles Taze Russell, USA

1878 Salvation Army founded by William Booth, UK
1910 International Missionary Conference marks first attempt in nearly 1,000 years to reunite churches
1948 World Council of Churches founded
1962–65 Second Vatican Council radically reforms the Catholic Church worldwide

1992 Church of England votes to allow women priests
2007 Boris Yeltsin's Russian Orthodox funeral is the first of a head of state in Russia since 1894

See also
History timeline: page 104

Buddhist festivals

There are a number of Buddhist traditions, and Buddhists in different countries have their own festivals on different dates. These are the most important Buddhist festivals.

● Wesak, held on the full moon in May, is the most important Buddhist festival and celebrates the birth of Buddha.

● Dharma Day celebrates Buddha's teaching and is held on the full moon of July. On Dharma Day there are readings from Buddhist scriptures, and people spend time reflecting on what they mean.

● Sangha Day is held on the full moon in November and celebrates the spiritual Buddhist community. Buddhists traditionally give presents on this day.

● Parinirvana Day, also known as Nirvana Day, marks the death of Buddha. Celebrations vary from place to place, but generally Buddhists go to temples or monasteries on this day, or meditate.

Losar

Losar is a Tibetan Buddhist festival. It is held in February and marks the New Year. The festival lasts for three days, when people go to monasteries, visit friends and family and exchange gifts.

Tibetan monks blowing horns to celebrate the Buddhist festival of Losar

Christian festivals

Epiphany (also known as Twelfth Night)
6 January (18 January in Russia; 1 February in Ethiopia). The Epiphany (Epiphaneia: Greek for manifestation) celebrates three events that are all thought to have happened on this day: Jesus's appearance as a newborn to the Magi (three wise men); Jesus's baptism, when God acknowledged his son; Jesus's first public miracle, when he turned water to wine in Galilee.

Ash Wednesday
The first day of Lent (see below). Ash Wednesday is a day of repentance for Christians, when they make amends for the year's sins before the fasting of Lent. Anglican and Roman Catholic churches hold ceremonies at which churchgoers' foreheads are marked with crosses using ash.

Lent
The 44 days before Good Friday (including Sundays). Lent is a period of fasting when Christians identify with Jesus Christ's suffering. The day before the start of Lent is known as Shrove Tuesday or "Fat Tuesday" (Mardi Gras), when Christians traditionally eat up any leftover animal products (often in the form of pancakes), as these cannot be eaten during Lent.

Palm Sunday
The Sunday before Easter Sunday and the first day of Holy Week. Palm Sunday commemorates Jesus's arrival in Jerusalem, when the crowd threw palm leaves in front of his donkey. Later that week, many in the cheering crowd were calling for Christ's execution.

Maundy (or Holy) Thursday
The Thursday before Easter Sunday. Maundy Thursday commemorates the Last Supper, which established the ceremony of Holy Communion, when bread and wine became identified with Jesus's body and blood. It was also the day when Jesus washed the feet of his disciples. At Roman Catholic church services on Maundy Thursday the priest ceremonially washes 12 people's feet.

Good Friday
The Friday before Easter Sunday. Good Friday ("good" meant "holy" in Early Modern English) commemorates the day when Jesus Christ was crucified. The symbol of the cross is an important part of church services on Good Friday, and churchgoers read the psalms and the gospels to remember Christ's experience.

Easter Sunday
The Sunday that follows the first full moon after the 21 March (the spring equinox). Easter always falls between 22 March and 25 April in the Western calendar. Easter is up to two weeks later in Orthodox Churches. Easter Sunday is the most important day in the Christian calendar, as it celebrates Jesus's resurrection from the dead. Easter Sunday is a day of joy for Christians.

Pentecost/Whitsunday
Fifty days after Easter Sunday. Pentecost celebrates the day the Holy Spirit entered the Apostles, enabling them to speak many new languages and spread the word of God. This event is considered by most Christians to mark the birth of the Church.

Christmas
Christmas is the celebration of the birth of Jesus on 25 December (6 January in Russia and 17 January in Ethiopia). It comes in midwinter, a time of the year when many faiths hold festivities.

Jewish festivals

The main Jewish festivals celebrate the great events in the history of the people of Israel. The Jewish month in which they fall is given here, with an approximate equivalent in the Gregorian calendar.

Tishri (September/October)
Rosh Hashana: New Year
Yom Kippur: Day of Atonement
Sukkoth: Feast of Tabernacles
Shemini Atzeret: 8th Day of the Solemn Assembly
Simhat Torah: Rejoicing of the Law
Kislev (November/December)
Hanukkah: Feast of Dedication
Adar (February/March)
Tanrit Esther: Fast of Esther
Purim: Feast of Lots

Nisan (March/April)
Pesach (Passover)
Holocaust Remembrance Day
Iyar (April/May)
Lag B'Omer: Counting Day of Barley Sheaves
Sivan (May/June)
Shavuoth: Feast of Weeks
Tammuz (June/July)
Shiva Asar be-Tammuz: Fast of 17th Tammuz
Av (July/August)
Tisha be-Av: Fast of 9th Av

Muslims at the Grand Mosque in Makkah before pilgrimage (Hajj) month

Sky lanterns lit up in India for the Divali festival

Islamic festivals

Most Islamic festivals (see below) commemorate events in the life of the Prophet Muhammad. New Year's Day, for example, marks the day on which he set out from Makkah to Medina in the year 622. The month of the Islamic calendar in which the festival falls is given.

Every month starts approximately on the day of a new moon, or when a crescent is first seen after a new moon, so the calendar shifts and these festivals fall at different times every year according to the Gregorian calendar.

Islamic festival dates

New Year's Day 1 Muharram
Birthday of Muhammad, AD 572 12 Rabi I
Night of Ascent (of Muhammad to Heaven) 27 Rajab
Month of fasting during daylight hours 1 Ramadan
Night of Power (sending down the Koran to Muhammad) 27 Ramadan
Feast of Breaking of the Fast (Eid Ul Fitr) 1 Shawwal (end of Ramadan)
Pilgrimage (Hajj) **month** 8–13 Dhu-al-Hijja ceremonies at Makkah
Feast of the Sacrifice 10 Dhu-al-Hijja

Hindu festivals

These are the main Hindu festivals, held in honour of gods as well as to celebrate important events in mythology and in the heavens. The Hindu month in which they fall is given, with an approximate equivalent in the Gregorian calendar.

Chaitra (March/April)
Ramanavami: Birthday of Lord Rama
Asadha (June/July)
Rathayatra: Pilgrimage of the Chariot at Jaggannath
Sravana (July/August)
Jhulanayatra: Swinging the Lord Krishna
Rakshabandhana: Tying on Lucky Threads
Bhadrapada (August/September)
Janamashtami: Birthday of Lord Krishna
Asvina (September/October)
Durga-puja: Homage to Goddess Durga

Navaratri: Festival of Nine Nights
Lakshmi-puja: Homage to Goddess Lakshmi
Diwali, Dipavali: String of Lights
Magha (January/February)
Sarasvati-puja: Homage to Goddess Sarasvati
Maha-sivaratri: Great Night of Lord Shiva
Phalguna (February/March)
Holi: Festival of Fire
Dolayatra: Swing Festival

www.interfaithcalendar.org   search

The Labours of Hercules

The Greek hero Hercules killed his wife Megara and some of their children after being driven mad by his stepmother, the goddess Hera.

As a punishment he had to perform 12 dangerous tasks or labours. When he succeeded in all of them, he was granted immortality.

1 Slay the Nemean lion (its skin resisted weapons, so he strangled it)
2 Kill the Hydra (a many-headed monster) of Lerna
3 Catch the Arcadian stag
4 Destroy the giant Erymanthian boar
5 Clean the Augean stables
6 Destroy the cannibal birds of the Lake Stymphalis
7 Capture the fire-breathing Cretan bull
8 Catch the horses of the Thracian king Diomedes
9 Seize the girdle of Hippolyta, Queen of the Amazons
10 Capture the oxen of the monster Geryon
11 Obtain the golden apples of the Hesperides
12 Bring Cerberus from Hades (hell)

Unicorns

A unicorn has the body of a horse, a lion's tail, a goat's beard, an antelope's legs and a single, often twisted, horn growing from its forehead. The unicorn is a popular subject in medieval stories; it is ferocious but good, and can purify water – or neutralize poison – by dipping its horn into it. The way to catch a unicorn is to use a young girl as bait, as a unicorn will lie down peacefully next to a maiden.

Figurehead of *The Unicorn*, a former warship

Statue of Hercules fighting with the Cretan bull

Mythical creatures

Almost every culture on Earth has legends of imaginary beasts. Some are like humans with supernatural powers; some are part human, part animal; while others are unlike anything we know.

Giants

Giants or ogres are enormous human-shaped creatures. They are usually seen as fearsome but stupid monsters that feed on human flesh. Famous giants include Goliath in the Bible, and Cyclops, Atlas and the Titans in Greek mythology.

Leprechauns

Leprechauns are small Irish fairies who bring good luck. They are helpful creatures, usually shown wearing green clothes, with an apron, buckled shoes and a red cap. Their fun-loving nature means that leprechauns are fond of alcohol, music and sport, but they are also mischievous and love practical jokes. Other "little people", including elves, dwarfs, gnomes and pixies, appear in many European fairy stories.

Centaurs

A centaur is half-horse and half-man, with the head and arms of a man and the body of a horse. It is one of the best known of all Greek mythological creatures and is said to have come from Thessaly in northern Greece. The myth may have arisen because of the skilful horsemanship of the people there.

Fairies

Fairies also feature in many tales. They are usually sweet, kindly creatures. In the Middle Ages, however, people believed that fairies stole children and replaced them with fairy beings known as changelings.

Heroes of legend

King Arthur

Legend says that Arthur, king of the Britons, won the throne by pulling a sword – the famous Excalibur – from a stone. This was a feat that only the true king was able to achieve. Arthur ruled during a period of peace and prosperity in Britain. Some folk tales say that if Britain is in danger, Arthur will return with his knights to defend the nation.

Beowulf

Beowulf was a Scandinavian warrior and the hero of *Beowulf*, the oldest poem in the English language. Beowulf was loyal to his king and also extremely brave. He killed Grendel the ogre, Grendel's mother and finally a fearsome dragon, which cost him his own life.

Paul Bunyan

The lumberjack Paul Bunyan is a famous character in American folklore. It is said that he was so enormous, he created the Grand Canyon by dragging his pick behind him, and his giant footsteps formed the lakes of Minnesota. The legend came from stories told by the lumberjacks of the northern United States.

El Cid

El Cid really did exist and many legends have grown up around him. He was also known as El Cid Campeador (meaning my lord, the champion). His real name was Rodrigo Díaz de Vivar and he was a Spanish nobleman who was born in about 1040 and died in 1099. El Cid is a national hero in Spain because he is seen as a brave and accomplished warrior who fought to take control of

Mermaids

Mermaids are beautiful creatures with the head and body of a woman and the tail of a fish. The first mermaid legend is thought to have been the story of Atargatis, a Syrian moon goddess of about 1000 BC. Atargatis had a child with a human. She then killed her lover, abandoned the child and jumped into a lake, where she took the form of a mermaid.

Vampires

Vampires are the "undead" who drink the blood of the living to survive. Ideas about vampires include the belief that plunging a wooden stake through a vampire's heart can destroy it. Some people also think that you can protect yourself against vampires with garlic, holy water, crosses and bibles, and that a vampire cannot enter a home unless invited.

Werewolves

Werewolves, or lycanthropes, are mythical creatures in the folk tales of many cultures. They usually appear as men by day, but may turn into wolves on the night of a full moon. The werewolf is bloodthirsty and ruthless. It devours its prey and shows none of the remorse that it might have felt in human form.

Trolls

Trolls are grotesque, malicious, rather dim-witted creatures in Scandinavian folklore. They are said to steal sleeping children, sometimes replacing them with one of their own. Trolls have poor eyesight, and are active only at night because sunlight turns them to stone.

Dragon at the end of the Dragon Bridge in Ljubljana, Slovenia

See also
Monsters in the movies: page 272

Dragons
Dragons appear in the myths of many cultures, especially China, where the dragon was a symbol of the emperor. A typical dragon has a serpent-like body covered with scales, large wings, and can breathe fire. In legends, dragons often guard a cave of treasure.

Spain from the Muslims. Legend suggests that El Cid fought for both sides at different times.

St George
St George was a soldier for the Roman Empire who refused to take part in the Empire's persecution of Christians. He was executed for treachery and became a Christian martyr. Later, King Edward III made him the patron saint of England.

St George is the hero of a legend in which he slays a man-eating dragon that was guarding a city's water supply. The city's inhabitants were so grateful that they converted from paganism to George's Christianity.

Heracles/Hercules
According to Greek and Roman mythology, Hercules was born with superhuman strength. By the time he reached adulthood he had killed a lion. Hercules had a jealous stepmother, who drove him to madness. While in this state, Hercules killed his wife and children. In order to regain his honour, Hercules had to perform 12 difficult tasks (see p. 170).

Robin Hood
The Robin Hood of folklore was an English nobleman whose land was seized while King Richard the Lionheart was away fighting in the Crusades (1188–92). He became an outlaw in Sherwood Forest and led a band of Merry Men (and Maid Marian, his true love). They robbed the nobility who travelled through the forest and passed on the valuables they stole to the poor and needy. Robin Hood was a master of disguise and many stories describe how he dressed as somebody else in order to trick his enemies or rescue his friends.

Good and bad luck signs

Black cats
In the UK, people think black cats are lucky, particularly if they cross your path. The opposite is true in the USA and several European countries, where a black cat is seen as a bad omen. In the USA a white cat is very good luck, while in the UK it is a sign of bad luck.

Horseshoes
A horseshoe is a piece of metal fixed to a horse's foot. Some people think that if you find a horseshoe and the open space is facing you it will bring you luck. Traditionally, people also hang horseshoes above the doorway of their home to bring good luck. In many European countries, the horseshoe is hung downwards – that's believed to let the luck flow out into the house. In Britain and Ireland, the shoe must be hung with the opening at the top to keep the good fortune.

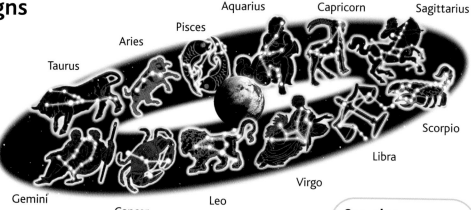

Aquarius
Capricorn
Sagittarius
Pisces
Aries
Taurus
Scorpio
Libra
Virgo
Gemini
Leo
Cancer

Lucky horseshoe

See also
Constellations: page 21

Clovers
Four-leaf clovers are very rare. Anyone who finds one is said to be able to recognize evil influences and avoid them.

Ladders
A ladder leaning against a wall forms a triangle. Some believe it is disrespectful, and unlucky, to walk underneath one because triangles symbolize the Holy Trinity. The bad luck is warded off by crossing the fingers or making a wish while under the ladder.

Magpies
Magpies are generally thought to be unlucky. This belief is said to come from the Bible, as the magpie was the only bird that refused to enter Noah's Ark. In China, however, the magpie is a good omen, and should never be killed.

Mirrors
Breaking a mirror is said to bring seven years' bad luck. This idea may come from the old belief that your reflection is an image of your soul, so anything that changes the reflection may bring evil. The length of the period of bad luck may come from the Roman belief that life renews itself every seven years.

Spilling salt
Salt was once valuable and spilling it was thought to cause bad luck, unless the person who spills it throws a pinch over their left shoulder. In his painting of the Last Supper, Leonardo da Vinci shows Jesus's betrayer Judas knocking over the salt cellar.

The signs of the zodiac

In Western astrology the zodiac has 12 parts. Each is named after a constellation and corresponds to a different time of year. Astrologists believe that the movements of the planets influence what happens on Earth, and that people born under the different signs have certain characteristics.

Aries, the ram
21 March–19 April
Creative, impatient, masculine, competitive, warrior-like, independent, outspoken

Taurus, the bull
20 April–20 May
Determined, resourceful, materialistic, touchy, ruthless, entrepreneurial

Gemini, the twins
21 May–21 June
Intellectual, shallow, inquisitive, selfish, talkative, witty, indecisive, irritable

Cancer, the crab
22 June–22 July
Emotional, sympathetic, moody, sensitive, home-loving, romantic, loyal, tactless

Leo, the lion
23 July–22 August
Generous, creative, broad-minded, patronising, bossy, extroverted, idealistic, arrogant

Virgo, the virgin
23 August–23 September
Diligent, intelligent, modest, conservative, overcritical, pedantic, affectionate, methodical

Libra, the scales
24 September–23 October
Charming, sociable, gullible, flirtatious, attractive, objective, artistic

Scorpio, the scorpion
24 October–22 November
Forceful, passionate, jealous, obsessive, secretive, intense, outspoken, extreme, rebellious

Sagittarius, the archer
23 November–21 December
Optimistic, honest, philosophical, careless, irresponsible, energetic, adventurous

Capricorn, the goat
22 December–20 January
Disciplined, economical, patient, reserved, pessimistic, serious, organized, rational

Aquarius, the water bearer
1 January–19 February
Inventive, friendly, independent, unpredictable, serious, intelligent, eccentric

Pisces, the fishes
20 February–20 March
Imaginative, compassionate, vague, gentle, sensitive, creative, spiritual, easygoing

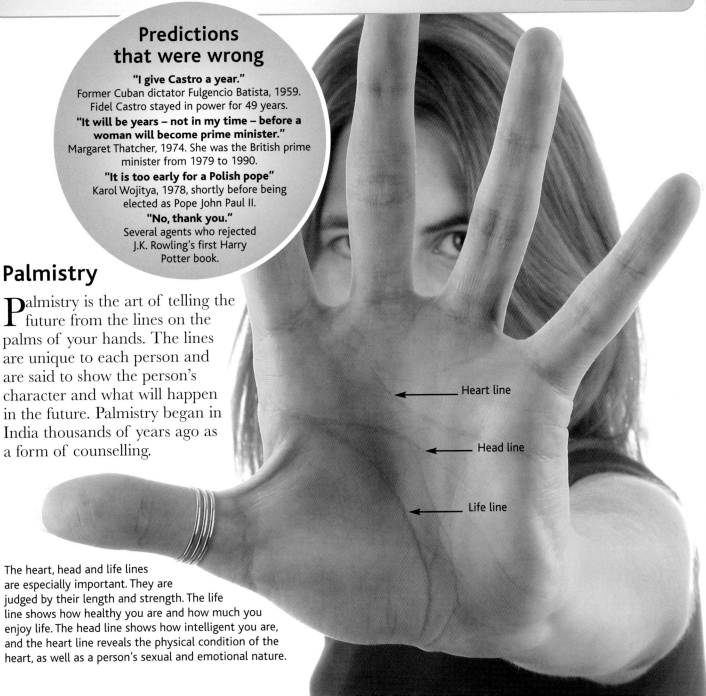

Number 13

The belief that the number 13 is unlucky is very ancient. The Romans believed the number 13 was a symbol of death and destruction. Norse legends claimed that the thirteenth guest at a banquet is the spirit of evil.

The Christian belief that the number brings bad luck is often said to come from the Last Supper, when Christ sat down with his 12 disciples – making 13 people. Some people think that the first person to leave a dinner table at which there are 13 diners will die before the end of the year.

Unlucky for some?

● The thirteenth *Apollo* space mission was known as *Apollo 13*. On 13 April 1970, there was an explosion on board and the spacecraft began to leak oxygen. This happened two days after it took off at 13:13 (1:13pm). The spacecraft only just made it back to Earth.

● On Friday, 13 September 1928, a hurricane killed 2,000 people in Puerto Rico, Florida and the Virgin Islands, and caused approximately $25 million in damage.

● There is no building in Paris that bears the number 13.

● Italy omits the number 13 from its national lottery.

● The 13th of the month costs the USA about $1 billion a year through cancellations on trains and planes, absenteeism from work, and reduced business activity.

Lucky for others?

● The number 13 was sacred for the Mayans and Aztecs of Central America, and it is traditionally a lucky number in China.

● Buddhists pay homage to 13 Buddhas, and the orthodox Jewish prayerbook holds 13 principles of faith.

See also

The Last Supper: page 165

Predictions that were wrong

"I give Castro a year."
Former Cuban dictator Fulgencio Batista, 1959. Fidel Castro stayed in power for 49 years.

"It will be years – not in my time – before a woman will become prime minister."
Margaret Thatcher, 1974. She was the British prime minister from 1979 to 1990.

"It is too early for a Polish pope"
Karol Wojitya, 1978, shortly before being elected as Pope John Paul II.

"No, thank you."
Several agents who rejected J.K. Rowling's first Harry Potter book.

Palmistry

Palmistry is the art of telling the future from the lines on the palms of your hands. The lines are unique to each person and are said to show the person's character and what will happen in the future. Palmistry began in India thousands of years ago as a form of counselling.

Heart line

Head line

Life line

The heart, head and life lines are especially important. They are judged by their length and strength. The life line shows how healthy you are and how much you enjoy life. The head line shows how intelligent you are, and the heart line reveals the physical condition of the heart, as well as a person's sexual and emotional nature.

THE UNEXPLAINED

Mysterious places

The Nazca Lines
The Nazca Lines are enormous drawings on the ground (called geoglyphs) that stretch across the Nazca Desert in southern Peru. They show more than 300 geometric patterns, spirals and animals. The lines are so vast (one extends 65 km [40 miles]) that they can only be seen properly from a height of about 300 m (1,000 ft). Most experts agree that they were made by the Nazca Indians who lived in the region between 300 BC and AD 800, but there are many questions yet to be answered about them. For example, why were the pictures made and how are they so precise if their makers had no means to view them from the sky?

Stonehenge
Stonehenge is a circle of 17 upright stones called sarsens which stand on Salisbury Plain in southwest England. The stones weigh up to 50 tonnes and have other stones, called lintels, laid across the top. There is also an inner circle of smaller bluestones weighing up to 4 tonnes each. Stonehenge is the only stone circle in the world with lintels across the top of the stones, and experts think it was completed in about 1500 BC.
They believe that the sarsen stones were transported from 32 km (20 miles) away and the bluestones came from an incredible 250 km (155 miles) away. At least 600 men would have been needed to move each sarsen stone on some of the steepest parts of the journey. Nobody knows exactly why Stonehenge was built, but it may have been a druids' temple or even a kind of astronomical calendar.

Teotihuacán
In AD 600 Teotihuacán in Mexico was the sixth largest city in the world and about 200,000 people lived there. Just 150 years later, Teotihuacán was almost deserted, and plants had begun to grow over the city's huge pyramids. Nobody knows why Teotihuacán was abandoned, but it may have been devastated by a huge fire in AD 650.

Easter Island
Easter Island (or Rapa Nui) lies in the South Pacific between Chile and Tahiti, and is one of the most isolated islands in the world. By the 16th century, Easter Island had nearly 10,000 inhabitants, who made huge statues known as *moai*. The 887 *moai* were carved from the island's volcanic rock and have long, angular faces. Some have eyes made from coral. The average *moai* was about 4 m (13 ft) tall and weighed over 14 tonnes, so they would have been extremely difficult for the islanders to transport. Archaeologists believe that the statues symbolize the spirits of Easter Island's most important inhabitants.

The Bermuda Triangle
The Bermuda Triangle is an area of the Atlantic Ocean off the coast of Florida. It is famous for being the supposed site of many unexplained disappearances. The points of the triangle are Miami, Bermuda and San Juan in Puerto Rico. In the 15th century, Christopher Columbus claimed to have seen a "great flame of fire" falling into the ocean in the area. The Bermuda Triangle first began to attract attention in 1945, when Flight 19, a training mission of five US bombers, vanished off the Florida coast. The plane that was sent to find them also disappeared, and around 100 boats and aircraft have been lost there. Explanations include magnetic fields, sea monsters and abduction by aliens, but most experts agree the disappearances are due to bad navigation and/or extreme weather conditions.

See also
Aztec empire: page 107

Teotihuacán

Four of the huge moai figures on Easter Island

Crop circles

Crop circles are complicated geometric patterns, usually in wheat fields. Some people believe that the patterns are left by the imprint of an extra-terrestrial craft, or that they are a message from extra-terrestrials themselves.

Another theory is that natural forces such as tornadoes, heat or strong winds create the patterns by flattening the crops, but the regular shapes of most crop circles makes this unlikely. The most likely explanation is that the circles are made by people as a hoax. They gradually build up a design by flattening the wheat, using very basic equipment such as rope and planks of wood.

Crop circles in Slovenia

Mysterious monsters

The Loch Ness Monster
The Loch Ness Monster, nicknamed Nessie, is said to live in Loch Ness in Scotland. The monster is generally thought to be a long-necked creature with flippers, like a prehistoric reptile. Many people have reported seeing Nessie, and in 2006 it was claimed that it might have been a circus elephant swimming in the Loch! However, there is no real evidence that the creature exists.

Yeti
The Yeti, also called the Abominable Snowman, is believed to live in the Himalayan mountains. People say this legendary creature measures up to 1.4 m (8 ft), is covered in long brown hair, and walks upright like a human being. Everest mountaineers, including Sir Edmund Hillary and Sherpa Tenzing Norgay, have reported seeing mysterious footprints in the snow.

Bigfoot
Another legendary creature is said to live in the northwest of North America. People who claim to have seen Bigfoot say it is a large hairy creature that walks upright like the Yeti. There is no firm evidence that Bigfoot exists, but there are some fuzzy photos and videos that are supposed to show this mystery monster.

On the Moon, or is this photo a fake?

Conspiracy theories

Many people believe that certain well-known historical events have been manipulated by governments and other secret organizations to conceal the truth. Some of the better-known beliefs are:

● A secret society called the Illuminati controls the world. This shadowy organization features in Dan Brown's novel *Angels and Demons*. Other powerful secret societies, including Opus Dei and the Priory of Sion, feature in his bestselling *The Da Vinci Code*.

● Sinister groups were responsible for plotting the deaths of US President Abraham Lincoln, civil rights leader Martin Luther King, musician John Lennon and Princess Diana. Some people claim that the Mafia were responsible for assassinating US President John F. Kennedy. Others believe it was the work of Russian spies.

● Inventions have been hushed up by big businesses and oil companies who fear loss of income if new technologies become available. These include light bulbs that last for ever and ways of running cars on water.

● Aliens from other planets have crashed on Earth at Roswell, New Mexico. Their bodies and spacecraft have been secretly examined in a place in Nevada, USA, known as Area 51, and the US government has acquired advanced weapon and space travel technology from them.

● Photographs of the *Apollo* Moon landings (20 July 1969) were faked by NASA in a TV studio. Conspiracy theorists have produced "evidence" such as the wrong sort of shadows and a lack of stars in the photographs, which were supposedly taken on the Moon's surface. They have even suggested that some astronauts were killed as part of the cover-up.

Elvis sightings

Singing legend Elvis Presley died on 16 August 1977, but many people all over the world have claimed to have seen him since – in supermarkets, at petrol stations, even working in burger bars. There is a society devoted to Elvis sightings and an "Elvis is Alive Museum" in Wright City, Missouri, USA. If Elvis were alive today, he would be over 73 years old.

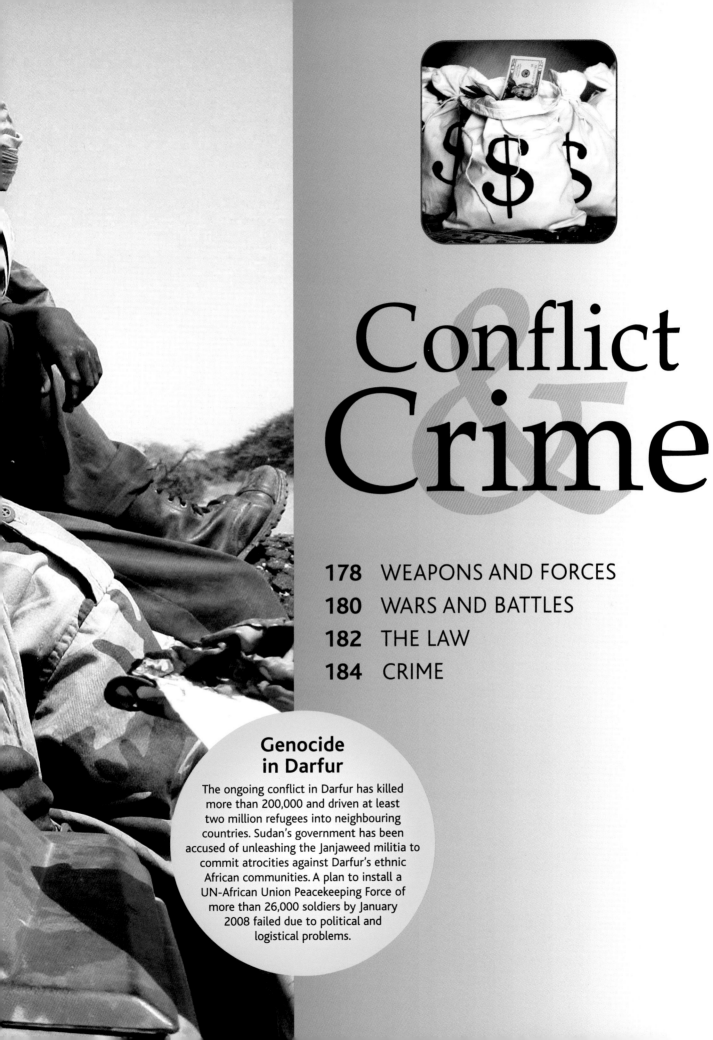

Conflict & Crime

Genocide in Darfur

The ongoing conflict in Darfur has killed more than 200,000 and driven at least two million refugees into neighbouring countries. Sudan's government has been accused of unleashing the Janjaweed militia to commit atrocities against Darfur's ethnic African communities. A plan to install a UN-African Union Peacekeeping Force of more than 26,000 soldiers by January 2008 failed due to political and logistical problems.

Weapons named after people

● Big Bertha
Big Bertha was a 144-tonne cannon used by the German army to shell Paris from a distance of 122 km (76 miles) during World War I. The name came from Bertha Krupp von Bohlen und Halbach (1886–1957), who inherited the German Krupp armaments business from her father.

● Browning pistol
Invented in America in 1896 by John Moses Browning (1855–1926), the Browning was an automatic pistol used by both civilians and military.

● Gatling gun
In 1862, Dr Richard Jordan Gatling (1818–1903) patented the hand-cranked machine gun with a fire rate of up to 350 rounds per minute. It appeared too late to be widely used in the American Civil War, and it was soon overtaken by more efficient weapons. The slang term "gat" for any gun derives from the name.

● Kalashnikov
This machine gun is named after its inventor, Russian Mikhail Kalashnikov (1919–). More than 70 million have been made.

● Lüger
Gunmaker Georg Lüger (1849–1923) pioneered the P-08 pistol that bears his name in 1898. It was adopted by the German army and was widely used during both World Wars.

● Mauser
The Mauser bolt-action rifle was developed in 1898 by German brothers Wilhelm (1834–82) and Peter Paul Mauser (1838–1914). They also invented an automatic pistol.

● Maxim gun
American (later British) inventor Sir Hiram Maxim (1840–1916), who was also an aviation pioneer, made this machine gun in 1884.

● Molotov cocktail
This was a crude but effective bomb made with a petrol-filled bottle and fuse. It was given its name by the Finns in about 1940 who used it during the war against Russia. They called it a cocktail for Molotov. Vyacheslav Mikhailovich Molotov (1890–1986) was the Soviet prime minister at the time.

● Shrapnel
This name was given to exploding shells invented by British officer Henry Shrapnel (1761–1842). Fragments of bombs are now also called shrapnel.

● Tommy gun
The Thompson sub-machine gun was invented by American army general John Taliaferro Thompson and US Navy commander John N. Blish. It became known as the Tommy gun and was popular with gangsters during the 1920s.

Nuclear explosion

Weird weapons

Combined gun and plough
This was patented by C.M. French and W.H. Fancher of Waterloo, New York in 1862. It was designed to be used by farmers so they could quickly turn their ploughs into powerful guns if they were attacked while ploughing.

Hard cheese
In 1865 during a war between Uruguay and Brazil, a Uruguayan ship ran out of cannon balls. Instead they fired stale Dutch cheeses, one of which dismasted an enemy vessel and killed two sailors.

Boomerang bullets
These bullets were invented in the USA in 1870, and were designed to fire in a curved line. The danger was that if they travelled in a complete circle, they could kill the person who fired them.

Countries with nuclear weapons

These numbers of nuclear warheads are as estimated by the Carnegie Endowment for International Peace. The total for Israel is not officially acknowledged.

Russia: 7,200–16,000
USA: 5,735–9,960
France: 350
UK: 200
India: 120–200
Israel: 75–170
China: 130
Pakistan: 30–92
North Korea: 1–10
World total: 27,600

Weapons milestones   1500s

500,000 BC Spears
250,000 BC Stone axes
25,000 BC Boomerang-like weapons (Poland) and knives
15,000 BC Spear-throwers
3000 BC Bows and arrows, shields and war chariots
2000 BC Armour and swords
865 BC Battering rams and other siege engines (Assyria)
3rd C BC Galleys, Crete
397 BC Catapults propelling darts
332 BC Catapults throwing stones
7th century Gunpowder (China)

8th century Viking longships
11th century Chain mail and crossbows
1150 Longbows
1221 Bombs (China)
1242 English monk Roger Bacon first describes gunpowder
1288 First guns (China)
1324 Cannon used at Battle of Metz
1346 Cannon (siege of Calais)
1370s Arbalests (crossbows)
1492 Leonardo da Vinci invents giant siege crossbows

1514 Man-of-war
1515 Wheel-lock muskets
1590 Bayonets made at Bayonne, France
1776 Submarine torpedoes
1784 Shrapnel shells
1835 Revolvers, Samuel Colt (US)
1838 Breech-loading rifles
1847 Guncotton, invented by Christian Friedrick Schönbein
1847 Nitroglycerine (explosive) invented by Ascanio Solaro
1850 Battleships

1860 Repeating rifle invented by Christopher Spencer (US)
1861 Metal gun cartridges and sea mines
1862 Gatling machine guns and Winchester repeating rifles
1866 Dynamite invented by Alfred Nobel (Sweden)
1872 Automatic pistols
1884 Maxim machine guns
1897 Dum-dum bullets (banned 1908)
1898 Lüger pistols
1901 Modern submarines

Largest armed forces

The number of personnel in the armed forces listed below are all active forces, but some countries have many reserves who can be called for service if needed. South Korea may have as many as 4.5 million reserve forces, Vietnam may have 5 million and China 800,000.

1 China 1,600,000 army, 255,000 navy and 250,000 airforce personnel. Total: 2,105,000

2 USA 593,327 army, 341,588 navy and 336,081 airforce personnel. Total: 1,498,157

3 India 1,100,000 army, 55,000 navy and 125,000 airforce personnel. Total: 1,288,000

4 North Korea 950,000 army, 46,000 navy and 110,000 airforce personnel. Total: 1,106,000

5 Russia 360,000 army, 142,000 navy and 195,000 airforce personnel. Total: 1,027,000

Some totals include other forces

Biological warfare

The aim of biological warfare is to infect enemies with deadly diseases. It is a modern form of warfare. However, in the Middle Ages the rotting carcasses of animals were catapulted into enemy castles to infect the inhabitants. In 1500 Leonardo da Vinci suggested using bombs containing saliva from mad dogs or pigs, or the venom of animals such as toads and spiders.

Gunner on a US army Black Hawk helicopter

2000s

1902 Armoured cars

1911 Aircraft carriers and bombers

1914 Zeppelin airships and large multi-engined aircraft able to carry heavy bombs used in aerial warfare

1914 Flechéttes first used – steel darts, designed to be dropped from aircraft on the enemy beneath

1915 Aircraft machine gun invented by German manufacturer Anthony Fokker

1915 Poisonous gases, such as mustard gas, chlorine, and tear gas, first used by German army at Ypres. Gas masks invented to combat them

1915 Rifles with periscopic sights (allowing users to remain hidden) invented by an Australian soldier

1917 Water-cooled Browning machine guns invented by John Browning. Tanks introduced as a way of getting through enemy barbed wire, and increasingly as a battlefield weapon

1936 Nerve gas (Tabun) and Spitfire fighter aircraft

1939 Military helicopters

1940 Bazookas and radar

1942 Napalm and V2 rockets

1942 Dam-buster bombs

1943 Jet bombers and fighters

1945 Atomic bomb

1952 Hydrogen bomb

1955 Nuclear submarines

1960 Harrier jump jets

1970 Exocet missiles

1982 Air-launched cruise missiles

1984 Stun guns

1988 Stealth bombers

1988 IMINT (Imagery Intelligence) satellites

2001 Heckler and Koch MP7 submachine guns

2003 Multiple JDAM (Joint Direct Attack Munition) air-launched smart bombs

2009 (Scheduled launch date) Boeing YAL–1 Airborne Laser (ABL) system capable of shooting down missiles

Great land battles

● **Marathon, Greece, September 490 BC**
The Athenians defeated an invading Persian army during the Battle of Marathon.

● **Hastings, England, 14 October 1066**
In the last successful invasion of England, the Norman and French army under William, Duke of Normandy, defeated the Saxons under King Harold. Harold was killed and William, known as William the Conqueror, was crowned King of England.

● **Agincourt, France, 25 October 1415**
Despite being heavily outnumbered (5,700 against 25,000), the English army under King Henry V defeated the French decisively. This gained them control of much of France.

● **Naseby, England, 14 June 1645**
In the English Civil War Oliver Cromwell's New Model Army defeated the Royalist army of King Charles I. The king was later taken prisoner and executed.

● **Blenheim, Bavaria, 13 August 1704**
This battle took place in the War of the Spanish Succession. English and Dutch troops crossed Germany and defeated the Franco-Bavarian army. The English and Dutch were led by John Churchill, later Duke of Marlborough.

● **Yorktown, America, 6–19 October 1781**
In the American War of Independence, the British were forced to surrender by the American army led by General George Washington, later the first president of the USA.

● **Waterloo, Belgium, 18 June 1815**
During the Napoleonic Wars, the Emperor Napoleon's army was defeated by the British and allies under the Duke of Wellington.

● **Gettysburg, USA, 1–3 July 1863**
During this important American Civil War battle, the Confederate (Southern) army under General Robert E. Lee was defeated by the Union army.

● **Somme, France, 1 July–18 November 1916**
In World War I, the British army under General Sir Douglas Haig tried to end the stalemate of trench warfare against the Germans. This led to the first of two battles of the Somme River. Neither side gained anything, and both suffered massive casualties.

● **El Alamein, Egypt, 1–27 July, 23 October–4 November 1942**
These two World War II battles were fought in the desert when the British 8th Army under Lieutenant-General Bernard Montgomery eventually crushed the German and Italian armies under Field Marshal Erwin Rommel.

● **Desert Shield/Storm/Sabre, Iraq/Kuwait, 16 January–27 February 1991**
These Gulf War campaigns were a response to Iraq's invasion of Kuwait. Coalition forces led by the USA drove the Iraqis out through a combination of air and land attack.

Stalingrad

During World War II, the German 6th Army was surrounded by the Soviet army in Stalingrad (now Volgograd), USSR, and suffered huge casualties in an extended siege from 19 August 1942 to 2 February 1943.

Worst battles

The Battle of Stalingrad was one of the longest and bloodiest battles of all time. It was fought between German and Soviet forces and continued from 19 August 1942 to 2 February 1943. The total number of casualties can only be estimated.

1 The battle of Stalingrad World War II, 1942–43; 2,000,000 casualties
2 The battle of the Somme River I World War I, 1916; 1,000,000 casualties
3 Po Valley World War II, 1945; 740,000 casualties
4 Moscow World War II, 1941–42; 700,000 casualties
5 Gallipoli World War I, 1915–16; 500,000 casualties
Figures are the estimated total of military and civilian dead, wounded and missing

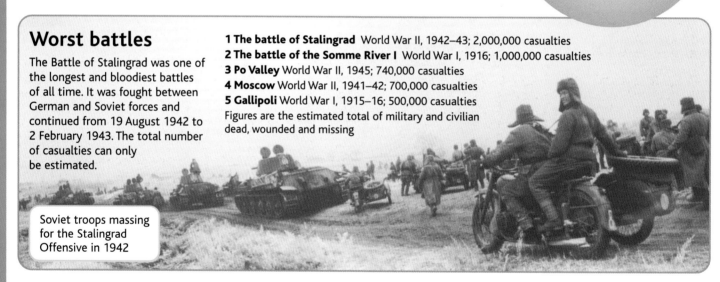

Soviet troops massing for the Stalingrad Offensive in 1942

Major wars   1600s

431–404 BC Peloponnesian War Sparta v Athens	**1618–48** Thirty Years War Catholic v Protestant forces in Europe	**1740–48** War of the Austrian Succession France, Spain, Bavaria, Prussia v Britain, Netherlands, Savoy	**1792–1815** Napoleonic Wars Britain, Austria, Russia, Sweden, Naples v France
264–146 BC Punic Wars Rome v Carthage	**1642–51** English Civil War Crown v Parliament	**1756–63** Seven Years War Austria, Russia, France, Sweden, Poland v Prussia, Britain, Portugal	**1812–15** War of 1812 USA v Britain
1095–1291 Crusades Christians v Muslims	**1701–14** War of the Spanish Succession France v Grand Alliance (of other European countries)	**1775–83** American War of Independence America v Britain	**1846–48** Mexico-American War Mexico v USA
1337–1543 Hundred Years War England v France			**1853–56** Crimean War Russia v Turkey, Britain, France, Sardinia
1455–85 Wars of the Roses York v Lancaster			

www.militaryhistoryonline.com   **search**

Trafalgar

On 21 October 1805, during the Napoleonic Wars, the British fleet under Lord Nelson won this sea battle against the French, although Nelson was killed.

The Battle of Trafalgar, painted by John Callow, 1875

Great sea battles

Salamis, 20 October 480 BC (Greco-Persian Wars)

The Greeks overcame a Persian fleet, saving Greece from conquest.

Aegosopotami, 405 BC (Peloponnesian War)

In this battle 180 Athenian triremes were faced with 170 Peloponnesian ships. The Athenians were conquered, and the Peloponnesian War ended.

Actium, 2 September 31 BC (Wars of the Second Triumvirate)

Mark Antony and the Egyptian fleet were defeated by the Romans during this battle.

Lepanto, 7 October 1571 (Cyprus War)

The Spanish force defeated the Turkish fleet, which lost 25,000 sailors in 250 galleys.

Spanish Armada, 29 July 1588 (Anglo-Spanish War)

In July 1588, 130 Spanish ships with 2,500 guns and 30,000 troops set out to attack England. The English fleet badly damaged the Spanish ships with their guns, and the rest of the fleet was destroyed by bad weather.

Jutland, 31 May 1916 (World War I)

During this engagement the Royal Navy took on the German fleet, which withdrew.

Guadalcanal, 9 August–30 November 1942 (World War II)

This series of six naval engagements between the USA and Japanese resulted in heavy losses on both sides.

Coral Sea, 8 May 1942 (World War II)

The US Navy took on the Japanese in the first major battle fought using aircraft from carriers.

Leyte Gulf, 22–27 October 1944 (World War II)

USA defeated Japan in this battle. The Japanese lost three battleships, four aircraft carriers, ten cruisers and nine destroyers.

Youngest medal winners

UK: Andrew Fitzgibbon, an Irish hospital apprentice, was awarded Britain's highest military honour, the Victoria Cross, when he was 15. He won the medal for bravery during action at Taku Forts, China, on 21 August 1860.

USA: William Johnston was a drummer who won the Congressional Medal of Honor, America's highest military award, when he was 12. The award was for bravery in action during the Seven Day Battle and Peninsular Campaign of 1862.

1900s

1861–65 American Civil War North v Confederate (Southern) states

1870–71 Franco-Prussian War France v Germany

1894–95 Chinese-Japanese War China v Japan

1898 Spanish-American War Spain v USA

1899–1902 Boer War Boers (South Africa) v Britain

1904–05 Russo-Japanese War Russia v Japan

1914–18 World War I Allies v Germany and others

1931–33 Chinese-Japanese War China v Japan

1936–39 Spanish Civil War Nationalists v Republicans

1937–45 Chinese-Japanese War China v Japan

1939–45 World War II Allies v Germany and others (Axis powers)

1950–53 Korean War North Korea (with Chinese aid) v South Korea (supported by USA)

1957–75 Vietnam War North Vietnam v South Vietnam (with US aid)

2000s

1982 Falklands War Argentina v Britain

1991 Gulf War Iraq v Allied forces

2001– "War on Terror" USA and allies v al-Qaeda, Taliban in Afghanistan

2003 Iraq War USA and allies v Iraq

Legal language

Accessory – someone who assists a criminal

Accomplice – a criminal's partner in crime

Acquit – to free or release from a charge, find not guilty

Affidavit – a written statement

Arson – deliberately setting a building on fire

Assault – is inflicting harm on another person

Bail – a sum of money paid to ensure a person appears in court. The money is forfeited if they fail to appear

Battery – unlawful assault

Blackmail – attempting to obtain money by threats

Burglary – breaking into a building to commit theft

Capital crime – a crime for which the penalty is death (abolished in the UK in 1965)

Civil law – disputes between individuals

Criminal law – deals with acts considered harmful to the community

Damages – money paid as compensation for injury or loss

Defamation – harming a person's reputation by libel or slander

Evidence – information presented to a court to prove or disprove a legal issue, such as a defendant's guilt or innocence

Fraud – deception to gain money, etc

Homicide – the unlawful killing of another person

Indictment – a written accusation

Kidnap – illegally carrying off a person, for example, to obtain ransom payment

Libel – defamation in writing, such as in a newspaper article

Manslaughter – taking another person's life without deliberate intent

Murder – the deliberate killing of another person

Oath – a promise to tell the truth in court, often sworn on a holy book such as the Bible

Perjury – a false statement made while under oath in a court

Probation – placing an offender under the supervision of a probation officer

Receiving – taking goods knowing that they are stolen

Robbery – theft with force or threat of violence

Slander – defamation of a person in spoken language

Sue – to bring legal proceedings against a person, organization, etc

Summons – an official order to attend court

Trespass – illegal entry of another person's property

Trial – the examination of a case in a court of law

Vandalism – deliberate damage to another's property

Verdict – the outcome of a trial, ie whether the accused is guilty or not guilty

Warrant – a legal document allowing for someone's arrest, the search of their property, etc

Law courts

This is the court system in England and Wales. The system differs in Scotland. Some countries follow the English system, but most have their own procedures. In many court rooms in the UK and elsewhere there is an image of justice as a woman, which dates from Roman times.

It traditionally shows her holding scales in one hand, to show that she is impartial, and a sword to represent the power of the law. Sometimes she is blindfolded to show that justice cannot be influenced.

County Court
Civil (non-criminal) cases are heard by a judge in a County Court.

Magistrates' Court
Criminal and civil cases are held before Justices of the Peace or District Judges, without a jury. There are limits on the sentences and fines they can impose. Youth Courts are part of Magistrates' Courts and hear cases involving young people between 10 and 17 years of age.

A statue of justice holding scales and sword on the roof of the Old Bailey, the Central Criminal Court in London

Crown Court
These hold trials by judge and jury for more serious criminal cases.

High Court
The High Court tries civil cases and hears appeals in criminal cases.

Court of Appeal
These hear appeals against civil and criminal cases following High Court and Crown Court convictions.

House of Lords
The House of Lords is the highest court in the land and hears appeals against judgements of the Court of Appeal.

Coroners' Courts
Coroners' courts investigate violent and unnatural deaths or sudden deaths in which the cause is unknown.

Scottish law

Scottish law differs from English law in a number of ways. The Procurator Fiscal presents the case for the prosecution in Sheriff Courts and in District Courts (where minor cases are tried). Advocates, instead of barristers, appear in Scottish courts. In Scottish law, if a person is charged with a criminal offence, they must be brought to trial within 110 days. If that does not happen, they are set free. In English courts juries can only find defendants guilty or not guilty, but in Scotland they may find a case "not proven".

The death penalty

The death penalty was once the most common punishment for murder and other serious crimes. It has been abolished in more than half the world's countries.

The electric chair at the State Penitentiary in Virginia, USA

● 133 countries have abolished the death penalty. Of these, 91 countries have abolished it for all crimes and 11 for ordinary crimes, but keep it for exceptional crimes, such as treason and war crimes.

● 62 other countries and territories officially retain the death penalty. Of these, 33 countries keep the death penalty in law, but have not carried out any executions for the past ten years or more.

● Uzbekistan was one of the most recent countries to abolish capital punishment, on 1 January 2008.

No executions took place in the USA from 1968 to 1976, when capital punishment was re-introduced. From 1977 to 2007, a total of 1,099 people were executed, including 11 women. Almost one third of them, a total of 405, were executed in the state of Texas.

Ways of execution

Methods used around the world include shooting (China, Vietnam), hanging (Iran, Singapore), beheading (Saudi Arabia), lethal injection and electric chair (USA).

Bear teeth

In Arkansas, USA, it is illegal to extract the teeth of a bear or otherwise surgically alter it.

Strange laws

● Members of parliament are not allowed to wear suits of armour in the House of Commons.

● A law passed by Oliver Cromwell banning the eating of mince pies on Christmas Day has not yet been repealed.

● Wyoming State Legislature banned the photographing of rabbits during January, February, March and April without an official permit.

● Anyone detonating a nuclear weapon within the city limits of Chico, California, USA, is liable to a $500 fine.

● Owners of monkeys in Indonesia must have an identity card for the animal, complete with a photo of the monkey.

● In France, no pig may be called Napoleon.

● No one may eat a rattlesnake in public on a Sunday in Kansas, USA.

● It is illegal to sell a teddy bear or play with a yo-yo on a Sunday in Memphis, Tennessee, USA.

● A law in Alderson, West Virginia, USA, says that "No lions shall be allowed to run wild on the streets".

● In Spades, Indiana, USA, you may not open a can with a revolver.

● In England it is illegal to impersonate a Chelsea Pensioner.

Who's who in court

Accused – a person charged with an offence.

Barrister – a lawyer qualified to appear in higher courts.

Defence – a barrister or solicitor who represents the defendant.

Defendant – a person accused of a crime.

Dock officer – an official who accompanies the defendant during a trial.

Judge – the public official in charge of a trial.

Jury – a group of 12 members of the public (jurors) chosen to hear the evidence and decide whether the defendant is guilty or not guilty.

Logger – a person who records the court proceedings using a stenograph or other equipment.

Magistrate/Justice of the Peace (JP) – a non-professional person qualified to try certain cases.

Plaintiff – a person bringing a civil action to court.

Prosecution – a barrister or solicitor who presents evidence against the defendant and has to prove his/her guilt beyond reasonable doubt (cases may be "not proven" in Scotland).

Solicitor – a lawyer who advises clients and prepares cases for barristers.

Usher – a court assistant who guides the jury and witnesses in and out of court and administers oaths.

Witness – a person who gives evidence in court – someone who saw the offence, a police officer, or a specialist such as a medical expert.

www.oldbaileyonline.org/schools   search

CRIME

Punishments

In most countries people who break the law are either fined or imprisoned, but through the ages there have been many other forms of punishment.

Flogging

Whipping or flogging was once common: mutinous sailors were whipped with a cat-o'-nine-tails or keelhauled (dragged beneath a ship on the end of a rope). Flogging was widely used in the USA. The last state to abolish it was Delaware – but not until 1972!

Stoning

Even today, some countries punish people by pelting them with stones, usually resulting in the victim's death.

Alcatraz, in the bay of San Francisco, is no longer used as a prison.

Mid 19th-century ball and chain used as restraints when transporting prisoners

Stocks and pillory

Stocks were wooden structures which held the seated victim by the ankles. People threw things at them and ridiculed them – they were literally made a laughing stock.
The pillory held victims in place by the neck and wrists. It was worse than the stocks as people could not use their hands to protect their faces from things thrown at them, and could be blinded or even killed. The last person to be pilloried in England was Peter James Bossy in London on 22 June 1830. A Chinese version, a sort of heavy wooden collar, was known as the Winged Tiger.

Ducking stool

This punishment was used in England and America. The victims were usually women. They were strapped into a special chair and plunged into a river or pond. The last person to be punished this way in England was Jenny Pipes in Leominster, Herefordshire, in 1809.

Chain gang

Chain gangs, in which prisoners were chained together as they did heavy labour, such as breaking rocks, were used across the USA until 1955. In recent years they have been reintroduced in some prisons.

Burning at the stake

Many famous people were burned at the stake, including the French patriot Joan of Arc in 1431 and Protestant martyrs in England. In Germany up to 100,000 people accused of witchcraft and other crimes were burned during the 16th, 17th and 18th centuries. In 1589 133 people were burned in a single day. Witches were rarely burned in England, and never in America, where hanging was the usual punishment.

Great robberies

Mona Lisa
Leonardo da Vinci's famous painting was stolen from the Louvre Museum, Paris, on 21 August 1911 by Vicenzo Peruggia. He kept it for two years, but when he tried to sell it he was caught and jailed.

Art theft
On 18 March 1990 two thieves disguised as policemen stole 12 works of art by Rembrandt, Degas, Vermeer and others from the Isabella Stewart Gardner Museum, Boston. The paintings were valued at $300 million and have never been recovered.

Dunbar Armored robbery
Believed to be the USA's biggest cash robbery, an estimated $8.9 million was stolen in an armed hold-up at the Dunbar Armored facility in Los Angeles, California, on the night of 13 September 1997. The gang leader was caught and jailed for 24 years, but most of the money has not been found.

Iraq Central Bank
In March 2003, just before the USA-led invasion of Iraq, President Saddam Hussein removed almost $1 billion in cash from the Iraq Central Bank. About $650 million was later discovered in his palace, but the rest has never been located.

Securitas depot robbery
On 22 February, 2006, Britain's biggest ever robbery took place at the Securitas depot, Tonbridge. The gang kidnapped the family of the depot manager and got away with £53,116,760 in cash. Following a series of police raids, some of the cash was recovered and several people were arrested.

See also
Crime and punishment
lasts: page 306

Science and crime detection

Modern detectives use a wide range of scientific techniques to help them identify and catch criminals.

Fingerprinting
Fingerprints have been used for more than 100 years to prove whether someone was at a crime scene or held a weapon. Experts dust areas for hidden prints, which can also be revealed under special lights or on contact with certain chemicals. Faint prints can be improved by laser image enhancement.

DNA testing
Now forensic scientists use DNA testing or genetic fingerprinting to prove or disprove a suspect's connection with a crime. Everyone's DNA is unique and even the smallest samples – a single hair or a trace of saliva – can provide evidence.

Psychological profiling
Experts prepare profiles that suggest certain features of the killer, based on the nature of their murders. The profile may give likely age, background and habits. This builds a portrait of the criminal and helps detectives track him or her down.

Ballistics
All guns have a unique "fingerprint" – the marks made on a bullet as it leaves the barrel. Ballistics specialists examine these with microscopes and compare bullets used in crimes with those fired from a suspect's gun to find out whether they are identical.

Identikit
The Identikit system, which was developed in the USA in the 1940s, used transparent layers to build up a picture of a suspect's face. Witnesses' descriptions of eye colour, hair styles, etc, were laid over a basic face shape. Modern developments include Photofit and computerised E-fit (Electronic Facial Identification Technique).

Surveillance
Crime-fighters increasingly use electronic methods to spy on suspects. They can plant bugs (hidden microphones and video cameras) and intercept telephone calls and computer data.

Prison fact file

Longest jail sentence
In Thailand on 27 July 1989, fraudster Chamoy Thipyaso and her seven accomplices were each sentenced to 141,078 years.

Longest in jail
Paul Geidel, a New York State prisoner, was sentenced for murder on 5 September 1911 at the age of 17. He came out on 7 May 1980 at the age of 85, having served 68 years 245 days.

Famous prisons

Newgate
This was once London's most notorious prison. Public hangings took place outside its gates, and it features in several of Charles Dickens's novels. Newgate was rebuilt several times, and finally demolished in 1902. The Central Criminal Court (Old Bailey) was built on the site of the prison.

Dartmoor
Dartmoor was first used for prisoners of war during the Napoleonic Wars and has served as a high-security, long-term prison ever since. The prison is miles from anywhere on a bleak Devon moor so if prisoners escape, they are usually recaptured quickly.

Guantanamo Bay
Since 2002, the detainment camp on the US Navy base at Guantanamo Bay, Cuba, has held hundreds of al-Qaeda and other prisoners captured in Afghanistan and elsewhere. The camp has been criticized by human rights groups and legal arguments about the status of the prisoners are ongoing.

Alcatraz
This island in San Francisco Bay, California, USA, is often known as The Rock, but was originally called Isla de los Alcatraces (Isle of the Pelicans). It was first used as a military prison, but then became a prison for the country's most dangerous criminals, among them Al Capone. Robert Stroud, a bird expert who became famous as the Birdman of Alcatraz, spent many years there.

Sing Sing
This New York prison was named after the Sin Sinck Native Americans who originally lived there. It was built from 1825 to 1828, and from 1891 onwards many murderers were electrocuted in the electric chair at Sing Sing. In 1969 the prison was renamed Ossining Correctional Facility.

Most wanted
Since 1950, the FBI (Federal Bureau of Investigation) in the USA, has issued a list of its "ten most wanted" criminals. Osama bin Laden, the international terrorist and al-Qaeda leader, is currently at the top of the list. There is a $50 million (£25.6 million) reward to anyone who provides information that leads to his capture.

WANTE[D]
DEAD or ALIV[E]

Osama bin Laden
For mass murder in New York City

Work & Home

Playtime

The famous plastic toy Lego – Danish for 'play well' – turned 50 in 2008. One of the first ever plastic toys to be created, Lego is still popular all over the world. The factory, in Denmark, makes 2 million pieces every hour.

The first vacuum cleaner

In 1901, Englishman Hubert Cecil Booth invented the first successful vacuum cleaner. The machine worked well and was popular with rich people. It was also used in places such as Westminster Abbey, Buckingham Palace and Windsor Castle. Booth's cleaner was so large that it had to be pulled along by a horse, and six people were needed to operate it. The machines were only hired out, never sold.

The upright vacuum cleaner was invented by an American named James Murray Spangler in 1907. Spangler realized that his asthma was made worse by dust, and wanted to find a more effective way of sweeping. He made the first upright vacuum cleaner with the help of a pillowcase tied to a broom handle and an electrical pump. Spangler sold the patent to his cousin William H. Hoover, who improved the invention and started a very successful business selling vacuum cleaners.

Fussy sleepers

British statesman Winston Churchill and American Benjamin Franklin always slept in rooms with two beds. They both liked to move into a fresh bed during the night. Author Charles Dickens always placed his bed north to south and carried a pocket compass so that he could adjust it.

Great Bed of Ware

Amazing beds

One of the largest beds in the world is the Great Bed of Ware. It is 3.26 m (10 ft 8.5 in) wide, 3.38 m (11 ft 1 in) long and was made in about 1580. The bed is mentioned by Shakespeare in *Twelfth Night*. It is now in the Victoria and Albert Museum in London.

In 1882 an Indian maharajah had a bed made of solid silver. At each corner there was a life-sized statue of a naked woman holding a fan. When the maharajah lay on the bed, his weight started a mechanism that made the women wave their fans.

Toilet paper

● Before the invention of toilet paper, people improvised with many different things. The rich used wool or lace, but the poor used anything they could find, including wood shavings, grass, stone, sand, leaves, corn cobs, moss, seashells, water or snow, as well as their hands. Later people began to use newspapers or telephone directories as toilet paper.

In the kitchen

The first washing machine
A washing machine was made in about 1677 by an Englishman named John Hoskin. Fellow Englishman William Bailey made a more efficient version in 1758. The first mass-produced washing machine was invented by American Alva J. Fisher in 1907, and was called the Thor.

The first microwave oven
The Raytheon Company in the USA began using microwave ovens in 1947 to cook food commercially. The idea came from one of their scientists, Percy Spencer. He had been standing near a microwave tube and noticed that a chocolate bar in his pocket had melted, although he had not felt any heat. The first home microwave appeared in 1952 and cost $1,295 (£465).

The first refrigerator
People used to pickle, smoke, dry and salt food so they could store it. During the 19th century some households began to use large boxes filled with blocks of ice, and the first electric fridge was made in 1913. It was called the Domelre (Domestic Electric Refrigerator) and was for home use, although it was very bulky. Refrigerators did not really become popular until after World War II, when the design was improved.

The first pop-up toaster
Charles Strite, a US mechanic, invented the pop-up toaster in 1919. There were toasting machines before then, but they had to be watched carefully all the time so the toast didn't burn. Strite worked out a way to put a timer and springs into the design. His first toasters were large machines, used by restaurants, but in 1926 he launched a smaller version called the Toastmaster.

1903 advertisement for refrigerators

● Chinese emperors used toilet paper in the 14th century, but the first commercial toilet paper was produced in 1857 by Joseph Gayetty, an American businessman. Gayetty's paper was sold as individual sheets with his name on them.

● Every person in the UK spends an average of £16.08 on toilet paper every year, compared with the average American's £12.60. The world average is £2.00 per person.

Home accidents

We think of our homes and gardens as safe places, but a surprising number of accidents are caused by everyday things. These UK figures record the number of people in a year who needed hospital treatment after accidents at home.

Sport/leisure items
Footballs and basketballs 13,695
Swings 6,528
Slides 5,801
Climbing frames 3,743
Bouncy castles 3,690
Rollerblades 2,874
Skateboards 2,643
Cricket bats 621
Cricket balls 461
Golf balls 355

Containers/packaging
Boxes 8,764
Glass bottles 8,249
Plastic bottles 2,448
Corned beef tins 2,147
Plastic bags 2,111
Aerosols 1,348
Tubes 745
Ring pulls 621
Lollipop sticks 160
Paper bags 8

Animals
Dogs 66,915
Cats 16,126
Bees and wasps 11,123
Rabbits, hamsters, etc 3,264
Wild birds 745
Pet birds 692
Snakes and other reptiles 426
Pet fish 106

Toilet fact file

● In medieval Europe people used chamber pots which they emptied out of the window. In castles there would be a garderobe – a small cupboard with a hole that let waste out into the moat.

● Throwing waste out of the windows into the street or rivers that provided drinking water, spread disease. The worst epidemic was the Black Death in the 14th century, which killed about a quarter of the people in Europe.

Accidents in a year in the UK involving clothing or personal effects
Trainers 60,830
Slippers 60,493
Jewellery 13,695
Socks, tights, etc 11,726
Wellington boots 4,364
Trousers 3,885
Shirts/T-shirts 1,472
Coats 1,401
Hairbrushes 1,224
Toothbrushes 763
False teeth 532

The right path
During the 16th and 17th centuries it was good manners for a gentleman to walk closest to the street when escorting a lady. This meant that he was more likely to be in the path of sewage as it was thrown into the street!

● In London a gigantic cesspit was built under 200,000 houses and it often overflowed into them. Cesspits in London were abolished in 1847 and every home had to have a lavatory. However, sewage was still diverted into the River Thames, which resulted in the "Great Stink" in the summer of 1858 – the worst smell in the city's history.

● Europe's major cities and the biggest cities in the USA started building sewers in the 19th century. Many of these early systems are still in use today. "Sewer tours" are popular in Paris, France, and in Brighton, UK. The systems are such amazing works of engineering that people travel to these cities just to visit them!

● Today, Japan makes the most advanced toilets. Known as "washlets", they have control panels, water jets, heated seats, driers and telephones. More improvements are being developed, including voice-activated toilets and some that can do medical tests.

www.geffrye-museum.org.uk/kidszone   search

Valuable toys

Some wealthy collectors prize rare toys, especially those that are in good condition – in their original box, and never played with. These are just some of the toys that may have cost very little when they were made, but now sell for high prices.

- GI Joe prototype was sold by Heritage Galleries & Auctioneers of Dallas, Texas for $200,000 (£126,580) in 2003.

- A Kämmer and Reinhardt doll was sold at Sotheby's, London, on 8 February 1994 for £188,500 ($277,981).

- Titania's Palace, a doll's house with 2,000 items of furniture, was sold at Christie's, London, in 1978 for £135,000 ($258,728).

- Dingley Hall, a doll's house dating from 1877, was sold at Christie's, London, in 2003 for £124,750 ($211,938).

- A 1906 train set made by German toymaker Märklin was sold at Christie's, London, in 2001 for £113,750 ($165,290).

- A black mohair Steiff teddy bear, made in about 1912, was sold at Christie's, London, in 2000 for £91,750 ($132,157). It was one of only 494 black Steiff bears made as a mark of respect after the sinking of the *Titanic*. They are known as "mourning teddies".

- A tinplate clockwork motorcycle with Mickey Mouse and Minnie from about 1930, was sold at Christie's, London, in 1997 for £51,000 ($83,650).

"Teddy Girl" teddy bear made in 1904

Birth of Barbie

The first Barbie doll appeared in February 1959. It was made by Ruth and Elliot Handler, co-founders of American toy manufacturers Mattel, and they named the doll after their daughter Barbara. The doll was dressed in a black and white striped swimsuit, with sunglasses, high heels and gold hoop earrings. In the first year a total of 351,000 Barbies were sold at $3 (£1) each. The doll went on to become one of the bestselling toys of all time.

The first Barbie dolls, in the Barbie Museum, Palo Alto, California

Top Teddy

"Teddy Girl" is a teddy bear made by the German manufacturer Steiff in 1904. It was sold at Christie's, London, on 5 December 1994 for a record £110,000 ($171,600). A Japanese collector named Yoshiro Sekiguchi bought the bear for his teddy bear museum near Tokyo.

Toy-buying countries

Forecast sales of traditional toys (eg construction toys, model vehicles, indoor games, dolls and teddy bears) and video games in 2008 are estimated to average £16.9 ($33) for every person on the planet. There are huge differences between countries: North Americans spend the most and people in African countries the least per child.

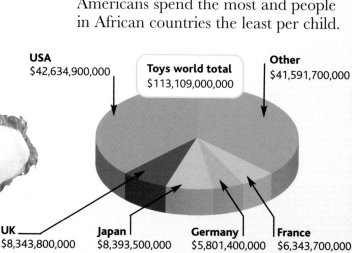

USA
$42,634,900,000

Toys world total
$113,109,000,000

Other
$41,591,700,000

UK
$8,343,800,000

Japan
$8,393,500,000

Germany
$5,801,400,000

France
$6,343,700,000

Computer games

The first computer games were played on televisions and appeared in the 1970s. They were basic arcade games like *PONG* (1972), an electronic table-tennis game, and *Pac-Man* (1980), in which a yellow blob is steered round a maze, gobbling up everything in its path.

As computer technology advanced, games and consoles improved, with better graphics, sound and choice of themes. Second generation 8-bit games had removable cartridges, while the fifth 32-bit and 64-bit generation games could be played in 3D. Sixth and seventh generation games are more realistic than ever before and can be played online with anyone around the world. These are popular consoles of different generations.

First generation Atari *PONG* (1975)

Second generation Atari 2600 (1977)

Third generation Nintendo Entertainment System (1983), Nintendo Game Boy (1989)

Fourth generation Sega Mega Drive (1988), Super Nintendo (1990)

Fifth generation
Nintendo 64 (1986),
Sony PlayStation (1994)

Sixth generation
Sega Dreamcast (1998),
Sony PlayStation 2
(2000),
Microsoft Xbox
(2001)

**Seventh
generation**
Xbox 360 (2005),
PlayStation 3 (2006),
Nintendo Wii (2006)

Scrabble

Scrabble was invented in the USA during the 1930s by an architect named Alfred Mosher Butts. First he called it Lexiko, then It and Criss-Cross, before hitting on the name Scrabble. Well over 100 million sets have been sold in more than 130 countries. The numbers of letters included vary according to the language. In Dutch, for example, there are 18 Es, 10 Ns and two Js. The Slovak version has 41 different letters – more than any other version.

Monopoly®

Monopoly was invented in 1934 by an unemployed engineer called Charles Darrow, who lived in Philadelphia, USA. In his first version of the game he used street names from Atlantic City in New Jersey because he dreamed of going there, but could not afford the fare. The game was so successful that Darrow became a millionaire and spent the rest of his life travelling and growing rare orchids.

There are many national and local versions around the world, as well as specialized versions including those for animal lovers, Birdopoly, Dogoploy and Horse-opoly, based on films such as James Bond and Shrek, as well as Bible-opoly and Elvis Monopoly. Parkers, the US manufacturers of the game, print more Monopoly money than the US Treasury prints dollars.

Monopoly® around the world

Country	City*	Mayfair becomes	
Australia	Canberra + state capitals	Kings Avenue	
Canada	Vancouver, etc	Robson Street	
China	Hong Kong	Victoria Peak	
Egypt	Cairo	Shari Qasr El Nil	
France	Paris	Rue de la Paix	
Germany	Munich	Schlossallee	
Ireland	Dublin	Shrewsbury Road	
Netherlands	Amsterdam	Kalverstraat	
New Zealand	Auckland	Queen Street	
Portugal	Lisbon	Rossio	
Russia	Moscow	Arbat	
Singapore	Singapore	Queen Astrid Park	
South Africa	Johannesburg	Eloff Street/Eloffstraat	Russian
Spain	Madrid	Paseo Del Prado	Monopoly
Switzerland	Zurich, etc	Paradeplatz	board
US	Atlantic City	Boardwalk	

* Some feature streets from more than one city

Diamond fact file

● The weight of diamonds is measured in carats. The word comes from the carob which has an amazingly consistent weight of 0.2 g (0.007 oz). There are five carats to a gram and about 142 carats to the ounce.

● Fewer than 1,000 rough diamonds weighing more than 100 carats have ever been found.

● The first ever reference to diamonds is in the Bible in Exodus xxviii.18 and xxxix.11. It mentions a diamond mounted on a priest's breastplate.

● In 1796, Smithson Tennant (1761–1815), a British scientist, was the first person to show that diamonds are made of carbon. The diamond is the only gem in the world made of a single element.

● Diamonds are 180 times harder than emeralds.

● Diamonds melt at 6,900°C (12,452°F), which is two and a half times the temperature needed to melt steel.

● Diamonds come from a rock called kimberlite. About 200 tonnes of kimberlite are mined for every carat of polished diamond.

● The largest diamond ever found is called the Cullinan after Thomas Cullinan, who was president of the diamond company De Beers. The stone weighed 3,106 carats (621 g [almost 22 oz]) and was found in South Africa in about 1905. It was presented to King Edward VII, who had it cut into 105 separate diamonds. One of the largest of these weighs 317.4 carats and is set in the British Imperial State Crown.

British Imperial State Crown

What's a million?

If you earned £100 a week, it would take you 192 years to earn £1 million. £1 million in £1 coins would weigh 9.5 tonnes. If they were in a line edge to edge they would stretch 225 km (140 miles). £1 million in 1p coins would weigh 356 tonnes.

A 2-euro coin (left) and US 1-dollar coin

Valuable coin

In 1933, 445,500 Double Eagles, gold $20 coins, were minted. They were never officially issued and most were later melted down, but a few found their way into private hands. The only one legally sold fetched $7.59 million in 2002, the highest price ever paid for one coin. In 2005, 10 were returned to the US Mint and are the subject of a legal dispute about their ownership.

Money facts

The first coins Coins made from gold and silver were used in Lydia, an ancient Middle Eastern kingdom, in about 687–652 BC. The coins were known as staters.

Smallest coins The silver quarter-jawa was made in Nepal in about 1740 and weighed only 0.002 g (0.00007 oz).

Largest coins Swedish 10-daler copper coins (made in 1644) weighed 19.71 kg (43.45 lb).

Most coins made The US Mint makes up to 20 billion coins every year. In 2007 the US Mint made 7,401,200,000 one cent coins, worth $74,012,000. There are 27 billion UK coins in circulation.

Banknotes Paper money was first made in China in the 13th century. The first European notes were made in Sweden in 1548. Banknotes were issued in 1690 in America and 1695 in England.

Largest banknotes One-guan Chinese notes from the late 14th century measured 22.8 x 33 cm (9 x 13 in) – bigger than a page of this book.

Smallest banknotes Romanian 10-bani notes of 1917 had a printed area of just 27.5 x 38 mm (1.08 x 1.5 in) – not much bigger than a postage stamp.

Golden treasures

Gold mask of Tutankhamun

Buddha statue

A 15th-century statue of Buddha is the largest gold object in the world. It is in the Wat Traimit temple, Bangkok, Thailand, stands 3 m (10 ft) tall and weighs 5.5 tonnes.

Gold salt cellar

This was made by Benvenuto Cellini for Francis I of France in about 1540. It is made of solid gold, elaborately decorated, and is one of the greatest works of the goldsmith's art. It is now in the Kunsthistorisches Museum, Vienna.

Gold stores

The United States Bullion Depository at Fort Knox, Kentucky, USA, contains 4,570 tonnes of gold and the Federal Reserve Bank of New York holds about 5,000 tonnes, the largest amount of gold in one place anywhere in the world.

Gold fact file

● People have prized gold since ancient times. It is easy to work with and makes beautiful objects that do not corrode. Even coins and jewellery that have been buried for thousands of years are as bright as the day they were made.

● Gold is rare – it is only the 73rd commonest element in Earth's crust. There are more than ten million tonnes of gold in the world's seas, but it would cost too much to get it out.

● Gold is very heavy. A cup of gold would weigh 19.3 times as much as the same cup filled with water.

● Gold can be stretched into very thin wire. Just one gram of gold makes a wire 2.4 km (1.5 miles) long and 5 microns (0.0002 in) thick.

Tutankhamun's mask

Tutankhamun was king of Egypt in the 14th century BC. In 1922 fabulous treasures were found in his tomb by archaeologist Howard Carter. They are now in the Cairo Museum, Egypt. They include a gold mask, which weighs 10.23 kg (22.7 lb). It was found inside a solid gold coffin weighing 110.4 kg (243 lb).

● More than 90 per cent of all the gold mined in the past 6,000 years has been extracted since 1848.

● Gold is used for making coins and jewellery. It is also used in electronics, dentistry and for making special products such as the coating on astronauts' visors that protects them against harmful radiation.

● Gold bars like those in films about bank robberies are known as "London Good Delivery Bars". They measure 17.8 x 8.2 x 4.4 cm (7 x 3.6 x 1.75 in) and weigh 12.5 kg (27 lb), about six times as much as a house brick.

● The largest gold nugget ever was found at Moliagul, Australia, in 1869. It is known as Welcome Stranger and weighs 70.92 kg (156 lb).

Cheques The first cheque was issued in London on 22 April 1659. It was for £10 and made payable to the bearer by Nicholas Vanacker. It was drawn on the bank of Clayton & Morris. The original cheque was sold for £1,200 ($2,160) at Sotheby's, London in 1976.

Credit cards The first credit card was invented by Frank X. McNamara in the USA and issued in 1950 by Diner's Club. Holograms were first used for security on Visa cards in the US in 1984. Smart cards (cards with built-in microchips) were introduced in France in 1975. There are 142.8 million payment cards in the UK:

69.5 million credit cards, 4.9 million charge cards and 68.3 million debit cards. There are more than 1 billion credit cards in use in the USA.

ATM The world's first ATM (Automated Teller Machine, or cashpoint) began operation on

27 June 1967 at Barclays Bank, Enfield, London.

Euro The new European currency was introduced in 1999 and was taken up by most European Union countries on 1 January 2002.

www.gold.org   search

ENERGY

Top energy users

These countries guzzle more energy than any others in the world. The figures below show the amount of gas, coal or other power needed to produce the same amount of energy as a tonne of oil. This is the standard way of comparing energy produced and consumed from different sources.

- **Other** Oil 1,601.6, Gas 1,136.4, Coal 636.6, Nuclear 114.7, HEP* 338.8, Total 3,817.3
- **USA** Oil 938.8, Gas 566.9, Coal 567.3, Nuclear 187.5, HEP* 65.9, Total 2,326.4
- **China** Oil 363.0, Gas 52.2, Coal 1,198.8, Nuclear 12.3, HEP* 94.3, Total 1,720.6
- **Russia** Oil 128.5, Gas 388.9, Coal 112.5, Nuclear 35.4, HEP* 39.6, Total 704.9
- **Japan** Oil 235.0, Gas 76.1, Coal 119.1, Nuclear 68.6, HEP* 21.5, Total 520.3
- **India** Oil 120.3, Gas 35.8, Coal 237.7, Nuclear 4.0, HEP* 25.4, Total 423.2
- **Germany** Oil 123.5, Gas 78.5, Coal 82.4, Nuclear 37.9, HEP* 6.3, Total 328.5
- **Canada** Oil 98.8, Gas 87.0, Coal 25.0, Nuclear 22.3, HEP* 79.3, Total 322.3
- **France** Oil 92.8, Gas 40.6, Coal 13.1, Nuclear 102.1, HEP* 13.9, Total 262.6
- **UK** Oil 82.2, Gas 81.7, Coal 43.8, Nuclear 17.0, HEP* 1.9, Total 226.6

Energy consumption 2006 World total
Oil 3,889.8 Gas 2,574.9 Coal 3,090.1 Nuclear 635.5 HEP* 688.1 Total 10,878.5
* Hydroelectric power

See also
Pollution fact file: page 70

Oil well pump at work

Top coal producers

	Country	2006 production (tonnes oil equivalent)
1	China	1,212,300,000
2	USA	595,100,000
3	India	209,700,000
4	Australia	203,100,000
5	South Africa	144,800,000
	UK	*11,300,000*
	World total	3,079,700,000

Top oil producers

	Country	2006 production (tonnes)
1	Saudi Arabia	514,600,000
2	Russia	480,500,000
3	USA	311,800,000
4	Iran	209,800,000
5	China	183,700,000
	UK	*76,600,000*
	World total	3,914,100,000

Top natural gas producers

	Country	2006 production (tonnes oil equivalent)
1	Russia	550,900,000
2	USA	479,300,000
3	Canada	168,300,000
4	Iran	94,500,000
5	Norway	78,900,000
	UK	*72,000,000*
	World total	2,586,400,000

Nuclear power

Countries that consume the most energy produced by nuclear power.

	Country	2006 consumption (tonnes oil equivalent)
1	USA	187,500,000
2	France	102,100,000
3	Japan	68,600,000
4	Germany	37,900,000
5	Russia	35,400,000
	UK	*17,000,000*
	World total	635,500,000

Hydroelectricity

Countries that consume the most energy produced by hydroelectric power.

	Country	2006 consumption (tonnes oil equivalent)
1	China	94,300,000
2	Canada	79,300,000
3	Brazil	79,200,000
4	USA	65,900,000
5	Russia	39,600,000
	UK	*1,900,000*
	World total	688,100,000

Wind farm in California, USA

Wind energy

Windmills were used in Persia (now Iran) in the 7th century, and in Europe since the 12th century, but they were first used for making electricity in the late 19th century. Today, California, USA, is the world's leading area for wind-generated electricity. Tehachapi Wind Resource, California, produces as much wind energy as the rest of the USA combined.

How much power?

All electrical appliances use energy. The amount depends on their size and purpose: an electric heater might use ten times as much energy as a single light bulb.

The energy an appliance uses is measured in watts. These are named in honour of Scottish engineer James Watt (1736–1819), who first worked out how to measure energy.

Air conditioner 2500–3000 watts
Central heating pump 800 watts
Coffee percolator 500–750 watts
Computer 400 watts
Cooker 10,000 watts
Deep freeze 1000–2000 watts
Dishwasher 2000–2500 watts
Electric blanket 50–150 watts
Electric kettles 2200–3000 watts
Electric razor 6 watts
Fan 50–100 watts
Fluorescent light 60 watts
Food mixer 450 watts
Hair dryer 1000–1500 watts
Iron 1000–1500 watts
Light bulb 100 watts
Microwave oven 1500 watts
Photocopier 1500 watts
Printer 350 watts
Radiator (oil filled) 1000–2000 watts
Radio, CD player, etc 40–200 watts
Refrigerator 1000 watts
Sewing machine 100 watts
Toaster 750–1500 watts
Tumble dryer 2400 watts
TV (colour) 250 watts
Vacuum cleaner 800–1400 watts
Washing machine 3000–4000 watts

The world's energy sources

A century ago, few homes had electricity and cars were a rare sight. Today, much of the world's energy is turned into electricity for homes, to power equipment in factories, and to fuel our cars, buses, aircraft and other transport. These are some of the main sources of this energy.

Oil

The first oil wells were drilled less than 150 years ago but oil, and petroleum which comes from it, has become the most important energy source. Almost 36 per cent of the world's energy supply comes from oil. Most oil is found in the Middle East and has to be taken by tankers or pipelines to places where it is used around the world.

Coal

Coal is the world's second most important source of energy. It makes up over 28 per cent of the total. Coal is a fossil fuel and is made from plants that lived and died 300 million years ago. The world's coal reserves will last about another 145 years. This is more than twice as long as gas (61 years) and almost four times as long as oil (38 years).

Natural gas

The third main source of power comes from gas that occurs naturally beneath the Earth's surface. It accounts for 24 per cent of the world total. The gas is mainly methane, with some ethane, propane and other gases. It is collected and taken to where it is needed by pipelines.

Grand Coulee Dam, Washington, USA

Hydropower

Flowing water has been used as a power source since the Middle Ages. Modern hydropower uses water flowing through turbines in dams to produce electricity.

Nuclear power

The fifth most important power source (just under 6% of the world total) is nuclear power. A nuclear reaction releases huge amounts of heat which in turn heats water or other liquid and drives a turbine to produce electricity. The first nuclear power station to produce electricity for public use was Calder Hall, UK, which opened in 1956.

Solar energy

The Sun's warmth can be stored to produce energy. Mirrors and glass were used to collect heat in ancient times, but the first houses to use solar heating were not built until 1955. Solar energy is becoming more popular and the technology is getting better all the time. The world's largest solar energy generating plants are in the Mohave Desert, California, USA. They are designed to use the Sun's rays to heat oil which drives a generator. Each produces enough electricity to power a small town.

Tidal energy

Using waves and marine currents to release energy is expensive and as yet small-scale. The first and largest tidal power station on the Rance river, St Malo, France, was completed in 1967. It can produce enough energy every year to supply power to 120,000 households.

Buildings & Structures

Rising ambition

The new headquarters of China Central Television in Beijing is scheduled to be completed in time to broadcast the 2008 Olympic Games. It is not a traditional tower but a continuous loop and has taken careful planning as Beijing has strict building regulations given seismic instability in the area.

Western architecture

Below are the main styles of Western architecture, from prehistory to the present day and famous examples of each. Styles did not stop and start abruptly; one style blended into another, so all dates are approximate.

Before the Renaissance most buildings had several architects or the architect's name was not recorded. The names of the architects of more recent buildings are given in brackets.

Prehistoric
Wooden post buildings, simple stone buildings, stone circles
Stonehenge, Wiltshire, UK

Ancient 3000–337 BC
Ancient Egyptian pyramids, tombs and temples
Great Pyramid, Giza, Egypt

Etruscan 700–200 BC
Alatri Temple, Villa Giulia, Rome, Italy

Greek 600–100 BC
Parthenon, Athens, Greece

Roman 100 BC–AD 370
The Baths of Caracalla, Rome, Italy
The Pantheon, Rome, Italy
The Colosseum, Rome, Italy
Maison Carrée, Nîmes, France

Byzantine 330–1450
Hagia Sophia, Istanbul, Turkey
St Mark's, Venice, Italy

Pre-Columbian 300–1540
Mayan, Aztec, Inca South and Central American
Mayan temples at Tikal, Guatemala

Carolingian 751–987
Chapel Palatine (now part of cathedral), Aachen, Germany

Romanesque 800 to 1200
St James, Santiago de Compostela, Spain
Tournai Cathedral, Belgium

Moorish/Islamic from 8th century
Great Mosque, Cordoba, Spain

Norman 1045–1180
Durham Cathedral, Durham, UK
Ely Cathedral, Ely, UK

Gothic 1140–1534
Cologne Cathedral, Cologne, Germany
Notre Dame Cathedral, Paris, France
Chartres Cathedral, Chartres, France
Salisbury Cathedral, Salisbury, UK

Renaissance 1400–1600
Hampton Court Palace, London, UK
Little Moreton Hall, Cheshire, UK
Florence Cathedral, Florence, Italy (Filippo Brunelleschi)
Ducal Palace, Urbino, Italy (Luciano Laurana)
Château de Chambord, France (Domenico da Cortona)

Baroque 1585–1750
St Paul's Cathedral, London, UK (Sir Christopher Wren)
Versailles Palace, France (Louis Le Vau and Jules Hardouin Mansart)
Greenwich Hospital (Royal Naval College), London, UK (Inigo Jones and Sir Christopher Wren)
Blenheim Palace, Oxfordshire, UK (Sir John Vanbrugh)

American Colonial 1600–1780
Governor's Palace, Williamsburg, Virginia, USA (rebuilt 1930)

Jacobean 1618–25
Ham House, Twickenham, Middlesex, UK
Blickling Hall, Norfolk, UK

Rococo 1650–1790
Vierzehnheiligen Church, Banz, Germany (Johann Balthasar Neumann)

Georgian 1714–1837
The Circus, Bath, UK (John Wood, Sr and Jr)
Charlotte Square, Edinburgh, UK (Robert Adam)

Neoclassical/Federalist US 1750–1880
Panthéon, Paris, France (Germain Soufflot)
Brighton Pavilion, Brighton, UK (John Nash)
University of Virginia, Charlottesville, Virginia, USA (Thomas Jefferson)

See also
Mysterious places: page 174

The Parthenon

Greek
The Parthenon, Athens, Greece, 447–438 BC.
Doric is the first and simplest classical Greek building style and this is the finest Doric building still standing. When it was first built, the Parthenon was decorated with marble sculptures painted in bright colours. Some of these, known as the Elgin Marbles, were removed and are now in the British Museum, London.

www.greatbuildings.com   search

Skyline of Chicago, USA, with skyscrapers and other modern buildings

Victorian 1837–1901

Houses of Parliament, London, UK (Sir Charles Barry and A.W.N. Pugin)
Crystal Palace, London, UK (Joseph Paxton)
American Surety Building, New York, USA (Bruce Price)

Arts and crafts 1860–1900

The Red House, Kent, UK (Philip Webb)

Art Nouveau 1890–1905

Glasgow Art School, Glasgow, UK (Charles Rennie Macintosh)
Paris Metro stations (Hector Guimard)
La Sagrada Familia, Barcelona, Spain (Antonio Gaudí)
Secession Building, Vienna, Austria (Joseph Maria Olbrich)

Art Deco 1925–35

Chrysler Building, New York, USA (William Van Alen)

Bauhaus 1919–37

Bauhaus, Dessau, Germany (Walter Gropius)

International modernism 1920–50

Fallingwater, Pennsylvania, USA (Frank Lloyd Wright)

Brutalism 1950s

Unité d'Habitation, Marseilles, France (Le Corbusier)
Seagram Building, New York, USA (Mies van der Rohe)

High-tech 1970s–

Centre Georges Pompidou, Paris, France (Richard Rogers and Renzo Piano)
Swiss Re Building (The Gherkin), London, UK (Norman Foster)

Post-modern 1970s

Staatsgalerie, Stuttgart, Germany (James Stirling)

Deconstruction 1990s–

Guggenheim Museum, Bilbao, Spain (Frank Gehry)

Art Deco

Chrysler Building, New York, USA, 1930.
The Chrysler is one of the best-known Art Deco buildings. The gleaming metal spire was based on the Chrysler cars of the time and skyscrapers are still a key feature of the New York skyline.

High-tech

Swiss Re Building (The Gherkin), London, 2004.
This building is London's first eco-friendly skyscraper. Its shape allows maximum natural light and ventilation inside so it uses only half the amount of energy consumed by a normal office block.

Japanese architecture

Eastern countries, such as Japan, had their own strong traditions of architecture. The Katsura Palace in Kyoto was built in the early 17th century, at the time of baroque and Jacobean architecture in Europe. It is a simple, elegant building and one of the most perfect examples of traditional Japanese architecture.

American Colonial

Governor's Palace, Williamsburg, Virginia, USA, 1722
European settlers in the New World used architectural ideas from their home countries. The historic district of Williamsburg in Virginia has some of the most famous colonial buildings, dating from before the War of American Independence. The Governor's Palace is one of the finest.

Great religious buildings

The world's major religions, including Christianity, Islam, Judaism, Buddhism, Hinduism and Sikhism, have inspired many of the world's greatest buildings. Some are shrines to the religion's founders. Others are places of pilgrimage. Several are among the world's largest structures. These are the tallest churches.

1 The Chicago Methodist Temple* Chicago, USA, built 1924, 173 m (568 ft)
2 Ulm Cathedral Ulm, Germany, built 1890, 161 m (528 ft)
3 Notre Dame de la Paix Yamoussoukro, Côte d'Ivoire, built 1989, 158 m (519 ft)
4 Cologne Cathedral Cologne, Germany, built 1880, 156 m (513 ft)
5 Rouen Cathedral Rouen, France, built 1876, 148 m (485 ft)
* Built on top of a 25-storey, 100 m (328 ft) building

Sagrada Familia

Spanish architect Antonio Gaudí's Sagrada Familia Cathedral in Barcelona, Spain, was begun in 1883, but it is still not finished. Its tallest spires are planned to be 170 m (558 ft).

Sagrada Familia Cathedral, Barcelona

Largest churches

Salt Lake Temple, Utah, USA (1893) has a floor area of 23,506 sq m (253,015 sq ft). St Peter's in the Vatican (1612), the centre of the Roman Catholic Church, is 218.7 m (717.5 ft) long and covers an area of 23,000 sq m (247,572 sq ft). It was the largest Christian cathedral in the world until 1989, when it was overtaken by the 30,000 sq m (322,917 sq ft) basilica in Yamoussoukro, Côte d'Ivoire.

Tallest mosques

The Great Hassan II Mosque, Casablanca, Morocco (1993) is the tallest mosque at 210 m (689 ft). The Saddam Mosque, Baghdad, Iraq was designed to be the largest in the Middle East, with a record-breaking 280 m (919 ft) minaret, but it has not been completed.

Largest mosque

The Masjid al Haram is the holy mosque of Makkah (formerly Mecca), the birthplace of the prophet Muhammad. Millions of Muslim pilgrims visit the mosque every year. The mosque covers 82,000 sq m (882,640 sq ft) and the surrounding yards cover another 985,000 sq m (10,602,442 sq ft). Together they can accommodate up to 1.2 million worshippers.

Largest Buddhist temple

The largest Buddhist temple in the world is Borobudur (many Buddhas), near Yogyakarta, Java, Indonesia. It was built between AD 750 and 842. The temple covers 60,000 sq m (645,834 sq ft) and contains 56,634 cu m (2 million cu ft) of stone.

Largest Hindu temple

Angkor Wat, Cambodia, built between 879 and 1191, is the largest religious structure in the world. The complex of buildings inside its walls and moat covers 83,110 sq m (894,588 sq ft).

Largest synagogue

The world's largest synagogue is Temple Emanu-El, New York City, USA. It opened in 1929 and occupies an area of 3,523 sq m (37,921 sq ft).

Lighthouses

Tallest in the world

The biggest lighthouse ever built was the Pharos of Alexandria, which stood 124 m (407 ft) tall. It was one of the Seven Wonders of the world. The world's tallest lighthouse today is in Yamashita Park, Yokohama, Japan, and is 106 m (348 ft) tall.

Tallest in the UK

The Bishop Rock lighthouse off the Scilly Isles, built in 1858, is 49 m (161 ft) tall and has a helipad on top. The equally tall Eddystone lighthouse, off Plymouth, was originally made of wood. The one there now is the fifth on the site, and was opened in 1882.

Tallest in the US

The Cape Hatteras lighthouse in North Carolina was built in 1870. It is the tallest in the USA at 59.7 m (196 ft). The lighthouse was being eroded by the sea so between 1999 and 2000 the entire 2,540-tonne building was moved 884 m (2,900 ft) inland, very slowly, on tracks.

See also

Holy places: page 162

Millennium Dome, London, UK

Biggest domes and roofs

In 1434, the Duomo Cathedral in Florence, Italy, had the largest dome in the world. It was 45.5 m (149.3 ft) across and was still the world's largest dome 400 years later.

The diameter of the Millennium Dome is almost eight times greater, thanks to modern building techniques and materials. Some of the domes in the list below are supported by struts and cables, others are free-standing. Some can even be opened.

The O₂ (formerly the Millennium Dome), London, UK, was completed in 1999. It measures 358 m (1,175 ft) in diameter. The span is supported by steel masts that project through the dome.

Wembley Stadium, London, UK, was completed in 2007. It has the largest single-span roof in the world (supported only at the sides). It measures 315 m (1,033 ft) in diameter.

The Georgia Superdome, Atlanta, Georgia, USA was completed in 1992 with a diameter of 256 m (840 ft). It has the world's largest cable-supported fabric roof.

The Fantasy Entertainment Complex, Kyosho, Japan, was completed in 2002. It has a diameter of 216 m (710 ft).

The Houston Astrodome, Houston, Texas, USA, was completed in 1966. It measures 216 m (710 ft) in diameter.

The Louisiana Superdome, New Orleans, Louisiana, USA, was completed in 1975. It measures 207 m (680 ft) in diameter.

SkyDome, Toronto, Canada, was completed in 1989 with a diameter of 205 m (674 ft). It has the world's largest retractable roof.

The Multi-Purpose Arena, Nagoya, Japan, was completed in 1997. It measures 187 m (614 ft) in diameter.

Tacoma Dome, Tacoma, Washington, USA, was completed in 1983 with a diameter of 162 m (532 ft).

The Superior Dome, Marquette, Michigan, USA, was completed in 1991 and has a diameter of 160 m (523 ft).

Obelisks and columns

Obelisks are stone columns made in ancient Egypt almost 4,000 years ago. Some were taken as trophies by invading armies and are now in cities such as Istanbul, Rome, London, Paris and New York. More recently, people have built memorials based on the design of obelisks.

● A column commemorating the battle of San Jacinto (1836) near Houston, Texas, USA, is the world's tallest monument at 174 m (570 ft). It was completed in 1939.

● The Washington Monument, Washington DC, USA, was completed in 1884. It is 169 m (555 ft) tall, made of 36,491 stone blocks on an iron frame and weighs 82,421 tonnes. It was the world's tallest structure for five years until it was overtaken by the Eiffel Tower in 1889.

● The Wellington Monument in Dublin, Ireland is a stone obelisk made to celebrate the victories of the Duke of Wellington. It was completed in 1861 and is Europe's tallest obelisk at 63 m (206 ft).

● The Monument in London commemorates the Great Fire of London in 1666. It was built in 1667 and is 62 m (202 ft) tall.

● Nelson's Column in Trafalgar Square, London, was completed in 1842 to celebrate Britain's great naval commander. The column is 44 m (145 ft) high and has a 5 m (17 ft) statue of Nelson on top.

● The tallest Egyptian obelisk is in the Piazza San Giovanni in Laterano, Rome, Italy. It measures 32 m (106 ft). The tallest still in Egypt is in Karnak and is 30 m (97 ft) tall. The ancient Egyptian obelisk in New York is 22 m (73 ft) and the London obelisk, Cleopatra's Needle, is 21 m (69 ft).

Modern pyramids

The ancient Egyptian pyramids are the best known, but this style of building has also been used in modern times.

"Mad Jack" Fuller's tomb, Brightling, East Sussex. Jack Fuller, an eccentric landowner and Member of Parliament, had his own 8 m (25 ft) pyramid tomb built in 1811. It is said that his body is inside, wearing a top hat!

Louvre Museum Pyramid, Paris, France The architect I.M. Pei designed the 22 m (71 ft) glass pyramid which was built in 1989 as the main entrance to the Louvre Museum, Paris, France.

Christa McAuliffe Planetarium, Concord, New Hampshire, USA Christa McAuliffe was killed in the *Challenger* space shuttle disaster. The pyramid-shaped planetarium named after her opened in 1990.

Luxor Hotel and Casino, Las Vegas, Nevada, USA This was opened in 1993. It is 107 m (350 ft)-tall and at its entrance is a sphinx that shoots laser beams from its eyes.

Rainforest Pyramid, Galveston, Texas, USA This 38 m (125 ft)-tall pyramid, finished in 1993, houses one of the world's largest indoor rainforests.

SKYSCRAPERS

Tallest skyscrapers over the last 100 years

New York's 119.2 m (391 ft) Park Row Building was the tallest office or apartment building in the world when it was completed in 1899. Since then it has been overtaken many times by the progressively taller skyscrapers on this list. The latest world record-holder, the Burj Dubai, is more than five times as tall as the Park Row Building.

	Building	Year completed	Floors	Height m/ft*	
1	Metropolitan Life, New York, USA	1909	50	213.4	700.1
2	Woolworth Building, New York, USA	1913	57	241.4	792.0
3	The Trump Building, New York, USA	1930	70	282.5	926.8
4	Chrysler Building, New York, USA	1930	77	318.8	1,045.9
5	Empire State Building, New York, USA	1931	102	381.0	1,250.0
6	One World Trade Center, New York, USA#	1972	110	417.0	1,368.1
7	Sears Tower, Chicago, USA	1974	108	442.0	1,450.1
8	Petronas Towers, Kuala Lumpur, Malaysia	1998	88	451.9	1,482.6
9	Taipei 101, Taipei, Taiwan	2004	101	509.0	1,669.9
10	Burj Dubai, Dubai, UAE	2008	164	620.0	2,034.0

* Excluding masts, etc
# Destroyed in terrorist attack of 11 September 2001

Until 1930 the Eiffel Tower, Paris, was the world's tallest building.

See also
Cities of the World: pages 118–19

Tallest structure

The world's tallest free-standing structure is the CN Tower in Toronto, Canada. It measures a mighty 553.33 m (1,815 ft) to the tip of its antenna. There are taller masts, but they are supported with guy wires. The CN Tower also has the world's highest graffiti. It was painted – with permission – in 1976 by 20,000 children before the antenna was lifted into position by helicopter.

The Eiffel Tower

The Eiffel Tower in Paris, France, was built as a temporary structure for the Universal Exhibition held in Paris in 1889. The tower was so popular that it has been there ever since.

● Engineer Gustave Eiffel (1832–1923) also built the framework of the Statue of Liberty. A workforce of 300 steelworkers completed the tower in two years, two months and five days.

● The Eiffel Tower contains 18,038 pieces of steel, weighing a total of 7,175 tonnes. They are connected by 2.5 million rivets.

● The tower's 220,000 sq m (2,368,060 sq ft) of surfaces are hand-painted every ten years (last in 2003) with 60 tonnes of paint.

● The tower is 300.5 m (986 ft) tall – 320.8 m (1,052 ft) with its antenna – but it can expand or shrink by up to 15 cm (6 in) depending on how hot or cold it is. It was the world's tallest structure until the Chrysler Building in New York overtook it in 1930.

● The tower is lit by 352 1,000-watt projectors and 20,000 lights (installed in 2003). These are switched on after dusk for the first ten minutes of every hour.

● More than 200 million people have visited the tower. Most take the lifts, although there are 1,665 steps for the very energetic. It also attracts publicity-seeking climbers. Birdmen, parachutists and even cyclists have made descents – some of them fatal.

● The Eiffel Tower features in many films, including the James Bond film *A View to a Kill* (1985).

Cities with most skyscrapers*

1 Hong Kong, China 199
2 New York City, USA 190
3 Chicago, USA 90
4 Shanghai, China 71
5 Tokyo, Japan 69

* Habitable buildings of more than 152 m (500 ft)

A view of the skyscrapers of Hong Kong from Victoria's Peak

Taller and taller

Scheduled for completion in 2009, the Burj Dubai, Dubai, United Arab Emirates, is planned to be over 620 metres (2,034 ft) tall, with a spire reaching 818 m (2,684 ft), making it the highest structure in the world. It cost more than $4 billion to build

Currently, the world's tallest building is the Taipei 101 in Taipei, Taiwan. It is so-called because it has 101 storeys above ground level. Some experts consider that its spire should not be included in its total height, but international rules count all parts of a skyscraper except masts, antennae and flagpoles. So this building qualifies as the tallest. It also has the highest occupied floor of any building.

The Empire State Building

New York's tallest building is the Empire State Building, which stands on Fifth Avenue, New York, between 33rd Street and 34th Street. It was built on the site of the Waldorf-Astoria Hotel and took 410 days at a rate of 4½ floors a week to complete. The building was opened on 1 May 1931 by remote control, when President Herbert Hoover pressed a button in Washington DC.

The Empire State Building towers 381 m (1,250 ft) above ground – and measures 443.2 m (1,454.1 ft) to the top of the TV tower. A further 16.7 m (54.8 ft) is below ground. The spire on top was designed as an airship mooring mast, but after a German airship, the *Hindenburg*, burned at its mooring mast in New Jersey in 1937, the mast was never used. For more than 40 years, the Empire State held the record as the world's tallest office or apartment building, until the twin towers of the World Trade Center were completed. Since their destruction in 2001, it is once again New York's tallest. More than 2.5 million tourists a year go up to the observatories on the 86th and 102nd floors.

- The workforce – 3,400 at its peak – took seven million man-hours to complete the building.

- The cost was $40,948,900 including the land (the building cost only $24,718,000).

- It weighs 331,122 tonnes, including a 54,431-tonne steel frame, 10 million bricks and 662 tonnes of aluminium and stainless steel.

- The Empire State is served by 73 lifts and contains 3,194,547 light bulbs, 80 km (49.7 miles) of radiator pipes and 113 km (70.2 miles) of water pipes.

- The lightning conductor was struck 68 times in the building's first ten years.

- In 2003 Australian runner Paul Crake broke his own record for racing up the 1,575 steps to the 86th floor in 9 min 33 sec.

- On 28 July 1945, a B-25 bomber crashed in fog between the building's 78th and 79th floors, killing the pilot and 13 other people. It happened on a Saturday so most offices were empty, or the casualties would have been higher.

- On St Valentine's Day, couples can marry on the 80th floor.

- The building's coloured lights are changed for seasonal celebrations. They are red, white and blue on Independence Day and green on St Patrick's Day. The lights are turned off when birds are migrating to avoid confusing them.

Bridge types

Arch An arch bridge is a very strong curved structure made of stone, concrete or steel. It is firmly supported on both sides.

Bascule A bascule bridge has a central section that opens to allow tall ships to pass. London's Tower Bridge is one of the most famous bascule bridges.

Beam A beam bridge is supported by the shore at both ends. This is the simplest and oldest type of bridge – a log across a stream is a very simple beam bridge. It is not very strong and may need to be strengthened by supports underneath.

Cantilever This type of bridge has two long arms held in place at the ends by anchors. Some can swing to let large ships through. Cantilever bridges are closest in length to suspension bridges.

Suspension This bridge is supported by steel cables fixed to high towers on the banks. All the world's longest bridges are suspension bridges because they are very strong.

Swing A swing bridge can be swung to one side to allow ships through. The Gateshead Millennium Bridge across the Tyne is a unique swing bridge, which rotates upwards to allow boats to pass beneath.

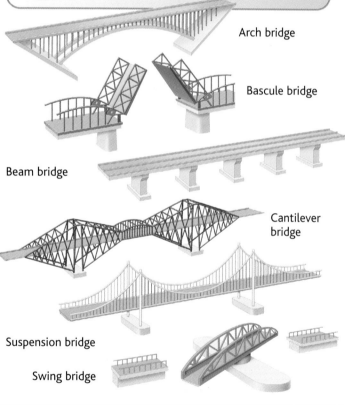

Arch bridge

Bascule bridge

Beam bridge

Cantilever bridge

Suspension bridge

Swing bridge

Famous bridges

Pont d'Avignon, France
This bridge was built in the 12th century. It was made famous by the song "Sur le Pont d'Avignon" (On Avignon Bridge).

Bridge of Sighs, Venice, Italy
The Bridge of Sighs was designed in 1560. It connects the Doge's Palace with the city jail, and prisoners who had been sentenced to death had to cross the bridge to reach the jail. Its name is said to come from their sighs of despair.

Pont Neuf, Paris, France
Pont Neuf was completed in 1604. The bridge is in two halves and links the Right and Left Banks of the River Seine to Ile de la Cité, the island on which Notre Dame Cathedral stands.

Kintai-Kyo Bridge, Iwakuni, Japan
This wooden arch bridge was built across the Nishiki River in 1673. It has been damaged and rebuilt many times.

Iron Bridge, Shropshire
The Iron Bridge was completed in 1781 and was the first bridge built of iron.

Longest bridges

1800s

All these bridges were the world's longest when they were built. Today's longest, the Akashi Kaikyo in Japan, is nearly 54 times longer than the Martorell bridge in Spain.

† No longer standing

217 BC Martorell, Spain
A stone arch bridge with a span of 37 m (121 ft)

27 BC Augustus, Narni, Italy
A stone arch bridge with a span of 43 m (142 ft)

AD 104 Trajan, Danube, Romania
A timber arch bridge with stone piers and a span of 52 m (170 ft)

1371 Trezzo, Adda, Italy †
A stone arch bridge with a span of 72 m (236 ft)

1757 Schaffhausen, Switzerland †
A timber bridge with a span of 119 m (390 ft)

1816 Schuylkill Falls, Philadelphia, USA †
A suspension bridge with a span of 124 m (407 ft)

1820 Union/Tweed, Berwick, UK
An iron chain suspension bridge with a span of 137 m (449 ft)

1826 Menai Strait, Anglesey, UK
A chain suspension bridge with a span of 177 m (580 ft)

1834 Fribourg, Switzerland †
Wire-cable suspension bridge with a span of 273 m (896 ft)

1849 Wheeling, West Virginia, USA
A suspension bridge with a span of 308 m (1,010 ft) long

1851 Lewiston-Queenston, Niagara, USA
A suspension bridge with a span of 318 m (1,043 ft)

The Golden Gate Bridge, San Francisco, USA, was completed in 1937. It was the world's longest bridge for many years.

Road and rail tunnels

The first tunnel built specially for passenger trains was the 766 m (2,513 ft) Tyler Hill Tunnel in Kent, UK. It opened on 4 May 1830. The first underwater rail tunnel was the Thames Tunnel, London, UK, which opened in 1869.

Some of the most amazing tunnels are made under the sea. The Seikan tunnel was built to link the Japanese islands of Honshu and Hokkaido; 23.3 km (14.5 miles) is below the sea bed. The Channel Tunnel has 38 km (23.6 miles) under the sea. The tunnels listed are all for railways, except the Laerdal in Norway, which is a road tunnel.

Longest tunnels

1 Gotthard Base Tunnel (Alp Transit Link) Switzerland, 2018* will be 57.07 km (35.46 miles)

2 Seikan Japan, 1988 is 53.85 km (33.46 miles)

3 Channel Tunnel France/England, 1994 is 50.45 km (31.35 miles)

4 Moscow Metro (Serpukhovsko-Timiryazevskaya line) Russia, 1983 is 38.90 km (24.17 miles)

5 Lötschberg Base Tunnel Switzerland, 2007 is 34.58 km (21.49 miles)

6 Guadarrama Spain, 2007 is 28.38 km (17.63 miles)

7 London Underground (East Finchley/Mordern, Northern Line) UK, 1939 is 27.84 km (17.29 miles)

8 Hakkoda Japan, 2010* will be 26.46 km (16.44 miles)

9 Iwate Japan, 2002 is 25.81 km (16.04 miles)

10 Pajares Spain, 2011* is 24.67 km (15.33 miles)

* Still being built

One and only

London Bridge was taken from the UK to the USA. The five-arched stone bridge was made between 1823 and 1831. In the 20th century, London Bridge needed to be replaced by one better suited to modern traffic. American businessman Robert P. McCulloch bought it for £1 million ($2,460,000). The bridge was shipped out stone by stone. It was rebuilt in Lake Havasu City in Arizona and completed in 1971. It is the largest structure ever moved and the largest antique ever sold!

Tower Bridge, London
Tower Bridge was completed in 1894. It opens and lifts in the middle to allow tall ships to pass underneath.

Brooklyn Bridge, New York, USA
After many setbacks, Brooklyn Bridge was finally opened in 1883. For a short time it was the world's longest bridge.

Sydney Harbour Bridge, Sydney, Australia
Sydney Harbour Bridge was built in 1932 to carry road and rail traffic across the harbour. It is a famous feature of the Sydney harbour skyline.

Tower Bridge, London, UK

1990s

1867 The Cincinnati-Ohio River, Covington, USA
A suspension bridge with a span of 322 m (1,057 ft)

1869 Niagara-Clifton, Niagara, USA/Canada †
A suspension bridge with a span of 387 m (1,268 ft)

1883 Brooklyn, New York
A suspension bridge with a span of 486 m (1,596 ft)

1890 Firth of Forth Rail, Scotland
A cantilever bridge with a span of 521 m (1,710 ft) long

1917 Quebec Rail, Canada
A cantilever bridge with a span of 549 m (1,800 ft)

1929 Ambassador, Detroit, USA/ Windsor, Canada
A suspension bridge with a span of 564 m (1,850 ft) long

1931 George Washington, New York
A suspension bridge with a span of 1,067 m (3,500 ft)

1937 Golden Gate, San Francisco, USA
A suspension bridge with a span of 1,280 m (4,200 ft)

1964 Verazzano Narrows, New York, USA
A suspension bridge with a span of 1,298 m (4,260 ft)

1980 Humber Estuary, Hull, UK
A suspension bridge with a span of 1,410 m (4,626 ft)

1997 East Bridge, Denmark
A suspension bridge with a span of 1,624 m (5,328 ft)

1998 Akashi Kaikyo, Japan
A suspension bridge with a span of 1,990 m (6,529 ft)

See also

Rail Transport: pages 214–15

The Seven Wonders of the ancient world

Early Greek writers drew up lists of the most important buildings in the world they knew. Of these only the Great Pyramid survives, but we know about the others from writers' accounts and archaeologists.

The Great Pyramid of Giza

The Great Pyramid of Giza, Egypt, is the oldest, and the only one of the Seven Wonders to survive. It was made as a tomb for King Khufu, who ruled Egypt from about 2551 to 2528 BC, and it is the largest stone structure ever built. Its sides are 230 m (754 ft) long and it covers an area the size of 200 tennis courts.

The Hanging Gardens of Babylon

The legendary gardens of King Nebuchadnezzar II may not have existed. Some people believe they were created in about 600 BC in Babylon, 88 km (55 miles) south of present-day Baghdad, the capital of Iraq. "Hanging" suggests that they were a series of terraces made of bricks, some glazed and brightly coloured.

The Statue of Zeus at Olympia

This was an enormous statue of the Greek god, carved by the sculptor Phidias. It was inside the Temple of Zeus, built about 466–456 BC. The statue was 13 m (43 ft) high and one of the largest indoor sculptures ever made. Today little remains of the temple and nothing of the statue.

The Temple of Artemis

The Temple of Artemis at Ephesus, Turkey, was built to honour the Greek goddess of hunting and nature. The temple was completed in 550 BC. It was the largest of all ancient Greek buildings and measured 114 by 55 m (375 x 180 ft). Archaeologists have found the foundations and some columns of this ancient wonder.

The Mausoleum at Halicarnassus

This was the tomb of Persian ruler Mausolus, who ruled part of the Persian empire from 377 to 353 BC. Halicarnassus (modern-day Bodrum) in Turkey was his capital. After his death his widow built this magnificent tomb, which measured 105 by 242 m (344 x 794 ft) and was 43 m (140 ft) high. It was damaged by an earthquake and demolished in 1522. The word mausoleum has come to mean any great tomb.

The Colossus of Rhodes

The huge statue of sun god Helios stood in Rhodes harbour, Greece. In 305–304 BC warrior king Demetrius Poliorcetes attacked the city of Rhodes. When he abandoned his siege, the people built the giant statue as an offering to the god Helios. It took 12 years to build and stood 33 m (110 ft) high, but in 226 BC it was destroyed by an earthquake.

See also
Holy places: page 162

The Great Wall of China can be seen from space.

Seven modern wonders

There are many candidates for this list and here is a selection.

Hoover Dam, USA
When it was built in 1936, the 221 m (725 ft) high Hoover Dam was the largest in the world. A record 3.63 million m³ (128.19 million ft³) of concrete were used to make the structure, which controls the flooding of the Colorado River.

Deltawerken flood barrier, Netherlands
After a disastrous flood in 1953, engineer Johan van Veen designed the Delta Project, or Deltawerken. This is a series of interconnected dams that forms a movable sea barrier while preserving the habitat and sea life within it.

Kansai International Airport, Japan
This airport was opened in 1994. It stands on a 4 x 1.2 km (2.5 x 0.75 miles) island which is entirely man-made. It was built with 48,000 huge blocks, made from earth excavated by flattening three mountains, and designed to withstand typhoons and earthquakes. Its terminal building was designed by Italian architect Renzo Piano.

Channel Tunnel, England/France
Work on the second longest underwater rail tunnel in the world began in 1987. It took seven years and 15,000 workers to create the 50.45 km (31.35 miles) tunnel (38 km [23.6 miles] under sea), which opened in 1994. The tunnel links Folkestone in England to Sangatte, France.

Guggenheim Museum, Bilbao, Spain
The Guggenheim was built in 1997 to the design of Canadian-born architect Frank Gehry. It houses a collection of modern art in a striking, ultra-modern setting. The structure combines limestone blocks of varied shapes, curved sections covered in panels of titanium (a light, strong metal) and large areas of glass.

The Eden Project, Cornwall, UK
About 1.8 million tonnes of earth were moved to make the foundations for the world's largest greenhouses. These are a series of domes, each devoted to a particular type of climate, and housing 100,000 plants. The Eden Project was designed by Nicholas Grimshaw and opened in 2001. It is one of the UK's most popular tourist attractions.

Panama Canal, Panama
It took 34 years, from 1880 to 1914, to build the ship canal that connects the Atlantic and Pacific Oceans. The 77-km (48-mile) canal was a remarkable feat of engineering, but cost the lives of up to 27,500 workers.

The Great Pyramid of Giza and the Sphinx

The Pharos of Alexandria
This was a lighthouse off the coast of the city of Alexandria. Work started on it in about 299 BC and it took about 20 years to build. It was 124 m (407 ft) tall – the tallest lighthouse ever made. It was damaged by earthquakes and in 1375 toppled into the sea. A few remains have been found.

Leaning Tower of Pisa

The Seven Wonders of the medieval world

People have never been able to agree on the Seven Wonders of the medieval world, and this is just one of several lists that have been made. It includes the Leaning Tower of Pisa (pictured right). In 2007, an organization produced a new list of Seven Wonders, according to a voting system, that included the Colosseum and the Great Wall of China, along with the Taj Mahal, India, Chichén Itzá, Mexico, Macchu Picchu, Peru, Petra, Jordan and the statue of Christ the Redeemer, Rio de Janeiro, which was completed as recently as 1931.

Stonehenge
The circle of huge stones was built in stages from about 3000 BC. The origin of the stones, how they were transported and the purpose of the site remain a mystery. It was possibly some sort of ancient observatory.

The Great Wall of China
This was a defensive wall designed to protect China from its warlike neighbours to the north. It was built in stages after 220 BC, using a huge labour force of as many as 300,000 workers. The main part is 3,460 km (2,150 miles) long and wide enough for an army to march along it ten abreast.

The Colosseum, Rome, Italy
This amphitheatre was opened in AD 80 with a huge spectacle lasting 100 days. It is oval and measures 48 m (157 ft) high, 188 m (617 ft) long and 156 m (512 ft) wide. It could hold up to 50,000 spectators and could be flooded for re-enactments of sea battles.

The Catacombs of Alexandria (Kom El Shoqafa), Egypt
These Roman tombs beneath the city of Alexandria, Egypt, were discovered in 1900 when a donkey fell into them. The beautifully preserved, carved catacombs had been made in solid rock during the 2nd century AD.

Hagia Sophia, Istanbul, Turkey
Hagia Sophia (Holy Wisdom), Istanbul, Turkey, was originally built in AD 360 by the Emperor Constantius. It was later rebuilt as one of the world's finest churches, with many mosaics and ornate details. In 1453 the church was converted into an Islamic mosque.

The Porcelain Pagoda of Nanking, China
The Porcelain Pagoda was built in about 1412 by Emperor Yung-lo. It was an eight-sided structure covered in glazed tiles, and soared to 79 m (260 ft). It was destroyed during a rebellion in 1853.

Leaning Tower of Pisa
Building began on the bell tower of Pisa Cathedral, Italy, in 1173. Soon the foundations began to sink on one side. The design was adjusted, but by the time the tower had reached its full height of 55 m (179 ft) it was leaning sharply. The tilt increased over the centuries and it is amazing that the 14,000-tonne structure is still standing.

Transport & Travel

Green car

This battery-powered Subaru is one of the new generation of environmentally-friendly cars, invented in response to the rapidly-changing natural world. Attempts to make functional and popular alternatives to the internal combustion engine have been going on for many years. At least 11 companies are planning to release electric cars between 2008 and 2011.

Types of ship

Passenger and commercial ships

Barge
This name is used for various types of ship, ranging from a slow canal boat to a small sailing cargo boat or a decorated rowing boat used by royalty.

Catamaran
A boat with two hulls side by side. There are different types of catamaran, including ferries and yachts.

Container ship
A cargo ship designed to carry standard-sized containers, making it easy to load and unload.

Ferry
A ship that takes passengers and vehicles from one port to another.

Galleon
A medieval sailing ship. The word was first used in 1529.

Galley
An ancient warship driven by oars. Biremes have oars on two levels, and triremes on three.

Hydrofoil
A boat with a special device to lift its hull out of the water, so increasing speed.

Junk
A high-sterned (the stern is the aft or back end), flat-bottomed, Chinese or Japanese sailing ship with two or three masts.

Liner or cruise ship
An ocean-going ship once used to take passengers on long journeys, such as across the Atlantic. Cruise ships are luxury liners designed to take people on pleasure cruises.

Oil tanker
A large vessel that carries oil from oil fields to refineries in other countries.

Yacht
A sailing or engine-powered ship used for pleasure cruises or racing.

Skyscraper?
During the 18th century, a skyscraper was a small triangular flag flown from the tip of a sailing ship's main mast. In the 19th century, the word began to be used to describe a tall horse or even an exceptionally tall person. And when the first very tall buildings were constructed in the 1890s people called them skyscrapers.

Sailors racing a catamaran at top speed

Top speeds

Rowing eight
The Oxford and Cambridge Boat Race is rowed annually on the River Thames, London, and covers 6.8 km (4.25 miles). The Oxford crew won in 1998 in a record time of 16 minutes 19 seconds, equivalent to a speed of 25 km/h (15.5 mph).

Aircraft carrier
The US Navy's Nimitz class nuclear-powered aircraft carriers can travel at more than 56 km/h (34.8 mph).

Submarine (submerged)
Russian Alfa class nuclear submarines could probably travel at 83.4 km/h (51.8 mph), but these are no longer in use. US Navy Los Angeles class subs are said to achieve 74 km/h (46 mph), but the precise figures are military secrets.

Sailing vessel
During the 19th century clippers could average 36.63 km/h (22.76 mph). The modern sailing yacht record is held by Simon McKeon and Tim Daddo of Australia. On 26 October 1993 they sailed their *Yellow Pages Endeavour* at 86.21 km/h (53.57 mph).

Car ferry
The Spanish-built Australian catamaran *Luciano Federico L* can carry 52 cars and 450 passengers at a top speed of 107 km/h (66.5 mph).

Hovercraft
On 25 January 1980 a US Navy Bell SES-1008 experimental vehicle achieved a speed of 170 km/h (105.6 mph).

Hydroplane
These super-fast racing motor boats are capable of great speeds: Dave Villwock set a record average speed of 343.5 km/h (213.4 mph) in *Miss Budweiser* at Oroville, California, USA, on 13 March 2004.

Ocean liners
Steam ships began carrying passengers across the Atlantic between Europe and the USA in 1838. In the early years, the journey (about 4,828 km [3,000 miles]) could take 18 days or longer. Shipping companies competed with each other and the fastest ship carried a blue flag, or Blue Riband. There were separate Blue Ribands for westbound and eastbound crossings, and after 1934 an award, the Hales Trophy, was presented to the ship with the fastest average speed. In 1952 the newly launched liner *SS United States* won both the westbound and eastbound Blue Riband with a time of 3 days 10 hours 40 minutes, and the Hales Trophy with an average speed of 65.9 km/h (40.95 mph). *Cat-Link V*, a Danish catamaran ferry, is the current Blue Riband and Hales Trophy holder. In 1998, it set a new transatlantic record of just 2 days, 20 hours and 9 minutes, and an average speed of 76.5 km/h (47.5 mph).

Warships

Aircraft carrier A warship from which aircraft can take off and land.

Cruiser A medium-sized, fast, long-range warship.

Battleship A large armoured warship.

Destroyer A small fast warship.

Frigate A warship that escorted cargo convoys to protect them from attack by submarines, introduced during World War II.

Minesweeper A naval ship designed to find and destroy mines.

Submarine Military submarines can travel long distances under water to avoid detection, and can fire torpedoes and missiles. Special civilian submarines are used for undersea research.

See also
The World's Oceans: pages 40–41

Biggest ships

All the ships listed here held the record as the biggest ship in the world when they were launched. The first, the *Great Western*, was less than ⅕ the length and ¹⁄₁₂₀ the tonnage of the current record holder *Liberty of the Seas*, which is 339 m (1,112 ft) long. The *Great Eastern* measured 211 m (692 ft) and the *Titanic* was 269 m (882 ft) long.

Some of these ships are still sailing, but many have been scrapped. The *Titanic* and *Lusitania* sank with the loss of many lives.

Great Western (launched in1838) gross tonnage*: 1,340

President (1840) gross tonnage: 2,360

Great Britain (1845) gross tonnage: 3,448

Great Eastern (1858) gross tonnage: 18,914

Oceanic (1899) gross tonnage: 17,274

Baltic (1904) gross tonnage: 23,884

Lusitania (1907) gross tonnage: 31,550

Mauretania (1907) gross tonnage: 31,938

Titanic (1912) gross tonnage: 46,232

Bismarck/Majestic/Caledonia†, (1922) gross tonnage: 56,621

Normandie/Lafayette† (1935) gross tonnage: 79,301

Queen Elizabeth (1938) gross tonnage: 83,673

Voyager of the Seas (1999) gross tonnage: 137,276

Explorer of the Seas (2000) gross tonnage: 137,308

Navigator of the Seas (2002) gross tonnage: 138,279

Queen Mary 2 (2003) gross tonnage: 142,200

Liberty of the Seas (2007) gross tonnage: 160,000

Genesis class (2009) gross tonnage: 220,000

* Weights given are the weight of the ship when empty, without cargo, crew, supplies or passengers.

† Renamed

World's biggest ship

Built in Finland, *Liberty of the Seas* is 339 m (1,112 ft) long and carries 4,370 passengers and a crew of 1,360. Among its luxurious facilities are an ice-skating rink and a water park with a wave-generator that allows swimmers to surf.

Liberty of the Seas, launched in 2007

Famous ships

Some ships, such as the *Titanic*, are famous because they sank, but here are some famous ships that are celebrated for a variety of other reasons.

Niña, Pinta and Santa Maria
The three ships on Christopher Columbus's voyage of 1492 to America.

Mayflower
The ship that took the settlers known as the Pilgrim Fathers from Plymouth to America in 1620.

Endeavour
Captain James Cook's ship on his exploration of Australia and New Zealand in 1768–71.

Bounty
The crew of this British ship mutinied against Captain William Bligh in 1789.

Victory
Captain Horatio Nelson's flagship at the Battle of Trafalgar, 1805. It is now on display in Portsmouth.

Beagle
The research ship on which British scientist Charles Darwin visited the Galápagos Islands in 1835.

Cutty Sark
A tea clipper (a sailing ship designed to bring tea from China as fast as possible) launched in 1869. The ship is preserved in dry dock at Greenwich, London and was seriously damaged by fire in 2007.

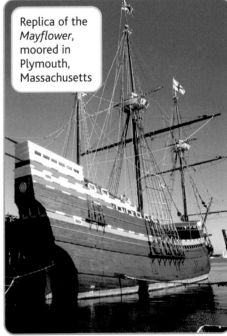

Replica of the *Mayflower*, moored in Plymouth, Massachusetts

Great Eastern
This ship was designed by Isambard Kingdom Brunel and launched in 1858. It laid the first transatlantic cable in 1866, but was scrapped in 1888.

Marie Celeste
A US ship found abandoned in the Atlantic in 1872. The fate of its crew remains a mystery.

Kon-Tiki
A balsawood raft on which Norwegian anthropologist Thor Heyerdahl sailed from South America across the Pacific to Polynesia in 1947. He made the voyage to prove his theory that Polynesian people came from South America.

Famous cars

● Mercedes

The German luxury car, which has been made since 1901, took its name from Mercédès, the daughter of Daimler car company director Emil Jellinek.

● Rolls-Royce

British car enthusiasts Henry Royce and Charles Rolls joined forces to form Rolls-Royce in 1906 and set new standards for a luxury vehicle. The company's engines are also used in many of the world's aircraft.

● Model T Ford

The first Model T Ford, nicknamed the Tin Lizzie, was made in the USA in 1908 by the Ford Motor Company, which was founded in 1903 by Henry Ford. By 1927, when production finished, a total of 16,536,075 had been built. At one point, more than half the new cars in the world were Model Ts.

● Aston Martin

This luxury sports car has been made in the UK since the 1920s. It became one of the most featured and gadget-laden cars in the James Bond films.

● Bugatti Royale

Only six Bugatti Royales (1926) were ever made. The Royale was designed by Italian Ettore Bugatti and was one of the largest vehicles of all time. It was 6.7 m (22 ft) long with a 12.7 litre (777 in^3) engine originally designed for aircraft. In 1980 one of these rare vehicles set a new world record price when it was sold for $15 million (£9.1 million).

● Volkswagen Beetle

The Volkswagen Beetle was designed by Ferdinand Porsche and first manufactured

James Bond's Aston Martin

Top vehicle-owning countries

There are so many cars today that there is one car for every 10.2 people in the world. In the USA there are 2.2 people per car and in the UK 2.1, but in some countries the ratio is amazingly high. In Myanmar, for example, there are 6,203 people for every car!

Germany
Cars 46,090,303
Commercial vehicles 3,133,197

Italy
Cars 34,667,485
Commercial vehicles 4,422,269

France
Cars 29,990,000
Commercial vehicles 6,139,000

UK
Cars 30,651,700
Commercial vehicles 3,942,700

Japan
Cars 57,090,789
Commercial vehicles 16,733,871

USA
Cars 132,908,828
Commercial vehicles 104,788,269

World total
Cars 617,020,169
Commercial vehicles 245,108,745

Rest of the world
Cars 285,621,064
Commercial vehicles 105,949,439

Car timeline   1800s   1900s

1883 First experimental petrol-driven car (France)

1886 Karl Benz and Gottlieb Daimler (Germany) build first cars

1892 First US car built by Charles and Frank Duryea

1893 Rudolf Diesel patents engine

1894 First cars in UK

1895 First car race, Paris-Bordeaux-Paris, France, 1,178 km (732 miles)

1895 First car show in UK

1895 Michelin (France) makes first pneumatic car tyres

1896 First car theft (France)

1896 First motoring death (UK)

1897 First woman driver in UK, Minnie Palmer

1898 First woman driver in USA, Genevra Mudge

1899 Jacob German arrested for speeding in New York (12 mph/ 19.3 km/h)

1900 8,000 vehicles on the road in USA

1903 First driving licences issued, Paris, France

1903 Registration plates in UK

1903 National speed limit in UK 20 mph (32 km/h)

1903 30,204 vehicles made in France, 11,235 USA, 9,437 UK

1904 28,842 vehicles in UK

1907 First Rolls-Royce made, the Silver Ghost (UK)

1908 First Model T Ford made (USA)

1909 143,000 vehicles in UK

1910 468,500 vehicles in USA

1912 First petrol station built (USA)

1915 Headlamp dipping and stoplights introduced (USA)

1919 Mechanical windscreen wipers developed (USA)

1921 First autobahn (high speed road or motorway) built in Germany in Germany in 1937. When production ended in 2003 a total of 21,529,464 Beetles had been made, the last of them in Brazil and Mexico. A new version of the Beetle was introduced in 1998.

● **MINI**
The MINI was launched in the UK in August 1959, when it cost just under £500 ($1,400). It was designed by Alec Issigonis (1906–88). More than 5.3 million MINIs had been made by 2000. The new MINI was launched in 2001. By 2007 more than 1 million had been sold.

Fastest car

ThrustSSC is the most powerful car ever built. It uses two Rolls-Royce engines from Phantom fighter aircraft. In 1997, driven by Royal Air Force fighter pilot Andy Green, *Thrust* set a new land speed record of 1,227.986 km/h (763.035 mph). It was also the first road vehicle to break the sound barrier.

See also
ThrustSSC: page 15

Amazing vehicles

GM Terex
Titan load

Average truck load ➜

● **Longest limos**
The current record-holder, built by Jay Ohrberg of California, measures 30.5 m (100 ft) and has 26 wheels. It is so long that it has to be hinged in the middle to enable it to turn corners.

● **Biggest bus**
The articulated Super City Train Buses used in the Democratic Republic of Congo are 32.2 m (105.7 ft) long. They can carry 110 seated passengers and 140 standing in the first part, and 60 seated and 40 standing in the second, a total of 350 people.

● **Fastest electric car**
The *White Lightning Electric Streamliner* holds the official record for the fastest electric vehicle.

In 1999, driven by Patrick Rummerfield (USA), it went at a speed of 395.821 km/h (245.952 mph). It is powered by two 200 horse-power motors and a 420 volt battery pack.

Giant dumper truck tyre

Normal car tyre

● **Biggest tyres**
The largest road vehicle tyres are 3.82 m (12.5 ft) in diameter. They are made by the Bridgestone Corporation, Tokyo, Japan, for giant dumper trucks. Normal car tyres are 60 cm (23.6 in) in diameter.

Driving on the left

People in most countries drive on the right. But in more than 70 countries and territories they drive on the left. These include the UK, Japan, Australia, South Africa, Thailand, Ireland, Malaysia, Indonesia, India, New Zealand and Pakistan. The tradition of keeping to the left dates back to the time when most road users were on horseback. One explanation is that as most people are right-handed, riding on the left allowed them to use a sword to defend themselves against approaching riders.

● **Biggest dumper trucks**
The General Motors Terex Titan 33-19 mine truck, first made in 1974, can carry 317.5 tonnes. An average truck carries about 5 tonnes.

● **Biggest fire engines**
Fire trucks made by the Oshkosh Truck Corporation of Wisconsin, USA for airports have eight wheels, 860-horsepower engines and weigh 60 tonnes.

2000s

1930 First traffic light installed in New York
1933 First drive-in cinema built (USA)
1935 First parking meters installed in Oklahoma City, USA
1935 Driving tests introduced in UK
1939 3,148,000 vehicles in UK
1940 32,453,200 vehicles in USA
1955 Highway Code issued in UK

1958 First motorway built in UK (Preston by-pass)
1960 8,512,000 vehicles in UK
1960 73,868,600 vehicles in USA
1962 200 millionth car produced in USA
1969 Czechoslovakia becomes first country to make seat belts compulsory
1970 Unleaded fuel introduced in USA

1978 Bosch (Germany) patents first satellite navigation
1980 155,796,000 vehicles in USA
1980 19,199,000 vehicles in UK
1983 Seat belts made compulsory in UK
1985 Seat belts made compulsory in New York

2005 The Bugatti Veyron 16.4 is the fastest, most powerful and most expensive car ever built
2007 Tesla Roadster electric cars capable of 400 km (250 miles) on a single charge
2008 The Tata Nano, the world's cheapest car (£1,277/$2,500) is launched in India

Types of train

Not all trains are the same: these are just some of the variations around the world.

Rubber-tyred metro

These electric trains run along a tracked roadway. They are quiet, can accelerate quickly and tackle slopes. They first ran in Paris in the 1950s and have been introduced in other French cities and Santiago, Chile, Mexico City, and Montreal, Canada.

Funicular

Funiculars (from the Latin *funiculus*, a thin rope) are designed to go up and down steep hills or mountains. Cars are drawn up by cables and descend by gravity. Funiculars are used in mountain and other resorts, and in hilly parts of cities, such as Montmartre in Paris, and Montjuic in Barcelona. The steepest passenger funicular is the Katoomba Scenic Railway in New South Wales, Australia.

Cog railway

Cog or rack-and-pinion railways are used in mountains. The train has a rotating cog wheel that meshes with a rack rail, so the train can climb steep slopes. Mount Pilatus in Switzerland, has the world's steepest. The Snowdon Mountain Railway in Wales is the only one of this type in the UK.

Maglev

The name Maglev comes from the words magnetic and levitation. These trains do not run on a track, but float above it by means of magnetic repulsion. They can travel very smoothly at high speeds (up to 650 km/h (400 mph) – and use little energy. A new 160 km (99.4 miles) Maglev line is being built between Shanghai and Hangzhou, China – the first inter-city Maglev service.

Monorail

A monorail train runs on a single rail, instead of on a track or two rails. It is either suspended from the rail or straddles it. The Tokyo Monorail in Japan carries 100 million passengers a year. There are also monorails in Malaysia, Australia and the USA.

A Maglev train in Germany

One and only

The only time a train has been powered by fish was during a coal shortage in Turkestan in 1919. Dried fish, caught in the Aral Sea, were used as fuel. A total of almost 9,000 tonnes were used to stoke the train's boilers.

The Ghan on its first journey across Australia

Famous trains

Orient Express

The Orient Express began trips from Paris, France, to Bulgaria on 5 October 1883 and from 1889 went as far as Constantinople (now Istanbul), Turkey. It was the first trans-European train and travelled a total of 2,736 km (1,700 miles) across six countries. It stopped running in 1977, but was re-launched five years later.

20th Century Limited

The luxurious 20th Century Limited ran between New York and Chicago from 1902 to 1967.

Trans-Siberian Express

The Trans-Siberian Express travels 9,297 km (5,777 miles) between Moscow and Vladivostok. The line opened in 1914 and is the world's longest continuous rail line.

Flying Scotsman

The Flying Scotsman provided a luxurious non-stop journey from King's Cross, London to Edinburgh, Scotland. It ran for 40 years, from 1923 until 1963.

Golden Arrow

From 1929 to 1971, the Golden Arrow ran from Victoria, London to Dover on the south coast of England. From there passengers could sail across the Channel and then take the French Flèche d'Or to Paris.

Blue Train

This is one of the world's most luxurious trains and it has operated between Cape Town and Tshwane (Pretoria), South Africa since 1939. The train, carriages and decor are mainly blue – hence the name.

Underground railways

An underground railway is an urban train line that runs mostly, or completely, underground. The world's first underground system was the London Metropolitan Line, opened between Bishop's Road, Paddington, and Farringdon Street, in 1863.

Steam trains were used on this and London's Circle Line, completed in 1884. They had a device to absorb smoke so that passengers were not suffocated in their gas-lit carriages. During the 1890s, several inventions made deep tunnelling, electric motors, electric lights and lifts or escalators possible. After that, underground railways in London and other countries were electrified.

First underground railways

London, UK opened 10 January 1863
Budapest, Hungary opened 2 May 1896
Glasgow, UK opened 14 December 1896
Boston, USA opened 1 September 1897
Paris, France opened 19 July 1900

Longest underground rail networks

City (stations)	Total track length km (miles)
London, UK (268)	408 (254)
New York, USA (468)	368 (229)
Moscow, Russia (176)	293 (182)
Tokyo, Japan (282)	292 (182)
Seoul, South Korea (266)	287 (179)
Madrid, Spain (316)	282 (175)
Paris, France (369)	213 (132)

Busiest underground systems
Annual passengers
Tokyo 2,819,000,000
Moscow 2,603,000,000
Seoul 1,465,000,000
New York 1,449,000,000
Mexico City 1,442,000,000
Paris 1,336,000,000
London 976,000,000

Longest rail networks

These countries all have more than 10,000 km (6,214 miles) of railway. At the other end of the scale, Puerto Rico, Saint Christopher and Nevis, Paraguay and Nicaragua have less than 100 km (62 miles). Some countries have none at all.

USA: 226,612 km (140,810 miles)
Russia: 87,157 km (54,157 miles)
China: 75,438 km (46,875 miles)
India: 63,221 km (39,284 miles)
Germany: 48,215 km (29,959 miles)
Canada: 48,068 km (29,868 miles)

Australia: 38,550 km (23,954 miles)
Argentina: 31,902 km (19,823 miles)
France: 29,370 km (18,250 miles)
Brazil: 29,295 km (18,203 miles)
Japan: 23,474 km (14,586 miles)
Poland: 23,072 km (14,336 miles)

Ukraine: 22,473 km (13,964 miles)
South Africa: 20,872 km (12,969 miles)
Italy: 19,460 km (12,092 miles)
Mexico: 17,665 km (10,977 miles)
UK: 16,567 km (10,294 miles)
Spain: 14,974 km (9,304 miles)

Kazakhstan: 13,700 km (8,513 miles)
Sweden: 11,528 km (7,163 miles)
Romania: 11,385 km (7,074 miles)
World total: 1,370,782 km (851,764 miles)

Bullet Train
Japanese bullet trains (shinkansen) are the world's fastest scheduled rail services. They were introduced in 1964 to coincide with the Tokyo Olympic Games.

TGV
The French TGV (Train à Grande Vitesse, or high speed train) was launched in 1981 and is an electric train service between Paris and Lyon. A specially modified TGV, the Atlantique, set a world speed record of 515.3 km/h (320.2 mph) on 18 May 1990.

Eurostar
The Eurostar service was launched on 14 November 1994 to carry passengers between London, Paris and Brussels through the Channel Tunnel. It can reach speeds of 300 km/h (186 mph). In its first ten years it carried a total of 59 million passengers.

Ghan
The Ghan is the first rail service from Adelaide to Darwin on the north–south route across Australia. It was named after the camel trains that were once the only way to cross the desert. The first train ran in 2004. It had 43 carriages, measured more than 1 km (3,280 ft) in length, and carried 330 passengers.

 www.nrm.org.uk   search

Aviation pioneers

John Alcock
(UK, 1892–1919) and
Arthur Whitten Brown
(UK, 1886–1948)
On 14–15 June 1919,
they completed the first
ever non-stop flight
across the Atlantic
from Newfoundland
to Ireland.

Louis Blériot
(France, 1872–1936)
On 25 July 1909 Blériot
became the first person
to fly across the English
Channel.

Samuel F. Cody
(USA, c. 1861–1913)
The first person to
fly in England,
16 October 1908.

Glenn Curtiss
(USA, 1878–1930)
Rival to the Wright
Brothers, Curtiss made
the first public flight in
the USA on 4 July 1908.
He set up the first
aeroplane manufacturing
company in the USA.

Amelia Earhart
(USA, 1898–1937)
The first woman to fly
the Atlantic. She went on
to establish many flying

records but disappeared
during an attempt to fly
round the world.

Amy Johnson (UK,
1903–41)
She made the first solo
flight from England to
Australia in 1930.

Charles Lindbergh
(USA, 1902–74)
The first pilot to fly solo
across the Atlantic, from
New York to Paris,
20–21 May 1927, in
The Spirit of St Louis.

Harriet Quimby
(USA, 1875–1912)
America's first female
pilot. On 16 April 1912
she was the first woman
to fly the English
Channel – but on the
day the sinking of the
Titanic was reported,
so her triumph was
barely noticed.

Wilbur Wright (USA,
1867–1912) and
Orville Wright (USA,
1871–1948)
The Wright brothers, two
bicycle mechanics from
Dayton, Ohio, made the
first ever powered flights
on 17 December 1903.

Concorde

Concorde fact file

Concorde, the only
passenger aircraft ever
to fly faster than the speed of
sound, was first named in a
speech by General de Gaulle on
13 January 1963. The Anglo-French
project began the following year.

● The first prototype Concorde was shown at the Toulouse Air Show
on 11 December 1967.

● The first French flight took place on 2 March 1969.

● The first British flight took place on 9 April 1969.

● The first landing at London Heathrow was on 13 September 1970.

● The first Concorde landing in the USA was at Dallas-Fort Worth on
20 September 1973.

● The only Concorde crash was near Paris, 25 July 2000, when 109 passengers
and crew and four people on the ground died.

● Concorde's last flight took place on 24 October 2004. All surviving BA and
Air France Concordes are on public display in museums and airports in the
USA, UK, France, Germany and Barbados.

The Wright brothers demonstrate their
Wright Model A plane

The Wright brothers

Orville Wright was the first person to fly a
powered aircraft. He also became the first
to fly a plane for more than one hour, on
9 September 1908 at Fort Meyer, Virginia, USA.
His brother Wilbur became the first to fly for
more than two hours, on 31 December 1908
at Auvours, France. On 20 May 1909
French pilot Paul Tissandier became
the first person other than the
Wrights to fly for more
than an hour.

See also
Steve Fossett: page 153
Amelia Earhart: page 153

Breaking the sound barrier

Charles "Chuck" Yeager became the first person to break the sound barrier on 14 October 1947. His Bell X-1 rocket plane was dropped from a carrier aircraft above Muroc Dry Lake, California. At 12,800 m (42,000 ft) he reached a speed of 1,078 km/h (670 mph). He did not break the air speed record because only aircraft that take off and land under their own power are eligible. The speed of sound is not fixed and varies according to height and air conditions. In dry air at sea level the speed of sound is 1,229 km/h (763.67 mph), but at high altitudes, where air density is less, it is lower.

One and only

The only flight of the Hercules H-4 aircraft, known as the "Spruce Goose", took place on 2 November 1947. It was the largest flying boat ever built. It had the greatest wingspan (97.54 m/320 ft) of any aircraft and eight engines. Millionaire aviator Howard Hughes built and flew it himself, just 20 m (65.6 ft) above the water off Long Beach, California, USA. It travelled only 1.6 km (1 mile). The flight is recreated in the film *The Aviator* (2004).

🔍 www.flyingmachines.org **search**

First manned balloon flights

The first balloons worked on the principle that when air is heated, it rises. They were filled with hot air by burning things under them, such as paper, straw and wool – and even old shoes and rotten meat!

The balloons often caught fire and once the air cooled, they quickly came down. Soon after the first hot-air flights, people realized that the gas hydrogen could be used instead. Hydrogen is the lightest of all elements – almost 15 times lighter than air. Gas balloons can also be filled with helium, which is not as light as hydrogen but does not catch fire so easily. Most balloons today use hot air made by burning propane gas.

The first hot-air balloon flight
The Montgolfier brothers, Joseph and Etienne, tested their first unmanned hot-air balloon on 5 June 1783. On 21 November 1783, François Laurent, Marquis d'Arlandes and Jean-François Pilâtre de Rozier took off from the Bois de Boulogne, Paris, in a Montgolfier hot-air balloon. They travelled about 9 km (5.6 miles) in 23 minutes.

First hydrogen balloon flight
On 1 December 1783, Jacques Alexandre César Charles and Nicholas-Louis Robert made the first flight in a hydrogen balloon. They took off from the Tuileries, Paris, watched by a crowd of 400,000, and travelled 43 km (27 miles) north to Nesle in about two hours. Charles then took off again alone, so was the first ever solo pilot.

First British flight
On 27 August 1784 James Tytler, a doctor and newspaper editor, took off in a home-made balloon from Comely Gardens, Edinburgh. He reached an altitude of 107 m (350 ft) in a 0.8 km (0.5 miles) hop.

First Channel crossing
On 7 January 1785 Jean-Pierre Blanchard made the first Channel crossing in a balloon with Dr John Jeffries (the first American to fly). They also carried the first airmail letter. As they lost height, they had to reduce weight, so they threw almost everything overboard – including their clothes!

First flight in the USA
On 9 January 1793 in Philadelphia, Blanchard made the first balloon flight in America. He took a small black dog with him as a passenger.

First hot-air balloon flight

The flight was watched by George Washington, who gave Blanchard a passport permitting his flight, which was the first pilot's licence and America's first airmail document.

First non-stop solo flight
US adventurer Steve Fossett made the first non-stop solo and fastest round-the-world balloon flight, 19 June to 3 July 2002.

Shipwrecks

Shipping disasters as a result of collisions, storms, fires, explosions or military action are among the most famous of human tragedies. Some wrecks were carrying treasure that has since been recovered.

The *Mary Rose*, which sank in 1545

Mary Rose
This Tudor galleon sank in 1545 as Henry VIII watched from the shore. She was found in 1968, raised in 1982, and is exhibited in Portsmouth, UK.

Spanish Armada
Between August and October 1588 military action and storms combined to destroy the Spanish fleet off the British coast. About half the 130 ships that set out were wrecked, killing about 4,000 men.

St George, Defence and Hero
On 4 December 1811 these three British warships were stranded off the Jutland coast. More than 2,000 people died.

Tek Sing
This Chinese junk carrying 2,000 passengers and 350,000 pieces of porcelain sank in 1822. It was found in 1999 and its treasures sold for high prices.

Sultana
On 27 April 1865, the *Sultana*, a steamboat on the Mississippi River near Memphis, USA, was destroyed by a boiler explosion. This was the USA's worst ever marine accident and a total of 1,547 people died.

Princess Alice
On 3 September 1878 the pleasure steamer *Princess Alice* was taking people down the Thames in London. She collided with the *Bywell Castle* and 786 people died.

Titanic
On the night of 14 April 1912, the "unsinkable" *Titanic* struck an iceberg on its maiden voyage and sank the next day, killing 1,517. The wreck was discovered and explored by Robert Ballard in 1986.

Lusitania
The British liner was torpedoed off the Irish coast by a German U-boat on 7 May 1915, with the loss of 1,198 lives.

Wilhelm Gustloff
The German liner, laden with refugees, was torpedoed off Gdansk, Poland, on 30 January 1945 by a Soviet submarine, S-13. Between 5,348 and 7,800 people died, making this the worst ever marine disaster.

Dona Paz
The *Donna Paz* sank off the Philippines on 20 December 1987, killing up to 3,000 people. This was the world's worst passenger ferry disaster.

Kursk
This Russian nuclear submarine sank in the Barents Sea on 12 August 2000, with the loss of all 118 crew.

Rail disasters

Rail travel is one of the safest ways of journeying from place to place, taking into account the large numbers of passengers carried and distances travelled. But there have been accidents.

World's worst
At Telwatta, Sri Lanka, on 26 December, 2004, the *Queen of the Sea* train was struck by the Indian Ocean tsunami. The exact number killed is unknown, but is estimated to be between 1,700 and 2,000.

UK
On 22 May 1915 a troop train crashed head-on into another at Quintinshill near Gretna Green, Scotland. The wreckage was then struck by an express. The crashes and fire that followed left 227 dead and 246 injured.

USA
Two USA accidents resulted in 101 deaths. On 10 August 1887 a bridge at Chatsworth, Illinois caught fire and collapsed as a train was passing over. 101 people were killed and as many as 372 were injured. The second accident happened on 9 July 1918 at Nashville, Tennessee, when two trains collided head-on.

Underground
On 28 October 1995, at Baku, Azerbaijan, an underground train caught fire one evening killing more than 300 people.

British underground
Britain's worst tube disaster was on 8 March 1943 at Bethnal Green, London. About 173 people who were trying to enter the station during an air raid were killed in the crush.

American underground
America's worst subway accident was on 1 November 1918 at Brooklyn, New York. A train was derailed in the Malbone Street tunnel, leaving 97 dead.

Road disasters

Many people are killed and injured on the roads – more than 40,000 a year in the USA – but accidents involving more than a few drivers or pedestrians are rare.

Worst road disaster On 3 November 1982 a petrol tanker collided with a Soviet army truck and exploded in the 2.7 km (1.7 miles) Salang Tunnel in Afghanistan. At least 2,000, and perhaps as many as 3,000, people died as a result of the explosion, fire and fumes.

US road disaster The worst US road disaster took place on 15 December 1967. The Silver Bridge across the Ohio River from Kanauga, Ohio, to Point Pleasant, West Virginia, collapsed during heavy pre-Christmas rush hour traffic. About 60 vehicles plunged into the river and 46 people died.

British road accident On 27 May 1975 a coach crashed near Grassington, North Yorkshire, killing 33.

The Tay Bridge disaster

Britain's worst rail disaster during the 19th century took place on 28 December 1879. The Tay Bridge in Scotland collapsed as a train crossed, killing all 75 passengers and the crew of five.

The train itself was later recovered from the river. The bridge – the longest in the world at that time – had only been opened on 31 May the previous year. Queen Victoria had crossed it in a train soon afterwards.

Two hijacked planes crash into the World Trade Center, New York

Air disasters

Worst ever
Two terrorist attacks on the twin towers of the World Trade Center, New York, on 11 September 2001, killed everybody on both hijacked planes (92 on one and 65 on the other). More than 2,000 people also died in the buildings.

On the ground
On 27 March 1977, two Boeing 747s collided on the runway of Los Rodeos airport in Tenerife in the Canary Islands. The aircraft were carrying 614 passengers and 30 crew between them. A total of 61 people managed to escape.

Single-aircraft disaster
On 12 August 1985 a JAL Boeing 747 on an internal flight from Tokyo to Osaka crashed, killing 520.

Mid-air collision
At Charkhi Dadri, India, on 12 November 1996, a Saudi Airways Boeing 747 collided with a Kazakh Airlines Ilyushin IL-76 cargo aircraft. A total of 349 people died.

The Hindenburg disaster

The *Hindenburg* was the world's biggest airship at 245 m (804 ft) long. The airship made several successful transatlantic crossings, then flew from Frankfurt, Germany, to Lakehurst, New Jersey, USA. She arrived on 6 May 1937 after a three-day trip. As the airship was moored, she caught fire and turned into an inferno.

See also
Hydrogen: page 79

TOURISM

History of tourism

People have been travelling from place to place since ancient times. Nomadic people moved about to graze their livestock. Later people travelled to trade, or to seek their fortunes in gold rushes, and millions emigrated to other countries to escape persecution or to seek better lives.

Apart from a few historical examples, tourism – travelling for pleasure – is a relatively modern idea. Today, people spend nearly $500 billion a year on tourism.

Taking the waters
The Romans placed great value on bathing. They settled in many places with natural springs and developed cities as spas (the name comes from Spa in Belgium). In the 18th century, it became fashionable to visit these spas to "take the waters" – drinking and bathing as cures for various illnesses. Bath in England is a well-known Roman spa.

The Roman baths in Bath, England

Package tours
On 5 July 1841, British travel pioneer Thomas Cook took 570 members of the Temperance Society (an organization opposed to drinking alcohol) on the newly opened railway from Leicester to Loughborough. This was the first package tour, and the beginning of what was to become the world's best-known travel company. When the Paris Exhibition opened in 1851, Cook took "excursionists" abroad for the first time. By the time Thomas Cook died in 1892, he had made travel possible for the masses.

Exhibitions
During the 19th and 20th centuries, major exhibitions in Europe and the USA brought millions of people to the big cities of the world. Many had never travelled before. The Great Exhibition in London in 1851 had more than 6 million visitors. A century later, the 1951 Festival of Britain attracted 8.5 million. The Paris Exposition of 1889, for which the Eiffel Tower was built, had 28 million visitors, and more than 51 million visited the New York World's Fair of 1964–65.

Sleeping Beauty's Castle, Disneyland, Paris

Festivals
The world's major arts and music festivals receive millions of visitors. The annual Texas State Fair in the USA attracts as many as 3 million, and many other North American fairs receive 1 million or more. Festivals such as the carnival held in Rio De Janeiro, Brazil, and Mardi Gras in New Orleans, USA, are attended by large crowds.

Sport tourism
Winter sports such as skiing, water sports and adventure sports such as white-water rafting have become very popular. When the Olympic Games is held, the host country can expect a huge boost to its tourist industry.

Amusement parks
The world's most-visited amusement park is Disney World, Florida, USA, which attracts 16.64 million visitors a year. The total number of visitors at all Disney attractions around the world is 112.5 million a year. Britain's leading amusement park is Blackpool Pleasure Beach, with almost 6 million visitors a year.

Space tourism
The first fare-paying space tourist was American millionaire Denis Tito. In 2001 he paid $20 million to spend a week on the *International Space Station*. Anglo-South African Mark Shuttleworth paid a similar amount for a trip in 2002. Several companies, such as Virgin Galactic, are planning to take passengers to a height of about 100 km (62 miles) in 2009.

See also
Countries of the World: pages 116-117

Serengeti National Park, Tanzania

Serengeti National Park

This vast park in Tanzania was founded in 1951 and covers 14,763 sq km (5,700 sq miles). Wildebeest, gazelle and zebra graze here, along with lions, elephants, giraffe and other animals. It is one of Africa's most popular tourist attractions.

National parks

National parks are established by governments to preserve areas of land and the plants and animals they contain. Yellowstone National Park in the USA, set up in 1872, was the first. There are now more than 1,200 national parks in 100 or more countries. These are a few examples of the different types.

Everglades (founded 1934; 5,929 sq km/ 2,289 sq miles) The Everglades, USA is the only subtropical park in North America. Many different types of creatures live in its swamps, including alligators.

Great Barrier Reef (founded 1979; 343,800 sq km/ 132,742 sq miles) Australia's Great Barrier Reef, off the coast of Queensland, is the world's largest coral reef system, supporting many rare marine animals and plants.

Galápagos Islands (founded 1986; 6,937 sq km/ 2,678 sq miles) These volcanic islands off the coast of Ecuador are home to birds, seals and unique creatures including giant turtles and marine iguanas.

Lake District (founded 1951; 2,292 sq km/ 885 sq miles) The largest and most visited of Britain's national parks. The parks receive a total of 100 million visitors a year.

Wood Buffalo (founded 1922; 44,807 sq km/ 17,300 sq miles) This area of Canada contains forests, plains and many lakes. It has the largest herd of wild buffalo anywhere on Earth as well as many rare species such as the whooping crane.

Wrangell-St Elias (founded 1980; 33,820 sq km/ 13,057 sq miles) This national park in Alaska is the largest in the USA. It contains the most glaciers and peaks higher than 4,880 m (16,010 ft) in North America, as well as many wild animals, including bears, wolves and moose.

Yellowstone (founded 1872; 8,991 sq km/ 3,471 sq miles) This area of the Rocky Mountains in the USA is famed for its hot springs and geysers. Most famous is the Old Faithful geyser which sprays steam and water up to 56 m (184 ft) high.

Xingu (founded 1961; 22,000 sq km/ 8,494 sq miles) This large area of Brazilian rainforest is teeming with tropical wildlife. It is also inhabited by tribes of indigenous peoples who have little contact with outsiders.

Top tourist countries

In 2005, one in every eight people in the world travelled as tourists to another country – a total of 806 million. Of these, almost half visited the top ten destinations below. By the year 2020 the number of international tourists is likely to more than double to 1.5 billion.

Country	Visitors	% of world total
1 France	79,100,000	9.3
2 Spain	58,500,000	6.9
3 USA	51,100,000	6.0
4 China	49,600,000	5.9
5 Italy	41,100,000	4.9
6 UK	30,700,000	3.6
7 Germany	23,600,000	2.8
8 Mexico	21,400,000	2.5
9 Austria	20,300,000	2.4
10 Russia	20,200,000	2.4
Top 10 total	395,600,000	100.0

Language & Literature

Shaken not stirred

2008 was the centenary of the birth of Ian Fleming, creator of James Bond. Fleming's bestselling novels are still in print and James Bond is still the most famous fictional spy in the world. The latest film, *Quantum of Solace*, starred Daniel Craig in his second outing as Bond.

Most spoken languages

Chinese (Mandarin)
Approximately 885,000,000 speakers. Chinese has many dialects, but about two-thirds of the people speak Mandarin. Wu is the next most common dialect, with approximately 77 million speakers. At least 30 million people around the world are learning Mandarin Chinese because China is becoming an important economic power.

Spanish
Approximately 332,000,000 speakers. Spanish is one of the most widely used of all languages. It is spoken not only in Spain but also in South America, the west coast of Africa and the USA.

English
Approximately 322,000,000 speakers. Far fewer people have English as their main language than Chinese, but millions more know at least some English and it is spoken in every corner of the globe. The USA dominates cinema, television, pop music, technology (Internet) and business and this has increased the importance of the English language. At least 800 million people use the Internet and about 35 per cent of them communicate in English. There are probably more than one billion people worldwide learning English.

Arabic
Approximately 246,000,000 speakers. Arabic is the official language of 17 countries and it is also the language of the Muslim religion. As a result, many millions of Muslims in other countries have some knowledge of the language.

Hindustani
Approximately 182,000,000 speakers. Hindustani includes Hindi and Urdu, which are almost the same language. Hindustani is the official language of Pakistan, where it is written in modified Arabic script and called Urdu. It is also the official language of India, but there it is written in the Devanagari script and called Hindi.

Portuguese
Approximately 177,500,000 speakers. Portuguese is spoken as a first language by the people of Portugal and also by many of the inhabitants of Brazil, Angola and other former colonies in Africa and elsewhere. These stretch from the Caribbean to Macau, China.

Languages spoken in most countries

English: 57 countries
French: 33 countries
Arabic: 23 countries
Spanish: 21 countries
Portuguese: 7 countries

Other major languages

Bengali
Approximate number of speakers: 189,000,000

Russian
Approximate number of speakers: 170,000,000

Japanese
Approximate number of speakers: 125,000,000

German (standard)
Approximate number of speakers: 95,450,000

Chinese (Wu)
Approximate number of speakers: 77,200,000

French
Approximate number of speakers: 77,000,000

A stop sign in English and Inuktituk (the language of the Inuit people)

Disappearing languages

There are about 6,912 living languages but 516 of these are considered almost extinct as they are spoken only by a few elderly people.

Alphabets

An alphabet is the basis of a system of writing, using letters or characters to represent sounds or words. These are some of the oldest and most important alphabets.

Greek
The Greek alphabet is the oldest surviving European alphabet. The early Greek alphabet was written from right to left, but by about 500 BC it was written from left to right. The Greeks introduced an upper case (capital letters) and a lower case (small letters).

Cyrillic
The Cyrillic alphabet was invented in the 9th century by two Greek missionaries, St Cyril and his brother St Methodius. It is used for Slavonic languages such as Russian, Bulgarian and Ukrainian. The Russian Cyrillic alphabet originally had 43 letters, but the number was reduced to 33 after the Russian Revolution of 1917. Like the Greek alphabet, Cyrillic also has upper case and lower case versions of the alphabet.

Hebrew
Hebrew is written horizontally from right to left. Also, sometimes the letters are used as numerals.

Arabic
Arabic evolved from Aramaic in the 4th century, and is written from left to right. It consists of 28 consonants. Vowels are shown by marks placed above or below the consonants but are not always used. Arabic letters are

Braille

Braille is a system of raised dots that allows blind people to read by touch. It was invented in the 19th century by a blind Frenchman named Louis Braille. The dots are embossed on to paper, either by hand or using a machine. They are read by moving the fingers across the top of the dots.

written differently depending upon where they appear in a word. The positions of characters are known as final (end), medial (middle), initial (beginning) and isolated (on its own).

Chinese and Japanese
These are logographic writing systems. This means that each symbol represents a word, or part of a word, instead of a sound. The Chinese system has 40–50,000 characters and the Japanese system has 18,000, but you need to know only about 2,000 and 1,850 respectively to get by in these languages. In 1966 the Chinese language changed quite dramatically, when books and newspapers were printed with the characters running horizontally from left to right rather than vertically from right to left. There is now a phonetic alphabet known as pin-yin, made up of 25 letters taken from the Roman alphabet.

Most Chinese characters are made up of eight basic strokes. These are all in the character for eternity. Words in a Chinese dictionary are in order of the number of strokes they contain. Chinese verbs and adjectives usually contain only one character or syllable, but nouns often consist of two characters or more. The examples below show how some compound words are made up.

木	林	森
tree	woodland (2 trees)	forest (3 trees)

Chinese symbol in the background means eternity

Writing in Braille

The reader uses both hands – the right works out the message while the left feels ahead for the beginning of the next line. A skilled Braille reader can understand up to 150 words a minute, which is about half the speed of a sighted person reading ordinary text.

Braille cell

The basic unit of Braille is called a cell. It is made up of six dots, which allows for 63 possible combinations to represent letters, numbers and punctuation marks.

Phonetic alphabet

You may have heard pilots and soldiers on television and in films using the phonetic alphabet in radio messages. The alphabet is used to spell out parts of a message that might be difficult to recognize in unclear radio transmissions. The version generally used was developed in the 1950s.

It is known as the NATO (North Atlantic Treaty Organization) Phonetic Alphabet and was designed to be understood and easily pronounced by all NATO members. They chose words that were used in lots of different languages and could not be confused with other common words or those used for another letter. Aircraft and ship crews also use the phonetic alphabet. For example, in the phonetic alphabet "over and out" becomes Oscar Victor Echo Romeo Alpha November Delta Oscar Uniform Tango.

A Alpha	**K** Kilo	**U** Uniform
B Bravo	**L** Lima	**V** Victor
C Charlie	**M** Mike	**W** Whiskey
D Delta	**N** November	**X** X-ray
E Echo	**O** Oscar	**Y** Yankee
F Foxtrot	**P** Papa	**Z** Zulu
G Golf	**Q** Quebec	
H Hotel	**R** Romeo	
I India	**S** Sierra	
J Juliet	**T** Tango	

See also

Brainchildren: young inventors: page 81

Hieroglyphics on the pillars of Habu Temple in Luxor, Egypt

Hieroglyphics

The simplest of all writing systems use pictures. These are called pictograms and look like the things they describe – just like many road signs and computer icons today.

Writing or carving pictograms is very slow and a lot of work, so people began to use simpler versions of images, such as hieroglyphics. Ancient Egyptian hieroglyphics were used on obelisks, wall paintings, tombs and papyri (documents on a type of paper made from reeds). They are symbols that represent an object, a sound or an idea. They are not a code: you cannot simply convert an Egyptian hieroglyph into a letter and read it as we read words in a book. People stopped using hieroglyphics in the 1st century AD. From then on, no one could understand them until 1822 when French scholar Jean François Champollion worked out how to translate the text of the Rosetta Stone in the British Museum.

Morse code

By using Morse code you can send a signal in a series of dots and dashes. The signal can be sent by sound or by flashing lights. There are five parts to the code: a dot, a dash, a short gap or pause (between letters), a medium gap (between words) and a long gap (between sentences).

Morse was created by and named after American artist and inventor Samuel Finley Breese Morse (1791–1872). He sent the first Morse code message from Washington DC, to Baltimore, Maryland, on 24 May 1844. It read "What hath God wrought!" An international version of Morse code became widely used to send telegrams by wire. Once people could send messages by radio transmissions they still used Morse code in situations such as warfare, when clear voice signals were not always possible.

A ·–	N –·	0 –––––
B –···	O –––	1 ·––––
C –·–·	P ·––·	2 ··–––
D –··	Q ––·–	3 ···––
E ·	R ·–·	4 ····–
F ··–·	S ···	5 ·····
G ––·	T –	6 –····
H ····	U ··–	7 ––···
I ··	V ···–	8 –––··
J ·–––	W ·––	9 ––––·
K –·–	X –··–	
L ·–··	Y –·––	
M ––	Z ––··	

Keeping in touch

From cave paintings onwards, there have always been ways of conveying information and ideas to other people. Pictographs are pictures or symbols that represent words. Egyptian hieroglyphics are pictographs. They eventually developed into alphabets so that languages could be written down.

People have also used signs and flags to communicate with each other and found ways of turning language into codes to send messages quickly. Until inventions such as Morse code, the fastest anyone could send information from place to place was at the speed of a horse. Now electronic messages can be sent around the world instantaneously via e-mail.

Semaphore

In 1791 French inventor Claude Chappe (1763–1805) and his brothers developed a way of signalling called semaphore. They used two wooden arms which could both be set to seven positions. This made a total of 196 combinations, each representing a letter or other symbol. The signalling device was mounted on a high building. It could be seen from a distance by an operator viewing it through a telescope from the next semaphore station. From this, a system of signalling using human arms and flags was developed and used at sea to send information from ship to ship. This system was kept up to the 1960s, even after radio was commonly used to send messages at sea.

A and 1   B and 2   C and 3   D and 4   E and 5

Q   R   S   T   U

Deaf children learning sign language with their teacher

Sign language

Everyone makes hand gestures to show certain feelings: you might rub your stomach to show you are hungry, raise your fist as a threat or hold your thumb up to show approval.

Sign languages for the deaf were first used in 17th-century Europe. In the 18th century, schools were set up where national systems of sign language developed. Signers use the different finger positions, a variety of hand movements — upward, downward and so on — and make the signs against certain parts of the body such as the neck, arm and wrist. Sign languages differ around the world — some spell words with one hand, while others use both.

Post firsts

First air letter England to France, by balloon, 1785

First mail carried by rail UK, 1830

First postage stamps in regular use Penny Blacks, UK, 1840

First Christmas cards invented by Henry Cole, UK, 1843

First US stamps 1847

First perforated stamps Penny Reds, UK, 1847

First letter boxes in UK (St Helier, Jersey), 1852

London postal districts first used 1858

First postcard sent USA, 1861

First picture postcard Switzerland, 1872

First commemorative stamps Germany, 1887

First Christmas stamp Canada, 1898

First airmail service India, 1911

First transatlantic airmail service 1939

First zip (Zone Improvement Plan) codes, USA, 1963

First self-adhesive stamps Sierra Leone, 1964

First Internet-based SmartStamp™, 2004 and print-your-own stamps launched in the UK, 2006

A Morse key for sending messages

Swedish Treskilling Yellow stamp

Most valuable stamp

The world's most valuable single stamp is a Swedish Treskilling Yellow. It was issued in 1855 and used in 1857 to mail a letter. The stamp was printed with the wrong colour ink (yellow instead of green), so it is unique. It was sold for £1.4 million ($2.3 million) at an auction in Switzerland in 1996, making it the world's most valuable object by weight. The stamp is now part of a private stamp collection in Denmark.

F and 6   G and 7   H and 8   I and 9   J and alphabetic   K and 0   L   M   N   O   P

V   W   X   Y   Z   break   error   numerals

The Semaphore alphabet

The main reading room at the Library of Congress in Washington DC

Largest libraries

A library is a collection of books and other printed material. The word library can also be used to describe the building where a collection of books is kept, as well as manuscripts, maps, periodicals and photographs. Below are the world's largest libraries, each containing over 10 million books.

The Library of Congress, Washington DC, USA was founded in 1800 and holds 32,124,001 books.

The British Library*, London, UK was founded in 1753 and holds 29,000,000 books.

Library of the Russian Academy of Sciences, St Petersburg, Russia was founded in 1714 and holds 20,500,000 books.

National Library of Canada, Ottawa, Canada was founded in 1953 and holds 19,500,000 books.

Deutsche Bibliothek, Frankfurt, Germany was founded in 1990 and holds 22,200,000 books.

The Russian State Library, Moscow, Russia was founded in 1862 and holds 17,000,000 books.

Harvard University Library, Cambridge, Massachusetts, USA was founded in 1636 and holds 15,826,570 books.

* Founded as part of the British Museum, 1753; became independent in 1973

Page from the Codex Hammer

Valuable books and manuscripts

● The Codex Hammer (previously called the Codex Leicester) was sold in New York, USA, in 1994 for $28,800,000 (£18,643,190). It was bought by Bill Gates, the billionaire founder of Microsoft. The Codex is one of Leonardo da Vinci's notebooks and includes many of his scientific drawings and diagrams.

● John James Audubon's *The Birds of America* (1827–38) was sold in New York, USA in 2000 for $8,000,000 (£5,187,731), making it the most expensive printed book. Its giant pages feature more than 400 hand-coloured engravings of birds.

● One of the first-ever printed books was Geoffrey Chaucer's *The Canterbury Tales* (c. 1477). A copy was sold in London in 1998 for £4,621,500 ($7,570,941).

● A "first folio" (early edition) of the works of William Shakespeare dating from 1623 was sold in London in 2001 for £4,156,947 ($6,166,000).

● A rare copy of the Gutenberg Bible, one of the first books ever printed, was sold in New York, USA, in 1987 for $5,390,000 (£3,264,688).

Types of book

Almanac
This is an annual calendar of dates and events. It originally contained astronomical facts and figures, but now includes useful statistics and other information. Almanac is sometimes spelled almanack.

Anthology
A collection of writings by one author or on a theme, such as an anthology of animal poems.

Atlas
A book of maps.

Autobiography
An account of a person's life written by himself or herself. Sometimes a "ghost" writer may help someone write an autobiography.

Bibliography
A list of books or sources on a particular subject.

Biography
A book about someone's life written by another person.

Chronology
A dictionary of dated events.

Dictionary
An alphabetical list of words and their meanings. There are also dictionaries on a single subject, for example *Dictionary of Art*.

Dictionary of quotations
A listing of interesting remarks or extracts from the writings of famous people.

Directory
An alphabetical list of names and addresses of people or organizations.

Encyclopedia
A book of articles on many subjects, arranged alphabetically. Encyclopedias are often published in many volumes or, today, on CD-ROM or on the Internet.

Gazetteer
A book that lists and describes places (countries, cities, etc).

Glossary
A list of words and phrases used in a particular subject area, for instance *A Glossary of Computer Terms*.

Language dictionary
A dictionary that gives translations of words and phrases to and from other languages, for example a *French-English/English-French Dictionary*.

Monograph
A book on a specialized subject, such as the work of a particular artist.

Novel
A work of fiction, usually involving imaginary people. A historical novel may be about real historical characters.

Novella
A short work of fiction.

Phrasebook
A book for travellers, with translations of words and phrases into and from a foreign language.

Pop-up book
A book, usually for children, made so that pictures stand up or move when the pages are opened.

Thesaurus
A book organized to show words with similar meanings.

Travel guide
A book of information about a particular country or area.

Who's who or biographical dictionary
Alphabetical summaries of the lives of famous people, living or dead, sometimes by their subjects (such as a *Dictionary of Scientists*).

Yearbook
An annual reference book with information about the events of the previous year. Yearbooks containing statistical information about a country are often called *Abstracts*.

Book firsts and records

First printed books
Books were printed in China in the 8th century using woodblocks, and in 14th-century China and Korea using movable type.

First books printed in English
In 1474 William Caxton printed the first book in English, *Recuyell of the Historyes of Troye*. It was printed in Bruges, Flanders. Chaucer's *Canterbury Tales* was probably the first book in English to be printed in England, in about 1477.

First books printed in America
Massachusetts Bay Colony: The Oath of a Free-Man (1638) and *An Almanack for the Year of Our Lord* (1639) are the first two books known to have been printed in the new American colonies.

Longest novel
A science-fiction novel by French writer Georges-Jean Arnaud, *La Compagne des Glaces* (1980–92), runs to 62 volumes and has about 11,000 pages.

Electronic books

Electronic books, or eBooks, have been around for over 20 years. The earliest ones could not store much information and had tiny screens that were difficult to read, such as an electronic Bible (1991) that could display four lines at a time. The latest electronic books are small, light, and hold huge volumes of data that can be downloaded from the Internet.

First sequel
Daniel Defoe wrote *The Farther Adventures of Robinson Crusoe* in 1719, after the success of *Robinson Crusoe* earlier that year.

First American novel
The Power of Sympathy (1789) was the first novel published in America. It was published anonymously, but is believed to have been written by William Hill Brown.

First detective story
Murders in the Rue Morgue, by American author Edgar Allan Poe, was first published in *Grahame's Magazine* in 1841.

Smallest book
This was produced by a German typographer Josua Reichertand called *The World's Smallest Book*. It measures 2.4 x 2.9 mm (0.09 x 0.1 in) – the size of a match head.

Largest book
The largest book was published in 2003. It is a collection of photos called *Bhutan: A Visual Odyssey Across the Last Himalayan Kingdom*. When opened out it measures 2.1 x 1.5 m (7 x 5 ft) – almost the size of a table-tennis table! It costs $15,000 (£30,000) a copy.

The Amazon Kindle, launched in 2007, can hold the complete text of up to 200 novels.

www.acblack.com   search

Famous diaries

People have kept personal diaries for more than 500 years. Most were written as personal records about the times the writers lived through or events that happened to them, and they are often fascinating to read.

Samuel Pepys (1633–1703)
Pepys kept a diary for nearly ten years from 1660. He lived in London and wrote about events such as the Great Plague and Great Fire of London. He wrote in a special code, which was not translated until the 19th century. Pepys' original diaries are kept in the library of Magdalene College, Cambridge.

Anne Frank (1929–1945)
Anne Frank was forced to hide with her family in Amsterdam, Netherlands, during World War II, when Jewish people were being persecuted by the Nazis. Anne kept her diary while she was in hiding, but left it behind when she and her family were found. She was deported and died in a German concentration camp. Her father survived and edited her diary, which was published after the war. *The Diary of Anne Frank* became a bestseller and was translated into more than 55 languages. It has also been made into an award-winning play and a film. The house in which the Frank family hid is now a museum.

Adolf Hitler (1889–1945)
In 1993, the German magazine *Stern* paid 10 million marks (£4.0 million) to journalist Gerd Heidemann to publish extracts from what were claimed to be the diaries of the German dictator Adolf Hitler. The diaries were soon discovered to have been forgeries written by Konrad Kujau. He and Heidemann were imprisoned for their deception.

Bestsellers

These are some of the bestselling books ever. But the Bible has outsold them all. It is believed to have sold more than six billion copies in hundreds of versions and translations.

● One of the bestselling books of all time is a collection of quotations by Chinese leader Mao Zedong, known as his *Little Red Book*. Between 1966 to 1971 every Chinese adult had to own a copy and 900 million were printed.

● J.R.R. Tolkien's *The Lord of the Rings* trilogy was first published in 1954–55. It has sold well over 100 million and its sales received a further boost when the films based on the books were released between 2001 and 2003.

● *The American Spelling Book* by Noah Webster (1783) was used in American schools for generations. It has sold nearly 100 million copies.

● *The Common Sense Book of Baby and Child Care* by American doctor Benjamin Spock came out in 1946. Since then more than 50 million copies have been sold.

● British crime writer Agatha Christie has sold at least one billion copies of her novels in English and another billion in 45 foreign languages. In 1935 her novel *The Mysterious Affair at Styles* was one of the first Penguin paperbacks ever published.

● American author Margaret Mitchell's only book, *Gone With the Wind* (1936), has sold around 30 million copies. It is one of the bestselling novels ever.

Covers for two *Harry Potter* books

J.K. Rowling

J.K. Rowling was born on 31 July 1965 as Joanne Rowling (she later borrowed the name Kathleen from her grandmother to create a middle initial). Her first Harry Potter book, *Harry Potter and the Philosopher's Stone*, was published in 1997. It has been followed by six more books with sales now over 375 million copies in 64 languages. If all Harry Potter books ever sold were placed end to end, they would stretch 76,819 km (47,734 miles) – more than one and a half times round the Equator! Earnings from the book sales and films have made J.K. Rowling the richest author ever, and the first to make more than $1 billion (£509 million) from writing. She has given large amounts to charities. The final book, *Harry Potter and the Deathly Hallows*, was published on 21 July 2007.

Translations

These are the ten most translated authors in the world, according to UNESCO's *Index Translationum* (1979–2005).

Walt Disney Productions	8,677	Enid Blyton	3,433
Agatha Christie	6,362	Barbara Cartland	3,315
Jules Verne	4,021	Danielle Steel	2,767
V. I. Lenin	3,497	Hans Christian Andersen	2,624
William Shakespeare	3,435	Stephen King	2,591

Imaginary lands

Writers usually invent the characters in their books, but some have also created imaginary lands in which the action of the book takes place. These are some of the best known fictional worlds, and the books in which they first appeared. Some featured again in later books by their authors.

Thomas Moore – **Utopia**
in *Utopia* (1516)

Jonathan Swift – **Lilliput**
in *Gulliver's Travels* (1726)

Voltaire – **Eldorado**
in *Candide* (1759)

Lewis Carroll – **Wonderland**
in *Alice's Adventures in Wonderland* (1865)

Samuel Butler – **Erewhon***
in *Erewhon* (1872)

Anthony Hope – **Ruritania**
in *The Prisoner of Zenda* (1894)

L. Frank Baum – **Oz**
in *The Wonderful Wizard of Oz* (1900)

J.M. Barrie – **Neverland**
in *Peter and Wendy* (1911)

James Hilton – **Shangri-La**
in *Lost Horizon* (1933)

J.R.R. Tolkien – **Middle Earth**
in *The Hobbit* (1937)

C.S. Lewis – **Narnia**
in *The Lion, The Witch and The Wardrobe* (1950)

Terry Pratchett – **Discworld**
in *The Colour of Magic* (1983)

* An anagram for nowhere

Early cover for *The Lion, the Witch and the Wardrobe*

J.K. Rowling
Photograph
© Richard Young

Nobel Prize for Literature

Nobel prizes have been given every year since 1901 for achievements in different fields, including literature. Nobel Prize winners for literature include poets, playwrights and authors from all over the world. Below are some of the best known winners.

2007 Doris Lessing (UK, 1919–)
2006 Orhan Pamuk (Turkey, 1952–)
2005 Harold Pinter (UK, 1930–)
2003 J.M. Coetzee (South Africa, 1940–)
2001 V.S. Naipaul (UK, 1932–)
2000 Gao Xingjian (China, 1940–) first win by a Chinese writer
1999 Günter Grass (Germany, 1927–)
1995 Seamus Heaney (Ireland, 1939–)
1993 Toni Morrison (USA, 1931–)
1991 Nadine Gordimer (South Africa, 1923–)
1983 William Golding (UK, 1911–93) author of *The Lord of the Flies*
1973 Patrick White (Australia, 1912–90)
1970 Alexander Solzhenitsyn (Russia, 1918–)
1962 John Steinbeck (USA, 1902–68) author of *The Grapes of Wrath*
1958 Boris Pasternak (Russia, 1890–1960) author of *Doctor Zhivago*
1954 Ernest Hemingway (USA, 1899–1961)
1953 Winston Churchill (UK, 1874–1965) British prime minister and writer
1948 T.S. Eliot (US-born, UK, 1888–1965) author of the book that inspired the musical *Cats*
1938 Pearl Buck (USA, 1892–1973)
1932 John Galsworthy (UK, 1867–1933) author of *The Forsyte Saga*
1925 George Bernard Shaw (UK, 1856–1950)
1923 William Butler Yeats (Ireland, 1865–1939)
1907 Rudyard Kipling (UK, 1865–1936) author of *The Jungle Book*
1901 Sully Prudhomme (France, 1839–1907) the first winner

http//www.jkrowling.com   search

Children's firsts

First children's book
The first English children's book for entertainment (not a school book) was a collection of rhymes called *A Booke in Englyssh Metre, of the Great Merchante Man called Dives Pragmaticus, very preaty for Children to reade*. It was printed in London in 1563.

First children's book printed in the USA
John Cotton's *Milk for Babies* was printed in Cambridge, Massachusetts, America, in 1641–45.

First children's encyclopedia
Pera Librorum Juvenilium (Collection of Juvenile Books) was compiled in Germany by Johann Christoph Wagenseil in 1695.

First story for children
The History of Little Goody Two-Shoes was published by John Newbery in London in 1765. Some experts believe it was written by the famous British poet and playwright Oliver Goldsmith.

First nursery rhyme book
Tommy Thumb's Pretty Song Book was published in London in 1744. It contained well-known rhymes such as "London Bridge is falling down", "Hickory, dickory dock" and "Sing a song of sixpence".

First children's library
The Bingham Library for Youth was set up in Salisbury, Connecticut, USA, in January 1803 when Caleb Bingham, who came from the town, donated 150 books. In 1862 Britain's first library for children was created – an area set aside just for them inside the Campfield Reference Library, Manchester.

First children's book to win Whitbread Book of the Year Award (now Costa Book of the Year Award)
In 2001, British writer Philip Pullman won the Whitbread Children's Book of the Year Award and the Book of the Year Award for his novel *The Amber Spyglass* from *His Dark Materials* trilogy. It was the first time a children's book had won the overall prize.

Fairy tale authors

Fairy tales are fantastic stories for children that do not always involve fairies. They are traditional tales that were retold from generation to generation. The writers below collected the stories and wrote or re-wrote them in books that became hugely popular all over the world. Many fairy tales have been made into films – especially animated films by Disney.

Charles Perrault
French writer Charles Perrault (1628–1703) put together a collection of stories with the help of his son Pierre (1678–1700). Their collection contained *Cinderella*, *Little Red Riding-Hood*, *Sleeping Beauty* and *Puss in Boots*. The stories were translated into English in 1729. Later editions had the French title, *Contes de ma mère l'Oye*, or *Mother Goose's Tales*.

Brothers Grimm
German brothers Jacob Ludwig Carl Grimm (1785–1863) and Wilhelm Carl Grimm (1786–1859) were the authors of *Grimm's Fairy Tales*, which were first published for Christmas 1812. This was a collection of traditional stories, re-written for a young audience. It included many famous fairy tales, such as *Hansel and Gretel*, *Rumpelstiltskin* and *Snow White and the Seven Dwarfs*. They were translated into English in 1823 and became a worldwide bestseller.

Hans Christian Andersen
Danish author Andersen (1805–75) wrote 156 fairy tales, including *The Little Mermaid*, *The Emperor's New Clothes* and *The Ugly Duckling*. His stories first appeared in English in 1846.

> Illustration for *The Ugly Duckling*, a fairy tale by Hans Christian Andersen

Glass slippers
In Perrault's re-telling of the story of Cinderella, he used the French phrase *pantoufle de verre*, which means glass slipper. However, it may be that he mistook *verre*, glass, for *vair*, an old French word for fur, and what Cinderella was actually wearing were furry slippers!

Jacqueline Wilson
Jacqueline Wilson is one of the UK's bestselling authors. More than 15 million copies of her books have been sold and more people have borrowed her books from British libraries than those of any other writer. In 2002 her novel *The Story of Tracy Beaker* (1991) was made into a TV series.

Multi-million sellers

J.K. Rowling (UK, 1965–)
At the end of 2007, the seven Harry Potter books had sold more than 375 million copies worldwide. In 2007, *Harry Potter and the Deathly Hallows* sold 2,652,656 copies in the UK on its first day of release – the biggest one-day sale ever recorded.

Enid Blyton (UK, 1897–1968)
Enid Blyton wrote more than 700 children's books. Total sales of her works are more than 400 million. She was the bestselling English-language author until the arrival of J.K. Rowling.

René Goscinny (France, 1926–77) and Albert Uderzo (France, 1927–)
René Goscinny and Albert Uderzo created the comic-strip character Astérix the Gaul in 1959. They jointly produced 24 books, and Underzo went on to create 9 more after Goscinny's death. Their total worldwide sales are more than 330 million copies.

R.L. Stine (USA, 1943–)
The 138 books in R.L. Stine's *Goosebumps* series and its sequels have sold over 330 million copies worldwide.

Goosebumps HorrorLand (2008–09) is Stine's latest series.

Hergé (Belgium, 1907–83)
Georges Rémi was the author-illustrator who wrote under the pen-name Hergé. He created the comic-strip character Tintin in 1929. The boy detective's adventures have appeared in book form since 1948 onwards and have been

The Cat in the Hat, a character from one of Dr Seuss' most popular books

Famous illustrators

Below are some of the artists who have produced the best-loved illustrations for children's books. Some, such as Beatrix Potter, also wrote the books they illustrated.

Honor C. Appleton (American, 1879–1951) *Josephine and Her Dolls*

Quentin Blake (British, 1932–) Illustrated Roald Dahl's books and others

Raymond Briggs (British, 1934–) *The Snowman* and *Father Christmas*

Jean de Brunhoff (French, 1899–1937) *Babar the Elephant* series

Hergé (Belgian, 1907–83) the *Tintin* books

Tove Jansson (Finnish, 1914–2001) the *Moomin* series

Arnold Lobel (American, 1933–87) the *Frog and Toad* books

Henriette Willebeek Le Mair (Dutch, 1889–1966) *Our Old Nursery Rhymes*

© Hergé/Moulinsart 2005

Tintin by Hergé

Beatrix Potter (British, 1866–1943) the *Peter Rabbit* books and others

Arthur Rackham (British, 1867–1939) illustrated classics

William Heath Robinson (British, 1872–1944) illustrated classics

Maurice Sendak (American, 1928–) *Where the Wild Things Are* and others

Ernest Shepard (British, 1879–1976) *The Wind in the Willows, Winnie the Pooh*

Dr Seuss (Theodor Seuss Geissel; American, 1904–91) *The Cat in the Hat* and many others

Jessie Willcox Smith (American, 1863–1935) *The Water Babies*

Albert Uderzo (French, 1927–) the *Astérix* books

Chris Van Allsburg (American, 1949–) *Jumanji, The Polar Express*

Young authors

At the age of six, Dennis Vollmer (USA) wrote and illustrated his book *Joshua Disobeys*, published in 1988.

British author Libby Rees (born 1995) was only nine when she wrote *Help Hope & Happiness*, which was published in 2005.

---

translated into about 45 languages and dialects. Total sales are over 200 million.

Beatrix Potter (UK, 1866–1943) *The Tale of Peter Rabbit* (1901) and her other books have sold more than 150 million copies in 30 languages.

Lewis Carroll (UK, 1832–98) There are no world figures for sales of Lewis Carroll's books, *Alice in Wonderland* and *Alice*

Through the Looking Glass, but these two books have never been out of print. They have appeared in hundreds of editions and in many languages.

Dr Seuss (USA, 1904–91) *Green Eggs and Ham*, one of Dr Seuss' most popular books, has sold more than 8 million in the USA alone. Worldwide, he has sold more than 100 million copies of his books.

Rev. W. Awdry (UK, 1911–97) Rev. Awdry began writing his *Thomas the Tank Engine* books in 1946. The books have sold more than 90 million copies.

Mark Twain (USA, 1835–1910) Book sales in the USA were not accurately recorded before 1895. *The Adventures of Tom Sawyer* (1876) and *The Adventures of Huckleberry Finn* (1884) have probably each sold more than 20 million copies worldwide.

 http://www.ukchildrensbooks.co.uk   search

www.poetrysociety.org.uk   search

Ancient poems

Before stories and poems were written down they were passed on orally. Some of the most famous long narrative, or story, poems were passed on this way for hundreds of years before being written down by the poet who is now known as the author.

The Iliad – Homer

This Greek poem dates from 850 BC and tells the story of the final year of the war between the Greeks and the Trojans. It describes the great battle and the story of how beautiful Helen left her husband Menelaus for the Trojan prince Paris. It also tells us about the interference of the gods and their quarrels about the action on the battlefield below them.

The Odyssey – Homer

This describes Odysseus' journey home from the Trojan war. Odysseus features briefly in the *Iliad*. Again, human characters work side by side with the gods, who are given human characteristics. Although they are so powerful, the gods bear grudges, seek revenge and are very proud. The word odyssey has now come to mean any long, hard journey. The poem has strongly influenced other works of literature – most famously the novel *Ulysses* by the Irish writer James Joyce.

Rubáiyat

Omar Khayyám was a Persian writer, mathematician and astronomer who lived in the 11th and early 12th centuries. His *Rubáiyat* was introduced to the rest of the world in 1859, when it was translated by Edward Fitzgerald. Each verse contains a complete thought.

Beowulf

An epic poem of almost 3,200 lines written in Old English (or Anglo-Saxon). This is an early form of the English language that modern readers find hard to understand. The main theme is the struggle of the hero Beowulf with the water monster Grendel. Details of the poem's exact date and author are not known, but it may have been written in the 8th century by more than one person.

Sir Gawain and the Green Knight

This poem was written by a monk from the northwest of England during the second half of the 14th century. Its 2,530 lines describe events in King Arthur's court and the testing of Sir Gawain, a model knight. There are many opportunities for the character to fail, but he does not.

Famous poets and poems

Most poets write many poems. Below are some of the most famous poets and their best-known works.

Haiku

This is a traditional Japanese form of poetry which has 17 syllables, eg

Clouds appear
and bring to men a chance to rest
from looking at the moon.

Matsuo Basho

An illustration by William McLaren for *Sir Gawain and the Green Knight*

Charles Baudelaire (1821–67), France, wrote *Les Fleurs du Mal*

William Blake (1757–1827), England, wrote *The Tyger; London*

Matsuo Basho (1644–94), Japan, wrote numerous haiku

Elizabeth Barrett Browning (1806–61), England, wrote *How Do I Love Thee?*

Robert Burns (1759–96), Scotland, wrote *Tam o' Shanter*

Lord Byron (1788–1824), England, wrote *Don Juan*

Geoffrey Chaucer (c. 1343–1400), England, wrote *The Canterbury Tales*

Samuel Taylor Coleridge (1772–1834), England, wrote *Kubla Khan; The Rime of the Ancient Mariner*

Dante Alighieri (1265–1321), Italy, wrote *The Divine Comedy*

Emily Dickinson (1830–86), USA, wrote *Because I Could Not Stop for Death*

T.S. Eliot (1888–1965), USA/England, wrote *The Waste Land*

Robert Frost (1874–1963), USA, wrote *Stopping by Woods on a Snowy Evening; The Road Not Taken*

Seamus Heaney (1939–), Ireland, wrote *Death of a Naturalist*

Homer (c. 8th century BC), Greece, wrote *The Iliad; The Odyssey*

John Keats (1795–1821), England, wrote *Ode to a Nightingale; La Belle Dame Sans Merci; To Autumn*

Rudyard Kipling (1865–1936), England, wrote *If*

Mikhail Lermontov (1814–41), Russia, wrote *The Novice*

Li Po (701–762), China, wrote *Drinking Alone Under the Moon*

John Milton (1608–74), England, wrote *Paradise Lost; Paradise Regained*

Pablo Neruda (1904–71), Chile, wrote *Canto General*

Nezami (1140–c. 1217), Iran, wrote *Khamseh (or The Quinary)*

Ovid (43 BC–AD 17), ancient Rome, wrote *Metamorphoses*

Sylvia Plath (1932–63), USA, wrote *Ariel*

Arthur Rimbaud (1854–91), France, wrote *Une Saison en Enfer (or A Season in Hell)*

Christina Rossetti (1830–94), England, wrote *Remember*

William Shakespeare (1564–1616), England, wrote *Sonnet 18 (or Shall I Compare Thee to a Summer's Day)*

Percy Bysshe Shelley (1792–1822), England, wrote *Ozymandias*

Edmund Spenser (1552–99), England, wrote *The Faerie Queene*

Alfred Tennyson (1809–92), England, wrote *In Memoriam* and *The Lady of Shalott*

Dylan Thomas (1914–53), Wales, wrote *Fern Hill*

Virgil (70–19 BC), ancient Rome, wrote *The Aeneid*

Walt Whitman (1819–92), USA, wrote *Song of Myself*

William Wordsworth (1770–1850), England, wrote *The Prelude* and *Daffodils*

William Butler Yeats (1865–1939), Ireland, wrote *Sailing to Byzantium; The Lake Isle of Innisfree*

U.S. 10¢
Robert Frost
AMERICAN POET

Antique US stamp with a portrait of Robert Frost

Poets laureate

The word laureate means crowned with laurel. The expression dates back to ancient Rome, where a successful person was traditionally crowned with a wreath of laurel leaves.

In Britain, the position of poet laureate was created as a royal office in 1668 with the appointment of John Dryden by King Charles II. The position was traditionally held for life, but is now restricted to ten years. When it becomes vacant the prime minister has a list of names drawn up and the monarch chooses a new laureate. The poet laureate's main task is to write odes to celebrate royal birthdays, marriages and important state occasions. Poets laureate receive a salary of £70 per annum – the same as in the 17th century! Some famous poets laureate in the UK include William Wordsworth, Alfred Tennyson, Sir John Betjeman and Ted Hughes. The present laureate is Andrew Motion.

In the United States the first poet laureate (Joseph Auslander) was appointed in 1937. A new laureate is appointed every year. He or she serves from October to May and is paid $35,000 (£17,500).

Statue of Dante Alighieri in Florence, Italy

Most valuable comics

Copies of American comic books with the first appearances of superheroes Superman and Batman are the most valued by collectors. In perfect condition, an *Action Comics* No. 1, with the first Superman story, could be worth up to $5,800,000 (£2,944,000). *Detective Comics* No. 27, the first to feature Batman, is valued at up to $4,000,000 (£2,031,000).

All about comics

Comic strips

A comic strip is a story told in a series of pictures published in a newspaper. The New York *Daily Graphic* was the first newspaper to feature a comic strip. It started on 11 September 1875 with *Professor Tigwissel's Burglar Alarm*. The first regular strip was The Yellow Kid, which began in a supplement of the New York World on 5 May 1895. A syndicated comic strip is one that appears in more than one newspaper. Some appear in hundreds of papers all over the world.

Comics

In the UK, weekly collections of cartoon strips and jokes began to appear in the 1880s and 1890s. Comics such as *Dandy* (1937) and *Beano* (1938) are still published today. From the 1890s in the USA, series of cartoon strips began to appear in newspapers and were syndicated nationwide. *Katzehjammer Kids*, which was first published in 1897, still appears in many newspapers and magazines.

Comic books

The first American comic book was called *Funnies on Parade* and came out in 1933. The first to be published regularly was *Famous Funnies* in 1934. Many comic books were about the adventures of a single superhero, such as Batman or Superman, who used special powers to fight crime and defeat evil villains.

Captain America

Top newspaper-reading countries

1 Norway 626*
2 Japan 634*
3 Finland 518*
4 Sweden 481*
*daily copies per 1,000 people

See also

Book firsts and records: page 229

Newspaper fact file

First newspapers

From 59 BC onwards Roman emperor Julius Caesar had handwritten reports on news posted in public places in Rome. China had newspapers from about AD 713. The first European printed newspapers appeared in Germany in 1609.

The first daily newspaper, *Einkommende Zeitungen*, also started in Germany, in 1650. Britain's first daily paper was the *Perfect Diurnall*, published in London in 1660. America's first successful newspaper was the *Boston News-Letter*, which appeared in 1704.

Smallest

Newspaper publishers sometimes produce miniature editions for publicity purposes. The smallest regular publication was the *Daily Banner*, published in 1876 in Oregon, USA. It measured just 9.5 x 7.6 cm (3.75 x 3 in).

Largest

The edition of the Belgian newspaper *Het Volk* published on 14 June 1993 had pages measuring 142 x 99.5 cm (55.9 x 39.2 in), which is more than six times the area of an ordinary broadsheet (large page size) newspaper.

First appearances

Some comic strip and comic book characters are older than you might think. Below is a list of some famous comic characters' first appearances.

Rupert Bear appeared as a strip in the *Daily Express* (UK) on 8 November 1920

Tintin *Le Vingtième Siècle* (Belgium) on 10 January 1929

Popeye appeared as a strip in *Thimble Theatre* (USA) on 17 January 1929

Dick Tracy appeared as a strip in the *Chicago Tribune* (USA) on 4 October 1931

Flash Gordon appeared as a syndicated strip (USA) on 7 January 1934

Desperate Dan *Dandy* (UK) on 4 December 1937

Superman *Action Comics* No. 1 (USA) in June 1938

Batman *Detective Comics* No. 27 (USA) in May 1939

Captain Marvel *Whiz Comics* No. 1 (USA) in Februrary 1940

The Green Lantern *All American Comics* No. 16 (USA) in July 1940

The Flash *Flash Comics* No. 1 (USA) in January 1940

Robin (Batman's assistant) *Detective Comics* No. 38 (USA) in April 1940

Wonder Woman *All-Star Comics* No. 8 (USA) in December 1941

Captain America *Captain America Comics* No. 1 (USA) in March 1941

Dan Dare *Eagle* (UK) on 14 April 1950

Peanuts appeared as a syndicated strip (USA) on 2 October 1950

Dennis the Menace (USA) appeared as a syndicated strip (USA) on 12 March 1951

Dennis the Menace (UK) *Beano* (UK) on 17 March 1951

Astérix the Gaul *Pilote* (France) on 29 October 1959

Supergirl *Action Comics* No. 252 (USA) in May 1959

Spiderman *Amazing Fantasy* No. 15 (USA) in August 1962

The Incredible Hulk* *Hulk* (USA) in March 1962

X-Men *The X-Men* (USA) in September 1963

Daredevil *Daredevil* (USA) in June 1964

* The Hulk had grey skin in March 1962, but became The Incredible Hulk, with green skin, in the May issue two months later.

Magazine fact file

First-ever popular magazine
Mercure Galant, a gossip magazine, was first published in Paris in March 1672.

First women's magazine
The Ladies' Mercury was first published in London on 27 June 1693.

First American magazine
The American Magazine, published in Philadelphia, probably began on 13 February 1741.

First children's magazine
The *Lilliputian Magazine* appeared in the UK in June 1751 and ran for just over a year. The first in the USA was the *Children's Magazine*, published in January 1789.

First fashion magazine
The Paris magazine *Le Cabinet des Modes* was first published in 1785.

Longest-running US magazine
Scientific American was launched on 28 August 1845 and is the longest continuously published magazine in the USA. At first, it was a four-page newspaper and included features on science and technology as well as topics such as religion and poetry. Later it began to focus on science and is now the world's most popular scientific journal.

First photograph in a magazine
Each copy of the June 1846 issue of the *Art Union* (UK) contained a photograph by Henry Fox Talbot, one of the inventors of photography.

Heaviest
The Sunday edition of the *New York Times* for 14 September 1987 contained 1,612 pages and weighed 5.4 kg (12 lb). At one time 127 hectares (314 acres) of forest containing almost 63,000 trees had to be chopped down to make one edition of the paper. Nowadays, much of the paper used for newspapers is recycled.

Top selling
The *Yomiuri Shimbun* (Japan) sells more than 14.2 million copies a day. *Bild-Zeitung* (Germany) is the highest-circulation newspaper outside Japan, selling more than 4.2 million copies a day. *The Sun* (UK) sells 3.4 million copies, more than any other English-language newspaper in the world. The USA's biggest-selling newspaper is *USA Today*, which sells 2.6 million a day.

Most mistakes
The Times (UK) of 22 August 1978 contained 97 misprints in one story about the Pope. He was called "the Pop" throughout the article.

Education & the Arts

On the march

In 2007, the Terracotta Army was the focus of an exhibition in London that boasted the biggest loan of these magnificent, life-sized and individual figures ever to leave China. The exhibition at the British Museum received over one million visitors and sparked a new interest in Chinese culture.

Students in further education

The figures give the percentage of school leavers enrolled in further education. These countries have the highest number of students, but information is not available for all countries.

Country	%	Country	%	Country	%	Country	%
Finland	92	Lithuania	73	Belgium	63	Libya	56
South Korea	91	Australia	72	Poland	63	Portugal	56
Greece	89	Iceland	71	Belarus	62	Japan	55
USA	83	Russia	71	Canada	62		
New Zealand	82	Ukraine	69	Cuba	61	*World average*	*24*
Sweden	82	Spain	67	Netherlands	61		
Slovenia	81	Estonia	66	UK	60		
Denmark	80	Italy	66	Ireland	59		
Norway	80	Argentina	65	Israel	58		
Latvia	74	Hungary	65	France	56		

USA grade system

American children have 12 years of schooling. They start at five and the first year at school is called kindergarten. The grade system begins in the second year with first grade (six year olds) and continues to twelfth grade (18 year olds). In high schools, years have names instead of numbers: ninth grade is known as the freshman year, tenth as the sophomore year, eleventh as the junior year and twelfth as the senior year.

Harvard University, USA

Education timeline

1100s

3000 BC The Sumerians pioneer the idea of teaching. Education available only to those who could afford to pay a teacher for each lesson

590 BC The city of Athens becomes the first to offer public education to all men for a small fee. Free education available to the sons of war veterans

597 King's School in Canterbury opens – the first school in the UK

859 The world's first university still in existence is founded in Fez, Morocco

1064 The first European university is founded in Parma, Italy

1160 Oxford University becomes the first university in England

1538 The first university of the New World opens in Santo Domingo (now the Dominican Republic)

1635 The first publicly funded high school in the USA opens in Boston

1636 Harvard University becomes the first university in the USA

1760 The first school for deaf children opens in Paris. Pupils are taught an early version of sign language

1781 The first nursery school is opened in Scotland for parents who have to go to work

Children at a Chinese boarding school doing their morning exercises

Countries with the most...

Primary school pupils
The country with the most primary school pupils is India, where there are 140,012,901 children in primary school. In China there are 112,739,964 primary school children.

Secondary school pupils
China has the most secondary pupils – 100,631,925 – although not all children go on from primary to secondary school. In India there are 89,461,794 secondary school children.

University students
China recently overtook the USA for the number of students at university, 21,335,646 compared with the USA's 17,272,044. There are 11,777,296 at university in India and 9,019,556 in Russia.

Pupils per teacher at primary school
Primary school children in some African nations are taught in classes of more than 50: there are 72 pupils per teacher in Ethiopia and up to 83 in Congo. At the other end of the scale, there are only 10 per class in Italy, Norway and Sweden.

Pupils per teacher at secondary school
In secondary schools in Eritrea there are as many as 55 pupils for each teacher. The average class size in Malawi is 51. Schools in Azerbaijan, Belarus, Georgia, Greece, Montserrat, Norway and Portugal have only nine pupils, Lebanon eight and Andorra and Bermuda only seven.

See also
Largest countries: page 116

Schooling around the world

Time spent at school
● School children in China spend more time at school than children in any other country. They have 251 schooldays a year – 59 days more than British children, and 71 more than American children.

● In the United Kingdom, the United States, France, Canada, Germany, Belgium, the Netherlands, Australia and New Zealand children have 10, 11 or 12 years of education. In most African countries and parts of South America children spend just five or six years at school. Only two African countries, Gabon and Tunisia, have ten years of compulsory schooling.

● In Italy and China, children can legally finish school at the age of 14. In Myanmar, Angola and Pakistan, children are allowed to finish at the age of nine, after only four or five years at school. In several European countries, including Croatia, Denmark, Sweden and Switzerland, parents don't have to send their children to school until they are seven years old – two years later than in many other countries.

Largest school
The largest school in the world is the City Montessori school in Lucknow, northern India; it has more than 31,000 pupils.

1900s

1783 Poland becomes the first country to ban corporal punishment in schools

1784 The first school for blind children is started in Paris

1841 Oberlin College becomes the first university in the USA to award degrees to women

1871 A school in New York introduces the first distance-learning courses for young people who live too far away from schools to travel to them

1878 London University becomes the first UK university to award degrees to women

1987 Corporal punishment is banned in all UK state schools

1999 Corporal punishment is banned in all independent schools in the UK

2007 UK confirms intention to raise school leaving age to 18 years old in 2013

Most remote school
The world's most remote school is Kiwirrkurra Remote Community School in Australia. It is a 25-hour road journey from the nearest major town. The 100 pupils and seven teachers at another school in the region, Oombulgurri Remote Community School, can only get to school by light aircraft or by barge. The aircraft takes just 35 minutes, but the barge can take up to 12 hours.

Art Deco interior of Helsinki railway station, Finland

Stolen Screams

The Norwegian artist Edvard Munch painted several versions of *The Scream* (1893). One hung in the National Gallery in Oslo, Norway. In 1994 it was stolen and held to ransom for $1 million, but was recovered a few months later. Another version was stolen from the Munch Museum, Oslo, in 2004. The thieves were caught and jailed and the painting, which had been damaged, was recovered.

Cubism
An abstract style which is mostly about shape and colour.
Art Deco
An angular, decorative style popular in the 1920s and 1930s.
Surrealism
A style that emerged between the World Wars, in which artists explore dreams and fantasy.
Abstract art
Non-naturalistic art in which shapes, lines and colour are more important than the objects they represent.
Pop art
Style conceived in the 1950s, using images from popular culture such as comics and advertising.
Environmental art
Art in which the landscape is decorated or altered. The artist uses natural objects such as stones to create his work.
Britart
Modern art by a group of young British artists. The movement began in 1988.

Impressionism
This style of painting developed in France and was named in 1874. The aim was to convey an impression of what the eye sees rather than what the mind knows is there.
Symbolism
An attempt by late 19th-century artists to link the real and the spiritual worlds in their work.
Post-Impressionism
A development from Impressionism, which includes the Pointillism (dot painting) of Seurat and others. In Pointillism, small dots of colour are applied to the canvas. These appear to fuse when seen from a distance.
Art Nouveau
A flowing ornamental style of the late 19th/early 20th centuries, which influenced architects and furniture makers and painters.
Expressionism/abstract expressionism
Early 20th-century styles in which the emotions of the painter are powerfully expressed.

Giant eggs decorate the Dali museum in Rosas, Spain.

Western art styles

Medieval
Paintings, mosaics and miniatures in manuscripts, mostly of religious subjects.

Renaissance
The word means rebirth – the Renaissance art of the 15th and 16th centuries replaced medieval styles and revived the art of the Greek and Roman period.

Mannerism
A style of 16th-century Italian art, which uses bright colours and distorts scale and perspective.

Baroque/rococo
An ornate style that was popular in Italy during the 17th and 18th centuries.

Neoclassicism
A style of the 18th century modelled on classical (Greek and Roman) art.

Romanticism
This late 18th/early 19th-century style explores emotion and shows nature in its untamed state.

Realism/naturalism
19th-century style that showed real life, including its unpleasant side such as poverty.

Pre-Raphaelitism
This short-lived style, inspired by medieval history and myths, was invented in 1848. The aim was to go back to the simplicity of painting before Raphael.

Famous artists

Artist	Famous work
Fra Angelico (c. 1400–55) Italian	*Deposition of Christ*
Sandro Botticelli (1445–1510) Italian	*Birth of Venus*
Hieronymus Bosch (c. 1450–1516) Flemish	*Garden of Earthly Delights*
Leonardo da Vinci (1452–1519) Italian	*Mona Lisa*
Albrecht Dürer (1471–1528) German	*Four Apostles*
Michelangelo (1475–1564) Italian	Sistine chapel ceiling
Raphael (1483–1520) Italian	*Madonna*
Hans Holbein (1497–1543) German	*Sir Thomas More*
El Greco (1541–1614) Greek	*Burial of Count Orgaz*
Sir Peter Paul Rubens (1577–1640) Flemish	*Descent from the Cross*
Rembrandt Van Rijn (1606–69) Dutch	*The Night Watch*
Jan Vermeer (1632–75) Dutch	*Girl with a Pearl Earring*
Antonio Canaletto (1697–1768) Italian	*The Grand Canal and the Church of the Salute, Venice*

Artist	Famous work
Sir Joshua Reynolds (1723–92) British	*The Family of the Duke of Marlborough*
Thomas Gainsborough (1727–88) British	*Blue Boy*
Francisco Goya (1746–1828) Spanish	*Maja Nude/Clothed*
J.M.W. Turner (1775–1851) British	*Rain, Steam, and Speed*
John Constable (1776–1837) British	*The Haywain*
Dante Gabriel Rossetti (1828–82) British	*Proserpine*
Sir John Everett Millais (1829–96) British	*Ophelia*
Sir Edward Burne-Jones (1833–98) British	*The Golden Stairs*
Edgar Degas (1834–1917) French	*The Rehearsal*
James McNeill Whistler (1834–1903) American	*Symphony in White*

Art terms

acrylic
Quick-drying plastic-based paint

cartoon
A preliminary sketch for a painting

chiaroscuro
Light and shade in painting

collage
A work made from pieces of paper and other materials stuck on to a background

composition
The arrangement of the elements and colour within a work

fresco
A painting on a freshly plastered wall

gouache
Water-based paint

icon
A portrait of a religious subject, such as a saint

impasto
Thickly applied paint

landscape
A painting of the natural world

medium
The material used to create a work of art

montage
Cut-out objects mounted on a surface

palette
The surface used by an artist for mixing paints, but also used to refer to the selection of colours

pastel
Coloured pigments in stick form used for drawing

still-life
A painting of an object or a group of objects

tempera
Pigments mixed with egg yolk and oil or water

trompe l'oeil
A painting that plays tricks on the eye to look as if it is three-dimensional

watercolour
Coloured pigments mixed with water

Record price for a photograph

German photographer Andreas Gursky (born 1955) broke the world record for a photograph at an auction in London on 7 February 2007. His large double print, *9 Cent II*, which shows the interior of a supermarket, was sold for £1.7 million ($3.3m.). The previous record-holder was *The Pond – Moonlight* by Edward Steichen (USA), which was sold in 2006 for £1.68m. ($2.9m.).

www.artcyclopedia.com   search

Portrait of Dr Gachet (1890), by Vincent van Gogh

Most expensive paintings

Jackson Pollock's *No. 5, 1948*, was sold privately in New York in 2006 for a price believed to have been about $140 million (£75.7 million), making it the most expensive painting not sold at auction. Among the highest prices paid at auction are:

● Pablo Picasso, *Boy with a pipe*, $104.2 million (£58 million), May 2004

● Pablo Picasso, *Dora Maar with Cat*, $95.2 million (£53.6 million), May 2006

● Gustav Klimt, *Portrait of Adele Bloch-Bauer II*, $87.9 million (£47.4 million), November 2006

● Vincent van Gogh, *Portrait du Dr Gachet*, $82.5 million (£49 million), May 1990

● Pierre-Auguste Renoir, *Ball at the Moulin de la Galette, Montmartre*, $78.1 million (£46.5 million), May 1990

● Sir Peter Paul Rubens, *Massacre of the Innocents*, $75.9 million (£49.5 million), July 2002

Artist	Famous work
Paul Cézanne (1839–1906) French	*Large Bathers*
Claude Monet (1840–1926) French	*Waterlilies*
Berthe Morisot (1841–95) French	*The Cradle*
Pierre Renoir (1841–1919) French	*Luncheon of the Boating Party*
Mary Cassatt (1844–1926) American	*The Bath*
Paul Gauguin (1848–1903) French	*Nevermore*
Vincent van Gogh (1853–90) Dutch	*Sunflowers*
Georges Seurat (1859–91) French	*Sunday Afternoon on the Island of La Grand Jatte*
Henri de Toulouse-Lautrec (1864–1901) French	*Aristide Bruant* (poster)
Henri Matisse (1869–1954) French	*The Dance*
Piet Mondrian (1872–1944) Dutch	*Broadway Boogie Woogie*

Artist	Famous work
Pablo Picasso (1881–1973) Spanish	*Guernica*
Salvador Dali (1904–89) Spanish	*The Persistence of Memory*
Francis Bacon (1909–92) British	*Study after Velazquez's Portrait of Pope Innocent X*
Jackson Pollock (1912–56) American	*Number One 1948*
Lucien Freud (1922–) British	*Girl with Roses*
Roy Lichtenstein (1923–97) American	*Whaam!*
Jasper Johns (1930–) American	*Flag*
Andy Warhol (1930–89) American	*Marilyn Monroe*
David Hockney (1937–) British	*A Bigger Splash*
Damien Hirst (1965–) British	*The Physical Impossibility of Death in the Mind of Someone Living* (shark)

Art exhibitions and world fairs

Major art exhibitions and world fairs have been held for more than 200 years. Art exhibitions focus on a particular artist or style. World fairs promote the trade or image of a country and display new inventions.

Great Exhibition, London, 1851
This was a showpiece of the arts and industries of the world and the first exhibition of its kind in the UK. It was seen by 6,039,195 visitors.

First Impressionist Exhibition, Paris, France, 1874
Many Impressionist painters, including Claude Monet, first showed their work at this exhibition, which was shocking to many people.

Philadelphia Centennial Exposition, Philadelphia, USA, 1876
This first major show in the USA was held to celebrate the 100th anniversary of the Declaration of Independence. It was seen by 9,910,966 people. Inventor Alexander Graham Bell first demonstrated the telephone at the Exposition.

Exposition Universelle, Paris, 1889
The Eiffel Tower was built as a temporary exhibit for this show, which commemorated 100 years since the French Revolution. It attracted 28,121,975 visitors.

World's Columbian Exposition, Chicago, USA, 1893
This show celebrated the 400th anniversary of Columbus' discovery of America and had more than 27.3 million visitors. Many Americans experienced electricity and hand-held cameras for the first time.

Armory Show, New York, 1913
This was the first exhibition of modern art in the United States and included the work of Picasso. It influenced American artists, collectors and museums.

Exposition Internationale des Arts Décoratifs et Industriels Modernes, Paris, 1925
This exhibition of art marked the beginning of Art Deco style and attracted 5,852,783 visitors.

National Museum of the American Indian, in the Smithsonian Institution, Washington DC

World's Fair, Flushing Meadow Park, Queens, New York, 1939–40
The fair had 44,932,978 visitors and first introduced television to the public.

Festival of Britain, London, 1951
This was a celebration of post-war life, held 100 years after the Great Exhibition. It attracted 8.5 million visitors.

Treasures of Tutankhamen, British Museum, London, 1972–73
This was one of the most popular exhibitions of all time and attracted 1,694,117 visitors. The show went to New York in 1978–79, where it was seen by 1,226,467 people.

Expo 2005, Japan
22 million people visited the show, themed "Nature's Wisdom". All the exhibition pavilions were built from recycled materials.

Museum fact file

First museum open to the public
Uffizi Gallery, Florence, Italy, 1591.

First museum in England
The Ashmolean Museum, Oxford, opened in 1683 to display the collection of natural history exhibits, coins, weapons and other items belonging to the collector and antiquary Elias Ashmole (1617–92).

The first national museum
The British Museum, London, opened to the public in 1759.

First public museum in the USA
Charleston Museum, Charleston, South Carolina, opened 1773.

First open-air museum
Skansen, Stockholm, Sweden, opened in 1891.

First children's museum
Brooklyn, New York, USA, opened 1899 and was the first of more than 300 children's museums worldwide.

First interactive museum
The Exploratorium, San Francisco, California, USA, opened in 1969 and has hundreds of hands-on exhibits.

Largest museum complex
The Smithsonian Institution, Washington DC, USA, consists of 16 museums with a total of more than 140 million items in their collections.

The Buddhas of Bamian (Bamiyan)
Two giant buddhas 55 m (180.4 ft) and 37 m (121.4 ft) were carved into the side of a cliff in Afghanistan between the 5th and 9th centuries. They were listed as a UNESCO World Heritage site, but were blown up in 2001 by the Islamic fundamentalist Taliban who then ruled the country. A plan has been proposed to project laser images of the statues on the rock face where they once stood.

Giant statues

There are many larger-than-life statues and monuments around the world. Here are some of the largest and most famous.

Chief Crazy Horse, South Dakota, USA
This is the world's biggest monument. It is carved into Thunderhead Mountain and is 172 m (563 ft) high and 195 m (641 ft) long. Work on the carving started in 1948 and continues to this day.

Ushiku Daibutsu (Buddha), Tokyo, Japan
This was unveiled in 1993. It weighs 1,000 tonnes and is 120 m (394 ft) tall.

Leshan Giant Buddha, China
Work on this huge statue began in AD 713 and was completed 90 years later. It is 71 m (234 ft) high, with shoulders 28 m (92 ft) across. Its feet measure 8.5 m (28 ft) and the head is 15 m (48 ft) high, with ears 7 m (23 ft) long.

Statue of Liberty, New York, USA
This statue was presented to the USA by the people of France. It was shipped in sections and unveiled in 1886. The statue is made of sheets of copper on an iron frame, and weighs 229 tonnes. The height of the statue is 46 m (151 ft) from the base to the top of the torch. It stands on a massive pedestal which more than doubles the overall height to 93 m (305 ft). The hands are 5 m (16 ft 5 in) long, the eyes are 0.76 m (2 ft 6 in) across and the nose measures 1.48 m (4 ft 6 in). The statue was originally called Liberty Enlightening the World.

Angel of the North, Gateshead, UK
The Angel stands 19.8 m (65 ft) high, has a wingspan of 53.3 m (175 ft) and weighs 200 tonnes. It was designed by Antony Gormley and erected in 1998.

Antony Gormley's *Angel of the North* sculpture

Christ the Redeemer, Rio de Janeiro, Brazil
This statue stands high above the city. The figure of Christ is 38 m (125 ft) tall and weighs 1,163 tonnes. It was unveiled in 1931 by Guglielmo Marconi, who had designed its lighting. He unveiled it by sending a radio signal from his yacht in Genoa, Italy.

Sphinx, Giza, Egypt
This statue was carved in about 2500 BC. It is about 20 m (66 ft) high and 73 m (240 ft) long, and has the huge body of a lion, with the head of a pharaoh.

Mount Rushmore, South Dakota, USA
This is a massive sculpture of the heads of US presidents George Washington, Thomas Jefferson, Theodore Roosevelt and Abraham Lincoln. Each one is about 18.3 m (60 ft) high. It was carved out of a cliff face between 1927 and 1939.

Abu Simbel, Egypt
The four huge statues, each standing 20 m (66 ft) high, used to guard a temple. They were moved in 1966 when the Aswan High Dam was built and the area flooded.

Statues of Abu Simbel

Unusual museums

Cockroach Hall of Fame, Plano, Texas, USA
Record-breaking cockroaches, and insects dressed as famous people

Colman's Mustard Museum, Norwich, Norfolk, UK
Tells the fascinating history of mustard

The Museum of Dog Collars, Leeds Castle, Maidstone, Kent, UK
A collection of dog collars, some of them from the Middle Ages

Gallery of Also-Rans, Norton, Kansas, USA
A collection celebrating people who came second or lost political campaigns and other contests

The Lawnmower Museum, Trerice, Cornwall, UK
Mechanical lawnmowers through the ages

The Medieval Crime Museum, Rothenburg, Germany
Medieval crime, punishment and torture implements

National Wool Museum, Geelong, Australia
The only museum devoted to wool, opened in 1988

Nut Museum, Old Lyme, Connecticut, USA
Nut carvings, 2.4 m (7.9 ft)-long nutcrackers and other nut-related exhibits

Philips Mushroom Museum, Kennett Square, Pennsylvania, USA
A museum focusing on all types of mushrooms and other fungi

The Piggy Bank Museum, Amsterdam, Netherlands
Displays 12,000 piggy banks from all periods

Porter Thermometer Museum, Onset, Massachusetts, USA
More than 3,000 devices for taking temperatures

Amazing collectors

Louis XIV

The French king owned a collection of 413 ornate beds. He kept them in different places all over France, so wherever he travelled, he could sleep in his own bed.

The Schlumpf brothers

French factory owners Hans and Fritz Schlumpf built up one of the world's largest car collections. They had 427 vehicles, including 120 rare Bugattis. These are now on public display at the National Auto Museum of France in Mulhouse.

Sir Thomas Phillips

Eccentric English book collector Sir Thomas Phillips (1792–1872) wanted to own a copy of every book ever printed – and he almost succeeded. He acquired more than 50,000 books and 100,000 manuscripts. His collection plunged his family into debt, but he rescued many priceless treasures from destruction. Sales from his collection have continued almost every year since his death.

Robert Opie

Robert Opie began his collection in 1963 with the wrapper from a packet of sweets. He now owns the world's largest collection of British packaging and advertising material, a total of more than 500,000 items.

Henry Holt

Lancashire collector Henry Holt built up the world's largest collection of bricks. When he died in 1996 he left 7,000 of them to the local museum, stacked up in various locations. The museum has been puzzling over what to do with them ever since.

In 2005, George Barris the "King of Customizers" auctioned his film and television cars, including this one he made for Elvis Presley.

Unusual auction items

- In 1888 a cemetery containing 300,000 mummified cats was found in Egypt. Almost 20 tonnes of the mummies were shipped to Liverpool, UK, and sold at auction for £4 ($19.50) per tonne.

- The skull of the Swedish philosopher Emanuel Swedenborg was sold at Sotheby's, London in 1978 for £1,500 ($2,900). Stockholm Royal Academy of Science bought the skull and reunited it with the rest of his body, which was buried in Uppsala Cathedral.

- A pair of Napoleon's socks was sold at Sotheby's, London, in 1996 for £2,990 ($4,660).

- A burnt loaf from the Great Fire of London, 1666, was sold at Sotheby's, London, in 1996 for £322 ($500).

- A pair of Queen Victoria's underpants were sold at Sotheby's, London, in 1996 for £253 ($395). A pair of Victorian rollerblades dating from c. 1860 was sold at the same sale for £575 ($900).

- A dish containing a sample of penicillium mould prepared by penicillin inventor Alexander Fleming in 1935 was sold by Christie's, London, in 1997 for £14,950 ($23,770). At the same sale a box of 300 glass eyes was sold for £2,760 ($4,390).

- More than 2,000 items that had belonged to the singer Elvis Presley were sold at an auction in Las Vegas in 1999. These included clothing as well as letters, one of Elvis's school report cards and 29 dry-cleaning bills made out to Elvis.

- Several pairs of spectacles belonging to John Lennon of the Beatles have sold for up to $1.5 million (£750,000).

Young enthusiasts sorting a collection of baseball cards

Who collects what?

As soon as someone starts to collect something a word is invented to describe the collector. Most end in -ist, which means a person who does something (as a motorist is someone who drives a car or a violinist someone who plays a violin). Another ending is -phile or -philist, which means a lover of something.

Collectable	Collector
airmail	**aerophilatelist**
autographs	**philographist**
badges and patches	**scutelliphilist**
banknotes	**notaphilist**
beer bottle labels	**labeorphilist**
beer mats	**tegestologist** or **tegetologist**
books	**bibliophile** or **bibliophilist**
butterflies and moths	**lepidopterist**
cameos	**cameist**
cheese labels	**laclabphilist**
cigar bands	**brandophilist** or **cigrinophilist**
cigarette cards	**cartophilist**
coins, money, medals	**numismatist**
corkscrews	**helixophile**
dolls	**plangonologist**
eggs	**oologist** (illegal in many countries)
egg-cups	**pocillovist**
flags and banners	**vexillologist**
gramophone records	**discophilist**
keyrings	**copoclephilist**
keys	**cagophilist**
match books	**phillumenist**
matchboxes	**cumyxaphilist**
money boxes	**argyrothecologist**
postcards	**deltiologist**
prints and book illustrations	**iconophilist**
shells	**conchologist**
stamps	**philatelist**
sugar packets	**sucrologist**
teddy bears	**arctophilists**
telephone cards	**fusilatelist**

Stamp collection themes

Many philatelists (stamp collectors) follow topical philately, which means they collect stamps by theme.

They may acquire stamps from many different countries and periods. Here are some of the hundreds of popular themes.

aircraft	dinosaurs	medicine
animals	dogs	mountains
art and artists	dolls	mushrooms
authors	exploration	music
bicycles	famous people	Nobel Prize
birds	fish	Olympic Games
butterflies	flags	police
cars	flowers	railways
castles	food	religion
cats	heraldry	scouting
chess	horses	seashells
children	insects	ships
Christmas	lighthouses	space
cinema	literature	sports
costumes	maps	stamps
dance		theatre
		uniforms

Postage stamps from around the world

http://kids.si.edu/collecting **search**

A collection of shells

Music & Performance

The Motown Sound

The Tamla-Motown record label was founded 50 years ago, in 1959. Diana Ross and the Supremes were one of the label's first huge successes and the popularity of Motown sparked a movement in music that has influenced acts ever since, bringing black popular culture into the mainstream.

Musical instrument records

Double bass
A double bass 4.26 m (14 ft) long and weighing 590 kg (1,300 lb) was built by Arthur K. Ferris of Ironia, New Jersey, USA, in 1924.

Drum
The University of Texas Longhorn Band has a drum nicknamed Big Bertha which is 7.6 m (24.9 ft) in circumference.

Guitar
A giant version of a Gibson guitar 11.63 m (38.2 ft) long was made in 1991 by students at Shakamak High School, Jasonville, Indiana, USA. Large stringed instruments that are bigger than the span of human hands are difficult or even impossible to play.

Pianos
In 1935 in London, Charles H. Challen built a piano which is probably the largest in the world. It weighs 1.25 tonnes and is 3.55 m (11.6 ft) long. One of the lightest pianos ever made was a baby grand weighing just 180 kg (397 lb). It was made mostly of aluminium covered in yellow pigskin. It was made by the Blüthner company of Germany for the airship *Hindenburg*, and was destroyed when the airship exploded in 1937.

Tuba
In 1896 John Philip Sousa, who is the American inventor of the sousaphone, played a 2.28 m (7.48 ft) tuba on a world tour. This is the largest brass instrument ever made and had 11.8 m (38.7 ft) of tubing.

See also
Inventions: pages 80–81

Organs
The world's loudest instrument is the Auditorium Organ in Atlantic City, USA. It was built in 1930 at a cost of $500,000, has more than 32,000 pipes and is powered by a 365 horsepower blower.

The world's largest cathedral organ was built in St Stephen's Cathedral, Passau, Germany, in 1928. It has 17,774 pipes.

The world's largest church organ is in St Stephen's Cathedral, Passau, Germany.

Large orchestras
● In 1958, the Norwegian National Meeting of School Bands assembled 12,600 players at Trondheim, Norway.

● A total of 6,452 musicians from the Vancouver Symphony Orchestra and Canadian music students played together in Vancouver, Canada, on 15 May 2000.

● An ensemble of 1,013 cellists played on 29 November 1998 in Kobe, Japan.

● On 14 July 1999 Piers Adams conducted 710 recorder players performing "Roaring Rag" by Beverley Wragg at Cressing Temple Barn, Essex, UK.

Large choir
In 1872 Austrian composer Johann Strauss conducted an orchestra of 987 (including 400 first violinists) and a choir of 20,000. The performance was in Boston, USA.

Recording timeline

1800s

1877 Thomas Alva Edison first recorded a human voice (singing "Mary Had a Little Lamb") on a tinfoil cylinder phonograph
1878 Edison is granted phonograph patent
1885 "Graphophone" with wax cylinders is invented by Alexander Graham Bell and Charles Tainter

1888 "Gramophone", with 7-inch (17.8 cm) flat disk, is patented by Emile Berliner
1895 First spring-driven phonograph is sold by Edison
1896 Improved gramophone produced by Eldridge Johnson
1897 Shellac discs introduced

1898 First magnetic recorder, with steel wire, patented by Valdemar Poulsen
1904 First mass-produced, double-sided discs are sold in Germany
1925 First electrically-recorded discs make it possible to record entire orchestral works. Sound recordings for films are introduced

1900s

1927 First coin-operated juke box is produced
1931 Stereo recording introduced
1934 First hi-fi (high-fidelity sound) records are made
1935 "Magnetophone" (tape recorder) is demonstrated in Berlin

Musical terms

Many musical terms are derived from Italian words. Here are the meanings of some common ones.

Musical tempos

Tempo	Meaning
Larghissimo	As slow as possible
Largo	Very slow and solemn
Largementa	Slow, broad
Larghetto	Slightly less slow
Lento	Slow
Adagissimo	Very slow
Adagio	Slow (from the Italian for at ease)
Adagietto	Slightly faster
Andante	Moderately slow (from the Italian for walk)
Andantino	Slightly slower than andante
Moderato	At a brisk walking pace
Allegretto	Fairly lively
Allegramente	Lightly
Allegro	Lively, fast (from the Italian for cheerful)
Vivace	Fast
Vivacissimo	Very quick
Presto	Very fast
Prestissimo	Extremely fast

Other musical terms

Term	Meaning
Agitato	Agitated or excited
Brillante	Sparkling, brilliant
Brio	Spirit or vigour
Crescendo	Gradual increase in volume
Dolce	Sweet, soft and gentle
Dolente	Sad
Forte	Loud or strong
Fortissimo	Very loud
Grave	Slow and serious
Legato	Smoothly and evenly
Molto	Much or very
Pianissimo	Very soft
Piano	Soft
Ritenuto	Slowing in tempo
Scherzo	Lively
Sotto voce	Quiet and subdued
Tutti	All the players

Famous songs

Waltzing Matilda
"Waltzing Matilda" has been described as Australia's unofficial national anthem. The song was written in Australia in 1895 by Andrew Barton "Banjo" Paterson. He was inspired by events during a sheep-shearers' strike the previous year. The music is by Christina Macpherson and is based on a traditional Scottish song.

Auld Lang Syne
The words of this song come from verses written by Scottish poet Robert Burns in 1788. The music is based on an old ballad. "Auld Lang Syne" (meaning old long since) is traditionally sung at midnight on New Year's Eve, except in Taiwan where it is a graduation song.

Happy Birthday to You
In 1893 two American sisters, who were teachers, wrote this song to sing in school assemblies. Mildred J. and Patty Smith Hill originally called the song "Good Morning to You". After the words were changed in 1924, it became known the world over. The song will be in copyright until 2030, but only for commercial purposes. Singing it at a birthday party does not infringe copyright!

Thomas Edison (1847–1931) with his first phonograph

2000s

1948 First 12-inch (30.5 cm) 331/3 rpm, micro-groove LP vinylite record is produced, with 23-minute capacity per side
1949 First 7-inch (17.8 cm), 45 rpm, micro-groove EP (Extended Play) vinylite record and player is introduced
1958 First stereo LPs are sold
1963 First compact audio cassette is produced
1969 Dolby Noise Reduction is introduced
1979 First Sony Walkman portable audio cassette players are sold
1980 First camcorders are sold
1982 First CDs are sold
1987 DAT (Digital Audio Tape) players are launched
1992 Mini-discs are introduced
1997 MP3 format is launched
1999 DVD-Audio format is introduced
2001 Apple's iPod is launched
2006 MSI launches the solar-powered MP3 player
2007 It is estimated that 200 billion CDs have been sold since the format was launched 25 years ago.

www.recording-history.org search

Strings

Violin   Viola

The viola is larger and deeper-voiced than the violin, and is played in the same way.

Cello

Double bass

Harp

The violin has a hollow wooden body which resonates when the violinist pulls a bow over the four strings. There may be 30 or more violins in a modern orchestra.

The cello's full name is the violoncello. It is the third-largest member of the violin family and is played sitting down.

The largest and deepest stringed instrument in an orchestra is the double bass. Double bass players usually stand to play, pulling a bow across the strings, or plucking them.

The orchestral harp has 48 strings of different lengths, attached to the top and side, and seven pedals at the base.

Opera terms

aria
A song for a single voice
comic opera
Opera with a comic plot
finale
The ending, when the whole cast often sing together
libretto
The text of an opera, from the Italian for little book

operetta
A light (rather than serious) opera, usually with an amusing story
prima donna
First lady (from the Italian) – the main female singer, or diva
recitative
A part in an opera that is spoken rather than sung

Instruments of the orchestra

The range and number of instruments in a modern orchestra varies enormously. There may be as many as 100 or more, and less familiar instruments are brought in for special performances. The ones illustrated here are the most common instruments.

Brass

Trumpet

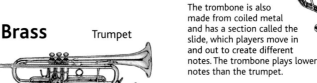

A trumpet is a tightly coiled metal tube with a cone called the bell at one end. Trumpets have three small buttons called valves which make different notes when pressed.

Flugelhorn

French horn

French horn players make different notes by changing the shape of their lips as they blow into the mouthpiece of this coiled metal tube.

The trombone is also made from coiled metal and has a section called the slide, which players move in and out to create different notes. The trombone plays lower notes than the trumpet.

Trombone

Tuba

Euphonium

There is usually just one tuba in an orchestra. It plays the lowest notes of all the brass instruments.

Singing parts

Name	Female voices
Soprano	The highest female voice
Mezzo soprano	Between a soprano and a contralto
Contralto	The lowest female voice
	Male voices
Alto	The highest male voice, traditionally sung by choirboys
Tenor	A high male voice. A countertenor voice is very high
Baritone	A voice higher than a bass, but lower than a tenor
Bass	The lowest male voice. Basso profundo is the lowest possible voice
Falsetto	An unnaturally high voice sung by tenors and basses

Woodwind

Piccolo

Flute

The concert flute is played through a blow hole at one end. Alto and bass flutes are larger versions which play lower notes. The piccolo is half the size of the concert flute and plays the highest notes in the orchestra.

Oboe

Oboe players blow through a double reed made from two small slices of cane tied together and inserted into the mouthpiece of the instrument.

Clarinet

The clarinet is also played through a reed. There are several different types of clarinet. B flat and A are played most often.

Bass clarinet

Bassoon

The bassoon plays the lowest notes of the woodwind instruments. It is a doubled-up wooden tube with a curved metal crook at one end, which holds the reed.

Cor anglais

Opera facts

Most-performed operas

Puccini's *La Bohème* is the most-performed opera in London and New York. It has been staged 545 times since 1897 at London's Royal Opera House, and 1,140 times at the Metropolitan Opera House in New York. *Aïda* and *Carmen* are the closest runners-up in both places.

Longest operas

Richard Wagner's *Gotterdämmerung* is the longest regularly performed opera. The opera can last up to six hours, including intervals.

Largest opera venues

The two largest opera houses where operas are regularly performed are in Italy and America. They are the Arena di Verona in Verona, which holds 16,663 people, and the Municipal Opera Theatre in St Louis, USA, which holds 11,745. The Teatro alla Scala, Milan, Italy, which has 3,600 seats, is one of the world's largest indoor opera theatres, although several US opera houses come close in size.

Nellie Melba

Grandest grand opera

The opera *Aïda* has often been performed on a grand scale, with a huge cast including elephants and other animals. It has been staged at the pyramids, Egypt, and in the year 2000 was performed in a football stadium in Shanghai, China, with a cast of 3,000 and an audience of 45,000.

Poster advertising *Madama Butterfly* by Puccini

MADAMA BUTTERFLY

Dame Nellie Melba

The real name of Australian opera singer Dame Nellie Melba (1881–1931) was Helen Mitchell. She was a great food-lover and inspired the famous chef Escoffier to create several new dishes for her at the Savoy Hotel, London. These included Peach Melba (a raspberry and redcurrant sauce poured over peaches and ice cream), Melba Toast (crisp dried bread) and Melba Garniture (chicken, truffles and mushrooms stuffed into tomatoes).

Percussion

Timpani/Kettledrums

Triangle

Cymbals

Side drum

Bass drum

Orchestras usually have three or four timpani or kettledrums. They are made of copper with a plastic skin stretched over the top.

Various other instruments are sometimes played in orchestras, including keyboards (piano, organ, celesta, etc), bells, castanets, glockenspiels, gongs, marimbas, rattles, tambourines, wind machines, wood blocks, xylophones, guitars, mandolins and saxophones.

Top singles of all time *

The numbers of singles sold outside the USA and some European countries have only been recorded fairly recently, so world sales here are estimates.

"White Christmas" was the world's bestselling single for more than 50 years until it was overtaken by Elton John's tribute to Princess Diana in 1997.

* These figures are only for singles sung in the English language.

Artist/single/year	Estimated sales (millions)	
	USA	World total
Elton John, "Candle in the Wind" (1997)/ "Something about the Way You Look Tonight" (1997)	11	37
Bing Crosby, "White Christmas" (1945)	n/a	30
Bill Haley and His Comets, "Rock Around the Clock" (1954)	n/a	17
Elvis Presley, "It's Now or Never" (1960)	1.0	12
The Beatles, "I Want to Hold Your Hand" (1963)	0.5	12
The Beatles, "Hey Jude" (1968)	4.0	10
Whitney Houston, "I Will Always Love You" (1992)	4.0	10

Downloads fact file

● In 2004 British rock band Arctic Monkeys released their songs only on the Internet.

● In 2004 download charts were published in the UK. Westlife had the first No. 1 downloaded single with "Flying Without Wings".

● By January 2005, digital downloads outsold physical singles in the UK for the first time. The official singles chart now included both downloads and sales of singles.

● In 2006, over 525 million individual tracks and 32.6 million full albums were downloaded in the USA.

● In 2006, "Keep Tryin'" by Utada Hikaru (Japan) set a new record for 2.5 million downloads.

● From 2003 to January 2008, iTunes had sold 4 billion downloads, over 70% of all online music sales.

Apple's iPod

The Beatles, 1963

See also

Entertainment lasts: page 306

One and only

The Beatles had all top 5 positions in the USA singles chart on 4 April 1964, with:

1 Can't Buy Me Love
2 Twist and Shout
3 She Loves You
4 I Want to Hold Your Hand
5 Please Please Me

Rock and pop facts

First CD single by a band
Dire Straits, "Brothers in Arms", 1985

Loudest rock band
During the 1960s and 70s, British group The Who played at 140 decibels – as loud as a jet at takeoff. Members of the band suffered hearing loss.

Biggest-selling group in the world ever
The Beatles' total sales of singles and albums on vinyl, tape and CD are well over one billion.

Biggest-selling album in the UK
The Beatles' *Sgt Pepper's Lonely Hearts Club Band* (1967) sold 250,000 in the UK in its first week and 500,000 within the month. It stayed at No. 1 for 27 weeks and total UK sales now exceed 4.5 million.

Most successive No. 1 albums by a solo artist (UK)
Robbie Williams had five No. 1 albums in the UK, 1997–2002. He won 14 BRIT awards, more than any other artist.

Albums longest in the charts
Pink Floyd's *Dark Side of The Moon* (1973) stayed in the UK charts for 741 weeks (14 years) and on the US Top 200 for 591 weeks. Fleetwood Mac's *Rumours* (1977) stayed in the UK charts for 477 weeks. It was also No. 1 in the US for 31 weeks, 19 of them consecutive, both a record for any group.

Biggest-selling album by a teenage solo singer
Britney Spears holds the record for her album *Baby One More Time* (1999). She is also the biggest-selling teenage artist – she'd sold more than 37 million records worldwide before her 20th birthday on 2 December 2001.

Bestselling single ever by a group in the UK
Queen's "Bohemian Rhapsody" (1975)

Major rock events

The following are among the best-attended rock events ever. The Live Aid concerts (13 July 1985) and Live 8 concerts (2 July 2005) had smaller audiences split over several venues but were reckoned to have had the greatest TV audiences of all time.

About 1.5 billion people, or a quarter of the world's population, watched Live Aid on television. The figure for Live 8 was over 2 billion.

Event/date	Est. audience
Rod Stewart, Copacabana Beach, Rio de Janeiro, Brazil, 31 December 1994	3,500,000
Golden Jubilee Concert, Buckingham Palace, London, 3 June 2002	over 1,000,000
Live 8, 10 free concerts in nine countries, 2 July 2005 (The largest single audience was 200,000 in Hyde Park, London.)	over 1,000,000
Garth Brooks in Central Park, New York, USA, 7 August 1997	750,000
US Festival, San Bernardino, California, 28–30 May 1982	725,000
Summer Jam, Watkins Glen, New York, 28 July 1973	600,132
Third Isle of Wight Festival, UK, 30 August 1970	up to 600,000
Simon and Garfunkel in Central Park, New York, USA, 19 September 1981	500,000
Rolling Stones Free Concert, Hyde Park, London, 5 July 1969	up to 500,000
Molson Canadian Rocks for Toronto, Toronto, Canada, 30 July 2003	489,176
Woodstock Festival, Bethel, New York, USA, 15–17 August 1969	over 400,000

Jimi Hendrix playing at Woodstock Festival, Bethel, New York, 1969

Top albums of all time worldwide

The USA has always led the world in album sales. Total worldwide sales are less easy to find, but using the best estimates available these albums can claim to be world-beaters.

Michael Jackson, *Thriller* (1982)
104 million copies (27 million USA)
Eagles, *Their Greatest Hits 1971–1975* (1976) 42 million copies (29 million USA)
AC/DC, *Back in Black* (1980)
42 million copies (21 million USA)
The Bodyguard (soundtrack) (1992)
42 million copies (17 million USA)
Backstreet Boys, Millennium (1999)
40 million copies (13 million USA)
Saturday Night Fever (soundtrack) (1977) 40 million copies (15 million USA)
Pink Floyd, *The Dark Side of The Moon* (1973) 40 million copies (15 million USA)

Shania Twain, *Come On Over* (1997)
39 million copies (20 million USA)
Meatloaf, *Bat out of Hell* (1978)
37 million copies (14 million USA)
Led Zeppelin, *Led Zeppelin IV* (1971)
32 million copies (23 million USA)
The Beatles, Sgt Pepper's Lonely Hearts Club Band (1967)
32 million copies (11 million USA)

John Lennon's Rolls-Royce

Bestsellers by a girl band
"Wannabe" (1996) by the Spice Girls is the bestselling single by a girl band in both the UK and USA. Their *Spice* (1996) is the bestselling album by a girl band in the UK, but the Dixie Chicks' *Wide Open Spaces* (1998) is the bestselling album by a girl band in the USA.

Girl group with most UK chart hits
Bananarama – 26
Band with most UK chart hits
Status Quo – 58, followed by The Rolling Stones – 51

www.theofficialcharts.com   search

Treasures of rock

Fans of rock music often like to buy items that belonged to their favourite singers and bands. The more successful the artist, the higher the price.

● 1965 Rolls-Royce Phantom V touring limousine, painted in psychedelic colours, owned by John Lennon of The Beatles. Sold at auction in New York, USA, on 29 June 1985 for £1,768,462 ($2,299,000).

● Steinway Model Z upright piano owned by John Lennon. Sold in an online auction on 17 October 2000 for £1,450,000 ($2,098,860).

● "Tiger" guitar owned by Jerry Garcia of Grateful Dead. Sold in New York, USA, on 9 May 2002 for £657,850 ($957,500).

● "Blackie" Fender Stratocaster guitar owned by Eric Clapton. Sold in New York, USA, on 25 June 2004 for £528,068 ($959,500).

● Bernie Taupin's handwritten lyrics for the re-written "Candle in the Wind", sung by Sir Elton John in Westminster Abbey at the funeral of Diana, Princess of Wales. Sold in Los Angeles, USA, on 11 February 1998 for £278,512 ($400,000).

Canadian circus troupe Cirque du Soleil (French for "Circus of the Sun")

A quick history of circus

Open air circuses with acrobats, chariot races, bareback riders and comedy acts were popular in ancient Rome. In the 18th century fixed buildings were used, and in the early 19th century travelling circuses appeared in Europe and America. Troupes moved from place to place, setting up a large tent, or "big top". The most famous American circus proprietor was Phineas T. Barnum (1810–91).

His shows were spectacular, with trick riding, juggling, trapeze acts, tightrope walking, strong men, and wild-cat tamers. They also featured "human oddities", or freak shows, in which Siamese twins, giants or bearded ladies were often paraded before the curious crowd. Since the 20th century, all-human Chinese and Russian circus companies have toured the world, as well as alternative circus troupes such as Circus Oz, Ra Ra Zoo and Archaos, whose acts have included juggling with chainsaws and jumping over blazing motorbikes.

See also
Tom Thumb: page 95

Famous playwrights and their famous plays

Aeschylus (Greek, c. 525–546 BC) – *The Oresteia*
J.M. Barrie (Scottish, 1860–1937) – *Peter Pan*
Samuel Beckett (Irish, 1906–89) – *Waiting for Godot*
Anton Chekhov (Russian, 1860–1904) – *The Cherry Orchard*
Noël Coward (English, 1899–1973) – *Private Lives*
Euripides (Greek, c. 484–406 BC) – *The Trojan Women*
Federico García Lorca (Spanish, 1898–1936) – *Blood Wedding*
Oliver Goldsmith (English 1728–74) – *She Stoops to Conquer*
David Hare (English, 1947–) – *Plenty*
Henrik Ibsen (Norwegian, 1828–1906) – *Hedda Gabler*
Ben Jonson (English, 1572–1637) – *The Alchemist*
Christopher Marlowe (English, 1564–93) – *Doctor Faustus*
Arthur Miller (American, 1915–2005) – *The Crucible*
Molière (French, 1622–73) – *Tartuffe*
John Osborne (English, 1929–94) – *Look Back in Anger*
Harold Pinter (English, 1930–) – *The Birthday Party*
Peter Shaffer (English, 1926–) – *Amadeus*
William Shakespeare (English, 1564–1616) – *Hamlet*
George Bernard Shaw (Irish, 1856–1950) – *Pygmalion*
Richard Brinsley Sheridan (English, 1751–1816) – *The Rivals*
Neil Simon (American, 1927–) – *Plaza Suite*
Sophocles (Greek, c. 496–405 BC) – *Antigone*
Tom Stoppard (Czech, 1937–) – *Rosencrantz and Guildenstern are Dead*
J.M. Synge (Irish, 1871–1909) – *The Playboy of the Western World*
John Webster (English, 1580–1625) – *The Duchess of Malfi*
Oscar Wilde (Irish, 1854–1900) – *The Importance of Being Earnest*
Tennessee Williams (American, 1911–83) – *A Streetcar Named Desire*

Theatre records

First actor
Thespis was the first performer ever recorded. He was an actor in Greece in 534 BC. At this time, Greek actors used masks, and Thespis was the first to use stage make-up.

World's oldest theatres
The oldest indoor theatre in the world is the Teatro Olimpico, Vicenza, Italy, which opened on 3 March 1585. London's oldest theatre is the Theatre Royal, Drury Lane, which opened on 7 May 1663. It burnt down in 1672 and was rebuilt by Sir Christopher Wren. In 1800 it became the world's first theatre to have safety curtains. The oldest surviving theatre in the USA is the Walnut Street Theatre in Philadelphia, Pennsylvania.

World's biggest theatres
The National People's Congress Building Theatre, Beijing, China was built in 1959 and can hold audiences of 10,000. The Perth Entertainment Centre, Australia (1976) has up to 8,500 seats, the Chaplin (originally Blanquetta), Havana, Cuba (1949) has 6,500 and Radio City Music Hall, New York, USA, has 6,200. The 3,483-seater Hammersmith Odeon is the largest theatre in Britain, but the Royal Albert Hall in London can hold up to 7,000, depending on the event and how the seating is organized.

The Teatro Olimpico in Vicenza, Italy

Worst disasters at a theatre

Fires, in which people were burned or trampled to death, have caused the worst disasters at theatres. The worst ever was at Canton (now Guangzhou), China, in 1845 when 1,670 died. Europe's worst was at the Ring Theatre, Vienna, Austria, in 1881, which killed at least 620 people. The worst in the USA was at the Iroquois Theatre, Chicago, in 1903, which left 602 dead. These are the worst single-building (rather than city or forest) fires in history.

Longest-running shows

The Golden Horseshoe Revue (Disneyland, California, 1955–86) 47,250 performances

The Mousetrap (London, 1952–) *23,026 performances

The Fantasticks (New York, 1960–2002) 17,162 performances

La Cantatrice Chauve (The Bald Soprano) (Paris, 1957–) *16,743 performances

Shear Madness (Boston, 1980–) *11,783 performances

Les Misérables (London, 1985–) *9,934 performances

The Mousetrap (Toronto, 1977–2004) over 9,600 performances

The Drunkard (Los Angeles, 1933–59) 9,477 performances

Cats (London, 1981–2002) 8,949 performances

Shear Madness (Washington, 1987–) *8,930 performances

The Phantom of the Opera (London, 1986–) *8,900 performances

Perfect Crime (New York, 1987–) *8,506 performances

The Phantom of the Opera (New York, 1988–) *8,355 performances

Blood Brothers (London, 1988–) *8,142 performances

Tubes (New York, 1991–2005) 8,006 performances

Shear Madness (Chicago, 1982–2007) 7,697 performances

* Still running, total as at 1 March 2008

Short runs

A play is expensive to stage, so everyone involved hopes that it will run for long enough to earn back the money spent on it. Shows that run for years earn back their initial investment many times over, but some fail on their first night, or even earlier!

● On 18 December 1816 the one and only performance of J.R. Ronden's The Play Without an A took place at the Paris Théâtre des Variétés. It was written with words without the letter "a", which made it very hard to perform and understand. The audience rioted and did not allow the play to finish.

● In 1888, at London's Shaftesbury Theatre, The Lady of Lyons failed to make its first night when the safety curtain jammed.

● The Intimate Revue opened and closed at the Duchess Theatre, London, on 11 March 1930. It was a disaster from start to finish. The scenery changes took so long that seven scenes were abandoned to allow the long-suffering audience to go home before midnight.

● Little Johnny Jones, a musical starring Donny Osmond, opened and closed at the Alvin Theater, New York, on 21 March 1982.

● Carrie closed in New York on 17 May 1988 after struggling through five performances. It is said to have cost the Royal Shakespeare Company, who performed it, $7 million.

Longest play

Neil Oram's The Warp was first performed at the ICA (Institute of Contemporary Art) in London from 18–20 January 1979. It lasted 18 hours and 5 minutes.

Oberammergau

Oberammergau is a town in Bavaria, Germany, where a Passion play (a play dealing with the crucifixion of Christ) is performed. The first play was put on in 1634 after an outbreak of plague in the town. The people vowed to repeat the play every ten years from then on. More than 2,000 people take part in the play, nearly all of them from Oberammergau, and the performance lasts six hours.

Scene from the Singapore production of Les Misérables

John Travolta in *Saturday Night Fever*, 1977

Highest-earning dance films

The most successful dance film of all time is *Saturday Night Fever*. It starred John Travolta as a talented disco dancer and has earned nearly $300 million around the world. Below are some of the other highest-earning dance films in the world.

1 *Saturday Night Fever* (1977) $285.4 million
2 *The Full Monty* (1997) $257.9 m.
3 *Dirty Dancing* (1987) $214.0 m.
4 *Shall We Dance* (2004) $170.1 m.
5 *Save the Last Dance* (2001) $131.7 m.
6 *Staying Alive* (1983) $127.6 m.
7 *Step Up* (2006) $114.2 m.
8 *Coyote Ugly* (2000) $113.9 m.
9 *Billy Elliot* (2000) $109.3 m.
10 *Flashdance* (1983) $94.9 m.

Girl breakdancing

Dance spectaculars

American choreographer Busby Berkeley (1895–1976) staged the most spectacular dance films ever made. He used his knowledge of organizing military parades during World War I to create dance numbers with casts of hundreds.

They were often photographed from cranes high above them, on huge sets and sometimes with giant mirrors so that they formed geometrical patterns apparently vanishing into infinity. His films included *42nd Street* (1933) and *Gold Diggers of 1933* (1933), which was hit by an earthquake during filming in Los Angeles. The quake cut all power and nearly collapsed the set.

Breakdancing

Breakdancing began in New York in the late 1970s and early 1980s. Some of its movements came from martial arts such as kung fu and from gymnastics. It became a feature of hip-hop culture.

Popular dances

Barn dances
These developed from traditional Scottish dancing. They were popular in the USA in the 1890s when they were held to celebrate the building of a barn on a farm. Barn dances are still held today in country areas.

Belly dance
The popular name of a style of dance that originated in the Middle East, especially Egypt. It was originally danced only by women, and men were not permitted to watch. An Essex woman named Eileen Foucher set a belly dance record. She danced for 106 hours, from 30 July to 3 August 1984.

The Charleston
The Charleston was named after the city in South Carolina, USA and was one of the most popular dances of the 1920s.

The conga
People dance the conga in a line, each dancer holding on to the person in front. The conga began in Latin American carnivals and spread to the USA in the 1930s. The Miami Super Conga was held on 13 March 1988. The conga line was made up of 119,986 people – only 14 short of 120,000.

The hula
The hip-swaying hula is danced by Polynesian islanders who settled in Hawaii. It was banned by Christian missionaries for a while, but became popular again in the late 19th century.

The limbo
This competitive dance comes from Trinidad. Dancers lean back to pass under a bar, which is placed lower and lower. The winner is the dancer who passes under the lowest bar. On 2 March 1991 Dennis Walston, known as King Limbo, (USA) limboed under a bar 15.25 cm (6 in) high.

Lindy Hop
The Lindy Hop was a version of the Charleston and another dance called the Breakaway. It was named after US aviator Charles Lindbergh (nicknamed Lindy). In 1927 he became the first person to fly solo across the Atlantic.

Morris dancing
This is a traditional English folk dance. Dancers wear special costumes with bells, and hold sticks, handkerchiefs and swords.

The polka
The polka was originally a Czech peasant dance which developed in Bohemia in the 1830s. It became popular in Paris in the 1840s and eventually spread worldwide.

Dance marathons

Dance marathons began in New York in 1923, when Alma Cummings won a contest by dancing for 27 hours with six different partners. Marathons were popular during the Depression years of the 1930s, when unemployed people danced non-stop for many days to win money.

The last couple standing won. Dancers were allowed only very short breaks and partners pinched and kicked each other to stay awake or tied themselves together to prevent one from falling down. Dance marathons were banned in many places because they were so dangerous for people's health.

Mike Ritof and Edith Boudreaux danced from 29 August 1930 to 1 April 1931 at the Merry Garden Ballroom, Chicago, USA, to win a prize of $2,000. They danced for a total of 5,154 hours 28 minutes 30 seconds (215 days) with only short rest breaks.

See also
Film winners: pages 268–69

Dance dummy

In 1921 Sidney E. Feist of Brooklyn, New York, USA, patented a female dummy to help men practise their ballroom dancing steps. The dummy partner had a telescopic leg with a rotating wooden ball at the end so that she could be wheeled around the floor.

The twist
The twist started when Hank Ballard recorded the song of this name in 1959. It became popular when Chubby Checker performed his cover version on US television on 22 October 1961. A woman called Ra Denny holds the twist record. She twisted for 100 hours at Christchurch, New Zealand, in March 1962.

The waltz
The waltz began in Austria in the late 18th century. Its name comes from a German word meaning to revolve. Many people were shocked by the dance when it first came to England in 1812 because it involved men and women dancing close to each other.

Flamenco dancing
Flamenco is popular in Andalusia, Spain, and comes from Moorish and gypsy dancing. It is lively and exciting; the dancers often play castanets and are accompanied by guitars, clapping and drumming.

www.streetswing.com/histmain.htm   search

Best-known ballets

Ballet	Composer	Choreographer	First performed
La Bayadère	Minkus	Petipa	1877
Cinderella	Prokofiev	Ashton	1948
Coppélia	Delibes	Saint-Léon	1870
The Firebird	Stravinsky	Fokine	1910
Giselle	Adam	Perrot/Coralli	1841
The Nutcracker	Tchaikovsky	Ivanov	1892
Romeo and Juliet	Prokofiev	Lavrovsky	1940
The Sleeping Beauty	Tchaikovsky	Petipa	1890
Swan Lake	Tchaikovsky	Petipa	1895
La Sylphide	Schneitzhoeffer	F. Taglioni	1832
Les Sylphides	Chopin	Fokine	1909

Best-known ballet companies

Alvin Ailey American Dance Theater (New York, USA), founded 1958
American Ballet Theater (New York, USA), founded 1940
Australian Ballet (Melbourne, Australia), founded 1962
Ballet Rambert (London, UK), founded 1926
Ballets Russes* (Moscow, Russia), founded 1909
Bolshoi Ballet (Moscow, Russia), founded 1776
Dance Theater of Harlem (New York, USA), founded 1961
English National Ballet (London, UK), founded 1950
Kirov/Marlinsky Ballet (St Petersburg, Russia), founded 1935
Martha Graham Dance Company (New York, USA), founded 1927
Merce Cunningham Dance Company (New York, USA), founded 1953
National Ballet of Canada (Toronto, Canada), founded 1951
New York City Ballet (New York, USA), founded 1948
Paris Opéra Company (Paris, France), founded 1669
Royal Ballet (London, UK), founded 1936
Royal Danish Ballet (Copenhagen, Denmark), founded 1748

* not in existence today

Ballet terms

arabesque
Position in which the dancer stands on one leg, with arms extended, the body bent forwards and the other leg stretched back

ballerina
A female ballet dancer

barre
The bar dancers hold on to while they practise, to help them balance

choreographer
The person who works out the steps and movements in a ballet

corps de ballet
Chorus of dancers (not those dancing solo)

entrechat
Rapid crossing and uncrossing of the feet during a jump

fouetté
A turn in which one leg is whipped round

glissade
A gliding movement

jeté
A jump from one foot to the other

pas
A dance step

pas de deux
A dance for two (usually the principal male and female dancers in the company)

pas seule
A solo dance

pirouette
A complete turn on one leg

plié
A knee-bending movement

pointes
On the tips of the toes. Dancers wear special point shoes with blocks in the toes to help them stand on their toes

positions
A range of five positions that are the basis of ballet dancing

prima ballerina
The leading ballerina in a company

tutu
The stiff skirt worn by ballerinas performing classical ballet

Sleeping Beauty by the Royal Ballet

See also
Famous last words: page 304

Darcey Bussell dancing with Igor Zelensky

Famous ballet dancers

Carlos Acosta (Cuban, 1973–) Trained in Cuba and became a principal dancer with the Royal Ballet in London. He has also staged his own show.

Mikhail Baryshnikov (Russian, 1948–) One of the greatest male dancers. He began with the Kirov in Russia but later joined the American Ballet Theatre.

Matthew Bourne (British, 1960–) Began as a dancer and became a famous choreographer and director. He is best known for his production of *Swan Lake*, in which all the swans are played by male dancers.

Darcey Bussell (British, 1969–) Became a principal dancer with the Royal Ballet at the age of 20. She is one of their most popular soloists, and in 1995 she was awarded an OBE for her work in dance. She retired in 2007.

Michael Clark (British, 1962–) Danced with the Royal Ballet and Merce Cunningham companies before becoming a choreographer and starting his own company. He is best known for his very original shows and for using music such as punk in his work.

Sir Anton Dolin (British, 1904–83) Originally danced with Diaghilev's Ballets Russes. He founded the London Festival Ballet (now English National Ballet).

Sir Anthony Dowell (British, 1943–) He was principal dancer with the Royal Ballet for many years and was Director of the Royal Ballet for 15 years from 1986.

Dame Margot Fonteyn (British, 1919–91) Royal Ballet prima ballerina, she is most famous for her long-term partnership with Rudolf Nureyev.

Dame Beryl Grey (British, 1927–) Prima ballerina at the Sadler's Wells Ballet, London and the first English ballerina to perform with the Bolshoi.

Sylvie Guillem (French, 1965–) Principal guest artist with the Royal Ballet, she is a versatile and athletic dancer, famous for her extraordinarily high leg extensions.

Dame Alicia Markova (British, 1910–2004) She danced with Anton Dolin and they are most famous for their *Giselle*. Dolin and Markova formed a ballet company.

Rudolf Nureyev (Russian, 1938–93) Former Kirov star who defected to the West and became the most popular male dancer of his generation.

Anna Pavlova (Russian, 1881–1931) Became the most famous ballerina of her generation through her world tours.

Dame Marie Rambert (Polish/British, 1888–1982) Dancer and teacher whose dance company promoted many new works.

Maria Taglioni (Swedish/Italian, 1804–84) One of the first ballet stars, famous for her role in *La Sylphide*.

Vaslav Nijinsky

(Russian, 1890–1950) One of most famous of all male dancers. He was a leading dancer with the Ballets Russes and best known for his performance in Stravinsky's *Rite of Spring*.

Ballet firsts and records

First ballet
In the late 16th century, performances that included dancing, music and acting were given at the French court of Henri II and Catherine de Médici. The *Ballet Comique de La Reine* (1581) was the first recorded.

First professional ballerina
On 21 January 1681 Mademoiselle de La Fontaine appeared in Jean Baptiste Lully's *The Triumph of Love* at the Paris Opéra.

First ballet in the USA
On 7 February 1827 Francisquy Hutin performed a ballet in the play *The Deserter* at the Bowery Theatre, New York. The women in the audience were so shocked by it that they fled from the theatre.

Most curtain calls for a ballet performance
In October 1964 Margot Fonteyn and Rudolf Nureyev received 89 curtain calls after their performance in *Swan Lake* at the Staatsoper, in Vienna, Austria.

Most pirouettes
Delia Gray (15) performed 166 consecutive turns at The Playhouse, Harlow, Essex, UK, on 2 June 1991.

First tutu and first on points
Ballerina Maria Taglioni (1804–84) wore a muslin dress known as a tutu when she danced in *La Sylphide* at the Paris Opéra on 12 March 1832. The dress allowed more freedom of movement so became popular in classical ballet. In the same ballet she danced on points without support – the first time any dancer had done so.

www.ballet.co.uk   search

Film, TV & Radio

Indiana's back!

Eighteen years after "Last Crusade" came the release of a fourth film in the Indiana Jones series. Harrison Ford was 65 years old when *Indiana Jones and the Kingdom of the Crystal Skull* was released – he first played the part in 1981. The first three films have earned more than $1.2 billion worldwide.

Poster advertising the Indian film *Ek Kali Muskai* (1968)

Top cinema-goers

1 India 3,997,000,000
2 USA 1,448,500,000
3 France 188,700,000
4 China 176,200,000
5 Mexico 165,500,000
6 Japan 164,300,000
7 S. Korea 163,900,000
8 UK 156,600,000
9 Germany 136,700,000
10 Spain 121,700,000

Top feature film-producing countries

Feature films produced (2005)			
● India	1,041	● Russia	160
● USA	699	○ Spain	142
● Japan	356	● UK	124
● China	260	● Germany	103
○ France	240	● Bangladesh	102

No. of films / Countries

Casts of thousands

About 200,000 of the extras in *Gandhi* were volunteers, but another 94,560 were paid a small fee. They appeared in the scene showing Gandhi's funeral, which lasted just two minutes and five seconds after editing.

In *Around the World in 80 Days* (1956), there were animal extras too – 3,800 sheep, 2,448 buffalos, 950 donkeys, 800 horses, 512 monkeys, 17 bulls, 15 elephants, 6 skunks and 4 ostriches. In recent films, such as the *Lord of the Rings* trilogy, scenes with thousands of people were computer-generated, so huge numbers of extras were not needed.

Film	Extras
Gandhi (UK, 1982)	294,560
Kolberg (Germany, 1945)	187,000
Monster Wangmagwi (South Korea, 1967)	157,000
War and Peace (USSR, 1968)	120,000
Ilya Muromets (*The Sword and the Dragon*) (USSR, 1956)	106,000
Dun-Huang (*Ton ko*) (Japan, 1988)	100,000
Razboiul Independentei (*The War of Independence*) (Romania, 1912)	80,000
Around the World in 80 Days (USA, 1956)	68,894
Intolerance (USA, 1916)	60,000
Dny Zrady (*Days of Betrayal*) (Czechoslovakia, 1973)	60,000

Who does what in a film?

Director The director controls everything, gives orders to the cast and crew and makes sure that the script is followed.

Producer(s) There can be more than one producer, who is responsible for raising the money to make the film and for other important activities, such as casting and controlling the costs.

Cast The actors and actresses who appear in the film.

Screenplay writer The person who writes the script. This gives the actors and actresses their lines and explains how the action takes place.

Extras The people who appear in crowd scenes but do not have speaking parts.

Animatronic engineer The person who makes the robotic creatures used in science-fiction and fantasy films.

Art director The art director coordinates the costumes, sets and make-up to set the overall style of the film.

Best boy The deputy electrician, assistant to the gaffer.

Casting director The person who chooses the actors for each role in the film.

Caterer The caterer supplies meals so that the cast and crew can work all day.

Cinematographer The person who directs the lighting and films the action, originally called the cameraman.

Clapper loader Details of each scene are written on a special board called a clapper board. The clapper loader snaps it shut in front of the camera as filming begins to record what is being filmed.

Film budgets

The production budgets of a film include the salaries paid to the director, writer(s), stars and crew, the designing and building of sets, costumes, the transport and location costs (filming away from the studio) and the cost of making and editing the film. Other costs include P & A (Prints and Advertising) – making thousands of copies of the film, distributing them to cinemas, and advertising the film in the press, on television and on the Internet.

An average Hollywood feature film takes eight weeks to film. It may cost $5 million or more a week, depending on how lavish the production is and how expensive the stars are. *Titanic* (1997) held the record for largest production budget ($200 million) until it was equalled by *Spider-Man 2* (2004), then broken by *King Kong* (2005) at $207 million. It has since been overtaken by *Superman Returns* (2006) at $270 million and *Spider-Man 3* (2007) at $258 million.

Most cinema screens

Country	Estimated number of screens (2006)
1 USA	38,415
2 China	37,753
3 India	11,183
4 France	5,632
5 Germany	4,848
6 Spain	4,299
7 Italy	3,987
8 Mexico	3,762
9 UK	3,569
10 Canada	2,986

Costs and income of a typical big-budget Hollywood film, *Spider-Man 2* (2004)

COSTS
Estimated cost ($US million)

Actors	17
Toby Maguire	7
Kirsten Dunst	3
Alfred Molina	3
Rest of cast	10
Director (Sam Raimi)	20
Story rights	10
Screenplay	15
Producers	45
Production costs	65
Special effects	5
Music	200
Total production budget	200
Prints and advertising	75
Income	374
US box office	410
Rest of world	
Home video/DVD sales and rentals	58.5
TV broadcast rights	15.0
Total	**784**
Profit	509

Video and DVD sales and rentals and TV broadcast rights would also add to the total income

La Géode cinema stands in the Parc de la Villette, Paris. Inside the enormous dome is a giant screen measuring 1,000 sq m (10,764 sq ft).

www.imdb.com   search

Composer The composer writes the music or adapts an existing score as a backing track for the film.

Costume designer The costume designer is responsible for designing and supplying the clothing worn by the cast.

Editor The editor cuts and connects the best versions of each section of film to create the final version.

Gaffer The chief electrician, who is responsible for lighting the set. The word may come from slang for grandfather – a senior person respected by everyone. Gaffer tape is the heavy-duty tape used on sets to secure cables and almost anything else.

Key grip A grip is responsible for moving the sets and for laying the tracks on which the camera runs. The key grip is in charge of all the other grips.

Make-up artist He or she applies the cosmetics which alter or improve an actor's looks under the studio lights.

Sound engineer This engineer makes sure that the dialogue and other sounds heard on the film are properly recorded and synchronized with the action.

Special-effects coordinator This person is responsible for creating spectacular scenes with photographic, mechanical and computer methods.

Stunt man/woman Specialists who perform the actions that are too difficult or dangerous for an actor. Stunt doubles are stunt men or women made up to look like the actors so it looks as though the actors have performed a feat themselves.

Wardrobe mistress The wardrobe mistress (or master) is in charge of the costumes, making sure they fit, are in good condition and available when they are needed for a scene.

R2D2 and C3PO, robots from the *Star Wars* films

Top documentary films

Documentary films present true factual situations and real people, instead of stories acted out by film stars.

These include the exploration of the world and space, and actual events filmed as they happen. Some of the most successful documentaries are IMAX (large format) films that have earned steadily over several years, unlike feature films, which have more limited runs.

Film	Subject	World total ($US million)
Grand Canyon: The Hidden Secrets* (1984)	Exploration	239.0
Fahrenheit 9/11 (2004)	War on terrorism	222.4
The Dream is Alive* (1985)	Space Shuttle	200.0
Everest* (1998)	Exploration	134.0
March of the Penguins (2005)	Nature	128.0
To Fly* (1976)	History of flying	120.7
Mysteries of Egypt (1998)	Historical	102.6
T-Rex: Back to the Cretaceous (1998)	Dinosaurs	97.0
Space Station 3D* (2002)	International Space Station	96.3
Jackass: Number Two (2006)	Comedy stunts	84.6
Jackass: The Movie (2002)	Comedy stunts	79.5
Blue Planet* (1990)	Earth from Space	71.9

*IMAX film

Highest-earning films

These films have made the most money at the box office.

Film	World total ($US million)
Titanic (1997)	1,845.0
The Lord of the Rings: The Return of the King (2003)	1,129.2
Pirates of the Caribbean: Dead Man's Chest (2006)	1,066.2
Harry Potter and the Sorcerer's Stone (2001)	985.8
Pirates of the Caribbean: At World's End (2007)	961.0
Harry Potter and the Order of the Phoenix (2007)	938.5
Lord of the Rings: The Two Towers (2002)	926.3
Star Wars: Episode I – The Phantom Menace (1999)	924.3
Shrek 2* (2004)	920.7
Jurassic Park (1993)	914.7
Harry Potter and the Goblet of Fire (2005)	896.0
Spider-Man 3 (2007)	890.9
Harry Potter and the Chamber of Secrets (2002)	879.0
The Lord of the Rings: The Fellowship of the Ring (2001)	871.4
Finding Nemo* (2003)	864.6
Star Wars: Episode III – Revenge of the Sith (2005)	850.0
Spider-Man (2002)	821.7
Independence Day (1996)	817.0
Star Wars: Episode IV – A New Hope (1977)	797.9
Shrek the Third (2007)	797.8
Harry Potter and the Prisoner of Azkaban (2004)	795.5
E.T. the Extra-Terrestrial (1982)	792.9
Spider-Man 2 (2004)	784.0
The Lion King* (1994)	783.8
The Da Vinci Code (2006)	758.2
The Chronicles of Narnia: The Lion, The Witch and The Wardrobe (2005)	744.8
The Matrix Reloaded (2003)	738.6
Transformers (2007)	706.5
Forrest Gump (1994)	677.4
The Sixth Sense (1999)	672.8
Pirates of the Caribbean: The Curse of the Black Pearl (2003)	654.3
Ice Age: The Meltdown* (2006)	651.6
Star Wars: Episode II – Attack of the Clones (2002)	649.4
The Incredibles* (2004)	631.4
Ratatouille* (2007)	620.6

* animated film

Computer games and films

Computer games are big business and a number of recent blockbuster films have been based on some of the most popular games.

These include *Lara Croft: Tomb Raider* (game 1996, film 2001), *Mortal Kombat* (game 1992, film 1995) and *Super Mario Bros* (game 1985, film 1993).

The link between films and games also works the other way, with games based on live-action and animated films – for example, *The Incredibles* (film and game 2004) and *The Lord of the Rings: Battle for Middle Earth* (2004) – a game based on *The Lord of the Rings* trilogy (2001–2003).

James Bond films

Including the latest, *Quantum of Solace*, Ian Fleming's 12 James Bond books have been made into 22 official and two unofficial films, the original *Casino Royale* (1967), a comedy starring David Niven, and *Never say Never Again* (1983), with Sean Connery as Bond, which was a remake of *Thunderball*.

Film	Bond actor	World total ($US million)
Quantum of Solace (not yet released)	Daniel Craig	
Casino Royale (2006)	Daniel Craig	594.2
Die Another Day (2002)	Pierce Brosnan	456.0
The World is Not Enough (1999)	Pierce Brosnan	390.0
GoldenEye (1995)	Pierce Brosnan	350.7
Tomorrow Never Dies (1997)	Pierce Brosnan	339.3
Moonraker (1979)	Roger Moore	202.7
For Your Eyes Only (1981)	Roger Moore	195.3
The Living Daylights (1987)	Timothy Dalton	191.2
The Spy Who Loved Me (1977)	Roger Moore	185.4
Octopussy (1983)	Roger Moore	183.7
Licence to Kill (1989)	Timothy Dalton	156.2
A View to a Kill (1985)	Roger Moore	152.4
Thunderball (1965)	Sean Connery	141.2
Live and Let Die (1973)	Roger Moore	126.4
Goldfinger (1964)	Sean Connery	124.9
Diamonds Are Forever (1971)	Sean Connery	116.0
You Only Live Twice (1967)	Sean Connery	111.6
The Man with the Golden Gun (1974)	Roger Moore	97.6
From Russia with Love (1963)	Sean Connery	78.9
On Her Majesty's Secret Service (1969)	George Lazenby	64.6
Dr No (1963)	Sean Connery	59.7

Daniel Craig as James Bond in the remake of *Casino Royale*

Quantum of Solace

Released in 2008, the 22nd official James Bond film takes its title from a short story in a collection by Bond creator Ian Fleming, *For Your Eyes Only* (1960). The film's events follow on from *Casino Royale* (2006), in which Daniel Craig first starred as Bond.

See also

All about comics: page 236

George Clooney as Batman

Top films based on comic books

Comic book characters have been popular subjects for film makers ever since the 1930s. The characters are already familiar, so are immediately appealing to audiences. The exploits of superheroes such as Superman and Batman are perfect for exciting action films, many of which have been hugely successful.

Film	Film released	Comic first published	World total ($US million)
Spider-Man 3	2007	1962	890.9
Spider-Man	2002	1962	821.7
Spider-Man 2	2004	1962	784.0
Men in Black	1997	1990	589.4
X-Men: The Last Stand	2006	1963	459.3
300	2007	1998	456.1
Men in Black II	2002	1990	441.8
Batman	1989	1939	413.4
X2: X-Men United	2003	1963	407.6
Superman Returns	2006	1938	391.1
Batman Begins	2005	1939	371.9
The Mask	1994	1991	351.6

The American Film Institute's top films

The American Film Institute has listed greatest films in a number of categories, based on the views of a panel of 1,500 film experts.

Funniest films

1. *Some Like It Hot* (1959)
2. *Tootsie* (1982)
3. *Dr Strangelove, or: How I Learned to Stop Worrying and Love the Bomb* (1964)
4. *Annie Hall* (1977)
5. *Duck Soup* (1933)
6. *Blazing Saddles* (1974)
7. *M*A*S*H* (1970)
8. *It Happened One Night* (1934)
9. *The Graduate* (1967)
10. *Airplane!* (1980)

Love stories

1. *Casablanca* (1942)
2. *Gone With the Wind* (1939)
3. *West Side Story* (1961)
4. *Roman Holiday* (1953)
5. *An Affair to Remember* (1957)
6. *The Way We Were* (1973)
7. *Doctor Zhivago* (1965)
8. *It's a Wonderful Life* (1946)
9. *Love Story* (1970)
10. *City Lights* (1931)

Thrillers

1. *Psycho* (1960)
2. *Jaws* (1975)
3. *The Exorcist* (1973)
4. *North by Northwest* (1959)
5. *The Silence of the Lambs* (1991)
6. *Alien* (1979)
7. *The Birds* (1963)
8. *The French Connection* (1971)
9. *Rosemary's Baby* (1968)
10. *Raiders of the Lost Ark* (1981)

Greatest American movies of all time

1. *Citizen Kane* (1941)
2. *Casablanca* (1942)
3. *The Godfather* (1972)
4. *Gone with the Wind* (1939)
5. *Lawrence of Arabia* (1962)
6. *The Wizard of Oz* (1939)
7. *The Graduate* (1967)
8. *On the Waterfront* (1954)
9. *Schindler's List* (1993)
10. *Singin' in the Rain* (1952)

Orson Welles in *Citizen Kane*

The Oscars®

What is an Oscar?

The Academy Awards or "Oscars" have been presented since 1929. The award is a gold-plated statuette made of tin, copper and antimony. It is 34.3 cm (13.5 in) high and weighs 3.8 kg (8.4 lb). Winning an Oscar is important because it encourages more people to see the film and helps the individual winners' careers.

Why is it called an Oscar?

According to legend, Academy librarian Margaret Herrick named it when she declared that the statuette looked like her Uncle Oscar!

Who decides who wins?

Members of the US Academy of Motion Picture Arts & Science members, including previous nominees and winners, vote to create a shortlist of five nominees in each of 24 categories, other than special, honorary and technical awards.

Who can win an Oscar?

The main categories are Best Picture, Best Director, Best Actor, Best Actress, Best Supporting Actor and Best Supporting Actress. There are other awards eg screenplay, cinematography, soundtrack, documentary, animated feature, foreign film.

Oscar® winners

These are the Best Picture, Best Actor and Best Actress winners for the last 25 years. The date given is the date of release. Oscars are awarded the following year.

Year	Best Picture	Best Actor	Best Actress
2007	No Country for Old Men	Daniel Day-Lewis	Marion Cotillard
2006	The Departed	Forest Whitaker	Helen Mirren
2005	Crash	Philip Seymour Hoffman	Reese Witherspoon
2004	Million Dollar Baby	Jamie Foxx	Hilary Swank
2003	The Lord of the Rings: The Return of the King	Sean Penn	Charlize Theron
2002	Chicago	Adrien Brody	Nicole Kidman
2001	A Beautiful Mind	Denzel Washington	Halle Berry
2000	Gladiator	Russell Crowe	Julia Roberts
1999	American Beauty	Kevin Spacey	Hilary Swank
1998	Shakespeare in Love	Roberto Benigni	Gwyneth Paltrow
1997	Titanic	Jack Nicholson	Helen Hunt
1996	The English Patient	Geoffrey Rush	Frances McDormand
1995	Braveheart	Nicholas Cage	Susan Sarandon
1994	Forrest Gump	Tom Hanks	Jessica Lange
1993	Schindler's List	Tom Hanks	Holly Hunter
1992	Unforgiven	Al Pacino	Emma Thompson
1991	The Silence of the Lambs	Anthony Hopkins	Jodie Foster
1990	Dances With Wolves	Jeremy Irons	Kathy Bates
1989	Driving Miss Daisy	Daniel Day-Lewis	Jessica Tandy
1988	Rain Man	Dustin Hoffman	Jodie Foster
1987	The Last Emperor	Michael Douglas	Cher
1986	Platoon	Paul Newman	Marlee Martin
1985	Out of Africa	William Hurt	Geraldine Page
1984	Amadeus	F. Murray Abraham	Sally Field
1983	Terms of Endearment	Robert Duvall	Shirley MacLaine

Highest paid actress

Julia Roberts earned a record $25 million for *Mona Lisa Smile* (2003). These are the highest-paid actresses per film in 2006.

	Pay per film $US million
Reese Witherspoon	15–20
Angelina Jolie	15–20
Cameron Diaz	15+
Sandra Bullock	10–15
Nicole Kidman	10–15
Julia Roberts	10–15
Renee Zellweger	10–15
Drew Barrymore	10–12
Jodie Foster	10–12
Halle Berry	10

Reese Witherspoon, Best Actress in 2006

See also
Awards: page 155

AFI's Top ten film songs

Song	Film
1 Over the Rainbow	*The Wizard of Oz* (1939)
2 As Time Goes By	*Casablanca* (1942)
3 Singin' in the Rain	*Singin' in the Rain* (1952)
4 Moon River	*Breakfast at Tiffany's* (1961)
5 White Christmas	*Holiday Inn* (1942)
6 Mrs Robinson	*The Graduate* (1967)
7 When You Wish Upon a Star	*Pinocchio* (1940)
8 The Way We Were	*The Way We Were* (1973)
9 Stayin' Alive	*Saturday Night Fever* (1977)
10 The Sound of Music	*The Sound Of Music* (1965)

Most wins

These three films have each won 11 Oscars, including Best Picture: *Ben-Hur* (1959), *Titanic* (1997) and *The Lord of the Rings: The Return of the King* (2003).

A no-win situation

The Turning Point (1977) and *The Color Purple* (1985) had 11 nominations each but neither of them won a single Oscar. *Gangs of New York* (2002) received 10 nominations, also without winning anything.

Long and short

Gone with the Wind (1939) was the longest film (238 minutes) and the first colour film to win Best Picture. *Marty* (1955) was the shortest Best Picture winner at 91 minutes.

Black and white

Marty was also one of the last black and white films to win Best Picture. *The Apartment* (1960) and *Schindler's List* (1993) are the only black and white films to have won since.

First appearances

These are the films in which some of the most famous animated characters made their first appearances.

Mickey Mouse *Plane Crazy* (1928)
Plane Crazy was Walt Disney's first Mickey Mouse cartoon and was silent. Two months later Mickey appeared in Disney's *Steamboat Willie*, the first Mickey Mouse cartoon with sound. Mickey starred in *Fantasia* (1940), and his *Lend a Paw* won an Oscar® in 1941.

Popeye *Popeye the Sailor with Betty Boop* (1933)
Popeye was born in 1929 as a newspaper comic strip by Elzie Crisler Segar. Animator Max Fleischer adapted it for the screen. Popeye cartoons were made for cinema and TV until the 1980s, and the live-action *Popeye* film was released in 1980.

Donald Duck *The Wise Little Hen* (1934)
Clarence Nash was the voice of Donald Duck for 50 years. The Donald Duck anti-Hitler film *Der Fuehrer's Face* (1942) won an Oscar.

Bugs Bunny *Porky's Hare Hunt* (1938)
A Wild Hare (1940) was the first cartoon in which Bugs Bunny said "Eh, what's up, Doc?" but he was not named until *Elmer's Pet Rabbit* (1941). *Knighty-Knight Bugs* (1958) won an Oscar.

Tom and Jerry *Puss Gets The Boot* (1940)
The very first Tom and Jerry cartoon was nominated for an Oscar. The characters also appeared in the 1992 film *Tom and Jerry: The Movie*. This full-length film is the only one in which they speak.

Casper the Ghost *The Friendly Ghost* (1945)
Casper starred in more than 50 cartoons and in a part live action/part computer animated feature film in 1995, which earned nearly $300 million around the world.

The Flintstones *The Flintstone Flyer* (1960)
This was the first episode of *The Flintstones* to be broadcast on TV. It went on to become the longest-running cartoon series until it was overtaken by *The Simpsons*. The live-action film *The Flintstones* (1994) was one of the top-earning films of the year.

Simpsons *Simpsons Roasting on an Open Fire* (1989)
Matt Groening's hugely successful animated series began in 1987 as short episodes screened on the Tracey Ullman Show. It was developed into longer weekly episodes and has become the longest-running and most successful cartoon series ever.

Walt Disney's first animated features

Walt Disney (1901–66) produced short animated films, including Mickey Mouse cartoons, before making main features. *Snow White* was Hollywood's first full-length animated feature film and earned Disney an honorary Oscar. The film made $188 million in the USA alone.

Film	First released in cinemas
1 *Snow White and the Seven Dwarfs*	21 December 1937
2 *Pinocchio*	7 February 1940
3 *Fantasia*	12 November 1940
4 *Dumbo*	23 October 1941
5 *Bambi*	9 August 1942

Walt Disney in his studio

Types of animation

A zoetrope – when the viewer spins the zoetrope and looks through a slit, the pictures inside appear to be moving.

The word animation comes from the Latin *animatus*, meaning filled with life. Even before the invention of cinema, people realized that if the human eye sees a series of images that change at a rate of at least 24 frames a second, the brain can be tricked into thinking it is seeing a live moving image. 19th-century optical toys such as zoetropes worked on this principle.

Traditional animation
Individual frames of a story are hand drawn on cels – transparent sheets of plastic. They are then photographed as a sequence against painted backgrounds.

Cut-out
In this type of animation, two-dimensional drawings are placed on a fixed background. These are moved and photographed to create the impression of movement.

CGI
CGI (Computer Generated Imagery) has been used since the 1970s, originally for short films. The 1989 film *The Abyss* used some CGI visual effects, but the hugely successful

A scene from
Ratatouille (2007)

That's all folks

Mel Blanc was the voice of many famous cartoon characters, from Bugs Bunny to the *Flintstones'* Barney Rubble. The headstone on his grave in the Hollywood Forever Cemetery has the sign-off line used at the end of Looney Tunes cartoons: "That's All Folks".

Most expensive animated films

Making animated films has become more and more expensive. In 1937 *Snow White and the Seven Dwarfs* cost $1.49 million – a record-breaking sum at the time. *Tarzan* (1999) and *The Polar Express* (2004) are the costliest films ever made and were more than 100 times as expensive as *Snow White*.

Film	Year	Budget ($US million)
The Polar Express	2004	170
Shrek the Third	2007	160
Bee Movie	2007	150
Ratatouille	2007	150
Shrek 2	2004	150
Tarzan	1999	145
Flushed Away	2006	143
Treasure Planet	2002	140

Toy Story (1995), from the Disney and Pixar Animation Studio, was the first CGI feature film. Another development known as 3D motion capture has been used in films such as *Beowulf* (2007), a $150 million budget film with Ray Winstone in the title role, in which the movements of the actors are converted into computer images.

Stop motion
This type of animation is created by moving three-dimensional figures and other objects a tiny amount between shots. This method has been used since 1925, but the best-known modern examples of this technique are the *Wallace & Gromit* films by Aardman Animation.

Scene from Wallace & Gromit: *The Curse of the Were-Rabbit* (2005)

Highest-earning animated films

Shrek 2 (2004) – $US 920.7 million
Finding Nemo (2003) – $US 864.6 m.
Shrek the Third (2007) – $US 797.8 m.
The Lion King (1994) – $US 783.8 m.
Ice Age: The Meltdown (2006) – $US 651.6 m.
The Incredibles (2004) – $US 631.4 m.
Ratatouille (2007) – $US 620.6 m.
Madagascar (2005) – $US 532.7 m.
Monsters, Inc. (2001) – $US 529.1 m.
The Simpsons Movie (2007) – $US 526.5 m.
Aladdin (1992) – $US 504.1 m.
Toy Story 2 (1999) – $US 485.0 m.
Shrek (2001) – $US 484.4 m.
Cars (2006) – $US 462.0 m.
Tarzan (1999) – $US 449.4 m.
Happy Feet (2006) – $US 384.3 m.

Marlene Dietrich

Top 10 screen legends

This is the Top 10 of the American Film Institute's list of the greatest American screen legends.

	Actor	Actress
1	Humphrey Bogart	Katharine Hepburn
2	Cary Grant	Bette Davis
3	James Stewart	Audrey Hepburn
4	Marlon Brando	Ingrid Bergman
5	Fred Astaire	Greta Garbo
6	Henry Fonda	Marilyn Monroe
7	Clark Gable	Elizabeth Taylor
8	James Cagney	Judy Garland
9	Spencer Tracy	Marlene Dietrich
10	Charlie Chaplin	Joan Crawford

Actors who have played Superman

Kirk Alyn (1910–99)
The Adventures of Superman (1948) and *Atom Man vs Superman* (1950), both made as cinema serials

George Reeves (1914–59)
Superman and the Mole Men (1951) and the *Superman* TV series (1953–57)

Christopher Reeve (1952–2004)
Superman (1978), *Superman II* (1980), *Superman III* (1983) and *Superman IV: The Quest for Peace* (1987)

Brandon Routh (1979–)
Superman Returns (2006)

Dean Cain (1966–)
Lois & Clark: The New Adventures of Superman (TV series, 1993–97)

Tom Welling (1977–)
Smallville: Superman the Early Years TV series (2001–) about Superman as a teenager

...and Supergirl
Helen Slater (1963–)
Supergirl (1984)

Top stars

Since the 1920s, cinemas across the USA have nominated the top stars of the year according to the number of people who pay to watch their films. These are the top stars of 2007.

1 Johnny Depp
2 Will Smith
2 George Clooney
4 Matt Damon
5 Denzel Washington
6 Russell Crowe
7 Tom Cruise
8 Nicholas Cage
9 Will Ferrell
10 Tom Hanks

Stars of the most $100 million-plus films

These are the stars who have appeared in the most films that have made more than $100 million at the US box office. A number of less well-known actors who have supplied their voices to animated films have made as many or even more high-earning films.

Johnny Depp

Star	$100 m. + films
Tom Hanks	17
Tom Cruise	15
Eddie Murphy	13
Jack Angel	12
Will Smith	11
Harrison Ford	11
Mel Gibson	11
Morgan Freeman	11
Robin Williams	11
Samuel L. Jackson	11

Movie monsters

Ever since cinema began, film-makers have played on everyone's fear of monsters. These are some of the most popular monster films.

Aliens
Hundreds of films have been made about alien monsters attacking Earth. The most successful of these was *Independence Day* (1996).

Dinosaurs
One of the first cartoons was *Gertie* (1914). It featured a drawing of a brontosaurus that comes to life. Dinosaur films *Jurassic Park* (1993) and its two sequels, *The Lost World: Jurassic Park* (1997) and *Jurassic Park III* (2001), are among the biggest blockbusters of all time.

Egyptian mummies
The Mummy (1932) featured an Egyptian mummy that comes to life and attacks people. *The Mummy* was remade in 1999 and its sequel, the comedy-adventure *The Mummy Returns* (2001), has made more than $433 million.

Frankenstein's monster
Frankenstein is the name of the creator of the monster, not the monster itself. The original story was written in 1816 by English writer Mary Shelley. It was first made into a silent film in 1910 by the inventor Thomas Edison and has been remade many times since. *Mary Shelley's Frankenstein* (1994) is the highest-earning of all the versions.

Stage names

Actors and actresses choose stage names for a variety of reasons. Their real names may be the same as or similar to those of other people, or they may be difficult to spell or pronounce.

Here are some famous performers who decided to change their names.

Film name	Real name
Woody Allen	Allan Stewart Konigsberg
Jennifer Aniston	Jennifer Linn Anastassakis
Mel Brooks	Melvin Kaminsky
Nicolas Cage	Nicholas Kim Coppola
Michael Caine	Maurice Joseph Micklewhite
Jackie Chan	Chan Kong-sang
Tom Cruise	Thomas Cruise Mapother IV
Kirk Douglas	Issur Danielovitch Demsky
Whoopi Goldberg	Caryn Elaine Johnson
Cary Grant	Archibald Alexander Leach
Richard E. Grant	Richard Grant Esterhuysen
Goldie Hawn	Goldie Jean Studlendegehawn
Hulk Hogan	Terry Gene Bollea
Angelina Jolie	Angelina Jolie Voight
Ben Kingsley	Krishna Bhanji
Queen Latifah	Dana Elaine Owens
Jet Li	Li Lian Jie
Marilyn Monroe	Norma Jean Baker
Demi Moore	Demetria Gene Guynes
Natalie Portman	Natalie Hershlag
Winona Ryder	Winona Horowitz
Susan Sarandon	Susan Abigail Tomalin
Christian Slater	Christian Michael Leonard Hawkins
Sigourney Weaver	Susan Weaver

Poster for the original horror-adventure film *King Kong* (1933); the film has been remade twice, most recently in 2005

Funny monsters
Some of the most successful cartoon monsters are those in *Monsters, Inc.* (2001). The monsters are led by Sulley, whose secret is that the monsters are scared of children!

Killer creatures
Giant ape King Kong is one of the most famous animal monsters and the star of the film *King Kong* (1933, 1976 and 2005).

Giant spiders have featured in films such as *Arachnophobia* (1990) and *Eight Legged Freaks* (2002). Harry Potter also meets an army of huge spiders in *Harry Potter and the Chamber of Secrets* (2002). Other famous killer creatures include sharks (*Jaws*, 1977), alligators (*Lake Placid*, 1999) and snakes (*Anaconda*, 1997 and *Snakes on a Plane*, 2006).

Vampires
Irish writer Bram Stoker's vampire novel *Dracula* was first published in 1897. Since then it has been made into countless films. The version starring Bela Lugosi (1931) is one of the most famous. *Bram Stoker's Dracula* (1992) and *Van Helsing* (2004) have been the most successful at the box office.

Zombies
Zombies are the "undead" – bodies that come out of their graves and terrorize the living. They have been the subject of many films, including *Night of the Living Dead* (1968) and the comedy *Shaun of the Dead* (2004).

This was billed as the first "Rom-Com-Zom" (Romantic Comedy Zombie film).

See also
Mythical creatures: pages 170–71

www.afi.com   search

Video and DVD fact file

- The terms video recording and videotape were first used in the early 1950s, but only among TV professionals.

- The abbreviation VCR (video cassette recorder) was first used in the UK and USA in 1971.

- The first domestic video cassette recorders were sold in 1974, but both machines and tapes were very expensive and few people bought them.

- The VHS (video home system) was launched in 1976 in the US and 1978 in Europe.

- By 1980 about 7,687,000 homes had video recorders; by 1996 the global figure was put at 400,976,000.

- DVD (digital video disc or digital versatile disc) players and discs were launched in Japan and the USA in 1997.

- Worldwide, sales of DVDs overtook video sales in 2002.

- By 2003 almost one in three UK households had a DVD player. In 2007 the figure increased to over 83 per cent, with sales of discs over £2.3 billion.

- In 2007, most major film studios stopped releasing films on video. DVD became the most popular format and the first HD (High Definition) DVD and Blu-ray high-density optical discs go on sale.

TV-owning countries

Country	TVs per 1,000 people in 2006	Country	TVs per 1,000 people in 2006
Norway	1,552	Latvia	859
Bermuda	1,070	Japan	843
UK	1,101	Netherlands	761
Denmark	975	Australia	724
Romania	893	Canada	706
USA	882	Ireland	694

A 1950s US magazine advertisement for TVs

First countries to have television*

The BBC's first broadcasts used Baird's mechanical television system. In this, spinning disks were used to scan images.

This was later dropped in favour of US inventor Philo Taylor Farnsworth's electronic system. Electronic television did not rely on moving parts, was more reliable and gave a better picture.

Country	Year
UK	1936
USA	1939
USSR	1939
France	1948
Brazil	1950

* High-definition regular public broadcasting service

TV viewing

- In the average US home, the TV is switched on for 7 hours 40 minutes a day.

- US children aged 2 to 17 watch an average of 19 hours 40 minutes' TV every week. That is 1,023 hours a year compared with 900 hours a year in school.

- In the UK children aged 8 to 15 spend an average of 2 hours 13 minutes a day watching TV and adults over 16 spend an average of 2 hours 23 minutes.

TV milestones   1930s

1922
18 October, BBC (British Broadcasting Company) founded
1929
First transmissions of Scottish inventor John Logie Baird's experimental mechanical television system and, in the USA, Philo T. Farnsworth's electronic TV system
1936
22 November, BBC opens the world's first regular high-definition television service, from Alexandra Palace, London

1937
21 June, Wimbledon Tennis Championships first broadcast
1938
30 April, television coverage of the FA Cup Final
31 May, first BBC TV panel game, *Spelling Bee*
1939
1 September, BBC television service is suspended throughout World War II
30 April, Franklin D. Roosevelt is the first president to appear on TV, opening the World's Fair in New York

10 June, the first king and queen on TV in the USA are King George VI and Queen Elizabeth, seen visiting the World's Fair
1941
1 July, the first ever TV commercial, for a Bulova clock, is broadcast by WNBT New York, during a game between the Brooklyn Dodgers and the Philadelphia Phillies
1946
1 June, first TV licences are issued in the UK (cost £2)
7 June, BBC television broadcasts resume

1940s

7 July, first British children's TV programme, *For the Children*, is broadcast
1947
21 February, America's first regular daytime serial, or soap opera, *A Woman to Remember*, begins its run
1948
29 July, London Olympic Games is televised
1951
24 December, in the USA *Amahl and The Night Visitors* becomes the world's first commercial colour broadcast

Radio milestones

1896
2 June, Italian inventor Guglielmo Marconi applies for first British "wireless" patent

1906
24 December, first radio programme (music and speech) broadcast by Professor Reginald Fessenden from the US coast and received by ships. The first radios were crystal sets, operated by adjusting metal wires known as cat's whiskers

1920
15 June, Marconi broadcasts a concert by opera singer Dame Nellie Melba

1922
18 October, BBC (British Broadcasting Company) founded. The first BBC broadcast was made on 14 November – the six o'clock news read by Arthur Burrows

1923
26 April, first daily weather forecast by the BBC

1926
24 January, launch of *The Week's Good Cause*, the BBC's longest-running programme

1933
28 August, first BBC woman announcer, Sheila Borrett

1939–45
During World War II the BBC provides information and stirring speeches from Winston Churchill and other wartime leaders

1951
1 January, launch of *The Archers*, longest-running BBC radio serial

1964
Pirate radio stations broadcast from ships to UK, encouraging the BBC to launch a pop music station (Radio 1, 30 September 1967)

1970
24 February, National Public Radio launched in the USA

1993
First Internet radio broadcasts

1995
First experimental DAB (digital audio broadcasting) in UK. DAB gives listeners better quality reception, easy tuning and text information

2002
BBC launches five new DAB channels

2005
BBC radio begins to make programmes available as podcasts that can be downloaded to computers, MP3 and DAB players

2007
Internet radio becomes available to mobile phones

www.bbc.co.uk   search

Why soap opera?

Radio (and later TV) serials about everyday life in the USA have been sponsored by soap manufacturers since the 1930s. They advertised their products during the shows. The name of these serials has been shortened to soaps since 1943.

Portable radio from the 1950s

2000s

1953
2 June, the coronation of Queen Elizabeth II is watched live by about 20 million people in the UK and 200 million worldwide

21 November, current affairs programme Panorama is launched; goes on to become the longest-running programme on British TV

1954
1 January, the *Tournament of Roses* parade at Pasadena, California, USA, becomes the first programme ever broadcast coast-to-coast

11 January, first TV weather forecast in the UK

9 April, Britain's first TV soap opera, *The Grove Family*

1955
22 September, first TV advert in the UK, for Gibbs SR toothpaste

1957
13 May, first schools programmes broadcast in UK

25 December, the Queen's first TV Christmas message broadcast

1958
16 October, *Blue Peter* starts, and becomes the longest-running children's programme

1969
21 July, first live broadcasts from the Moon (*Apollo XI*)

15 November, BBC1 and ITV start broadcasting in colour

1981
1 August, MTV launched; The Buggles' *Video Killed the Radio Star* the first music video to be broadcast

1989
5 February, Sky begins satellite broadcasting in the UK

1997
9 November, BBC1 begins broadcasting 24 hours a day, seven days a week (previously, TV closed down at night)

2000
18 July, UK launch of *Big Brother* starts a fashion for reality TV

2006
High Definition television (HDTV) becomes available in the UK and other countries

2008
The 108-inch (274-cm) flat screen LCD TV, the world's largest, is launched by Sharp

Sports

**Track
record**

2008 was the year of the 50th
Daytona 500, regarded by many as
the most important race on the
NASCAR calendar. The "golden
anniversary" of the race was won
by Lee Petty and the trophy
was plated in gold instead
of the usual silver.

Teams and competitors

Team sizes

These are the number of players allowed on a pitch at any one time. The full team can also include some substitutes. In American football, for example, there are 45 full-time team members. Different players come on the pitch for defensive and offensive moves.

Sport	Team on pitch
Australian Rules football	18
Gaelic football, hurling, Rugby Union	15
Rugby League	13
Canadian football, korfball, women's lacrosse	12
American football, bandy, cricket, field hockey, soccer, speedball	11
Men's lacrosse, slow-pitch softball	10
Baseball, rounders, fast-pitch softball	9
Tug-of-war	8
Team handball, netball, water polo	7
Ice hockey, volleyball	6
Basketball, roller hockey	5
Polo	4

Most competitors

● The Boston Marathon centenary race in 1996 attracted a record 38,706 competitors, the most ever for a marathon.

● The Athens Olympic Games (2004) had 11,099 competitors, the most of any Olympics.

● The world's biggest road race is the 12 km (7.5 miles) Bay to Breakers race in San Francisco, USA. It has been held every year since 1912. The 1988 race had a record 78,769 official entries, but the total number of people taking part was probably about 110,000, many of them in fancy dress.

● In 1929 the Grand National horse race had a record 66 runners, but only nine reached the finish line.

Most-watched sporting event

The 2000 Olympic Games in Sydney was the most-watched sporting event ever on television, with 3.7 billion viewers worldwide. 1,159,249 tickets for watching the events live were sold.

Sporting sizes

	Dimensions and distances
Blade of an ice skate (width)	33 mm (1.3 in)
Tenpin height	38 cm (15 in)
Parallel bars in gymnastics (distance between)	42 cm (16.5 in)
Dartboard diameter	45 cm (17.7 in)
Tennis net height (at centre)	91 cm (35.8 in)
Hurdles height (men's 400 m)	91.4 cm (36 in)
Cricket bat (maximum)	96.52 x 10.8 cm (38 x 4.3 in)
Water polo pool depth (minimum)	1 m (3.3 ft)
Women's javelin length (minimum)	2.2 m (7.2 ft)
Soccer goal height	2.44 m (8 ft)
Men's javelin length (minimum)	2.6 m (8.5 ft)
Table tennis table	2.74 x 1.52 m (9 x 5 ft)
Rugby goal crossbar height	3.05 m (10 ft)
Snooker table (full size)	3.66 x 1.86 m (12 x 6.1 ft)
Boxing ring	6.1 x 6.1 m (20 x 20 ft)
Soccer goal width	7.32 m (24 ft)
Marathon distance	42.195 km (26 miles 385 yd)
Australian Rules football pitch (oval)	135–185 x 110–155 m (442.9–607 x 360.9–508.5 ft)
Polo pitch	275 x 183 m (902.2 x 600.4 ft)
Formula One Grand Prix (Brazilian Grand Prix circuit)	306 km (190.1 miles)
Isle of Man TT motorcycle race (longest, 1957)	485.8 km (301.9 miles)
Longest hole in open golf (14th at St Andrews)	565 m (618 yd)
Iditarod dog sled race, Alaska north route (even-numbered years)	1,790 km (1,112 miles)
south route (odd-numbered years)	1,820 km (1,131 miles)
Le Mans 24 Hour race (greatest distance covered in the time, 1971)	5,333.7 km (3,314.2 miles)
Tour de France cycle race (record longest, 1926)	5,745 km (3,569.8 miles)
Tour d'Afrique, Cairo to Cape Town (longest cycle race)	10,500 km (6,524.4 miles)
Around alone (solo round-the-world yacht race)	46,276.7 km (28,754.6 miles)

Marathon sprint!

If an athlete could run a marathon at the same rate as a 100 m sprint, he would finish in 43 minutes. In reality, no one has run a marathon in under two hours.

Sport origins

Who invented baseball?

Baseball is a much older game than you might think. Medieval manuscripts show ball games with bats, while a game called "base-ball" appears in a picture published in London in 1744. Baseball is also mentioned in Jane Austen's novel *Northanger Abbey*, which she began writing in 1798. The game of rounders was first described 30 years later, and this or a similar game was known among British settlers in America. Abner Doubleday is sometimes said to have invented baseball in 1839, but Alexander Joy Cartwright Jr drew up the game's rules in 1845. He founded the first team, the Knickerbocker Base Ball Club of New York.

When did basketball start?

The inspiration for basketball may have been the Aztec game *ollamalitzli* and other ball and hoop games played by South American peoples. The modern game was invented in 1891 by Canadian physical education teacher Dr James A. Naismith at the International YMCA College at Springfield, Massachusetts. He wanted to find a game that could be played indoors during the winter. Peach baskets were originally used as goals – players had to climb a ladder to fetch the ball after scoring. Then someone hit on the idea of removing the bottom! The baskets were soon replaced by metal rings with netting.

Famous US basketball player Michael Jordan about to score

Sport top speeds

Sport	km/h	mph
Competition rifle bullet	3,787	2,353
Longbow arrow	547	340
Drag racer (0.4 km [0.25 miles] from standing start)	535	332
Free-fall skydiver	531	330
Pelota (jai-alai) ball	302	188
Indy 500 racing car (record, 1990)	299	186
Golf ball (leaving tee)	273	170
Downhill skier (record)	248	154
Squash ball (record, 1988)	243	151
Tennis serve (record, 2004)	241	150
Racing car (Formula One)	238	148
Water skiing (record, 1983)	230	143
Isle of Man TT race (record, 2006)	208	129
Snowboarding (record)	202	126
Ice hockey puck	190	118
Ski-bob (record, 1999)	185	115
Table tennis ball	170	106
Baseball (pitched)	162	101
Cricket bowl (record, 2003)	161	100
Luge	137	85
Frisbee	119	74
Cyclist (record)	105	65
Skateboard (record, 1998)	101	63
4-man bobsleigh	90	56
Racehorse	72	45
Greyhound	67	42
100-m sprinter	59	37
Boxing punch	56	35
Karate chop	51	32

Longest events

● In Formula One motor racing, the 18-race season (2008) is spread over seven-and-a-half months.

● The Tour d'Afrique cycle race includes 100 days of cycling and 20 days of rest.

● The Tour de France lasts 22 days (with rest days).

● The Iditarod dog sled race, held in Alaska, lasts nine days.

● The Global Challenge round-the-world yacht race covers some 54,000 km (29,000 nautical miles). The 22-m yachts are at sea for six months. The race has been held every four years since 1992, with the next in 2008–09.

● The longest boxing match with gloves was a 100-round bout between Andy Bowen and Jack Burke (both USA). It started at 9.15 pm on Thursday, 6 April 1893 and finished at 4.34 am on Friday, 7 April – a total of 7 hours 19 minutes.

Oldest sporting events

Doggett's Coat and Badge Race is the world's oldest continuous sporting event. It is a rowing contest held on the River Thames in England and has been held every year since 1715. The Newmarket Town Plate horse race is even older, but the race was discontinued for a while.

Event	First held	Event	First held
Newmarket Town Plate horse race	1665	Football League championship (England)	1888
Doggett's Coat and Badge Race (rowing)	1715	Stanley Cup ice hockey competition	1893
Real Tennis Championship	1740	US Open golf championship	1895
St Leger horse race	1776	Davis Cup tennis tournament	1900
Epsom Derby horse race	1780	Baseball World Series	1903
County Cricket Championship	1827	Tour de France cycle race	1903
Oxford and Cambridge Boat Race	1829	Ryder Cup golf tournament	1927
Grand National steeplechase	1836	FIFA Soccer World Cup	1930
Henley Regatta	1839	Formula One World Championship	1950
British Open golf championship	1860	Super Bowl (US football championship)	1967
Melbourne Cup horse race	1861	Cricket World Cup	1975
America's Cup yachting series	1870	Athletics World Cup	1977
Football Association Challenge Cup	1872	World Athletics Championships	1983
Kentucky Derby horse race	1875	Breeders' Cup horse race series	1984
Test Match cricket	1877	Rugby Union World Cup	1987
Wimbledon Lawn Tennis Championships	1877	Cricket World Twenty20 Cup	2007

Grand National steeplechase (19th century)

Top sporting events

These are the leading events in the world's most popular sports, in addition to the Olympic Games.

American football Super Bowl

Athletics IAAF (International Athletics Association Federations) World Championship

Grand Prix Auto racing (US) Indianapolis 500

Baseball World Series

Basketball NBA (National Basketball Association) Final

Cycling Tour de France

Golf British Open, US Open, Ryder Cup (every two years)

Horse racing Epsom Derby, Grand National, Breeders' Cup, Kentucky Derby

Ice hockey Stanley Cup

Motor racing World Formula One Championship

Rallying Dakar Rally

Rugby League Challenge Cup, Super League

Rugby Union Six Nations Tournament, World Cup (every four years)

Soccer UEFA Champions League, FIFA World Cup (every four years)

Tennis Wimbledon Championships, US Open

See also

Major rock events: page 255

Sports timeline

Experts argue about the exact origins of many sports. The dates here are generally agreed to be when these sports were first played or contested on an organized basis.

Athletics	3800 BC	Soccer	1848	Basketball	1891
Horse racing	AD 1540	Tenpin bowling	1850	Rugby League	1895
Boxing	1681	Show jumping	1864	Darts	1896
Rowing	1715	Cycling	1867	Motor cycling	1896
Ice skating	1742	Badminton	1873	Speedway	1902
Cricket	1744	Lawn tennis	1873		
Golf	1744	American football	1874		
Swimming	1791	Hockey (field)	1875		
Baseball	1839	Hockey (ice)	1887		
Rugby Union	1839	Motor racing	1887		

Bare-knuckle boxing match (1820)

Biggest soccer crowd

The biggest-ever crowd for a soccer match was at the 1950 World Cup Final. The match between Brazil and Uruguay at the Maracanã Stadium (now called the Journalista Mário Filho Stadium) in Brazil was watched by 199,854 people. The biggest crowd for a soccer match in Britain was at Hampden Park, Glasgow, on 17 April 1937. Scotland was playing England and 149,547 people paid to watch and another 10,000 may have got in without paying!

The Journalista Mário Filho Stadium in Rio de Janeiro, Brazil, was built for the 1950 World Cup and held almost 200,000 people.

Biggest crowds

In the past, more than 100,000 people at a time crammed into American football's Rose Bowl, the old Wembley Stadium and other venues across Europe to watch sport. Today, there are laws which limit the number of people allowed in a sports stadium. Outdoor events such as the New York City Marathon and the Tour de France now draw the biggest crowds. They are held over open roads and people don't have to pay to watch them.

● About 2.5 million people watch the New York Marathon – the biggest crowd for a single day at a sporting event. As many as 15 million people turn out to see the Tour de France during its three weeks.

● The record crowd for a golf tournament was set at the US Open, Flushing Meadows, 2005, which was attended by 659,538 people.

● In horse racing, more than 60,000 watch the Grand National and about 120,000 go to the Epsom Derby every year.

● Cricket attracts big crowds. Nearly a million people watched the 1936–37 series between Australia and England over its three months. More than 400,000 people watched the India v Pakistan Test match in Calcutta in 1998–99.

● Some of the biggest crowds at US sporting events are for Indy car races. About 270,000 fans attend the Indianapolis 500 every year and as many as 332,000 attended the 2006 Canadian Grand Prix in Montreal.

Strange sport

A world championship in mobile phone throwing has been held in Finland every year since 2000. Competitors take part in individual or team events. There is also an under-12 category. The current world record stands at 95.83 m (314 ft 4 in) for men and 53.52 m (175 ft 7 in) for women.

Sport on TV

TV audiences for many sporting events were larger 30 years ago than they are today. Fewer people had televisions, but there were not as many channels and no video recorders, so more people watched events live.

UK event	Audience*
World Cup Final, England v West Germany, 1966	32,500,000
World Cup, Brazil v England, 1970	32,500,000
FA Cup Final replay, Chelsea v Leeds United, 1970	32,000,000
World Heavyweight boxing match, Muhammad Ali v Joe Frazier, 1970	27,000,000

USA event	Audience*
Super Bowl XLII, New York Giants v New England Patriots, 2008	148,300,000
Super Bowl XXXVIII, New England Patriots v Carolina Panthers, 2004	143,600,000
Super Bowl XL, Pittsburgh Steelers v Seattle Seahawks, 2006	141,400,000
Super Bowl XLI, Indianapolis Colts v Chicago Bears, 2007	140,000,000
Super Bowl XXXVII, Tampa Bay Buccaneers v Oakland Raiders, 2003	138,900,000
Super Bowl XXX, Dallas Cowboys v Pittsburgh Steelers, 1996	138,488,000
Super Bowl XXVIII, Dallas Cowboys v Buffalo Bills, 1994	134,800,000
Super Bowl XXVII, Dallas Cowboys v Buffalo Bills, 1993	133,400,000

* Number of people who watched at least part of broadcast

Summer Olympics

The modern Olympic Games have been held every four years since 1896, except during World Wars I and II. Over this time the numbers of competitors, events and nations taking part have all increased dramatically.

Winter Paralympic events for athletes with disabilities have been held since 1976. The Summer Paralympics began in 1960 and were first held in conjunction with the regular Summer Olympics in 1988.

Year/City/country	Competitors	No. of nations	Events	Most golds	Most medals
1896 Athens, Greece	245	14	43	USA 11	Greece 47
1900 Paris, France	1,225	26	95	France 26	France 95
1904 St Louis, USA	687	13	91	USA 79	USA 245
1906 Athens, Greece	884	20	76	France 15	France 40
1908 London, UK	2,035	22	110	UK 54	UK 138
1912 Stockholm, Sweden	2,547	28	102	USA 25	Sweden 64
1920 Antwerp, Belgium	2,669	29	154	USA 41	USA 95
1924 Paris, France	3,092	44	126	USA 45	USA 99
1928 Amsterdam, Netherlands	3,014	46	109	USA 22	USA 56
1932 Los Angeles, USA	1,408	37	117	USA 41	USA 103
1936 Berlin, Germany	4,066	49	129	Germany 33	Germany 89
1948 London, UK	4,099	59	136	USA 38	USA 84
1952 Helsinki, Finland	4,925	69	149	USA 40	USA 76
1956* Melbourne, Australia	3,342	72	145	USSR 37	USSR 98
1960 Rome, Italy	5,348	83	150	USSR 43	USSR 103
1964 Tokyo, Japan	5,140	93	163	USA 36	USA 90
1968 Mexico City, Mexico	5,531	112	172	USA 45	USA 107
1972 Munich, West Germany	7,123	121	195	USSR 50	USSR 99
1976 Montreal, Canada	6,028	92	198	USSR 49	USSR 125
1980 Moscow, USSR	5,217	80	203	USSR 80	USSR 195
1984 Los Angeles, USA	6,797	140	221	USA 83	USA 174
1988 Seoul, South Korea	8,465	159	237	USSR 55	USSR 132
1992 Barcelona, Spain	9,367	169	257	EUN† 45	EUN 112
1996 Atlanta, USA	10,744	197	271	USA 44	USA 101
2000 Sydney, Australia	10,651	199	300	USA 39	USA 97
2004 Athens, Greece	11,099	202	301	USA 35	USA 103

* The equestrian events in 1956 were held in Stockholm, Sweden, from 10–17 June, because of quarantine restrictions in Australia at the time.

† The Unified Team (EUN) was made up of the former Soviet republics of Russia, Ukraine, Kazakhstan and Uzbekistan.

The big five

Only five sports have been contested at every Summer Olympics since the first Modern Olympics in 1896. These are cycling, fencing, gymnastics, swimming and track and field. Rowing would have been on this list, but the events in 1896 were cancelled due to bad weather.

Out of the Olympics

Various sports have been dropped from the Olympic Games over the years. These include croquet, underwater swimming, duelling pistol shooting, stone-throwing, lacrosse, archery with live birds, tug-of-war, club-swinging and rope climbing.

The Olympic flag

The five-ring Olympic flag was first raised at the 1920 Antwerp Olympics. The rings on the flag represent the five major regions of the world: the Americas, Europe, Asia, Africa and Australasia. At least one of the colours on the flag (blue, yellow, black, green and red) can be found on the flags of every nation in the world.

One and only

Softball is the only sport that women contest at the Olympics but men do not. The sport has been played at three Olympics (1996, 2000, 2004) and the USA has won gold each time.

Olympic firsts   1800s   1900s

1896 First modern Olympics. Doves released to symbolize peace

1896 First American gold medal winner, James Connolly (triple jump)

1896 First British gold medal winner, Launceston Elliot (weightlifting)

1900 First women competitors. First woman to win a gold medal, Charlotte Cooper from Great Britain for tennis

1908 First parade of athletes with national flags

1908 First athlete to win ten gold medals (in four Olympics, 1900, 1904, 1906 and 1908), Ray Ewry (USA)

1912 Electronic timing and photo-finish equipment first used

1920 Olympic oath, "We swear that we will take part in the Olympic Games in a spirit of chivalry, for the honour of our country and for the glory of sport", first taken, by Belgian fencer Victor Boin

1920 Olympic flag first raised

1924 First Olympics with more than 100 women competitors (there were 136 women and 2,956 men)

1924 First live radio transmissions of events

1928 First Olympic flame, large results display board first used

Olympic history

The ancient Olympic Games were dedicated to the Olympian gods and held at Olympia, on the border between Greece and Macedonia. They began in 776 BC and were held every four years. There were fewer events than now, and only Greeks could take part. The 293rd and last Olympiad was held in AD 392. After this, they were banned by the Emperor Theodosius. The games were revived in 1896 when the first modern Olympic Games were held in Athens.

Top medal winners

These athletes have won the most medals in the history of the Summer Olympics from 1896–2004.

Athlete	Sport	Years	Gold	Silver	Bronze	Total
Larissa Latynina (USSR)	Gymnastics	1956–64	9	5	4	18
Nikolai Andrianov (USSR)	Gymnastics	1972–80	7	5	3	15
Boris Shakhlin (USSR)	Gymnastics	1956–64	7	4	2	13
Edoardo Mangiarotti (Italy)	Fencing	1936–60	6	5	2	13
Takashi Ono (Japan)	Gymnastics	1952–64	5	4	4	13
Paavo Nurmi (Finland)	Athletics	1920–28	9	3	0	12
Sawao Kato (Japan)	Gymnastics	1968–76	8	3	1	12
Alexei Nemov (Russia)	Gymnastics	1996–2000	4	2	6	12

Athlete Ray Ewry (USA) won only ten medals but they were all gold! He still holds the record for the most individual gold medals. Ewry won his medals between 1900 and 1908 in the standing jump events: high jump, long jump and triple jump. Amazingly, Ewry had suffered polio as a child, but overcame his illness to become one of the greatest athletes ever.

The opening ceremony of the 2004 Olympics was watched by 72,000 spectators in the Olympic Stadium in Athens, Greece.

2000s

1928 First women competitors in track and field events

1932 First Olympic logo, three-tier victory stand, national anthem played and flag raised for winner

1936 Introduction of Olympic torch relay (from Olympia, Greece, to Berlin, Germany)

1936 Games televised for the first time

1956 Athletes enter closing ceremony together to symbolize unity

1956 First games in the southern hemisphere (Melbourne, Australia)

1960 First Summer Paralympics, held in Rome, Italy

1960 Worldwide TV coverage for the first time

1984 Professionals allowed to compete for the first time

2004 Women competed in freestyle wrestling for first time.

Ukraine, Japan and China all won gold medals

2004 First Olympics broadcast over the Internet

2008 BMX cycling events introduced

Q www.olympic.org/uk　　　　search

ATHLETICS

Running a mile

For decades, athletes struggled to run a mile in less than four minutes. At 6.07 pm on 6 May 1954, British runner Roger Bannister eventually broke the record. He ran a mile in 3 minutes 59.4 seconds at the Iffley Road track in Oxford.

Since that historic day, Bannister's record has been beaten many times. The current record speed for running a mile is 3 minutes 43.13 seconds.

Decathlon and heptathlon

The decathlon is a two-day event for men which first featured in the Olympic Games in 1912. The seven-event heptathlon is for women only. It was introduced in 1984, when it replaced the five-event pentathlon. Competitors score points for each event and the person with the highest total wins.

Decathlon events
Day 1: • 100 m • Long jump • Shot put • High jump • 400 m
Day 2: • 110 m hurdles • Discus • Pole vault • Javelin • 1500 m
The world record (9,026 points) is held by Roman Sebrle (Cze), which he achieved in 2001

Heptathlon events
Day 1: • 100 m hurdles • High jump • Shot put • 200 m
Day 2: • Long jump • Javelin • 800 m
The world record (7,291 points) is held by Jackie Joyner-Kersee (USA), which she achieved in 1988

Marathon

The race takes its name from a place called Marathon in Greece, which was the scene of a battle between Athenian and Persian troops in 490 BC.

The Athenians won and supposedly sent a messenger named Pheidippides from Marathon to Athens to spread the news – a distance of about 25 miles (40.23 km). It is said that Pheidippides dropped dead after delivering his message! The current marathon distance of 26 miles 385 yards (42.195 km) was first used at the 1908 Olympics in Britain. It was worked out so that the race from Windsor would finish in front of the Royal Box at the White City Stadium. This distance has been the standard for all marathons since 1924.

Marathon fact file

Hundreds of marathon races are held all over the world every year. There is an Antarctica Marathon, a Sahara Marathon and even a night-time marathon, run in Marburg, Germany. The following are some of the biggest and most popular events.

Boston Marathon
This race has been held since 1897 and is run on Patriots' Day every April. It is the oldest marathon in the United States and one of the world's most important road races. Clarence DeMar won it a record seven times between 1911 and 1930.

New York City Marathon
First held in 1970, the race goes through all five boroughs of New York and finishes in Central Park. It is usually held on the first Sunday in November. Norway's Greta Waitz won the women's race an amazing nine times between 1978 and 1988.

Chicago Marathon
The Chicago Marathon began in 1977. It was originally called the Mayor Daley Marathon after Chicago mayor Richard J. Daley, who died in office in 1976. Khalid Khannouchi of Morocco won the men's race a record four times between 1997 and 2002.

Track and field records

These are the current world records for major track and field events as at 1 January 2008. Most events have both male and female record holders. A few events are contested by only men or women.
For country name abbreviations, please refer to the list on page 318.

Event		Time (min:sec)	Record holder	Date
100 m	(m)	9.74	Asafa Powell (Jam)	2007
	(w)	10.49	Florence Griffith-Joyner (USA)	1988
200 m	(m)	19.32	Michael Johnson (USA)	1996
	(w)	21.34	Florence Griffith-Joyner (USA)	1988
400 m	(m)	43.18	Michael Johnson (USA)	1999
	(w)	47.60	Marita Koch (GDR)	1985
800 m	(m)	1:41.11	Wilson Kipketer (Den)	1997
	(w)	1:53.28	Jarmila Kratochvílová (Cze)	1983
1500 m	(m)	3:26.00	Hicham El Guerrouj (Mar)	1998
	(w)	3:50.46	Qu Yunxia (Chn)	1993
1 mile	(m)	3:43.13	Hicham El Guerrouj (Mar)	1999
	(w)	4:12.56	Svetlana Masterkova (Rus)	1996
5,000 m	(m)	12:37.35	Kenenisa Bekele (Eth)	2004
	(w)	14:16.63	Meseret Defar (Eth)	2007
10,000 m	(m)	26:17.53	Kenenisa Bekele (Eth)	2005
	(w)	29:31.78	Wang Junxia (Chn)	1993
3,000 m steeplechase	(m)	7:53.63	Saaeed Shaheen (Qat)	2004
	(w)	9:01.59	Gulnara Samitiva (Rus)	2004
110 m hurdles	(m)	12.88	Liu Xiang (Chn)	2006
100 m hurdles	(w)	12.21	Yordanka Donkova (Bul)	1988
400 m hurdles	(m)	46.78	Kevin Young (USA)	1992
	(w)	52.34	Yuliya Pechonkina (Rus)	2003
4 x 100 m relay	(m)	37.40	USA	1992/1993
	(w)	41.37	GDR	1985
4 x 400 m relay	(m)	2:54.20	USA	1998
	(w)	3:15.17	USSR	1988

Event		Ht/lgth (m)	Record holder	Date
High jump	(m)	2.45	Javier Sotomayor (Cub)	1993
	(w)	2.09	Stefka Kostadinova (Bul)	1987
Pole vault	(m)	6.14	Sergey Bubka (Ukr)	1994
	(w)	5.01	Yelena Isinbayeva (Rus)	2005
Long jump	(m)	8.95	Mike Powell (USA)	1991
	(w)	7.52	Galina Chistyakova (USSR)	1988
Triple jump	(m)	18.29	Jonathan Edwards (GBR)	1995
	(w)	15.50	Inessa Kravets (Ukr)	1995
Shot	(m)	23.12	Randy Barnes (USA)	1990
	(w)	22.63	Natalya Lisovskaya (USSR)	1987
Discus	(m)	74.08	Jürgen Schult (GDR)	1986
	(w)	76.80	Gabriele Reinsch (GDR)	1988
Hammer	(m)	86.74	Yuriy Sedykh (USSR)	1986
	(w)	77.80	Tatyana Lysenko (Rus)	2006
Javelin	(m)	98.48	Jan Zelezny (Cze)	1996
	(w)	71.70	Osleidys Menéndez (Cub)	2005

Florence Griffith-Joyner

World's fastest

The world's fastest man is Asafa Powell of Jamaica who ran the 100 metres in 9.74 seconds at Rieti, Italy, on 9 September 2007

The world's fastest woman was Florence Griffith-Joyner (USA), who died in 1998. She ran the 100 m in 10.49 seconds in Indianapolis in 1988. The fastest living woman is Marion Jones (USA). She ran the 100 m in 10.65 seconds in Johannesburg in 1998.

London Marathon
Dionico Cerón (Mexico) and António Pinto (Portugal) have each won the men's race a record three times. Ingrid Kristiansen (Norway) won the women's race four times between 1984 and 1988.

Marathon record holders
The current male record holder, Haile Gebreselassie (Ethiopia), ran the Berlin Marathon in 2 hours 4 minutes 26 seconds on 30 September 2007. The female record is held by Paula Radcliffe (GB), who ran the London Marathon on 13 April 2003 in 2 hours 15 minutes 25 seconds.

See also
Ancient Greece: page 106

 www.gbrathletics.com search

Yankees All-Star Alex Rodriguez

Baseball World Series

Major League baseball started in the USA when the National League was formed in 1876. The rival American League was started in 1901, and in 1903 the World Series, a best-of-nine game event, was held between the winners of each league's championship. In the first series the Boston Red Sox beat the Pittsburgh Pirates 5–3. The World Series has been a best-of-seven games series since 1905, except in 1919–21 when it went back to a nine-game series.

Most wins American League: New York Yankees – 26 between 1923 and 2000; National League: St Louis Cardinals – 10 between 1926 and 2006
Most consecutive wins New York Yankees – 5 (1949–53)

Baseball

Baseball is one of the most popular sports in the USA and is also played in Japan, Mexico, Cuba and a number of South American countries. It is played by two teams of nine players each.

Medieval manuscripts show ball games with bats, and a game called "base-ball" appears in a picture published in London in 1744. The game of rounders was first described in 1828, and this or a similar game was known among British settlers in America. The first rules were drawn up in 1845 by Alexander Joy Cartwright Jr and the first match under these rules played on 19 June 1846.

Golf majors

The four big competitions in golf are known as the majors. They are the US Masters, British Open, US Open and US PGA Championship, and are played in that order every year.

The Masters, founded in 1934, is the only one of the four played on the same course each year, at Augusta National in Georgia, USA. The oldest of the majors is the British Open, which was first held in 1860. It is also the only one played outside the USA. The US Open was first played in 1895 and the US PGA in 1916.

Tiger Woods

Players with most professional major wins

Jack Nicklaus (USA) 18:
3 British Open; 4 US Open;
5 US PGA; 6 Masters
Tiger Woods (USA) 13:
3 British Open; 2 US Open;
4 US PGA; 4 Masters
Walter Hagen (USA) 11:
4 British Open; 2 US Open;
5 US PGA

Ben Hogan (USA) 9:
1 British Open; 4 US Open; 2 US PGA;
2 Masters
Gary Player (S Africa) 9:
3 British Open; 1 US Open; 2 US PGA;
3 Masters
Tom Watson (USA) 8:
5 British Open; 1 US Open; 2 US Masters

Tiger Woods

At just 21 years, three months and 14 days, Tiger Woods was the youngest-ever Masters champion. In 2001 Tiger won his second US Masters and became the first player to hold all four professional major championships at the same time.

Basketball

Basketball is hugely popular in the USA and is now played in other parts of the world, as well as at the Olympics. The game is played by two teams of five players each, usually on an indoor court.

Players score points by shooting the ball through the basket. The National Basketball Association (NBA) in the USA was formed in 1949. It contains 30 teams divided into two conferences, Eastern and Western. At the end of the season the two conference winners meet in a best-of-seven series for the NBA Championship.

Corliss Williamson (Sacramento Kings) drives for the basket

Record breakers

Outstanding player Kareem Abdul-Jabbar (Milwaukee Bucks and Los Angeles Lakers) scored a record 38,387 points during his career.

Teams with most wins
Boston Celtics: 16
Minneapolis/Los Angeles Lakers: 14
Chicago Bulls: 6

Rugby

The game of rugby probably started in 1823 at Rugby School in England, when William Webb Ellis picked up a football and ran with it. The first rules were drawn up in 1848 and the Rugby Football Union (RFU) was formed by Edwin Ash in 1871.

Today's game of Rugby Union is played between two teams of 15 players. The two biggest events are the International Championship and the World Cup. The International Championship began in 1884 and was originally played by four teams: England, Ireland, Scotland and Wales. France joined in 1910 and Italy in 2000, making it a six-nation tournament. The Rugby World Cup was launched in 1987 and has been held every four years since then. In 2007, 20 teams took part and over 2.25 million people watched the 48 live matches at an average of 47,150 per game.

Rugby League

Rugby League dates from 29 August 1895, when 21 major clubs in the north of England formed a league outside the RFU. They were protesting against the RFU's refusal to pay players who had to take time off work. To make Rugby League less like Rugby Union they changed various rules, including reducing the team size from 15 to 13. Rugby League is now played in Australia, New Zealand, France, Russia and some Pacific nations, as well as in Britain. One of the major events in Rugby League is the Challenge Cup, open to British, French and Russian teams. There is also a Rugby League World Cup, which is in Australia in 2008.

Test cricket

Cricket is a bat and ball game played between two teams of 11 players. The aim is to score more runs than the opposing team. Among the major competitions are the Test matches, which are normally played over five days.

They are called Test matches because they were started as a test of the relative skills of the two sides. Test matches are played between teams representing their countries. There are currently ten countries that play Test cricket.

Australian Rules football

This is a tough, fast-moving game, in which players can kick, bounce, catch or punch the ball. It has been played in Australia since the Melbourne Football Club was formed in 1858. The season-long series of matches ends in the Grand Final at the Melbourne Cricket Ground.

There are 18 players in an Australian Rules team. This is more than any other team sport. The game is played on one of the biggest pitches. The oval-shaped area measures 135–185 x 110–155 m (443–607 x 361–508 ft). A professional soccer pitch measures 90–120 x 45–90 m (295–394 x 148–295 ft) wide.

The Ashes

Cricket's most famous trophy is the Ashes. England and Australia were the first two Test teams. When England lost to Australia at home in 1882, the *Sporting Times* joked that English cricket was dead and that its body would be cremated and the ashes taken to Australia. When the England team next visited Australia, it was presented with a tiny urn containing the burnt bails from the wicket used in the Third Test. Since then, whichever team wins an England-Australia Test series is said to have won the Ashes. The trophy is kept at Lord's Cricket Ground in London.

www.cricinfo.com   **search**

The World Cup

The first soccer World Cup was played in 1930 in Uruguay. Thirteen teams took part and the hosts beat Argentina 4–2 in the final in Montevideo.

They won the Jules Rimet trophy, named after the president of FIFA (Fédération Internationale de Football Association) when the competition began. Brazil were allowed to keep the trophy after winning it for the third time in 1970 and it was replaced by the FIFA World Cup trophy. The World Cup final takes place every four years.

The Italian team that won the 2006 World Cup

Winning country	Year	Winning country	Year
Uruguay	1930	Brazil	1970
Italy	1934	West Germany	1974
Italy	1938	Argentina	1978
Not held	1942	Italy	1982
Not held	1946	Argentina	1986
Uruguay	1950	West Germany	1990
West Germany	1954	Brazil	1994
Brazil	1958	France	1998
Brazil	1962	Brazil	2002
England	1966	Italy	2006

World Cup facts

● The first World Cup goal was scored by Lucien Laurent of France. The goal came 19 minutes into the first World Cup game on 13 July 1930.

● The first player to score four goals in a World Cup match was Ireland's Paddy Moore in a qualifying match against Belgium in 1934. It was the Republic's first ever World Cup match.

Most World Cup wins

Brazil	5
Italy	4
West Germany	3
Uruguay	2
Argentina	2

International caps

On 10 May 1886 the English Football Association decided: "That all players taking part for England in future international matches be presented with a white silk cap with red rose embroidered on the front. These to be termed International Caps."

This tradition has spread throughout world football. The number of caps show how many times players have represented their countries. The following footballers are the most-capped players in their countries, as at 1 January 2008.

Player	Country	Years	Caps
Mohamed Al-Deayea	Saudi Arabia	1990–2006	181
Claudio Suárez	Mexico	1992–2006	178
Cobi Jones	USA	1992–2004	164
Lothar Matthäus	Germany	1980–2000	150
Cafu	Brazil	1990–2006	142
Lilian Thuram	France	1994–2007	136
Luis Figo	Portugal	1991–2006	127
Paolo Maldini	Italy	1988–2002	126
Andoni Zubizarreta	Spain	1985–1998	126
Peter Shilton	England	1970–1990	125
Edwin van der Sar	Netherlands	1995–2007	122
Pat Jennings	Northern Ireland	1964–1986	119
Javier Zanetti	Argentina	1994–2006	117
Steve Staunton	Republic of Ireland	1989–2002	102
Kenny Dalglish	Scotland	1972–1987	102

Soccer timeline   1800s

500 BC Football (tsu chu, meaning to kick a ball) played in China

1314 First reference to football in England when Edward II prohibited the game because "too many people were bustling over footballs on London streets"

1848 The first rules of football drawn up at Cambridge University

1852 First inter-school football match, Westminster v Harrow

1855 Sheffield football club, the oldest still in existence, formed

1862 Notts County, the oldest current League club, formed

1863 Football Association (FA) formed

1870 First international match, England v Scotland, played at Kennington Oval

1871 FA Cup launched

1872 Corner kick introduced

1873 Scottish FA formed; Scottish Cup started

1874 Shin pads first worn

1875 The crossbar replaced a tape across the top of the goals

1876 Welsh FA formed

1878 Irish (now Northern Ireland) FA formed

1878 Referee's whistle first used

1885 Professional football legalized

1888 Football League formed

1889 The term "soccer" first used; May be an abbreviation of association football – the FA was formed to standardize the rules of the game

1890 Scottish League formed

1891 Goal nets first used

1891 Linesmen (now assistant referees) replace umpires

1891 Penalty kick adopted by the FA

American Football records

The first international American football game took place at Cambridge, Massachusetts, on 14 May 1874, between Harvard University and McGill University of Montreal, Canada.

The first Rose Bowl college football game was at Pasadena, California, on 1 January 1902 between the Universities of Michigan and Stanford. It has been held annually since 1916.

The New England Patriots (wearing blue and white) have won three Super Bowls this century.

American football

American football, or Gridiron, is the number one sport in the USA. The National Football League (NFL) is split into two conferences, the American Football Conference (AFC) and National Football Conference (NFC). Each conference is split into four divisions – North, South, East and West – and each division has four teams.

Each team plays 16 matches and the six teams with the best records in both the AFC and NFC take part in the play-offs, with the winner of each conference then meeting for the Super Bowl early in February. The Super Bowl winning team receives the Vince Lombardi Trophy.

No.	Year	Winners	No.	Year	Winners	No.	Year	Winners	No.	Year	Winners
I	1967	Green Bay Packers	XII	1978	Dallas Cowboys	XXIII	1989	San Francisco 49ers	XXXIII	1999	Denver Broncos
II	1968	Green Bay Packers	XIII	1979	Pittsburgh Steelers	XXIV	1990	San Francisco 49ers	XXXIV	2000	St Louis Rams
III	1969	New York Jets	XIV	1980	Pittsburgh Steelers	XXV	1991	New York Giants	XXXV	2001	Baltimore Ravens
IV	1970	Kansas City Chiefs	XV	1981	Oakland Raiders	XXVI	1992	Washington Redskins	XXXVI	2002	New England Patriots
V	1971	Baltimore Colts	XVI	1982	San Francisco 49ers				XXXVII	2003	Tampa Bay Buccaneers
VI	1972	Dallas Cowboys	XVII	1983	Washington Redskins	XXVII	1993	Dallas Cowboys	XXXVIII	2004	New England Patriots
VII	1973	Miami Dolphins	XVIII	1984	Los Angeles Raiders	XXVIII	1994	Dallas Cowboys	XXXIX	2005	New England Patriots
VIII	1974	Miami Dolphins	XIX	1985	San Francisco 49ers	XXIX	1995	San Francisco 49ers	XL	2006	Pittsburgh Steelers
IX	1975	Pittsburgh Steelers	XX	1986	Chicago Bears	XXX	1996	Dallas Cowboys	XLI	2007	Indianapolis Colts
X	1976	Pittsburgh Steelers	XXI	1987	New York Giants	XXXI	1997	Green Bay Packers	XLII	2008	New York Giants
XI	1977	Oakland Raiders	XXII	1988	Washington Redskins	XXXII	1998	Denver Broncos			

1900s

1904 FIFA formed in Paris; first international match outside Britain – Belgium v France played near Brussels

1907 Professional Footballers' Association (PFA) formed (as the Football Players and Trainers Union)

1921 FA of Ireland (Republic of Ireland) formed

1923 First Wembley Cup Final (Bolton v West Ham)

1928 Players' numbers introduced

1930 First World Cup in Uruguay

1932 Substitutes formally agreed by FIFA

1950 England's first World Cup (lost 1–0 to USA)

1954 Union of European Football Associations (UEFA) formed

1955 European Cup started

1960 Football League Cup started

1965 Football League agrees use of substitutes

1968 Red cards introduced (at the Mexico Olympic Games)

1975 Scottish Premier Division (now Premier League) formed

1981 Football League changed the number of points for a win from two to three

1982 Professional foul rule introduced

2000s

1992 FA Premier League formed

1993 Champions' League replaces the European Cup

2004 Greece are surprise winners of the European Championship

2007 David Beckham moves to Los Angeles Galaxy for $150 million over 5 years

2008 Fabio Capello (Italy) becomes England Manager

http://www.fifa.com   search

Badminton

Badminton probably came from an old children's game called "battledore and shuttlecock". The battledore is a small wooden bat which the player uses to hit the shuttlecock. The game was popular in India and other Asian countries, and the aim was to keep the shuttlecock in the air as long as possible. British army officers played the game in India in the 1860s and they added a net to hit the shuttlecock over. They called the game "poona".

When the officers returned to England they continued enjoying poona. The game was renamed badminton at a garden party at the home of the Duke of Beaufort in 1873. His home was called Badminton House. By 1877 the first official rules of the game were drawn up and in 1893 the first governing body, The Badminton Association of England, was set up. The Badminton Club of New York began in 1878, although the game did not become popular until the 1930s.

Badminton's greatest player
Rudy Hartono from Indonesia won the world's oldest badminton tournament, the All-England Championships, a record eight times between 1968 and 1976. He was also the 1980 world champion at the age of 32, and unbeaten in six Thomas Cup ties.

Pelota

Pelota is the name given to a variety of sports that are played by hitting a ball with the hand, a racquet, or a basket attached to the hand. Pelota and its variations were first played during the 13th century in the Basque region of Spain. There are variations of the game depending upon the equipment used.

- Played with the hand it is called *pelota mano*, or just pelota.
- Played with a racquet, it is called *frontenis*.
- Played with a hand basket, it is called *jai-alai*.

The game is similar to squash – players hit the ball against the end wall of a three-sided court, if possible, out of reach of their opponent. Pelota is popular in Spain, Mexico, South America, Cuba, Italy and many US states, including Florida.

New rules for table tennis
Traditionally, the winner of a table tennis game was the first player to score 21 points, but in 2001 the International Table Tennis Federation (ITTF) announced changes in the rules. These included a new scoring system in which the first player to score 11 points wins the game. In national and international tournaments all matches are played to either the best-of-5 games or the best-of-7.

Pelota player in action

Lawn tennis timeline   1800s   2000s

1877 First Wimbledon Championship
1881 First US Championship
1891 First French Championship – until 1925 for French nationals
1896 Tennis played at the first Modern Olympics in Athens
1900 Davis Cup began after Dwight F. Davis donated a trophy
1905 First Australian Open
1913 International Lawn Tennis Federation founded in Paris with 12 member countries

1922 Seeding (method of ranking players) first used, at the US National Championships
1923 Women's tennis became international with the launch of the Wightman Cup (named after US team captain Hazel Wightman)
1938 Donald Budge (USA) became the first player to complete the Grand Slam

1950 Louise Brough (USA) became the first woman to complete the Grand Slam
1963 The Federation Cup, the women's equivalent of the Davis Cup, began
1968 Tennis tournaments were opened to professional players, effectively ending the amateur game
1971 The tie-break was introduced by the British LTA as an experiment

1973 Introduction of official world rankings by the ATP and LTA
1988 Tennis revived as an Olympic sport after 64 years
2004 World ranking points first allocated to competitors in the Olympic Games
2008 On 1 January, Roger Federer achieved a recrod 205th consecutive week at No. 1 in the ATP rankings

Tennis scoring

No one knows exactly how the tennis scoring system came about, but it may have started in France in medieval times. People think the system may be based on the movement of the hand of a clock at one end of the court: on winning a point, the hand would be moved 15 minutes, or a quarter round the clock. Next comes 30, half the clock, and so on. As a player had to win four points to win the game, the first round the clock face won. The score 40 may be used instead of 45 because in French quarante (40) is easier to say than quarante-cinq (45). When both sides reach 40 the score is deuce. This comes from the French quarante à deux, or 40 to both, or simply from deux, two, as players must gain two points to win. "Love", the zero score, may come from the French word l'oeuf, meaning egg, as the symbol for zero is egg-shaped.

Serena and Venus Williams

Serena Williams (born 1981) has won 8 Grand Slam singles titles, which is two more than her older sister Venus (born 1980). Both players have been ranked World No. 1 and have each earned more than $18 million in prize money.

Serena Williams

Lawn tennis Grand Slam events

The Grand Slam consists of the Australian, French, Wimbledon and US Championships. A player is said to have completed the Grand Slam if he or she holds all four titles simultaneously, although not necessarily in the same year. These events were originally for amateur players but are now open to all, including professionals.

Wimbledon Championships

First held in 1877, Wimbledon is the world's most famous tennis championship. From 1877 to 1921 it was a challenge event with the defending champion qualifying for the next year's final. Women first took part in 1884. Since 1968 Wimbledon has been an open event. This means it is open to all players, including professionals.

US Open

This was first held in 1881. Until 1911, the US tournament operated as a challenge system, with the defending champion automatically going through to the following year's final. Women first competed in 1887. Two championships were held in 1968 and 1969, one for amateurs and an open championship. It became completely open in 1970.

French Open

The French Open was first held in 1891 and until 1925 it was only for French nationals. It became the French Open in 1968 and has been played at the Stade Roland Garros (named after a famous French aviator) since 1928. Women have competed since 1897.

Australian Open

This competition was first held in 1905 as the Australasian Tennis Championship. Women first competed in 1922. The competition became the Australian Championship in 1927, and since 1969 has been the Australian Open. It is played at Melbourne every January.

Most titles in Grand Slams

Australian Roy Emerson won 28 Grand Slam titles between 1961 and 1967. He is the only male player to win singles and doubles titles at all four Grand Slam events. Margaret Court (née Smith), also from Australia, won a record 62 Grand Slam titles, between 1960 and 1973.

Squash champions

Jahangir Khan

Jahangir Khan is the greatest male squash player of all time. He has won six World Open titles, three World Amateur titles, four World Masters and ten consecutive British Open titles. Khan was born in Karachi in 1963. His father Roshan was a British champion, as were Roshan's cousins Hashan and Azam. At one point in his career, Jahangir competed for an amazing five years and eight months without defeat, playing more than 800 matches. He was voted Pakistan's Sportsman of the Millennium and elected President of the World Squash Federation in 2002.

Heather McKay

Heather McKay (born Blundell) dominated ladies' squash during the 1960s and 1970s. She was born in New South Wales, Australia in 1942, the eighth of 11 children. Between 1962 and 1977 she won 16 consecutive British Open titles and remained undefeated for 17 years before her retirement. She lost just two games in her career. In 1999 Heather McKay became a founder member of the WISPA Hall of Fame, and was awarded the Australian Sports Medal in 2000.

Boxing weights

Boxing matches are held between two contestants of similar weight. The weight classes were first used in the 19th century and more were added during the 20th century.

Weight class	Max kg (lb)
Strawweight/Mini flyweight	48 (106)
Junior flyweight/ Light flyweight	49 (108)
Flyweight	51 (112)
Junior bantam/ Super flyweight	52 (115)
Bantamweight	54 (119)
Junior featherweight/ Super bantamweight	55 (121)
Featherweight	57 (126)
Junior lightweight/ Super featherweight	59 (130)
Lightweight	61 (134)
Junior welterweight/ Super lightweight	65 (143)
Welterweight	67 (148)
Junior middleweight/ Super welterweight	70 (154)
Middleweight	73 (161)
Super middleweight	76 (168)
Light heavyweight	79 (174)
Cruiserweight	91 (201)
Heavyweight	>91 (201)

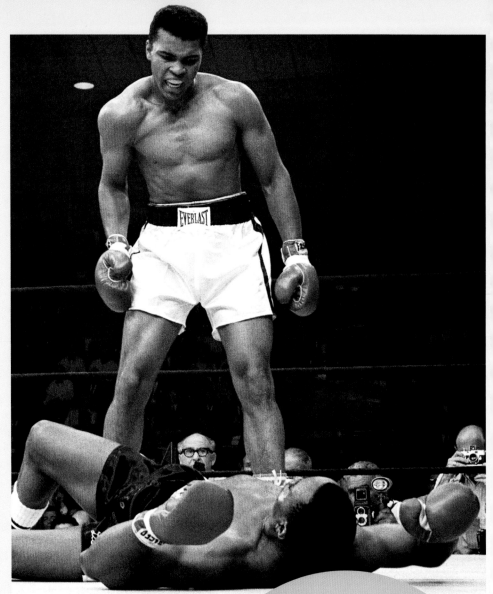

Muhammad Ali defeating Sonny Liston in 1965 to retain his world title.

Boxing's greatest champions

● "Sugar" Ray Robinson was one of the best boxers in any weight division. His first world title was at welterweight in 1946. Moving up a division, he beat Jake La Motta in 1951 to capture the middleweight title. He even had a crack at the light heavyweight title, but failed after a 14th-round knockout. Robinson was born in Detroit in 1920 and turned professional in 1940. He went on to have 201 fights and won 174 of them, 109 with knockouts.

● "Sugar" Ray Leonard was born in Wilmington, Carolina in 1956. He began boxing at 14 and in 1976 won the Olympic light welterweight title. He turned professional in 1977. Two years later he won the first of many world titles when he beat Wilfred Benitez to become welterweight champion. Leonard went on to become the first man to win world titles at five different weights, all within ten years. He held welterweight, light middleweight, middleweight, light heavyweight and super middleweight titles.

● Oscar de la Hoya from Los Angeles first became famous at the 1992 Barcelona Olympics – he won the USA's only boxing gold that year. La Hoya turned professional after the Olympics. He went on to become only the third man to capture world titles at five different weights, from junior lightweight to junior middleweight. His greatest win was beating his idol Julio Cesar Chavez in four rounds at Caesar's Palace, Las Vegas, in 1996.

Muhammad Ali

Muhammad Ali was born Cassius Clay in Louisville, Kentucky in 1942. He burst on to the boxing scene at the 1960 Rome Olympics where he took the light heavyweight gold medal. In 1964, aged 22, he won his first world heavyweight title by beating Sonny Liston. He beat George Foreman ten years later to become only the second man to regain his title. In 1978, at the age of 36, he beat Leon Spinks to become the first man to win the title a third time. He lost his last world title fight to Larry Holmes in 1980.

www.wwe.com · search

Snooker and pool

Snooker was first played by British army officers in India and later became popular in Britain, while pool began in America. One of pool's top events is the Mosconi Cup, named after the great American pool player and 14 times world champion Willie Mosconi. It is now an annual contest in the UK and pitches the best pool players from Europe against those from the USA.

Pool champion

Earl Strickland from Greensboro, North Carolina has won three world Nine-ball titles (1990, 1991, 2002). He has also been the US Open Nine-ball champion five times. Nicknamed "The Pearl", he has appeared in 11 Mosconi Cups, winning 37 matches out of 56.

Snooker champions

The greatest players of the modern game still playing are Steve Davis and Stephen Hendry. Between them they have won the Embassy World Professional Snooker title 13 times, and both have won all the other major trophies in the game. Davis won six world titles between 1981 and 1989. Scottish-born Hendry has won a record seven, including five consecutive titles between 1992 and 1996.

Hossein Rezazadeh

Hossein Rezazadeh (Iran) holds the men's weightlifting record. He lifted 472.5 kg (1,041.7 lb) at the Sydney Olympics in September 2000. This is heavier than a cow!

Wrestling

The World Wrestling Federation was started in the 1960s as the WorldWide Wrestling Federation (WWWF) by Vince McMahon. In the early 1980s Vince's son, Vince McMahon Jr, renamed it WWF.

The sport changed and became widely popular. Characters such as Hulk Hogan became household names, attracting huge crowds to live matches and millions of followers via TV. The WWF is now known as WWE®, World Wrestling Entertainment, Inc. The two biggest events in the WWE calendar are Wrestle Mania, which decides the world champions, and the Royal Rumble. The first WWF Wrestle Mania was at Madison Square Garden on 31 March 1985.

Top wrestlers

● Texan Shawn Michaels is one of the most popular of all wrestlers. He weighs in at about 116 kg (255.7 lb). Michaels has won the WWE title, WWE World Heavyweight title, the WWE World Tag Team title and twice won the Royal Rumble, among many other top honours and titles.

Hulk Hogan

Hulk Hogan's real name is Terry Bollea. He is 2.03 m (6.66 ft) tall and weighs a massive 122 kg (269 lb). His first ring name was Sterling Golden and then he became Terry Boulder before settling with Hulk Hogan. He played the wrestling villain Thunderlips in *Rocky III* in 1982. Hogan's latest film appearance is as Zeus in *Little Hercules in 3-D*, which is scheduled for release in 2008.

● The Rock (real name Dwayne Johnson) is 1.94 m (6.36 ft) tall and weighs 118 kg (260.11 lb). He has been the WWE Champion, the WWE World Tag Team Champion and was the winner of Royal Rumble 2000. He took to the sport after a brief professional football career, and has also appeared in several films, including *The Mummy Returns* (2001), *The Scorpion King* (2002), *The Game Plan* (2007), and *Get Smart* (2008).

● Triple H, or "The Game", made his WWE debut in 1995 as Hunter Hearst Helmsley. He weighs around 118 kg (260.11 lb). He has been WWE Champion, WWE World Heavyweight Champion, WWE World Tag Team Champion, King of the Ring and Royal Rumble. He is the only man to win the Grand Slam, King of the Ring and Royal Rumble.

Weightlifting records

In an Olympic weightlifting competition contestants perform two types of lifts, the snatch, and the clean and jerk. They have three attempts at each. The score is the total of the best of each type of lift.

In the snatch the contestant lifts the bar from the floor directly above the head and holds it for two seconds. In the clean and jerk the contestant first takes the bar from the floor to the shoulders and then above the head.

The women's world record stands at 319 kg (703.4 lb) set by Mu Shuangshuang of China on 26 September 2007.

Iranian weightlifter Hossein Rezazadeh

Olympic water sports

Sailing

The first Modern Olympics in 1896 should have included sailing, but the races could not be held because of bad weather. Sailing was included for the first time four years later in Paris and has been a full Olympic sport since 1908. Boardsailing made its debut in 1988. Men and women have competed together in sailing events over the years, but in 1988 women had events of their own. Until the 2000 Olympics, sailing was known as yachting.

Top gold-medal winning nations (1900–2004)
Great Britain 24
Norway 17
USA 17

Rowing

Rowing was to have been part of the 1896 Olympics, but the events were cancelled. It was first included in Paris four years later, and has appeared at every Olympics since. Women first competed in 1976.

The top gold-medal winning nations (1900–2004)
East Germany 33
USA 30
Germany/West Germany 27
Great Britain 22

Canoeing

Canoeing was first included as a demonstration sport in 1924, and did not become a full Olympic sport until 1936. Women took part for the first time in 1948.

Top gold-medal winning nations (1936–2004)
USSR/Unified Team 30
Germany/West Germany 28
East Germany 14
Hungary 17
Sweden 15

Michael Phelps swimming in the 2004 Olympic Games

Mark Spitz

When swimmer Mark Spitz took part in the 1968 Mexico Olympics he was already a record holder – he set a total 26 world records during his career. He predicted he would win six gold medals at the Olympics, but he won just two, both in relay events.

But in 1972, in Munich, Spitz became the first and only person to win seven gold medals at one Summer Olympics. He also set new world records with all his medals.

Mark Spitz's gold medals at the 1972 Olympics

Event	Time (min:sec)
200 m butterfly	2:00.70
4 x 100 m freestyle	3:26.42
200 m freestyle	1:52.78
100 m butterfly	0:54.27
4 x 200 m freestyle	7:35.78
100 m freestyle	0:51.22
4 x 100 m medley	3:48.16

Start of the men's coxless fours rowing final at the 2004 Olympic Games. Great Britain is the 3rd boat from the top.

Rowing knights

British rower Steve Redgrave won gold medals at five consecutive Olympic Games (1984–2000), while Matthew Pinsent won gold medals at four consecutive Games – in coxless pairs (with Steve Redgrave) in 1992 and 1996 and coxless fours in 2000 and 2004. Pinsent and Redgrave were knighted for their rowing achievements.

Olympic swimming

These are the top medal-winning Olympic swimmers. Totals include medals won in relays.

Swimmer	Gold	Silver	Bronze	Total
Men				
Mark Spitz (USA)	9	1	1	11
Matt Biondi (USA)	7	2	1	10
Aleksandr Popov (Russia)	4	5	0	9
Zoltán Halmay (Hungary)	3	5	1	9
Women				
Jenny Thompson (USA)	8	1	1	10
Dara Torres (USA)	4	1	4	9
Dawn Fraser (Australia)	4	4	0	8
Kornelia Ender (GDR)	4	4	0	8
Shirley Babashoff (USA)	2	6	0	8

www.fina.org   search

Olympic Tarzans

Johnny Weissmuller won the 100 metres freestyle at the 1924 Paris Olympics. He went on to win a total of five golds and one bronze medal during his Olympic career. While training for the 1932 Olympics, he was offered a $500-a-week contract to advertise swimwear. A Hollywood executive saw the adverts and offered Weissmuller the role of Tarzan. In 1932 he made his debut in the film *Tarzan the Ape Man*. He played the character in 11 more films over the next 16 years. He was the first of four Olympic medallists to play the film role. The others were Buster Crabbe (freestyle swimmer), Herman Brix (shot put) and Glenn Morris (decathlon).

The America's Cup

The America's Cup is the top sailing trophy and one of the best known trophies in the sporting world. It began in 1851 when the English Royal Yacht Squadron organized a 10-km (6-mile) regatta of 17 boats around the Isle of Wight. The 31-m American schooner *America* entered and won the trophy, then called the One Hundred Guinea Cup.

Competitors in the America's Cup, 2003

After *America*'s win, the trophy was re-named the America's Cup and given to the New York Yacht Club. There it remained unless won by a challenger. Over the next 132 years the New York Yacht Club successfully defended the trophy against 25 challengers, until in 1983 it was won by Australia. In 2003 the trophy returned to Europe when Russell Coutts in *Alinghi* won for Switzerland – a landlocked country! The latest Cup was held at Valencia, Spain, in 2007, and was again won by *Alinghi* for Switzerland.

Swimming strokes

Breaststroke

The breaststroke was the first stroke used in competitive and recreational swimming. It is also the stroke that most people learn when they first take up swimming. The first reference to the breaststroke was in a French book in 1696. The sidestroke, with a scissor leg action, developed from breaststroke. Top swimmers can swim the breaststroke at 1.37 m (4.5 ft) a second.

Backstroke

The backstroke is the only stroke in which the swimmers start in the water, rather than diving in. The stroke, in which swimmers lie on their backs and use their arms in a windmill style, was first made popular in the USA by Harry Hebner in 1912. An earlier form of the backstroke was first seen at the 1900 Olympics. For this fast stroke, top speed is about 1.52 m (5 ft) a second.

Butterfly

In this stroke, both arms enter and leave the water at the same time, while the legs perform a dolphin kick. It was developed in the 1930s and evolved from the breaststroke. Swimming coach David Armbruster developed the arm movement of the stroke at the University of Iowa in 1934 and the following year one of his swimmers, Jack Sieg, developed the foot and leg movements. The two combined produced the butterfly. The stroke was not officially approved until 1953 and became an Olympic event in 1956. Maximum speed is 1.67 m (5.5 ft) a second.

Front crawl/freestyle

In 1844 two native Americans competing in a swimming regatta in London introduced their new revolutionary overarm stroke. Flying Gull beat Tobacco to take the winner's medal. The stroke was later developed by Englishman John Trudgen, and then by Australian Richard Cavill, who realized the importance of kicking the feet at the same time as moving the arms. Front crawl is the fastest swimming stroke and has a maximum speed of 1.71 m (5.6 ft) a second.

Tour de France

The oldest and best-known of the world's great cycling tours is the Tour de France. The others are the Vuelta – Tour of Spain, and Giro – Tour of Italy.

● The Tour de France was first staged in 1903 when the course was made up of six stages over 2,428 km (1,508.7 miles). Now the race is 5,000 km (3,106.9 miles) or more and the course takes in more than 20 stages, often going into neighbouring countries.

● The famous yellow jersey (*maillot jaune*) is worn by the current overall time leader in a race. It was first worn in 1919.

● The longest race was in 1926 when Lucien Buysse of Belgium won after 5,745 km (3,569.8 miles).

● Around 15 million people every year line the streets to watch the Tour de France over its three weeks.

● The first US winner of the Tour de France was Greg LeMond who won it in 1986, and again in 1989 and 1990. He was also the first English-speaking winner of the race.

● Eddie Merckx has won more of the big three tours than any other man. He has won the Tour de France five times, the Giro five times and the Vuelta once.

Lance Armstrong

Lance Armstrong (USA) has won the Tour de France a record seven times, two more than Jacques Anquetil (France), Eddie Merckx (Belgium), Bernard Hinault (France) and Miguel Indurain (Spain).

Olympic cycling

Cycling was included in the first Modern Olympics in 1896. Léon Flameng (France) won the first cycling gold in the 100 km race. Only two men competed – Flameng and Georgios Kolettis of Greece – and they had to race around a 333.3 m (1,093.5 ft) track 300 times! During the race, Kolettis's bicycle needed repairing, so Flameng waited for him while the repairs were carried out. Cycling has been included in every Olympics since then. Below are the current Olympic events.

Men
Track
Sprint (1,000 metres)
Team Sprint (1,000 metres)
Individual pursuit (4,000 metres)
Team pursuit (4,000 metres)
Points race (40 kilometres)
Madison (60 kilometres)
Keirin (2,000 metres)
Road
Road race (individual)
Time trial (individual)
BMX (individual)
Mountain bike
Cross-country

Women
Track
Sprint (1,000 metres)
Individual pursuit (3,000 metres)
Points race (25 kilometres)
Road
Road race (individual)
Time trial (individual)
BMX (individual)
Mountain bike
Cross-country

Lance Armstrong

Mountain biking

Mountain biking, or off-road biking, was started in 1974 by a group of Californian enthusiasts, who modified their bikes. By 1977, there was so much interest in the sport that manufacturers started to produce mountain bikes, and in 1983 the National Off-Road Bicycle Association (NORBA) was formed.

There are two principal types of mountain bike competitions – downhill riding and cross-country – and the first world championships were held in 1990. Cross-country mountain biking was first held at the Olympics in 1996. Competitors ride over a hilly, sometimes mountainous, natural course. Men race 40 to 50 km (24.85 to 30.07 miles), and women 30 to 40 km (18.64 to 24.85 miles).

The top male and female riders are both French. Nicolas Vouilloz won seven men's downhill world titles between 1995 and 2002. Anne-Caroline Chausson (France) has won 16 World Championship titles. She won the downhill event every year from 1996 to 2003 and again in 2005.

Olympic women's mountain bike race

Formula One

The Formula One World Championship normally lasts from March until October. In 2008 the schedule consisted of 18 races. Since 2003 the points system has been:

winner – 10 points
2nd – 8 points
3rd – 6 points
4th – 5 points
5th – 4 points
6th – 3 points
7th – 2 points
8th – 1 point.

The driver with the most points at the end of the season is the champion. There is also a manufacturers' championship.

In 2007, in his first season in Formula One racing, British racing driver Lewis Hamilton (born 1985) won four Grand Prix races (Canada, USA, Hungary and Japan) and became the youngest ever to lead the Formula One World Championship.

World champion

German Michael Schumacher is the world's most successful Formula One driver. He has won a record seven world titles (1994, 1995, 2000, 2001, 2002, 2003, 2004) and also has the most race wins in a season – 13 in 2004.

Motor cycle racing

Grand Prix bikes come in engine sizes 125 cc, 250 cc and Moto GP (which replaced the old 500 cc event). Grand Prix bikes are made in small numbers just for racing. Superbikes are made in larger quantities and can be used on the road.

Top manufacturers

● An Aprilia machine first won at 250 cc in 1987, and the make is now dominant in both the 125 and 250 cc classes. They enjoyed their first Superbike success in 2000.

● Honda are the most successful manufacturer in motor cycle racing. They have won 48 Grand Prix world titles and have had 607 race wins. They are now also making a name for themselves in Superbike racing.

● Kawasaki bikes won their first world title (125 cc) in 1969. They have now won nine world titles in three classes as well as producing the 1993 Superbike world champion.

● The Yamaha company started in 1887 as musical instrument manufacturers and made their first motor cycle in 1955. They entered a bike in the 1961 French Grand Prix, but did not compete regularly until 1964, when they won the world 250 cc title.

● Suzuki began life as clothing makers before starting to make motor cycles. They won their first Grand Prix in 1962 and in the same year won the first ever 50 cc title.

● Ducati have been in Grand Prix racing since the 1950s. They are now by far the most successful manufacturer in Superbike history.

One and only

One of the great Indy 500 drivers was A.J. Foyt, the first of only three men to win the race four times. He won in 1961, 1964, 1967 and 1977. He drove a record 18,966 km (11,785 miles) in 34 Indy 500 races. Foyt started racing in 1953. He is the only man to win the Indy 500, the Daytona 500 and the Le Mans 24 Hour races.

Young winners

● In 2005 Fernando Alonso (Spain) became the youngest-ever winner of the Formula One World Driver's Championship aged 24 years, 2 months.

● In 1952 Troy Ruttman (USA) won the Indianapolis 500 (at that time part of the Formula One World Championship) aged 22 years, 3 months. Bruce McLaren (New Zealand) was the same age when he won the US Grand Prix in 1959.

● Other young Formula One World Champions are Emerson Fittipaldi (Brazil), aged 25 years, 9 months, in 1972; Michael Schumacher (Germany), who won in 1994 at the age of 25 years, 10 months.

Indianapolis 500

The biggest event in American motor racing is the Indianapolis 500, which is not just a race but a day-long carnival. The auto race is part of the Memorial Day celebrations at the end of May and crowds of 250,000 flock to the Indianapolis raceway from all over the USA.

The course, which opened in 1909, is known as The Brickyard because the original circuit was made out of thousands of bricks. The first Indy 500 was held in 1911 and was won by Ray Harroun in his Marmon Wasp. Contestants race over 200 laps of the 4 km (2.48 miles) oval circuit.

www.formula1.com   search

Winter Olympics

The Winter Games (officially the International Winter Sports Week, but later recognized as the first Winter Olympics) was first held in 1924. It included five events: Nordic skiing, figure skating, speed skating, bobsledding and ice hockey.

Winter Olympics were held in the same years as the Summer Olympics until 1992, but since 1994 they have taken place every four years between the Summer Games. The sports being contested at the 2010 Vancouver Games are:

- Alpine skiing
- Biathlon
- Bobsleigh
- Cross-country skiing
- Curling
- Figure skating
- Freestyle skiing
- Ice hockey
- Ice sledge hockey
- Luge
- Nordic combined
- Short-track speed skating
- Skeleton
- Ski-jumping
- Snowboarding
- Speed skating
- Wheelchair curling

Snowboarding

Snowboards were invented in the 1970s, and the sport started to become popular in the 1980s. In 1998 snowboarding was included in the Winter Olympics for the first time, with Halfpipe and Parallel giant slalom events. Snowboard cross was added in 2006.

Top medal winners at the Winter Olympics (1924–2006)

Athlete – Men	Sport	Gold	Silver	Bronze	Total
Bjorn Dählie (Norway)	Cross-country	8	4	0	12
Sixten Jernberg (Sweden)	Cross-country	4	3	2	9
Ole Einar Bjoerndalen (Norway)	Biathlon	5	3	1	9
Ricco Gross (Germany)	Biathlon	4	3	1	8
Kjetil André Aamodt (Norway)	Alpine skiing	4	2	2	8
Sven Fischer (Germany)	Biathlon	4	2	2	8

Athlete – Women	Sport	Gold	Silver	Bronze	Total
Raisa Smetanina (USSR/Unified Team)	Cross-country	4	5	1	10
Stefania Belmondo (Italy)	Cross-country	2	3	5	10
Lyubov Egorova (Unified Team/Russia)	Cross-country	6	3	0	9
Uschi Disl (Germany)	Biathlon	2	4	3	9
Claudia Pechstein (Germany)	Speed skating	5	2	2	9

Top medal-winning nations at the Winter Olympics (1924–2006)

Country	Gold	Silver	Bronze	Total
USSR/Unified Team/ Russia	122	89	86	297
Norway	96	102	84	282
USA	78	81	59	218
Germany/ West Germany	76	78	57	211
Austria	50	64	71	185

🔍 www.vancouver2010.org   **search**

Winter Olympic facts and figures   1900s

1924 Chamonix, France
There were 294 competitors from 16 nations. Norway won the most medals (17) and tied with Finland for gold medals (4).

1928 St Moritz, Switzerland
Twenty-five nations and 495 competitors took part. Norway won the most medals (15) and the most golds (6).

1932 Lake Placid, USA
A total of 306 competitors from 17 nations competed. USA won the most medals (12) and the most golds (6).

1936 Garmisch-Partenkirchen, Germany
There were 755 competitors from 28 nations. Norway won most medals (15) and most gold medals (7).

1948 St Moritz, Switzerland
A total of 28 nations and 713 competitors took part. Norway, Sweden and Switzerland tied for top medal position (10). Norway and Sweden tied for most golds (4).

1952 Oslo, Norway
A total of 732 competitors from 30 nations took part. Norway held both top medal (16) and top gold (7) position.

1956 Cortina D'Ampezzo, Italy
Thirty-two nations and 818 competitors took part. USSR were top medal winners (16) with the most gold wins (7).

1960 Squaw Valley, USA
Thirty nations took part with 665 athletes. USSR again won the most medals (21) and most golds (7).

1964 Innsbruck, Austria
Thirty-six nations and 1,186 athletes took part. USSR won most medals (25) and most golds (11) for the third time.

1968 Grenoble, France
A total of 1,293 athletes competed from 37 nations. Norway won most medals (14) and most gold medals (6).

Competitors in the Men's Snowboard Cross final at the Turin 2006 Winter Olympics

The Stanley Cup

Every player on the winning team takes the Stanley Cup home for 24 hours to show off to family and friends. New York Islander Clark Gillies used it in 1980 to feed his dog, and in 1996 Colorado Avalanche defenceman Sylvain Lefebvre baptized his daughter in it.

Ice hockey

Ice hockey probably developed from a game called bandy that was played on ice-covered pitches. The modern game is played over three 20-minute periods between two teams. Each team has six players on the ice at any one time. The object is to move the puck (a hard rubber disc) across the ice with a stick (maximum length 160 cm [63 in]) and put it into the opponent's goal.

The National Hockey League (NHL) was formed in 1917. Today the NHL is made up of 30 teams split into two conferences. The Eastern Conference has 15 teams divided into three divisions: Atlantic, North-East and South-East. The Western Conference is also divided into three divisions: Central, North-West and Pacific. At the end of season the leading teams in each conference play each other. The winner of each plays for the Stanley Cup.

NHL's top goalscorers

Player	Goals
Wayne Gretzky	894
Gordie Howe	801
Brett Hull	741
Marcel Dionne	731
Phil Esposito	717
Mike Gartner	708

Top teams Stanley Cup wins

Montreal Canadiens	24
Toronto Maple Leafs	13
Detroit Red Wings	10
Boston Bruins	5
Edmonton Oilers	5

Ice skating

Famous skaters

● Ulrich Salchow, born in Sweden in 1877, was the greatest men's figure skater of all time. He won the first Olympic skating title at the 1908 London Olympics and between 1901 and 1911 he was the world champion on ten occasions.

● Norway's Sonja Henie won Olympic golds in 1928, 1932 and 1936. She also won ten world titles. She won nearly 1,500 cups and medals during her career. After leaving the sport in 1936 she became a film star and appeared in 11 films.

Fastest speed skaters

● Finland's Pekka Koskela set a new men's world record at Salt Lake City, USA, on 10 November 2007 when he covered 1,000 metres in 1 minute 7 seconds, knocking 3/100ths of a second off the old record.

● Cindy Klassen of Canada set a women's world record of 1 minute 13.46 seconds for the 1000 m at Calgary on 24 March 2006. The next day, she lowered the record further to 1 minute 13.11 seconds.

Young star

The first athlete aged under 14 to win a Winter Olympic gold was Kim Yoon-mi of South Korea. She was in the winning 3,000 m speed skating relay team at Lillehammer, Norway in 1994.

Ski-jumping

In 2005 the world ski-jumping record was broken three times within 75 minutes! At the final meeting of the 2004–05 Ski Jumping World Cup Bjørn Einar Romøren (Norway) set a new mark at 234.5 m (769.3 ft). Then Matti Hautamaeki (Finland) put the record up to 235.5 m (772.6 ft) before Romøren re-took the record with a leap of 239 m (784.1 ft).

2000s

1972 Sapporo, Japan
There were 1,232 competitors from 35 nations. USSR were top of the overall medal table (16) and won most gold medals (8).

1976 Innsbruck, Austria
Thirty-seven nations and 1,128 athletes took part. USSR won most medals (27) and most gold medals (13).

1980 Lake Placid, USA
There were 1,067 competitors from 37 nations. USSR won most medals overall (22) and most golds (10).

1984 Sarajevo, Yugoslavia
A total of 1,278 competitors from 49 nations took part. USSR won most medals (25) but East Germany topped the gold medal table (9).

1988 Calgary, Canada
Fifty-seven nations fielded 1,423 athletes. USSR won most medals (29) and most golds (11).

1992 Albertville, France
Sixty-three nations with 1,801 competitors took part. Germany won most medals (26) and most gold medals (10).

1994 Lillehammer, Norway
1,739 athletes from 67 nations took part. Norway won most medals altogether (26) but Russia won most golds (11).

1998 Nagano, Japan
There were 72 nations taking part and 2,302 athletes. Germany won most medals (29) and most gold medals (12).

2002 Salt Lake City, USA
Seventy-eight nations fielded 2,399 athletes. Germany again won most medals (35) and most golds (12).

2006 Turin, Italy
A record 2,663 athletes from 82 nations took part. Germany were the top medal winners for the third time in a row (29) and also won most gold medals (11).

See also

The Olympics: pages 282–83

Greyhound racing

Dog racing has been popular since ancient times, when dogs were used for hunting. Modern greyhound racing takes place on an oval-shaped track over distances from 210 m (689 ft) to 1,097 m (3,599 ft). An electric "hare" goes round the track, and the dogs are released from traps to chase it.

In the UK most greyhound races are run with six dogs, but in the USA they are run with eight. There is a draw before the race to decide which trap each dog starts from. Each dog wears a coloured jacket which matches its starting trap.

Harness racing

In harness racing the horses pull the drivers who sit in a two-wheeled cart called a sulky. There are two forms of harness racing – pacing and trotting.

The difference between pacing and trotting is in the way the horse moves. A pacing horse moves its right front and back legs together, then its left front and back legs. A trotter moves its left front leg and right back leg at the same time, followed by its right front leg and left back leg.

Hambletonian harness race

Main races

The leading race for trotters is the Hambletonian. This race was first held at Syracuse, New York, in 1926 and is now run every year at The Meadowlands, East Rutherford, New Jersey. It is named after a trotter called Hambletonian. The leading race for pacers is The Little Brown Jug, named after a 19th-century horse. It has been held at Delaware, Ohio, every year since 1946.

Top drivers

Herve Filion, born in Quebec, Canada, is the most famous driver in harness-racing history and set many records in his 35-year career. In 1968 he became the first driver to win 400 races in a season. He went on to achieve 400 or more wins per season in 14 other years. He was forced to retire in 1995 but made a comeback in 2002. He achieved his goal of reaching 15,000 wins before finally retiring the following year with a total of 15,086 wins.

John Campbell, from Ontario, Canada, is the top money-winning jockey in the sport. He started driving in 1972 at the age of 17 and was the first man to pass the $100 million and $200 million milestones in career earnings. He won the Hambletonian six times.

Top horse

Moni Maker was the first horse to pass the $5 million mark. Remarkably, she achieved this during a four-year career between 1997–2000. She won 60 of her 91 trotting races and won the Horse of the Year Award in 1998 and 1999. In 2003, the Italian-bred horse Varenne surpassed Moni Maker's career winning record.

Rodeo

Professional rodeo developed from the early days of ranching, when bull riding and calf roping were common activities. The first known rodeo with prize money was held at Deer Trail, Colorado, in 1869. The All-Round Cowboy World Champion is decided each year – the champion is the cowboy who wins the most money over a series of events. Top cowboys win more than $250,000 a year.

Record horse jumps

● The highest officially recognized horse jump is 2.47 m (8.1 ft). The jump was made by Captain Alberto Larraguibel Morales (Chile) on Huasó on 5 February 1949 at Santiago, Chile. Richard "Dick" Donnelly (USA) claimed to have cleared 2.51 m (8.3 ft) on a horse named Heatherbloom in Richmond, Virginia, USA, in 1902, but this is an unofficial record.

● The world record height jump by a horse in a puissance competition (in which horses jump a limited number of obstacles) was set on 9 June 1991. German rider Franke Sloothaak on Obtibeurs Leonardo cleared 2.4 m (7.9 ft) in Chaudfontaine, Switzerland.

● The longest horse jump over water is 8.4 m (27.5 ft). The jump was made by André Ferreira (South Africa) on 25 April 1975 in Johannesburg, South Africa, on a horse named Something.

The Breeders' Cup

The Breeders' Cup Limited was started in 1982 to encourage thoroughbred racing throughout the USA. The first Breeders' Cup day was held on 10 November 1984 at Hollywood Park, Inglewood, California. Between 1984 and 2006 the championship was a single day event, but since 2007 has been spread over two days. It is held at a different course each year.

From 2008 there will be six races on the first day (Friday), and eight on the second (Saturday). The total prize-money for the 2008 Breeders' Cup is $25.5 million. The top race is the Breeders' Cup Classic which is run over one mile and two furlongs. The prize-money for this race in 2008 is $5 million with over $2.7 million for the winner.

Winner of the Breeders' Cup Classic 2002

Most successful jockey

Laffit Pincay Jr was the first man to win more than 9,500 races. He won the Breeders' Cup seven times. He retired in 2003 having won more than $225 m. In December 2006 Russell Baze (Canada) surpassed Pincay's record and on 10 January 2008 rode his 10,000th winner.

Top horse races

England
● The Epsom Derby was first held in 1780 and is now run over one-and-a-half miles at Epsom Downs each June. The first winner was a horse named Diomed. Jockey Lester Piggott won the Derby a record nine times.

● The Grand National is the world's best-known steeplechase, a horse race over a course with obstacles to be jumped. It was first run as the Grand Liverpool Steeplechase in 1839. The race now takes place every spring over four-and-a-half miles at Aintree in England and the winning horse has to clear 30 challenging fences. The famous horse Red Rum won the race a record three times between 1972–76.

France
● The Prix de L'Arc de Triomphe was first run in 1920. It takes place on the first Sunday in October every year and covers 2,400 m over the Longchamps race course, Paris. Alleged, ridden by Lester Piggott, won the race in 1977 and 1978 and was the last horse to win two years in a row.

Australia
● The most important horse race in Australia is the Melbourne Cup which dates from 1861. It is run on the first Tuesday in November at the Flemington Park race track in Victoria. Trainer Bart Cummings won the race a record 11 times between 1965 and 1999.

United States
● The Kentucky Derby was first held in 1875. It is run over one mile two furlongs at Churchill Downs, Kentucky, on the first Saturday in May and is the most famous of all US horse races. Eddie Arcaro and Bill Hartack have been the most successful jockeys with five wins each.

Breeders' Cup records
Most wins (jockey)	15 (Jerry Bailey)
Most prize money (jockey)	$23,033,360 (Pat Day)
Most wins (trainer)	18 (D. Wayne Lukas)
Most prize money (trainer)	$19,645,520 (D. Wayne Lukas)
Most used track	Churchill Downs, Kentucky, used in 1988, 1991, 1994, 1998, 2000, 2006

Breeders' Cup firsts
The 2003 Breeders' Cup produced two firsts. Julie Krone, who rode Halfbridled to victory in the Juvenile Fillies race, was the first woman to ride a winner at the event. One race ended in a dead heat – the first in Breeders' Cup history.

 http://www.bhs.org.uk   search

Last
Lists

Young loss

Australian actor Heath Ledger died in 2008, at the age of 28, from an accidental overdose of prescription drugs. One of Hollywood's brightest young stars, the Oscar-nominated actor's death was a huge shock to the world and highlighted the dangers of combining precription medication.

Unusual deaths

Aeschylus
Aeschylus was a famous Greek dramatist who died in 456 BC. A prediction that he would be killed by a blow from heaven came true when an eagle carrying a tortoise dropped it on his head.

King Alexander of Greece
He died after being bitten by his pet monkey in 1920.

Francis Bacon
This Elizabethan philosopher caught a chill while trying to deep-freeze a chicken by stuffing it with snow. He died in 1626.

Hilaire Belloc
Although born in France, Hilaire Belloc was an English writer and member of parliament. He died in 1953 after a burning coal fell out of his fire and set him ablaze.

Madéleine-Sophie Blanchard
Madame Blanchard was the widow of pioneer balloonist Jean-Pierre Blanchard. She was killed in Paris in 1819, when fireworks set fire to her balloon.

Jerome Cardan
Cardan was an Italian physician, mathematician and astrologer. He starved himself to death in 1576 to make sure that his own prediction of his death would come true.

Lord Carnarvon
Carnarvon was an amateur Egyptologist who financed the excavation of Tutankhamun's tomb in 1922. Several months after opening the tomb, Carnarvon died suddenly from a mosquito bite. This began the legend of the curse of Tutankhamun.

Isadora Duncan
This American dancer was strangled in 1927 by her scarf. It became caught in the wheel of a Bugatti sports car in which she was a passenger.

Anton Dvorák
The Czech composer died in 1904 of a chill which he caught while train-spotting.

Frederick, Prince of Wales
Frederick was the son of George II and heir to the British throne. He died in 1751 after being hit by a cricket ball.

Harry Houdini (Erich Weiss)
Houdini was a famous escapologist who claimed he could withstand being punched in the stomach. He died in 1926 – after being punched in the stomach.

William Huskisson
Huskisson was a British member of parliament. He was run down by a train during the opening of the first railway in 1830.

Jean-Baptiste Lully
This Italian-French composer died in 1687 after accidentally stabbing his foot with a stick while beating time. The short conductor's baton came into use soon afterwards.

Thomas Midgley
Midgley was an American inventor who was strangled in 1944 by a machine he had invented to help him move after contracting polio. He invented three products that have since been found to be environmentally harmful: lead in petrol, CFCs in fridges and aerosols, and the insecticide DDT.

Forever young

The following are some of the most famous people who died early and so remain forever young in our minds.

Name/cause/year	Age at death
King Edward V of England, murdered, 1483	12
Saint Agnes martyred, c. 304	13
King Edward VI of England, natural causes, 1553	15
Anne Frank German diarist, in concentration camp, 1945	15
Lady Jane Grey Queen of England, executed, 1554	16
Thomas Chatterton English poet, took poison, 1770	17
Anastasia Grand Duchess of Russia, assassinated, 1918	17
Ritchie Valens American rock singer, plane crash, 1959	17
King Tutankhamun Egyptian pharaoh, c. 1340 BC	18
Heliogabalus Roman Emperor, assassinated, 222	18
Joan of Arc French heroine, burned at the stake, 1431	19
Catherine Howard Queen of Henry VIII, beheaded, 1542	20
Billy the Kid (William H. Bonney) American outlaw, shot, 1881	21

Name/cause/year	Age at death
Eddie Cochran American rock singer, car accident, 1960	21
Pocahontas Native American Indian princess, smallpox, 1617	22
Buddy Holly American rock singer, plane crash, 1959	22
Aaliyah (Aaliyah Haughton) singer, plane crash, 2001	22
River Phoenix actor, drug overdose, 1993	23
Clyde Barrow US outlaw, shot by Texas Rangers, 1934	24
James Dean American film actor, car crash, 1955	24
Lee Harvey Oswald assassin of John F. Kennedy, murdered, 1963	24
John Keats English poet, tuberculosis, 1821	25
"Red Baron" Manfred von Richthofen German flying ace, shot down, 1918	25
Jean Harlow film actress, illness, 1937	26
Brian Jones Rolling Stones guitarist, drowned, 1969	26
Jimi Hendrix rock guitarist, drugs, 1970	27
Kurt Cobain Nirvana lead singer, shooting suicide, 1994	27
Anne Brontë British writer, tuberculosis, 1849	29

Famous last words

Julius Caesar, 44 BC
Roman emperor, who was assassinated by conspirators, including Brutus, a man he thought was his friend. According to legend and Shakespeare, Caesar said: "Et tu Brute?" (You as well, Brutus?)

Caligula, AD 41
Roman emperor who was assassinated: "I am still alive!"

Catherine de Medici, 1589
Queen of France: "Ah, my God, I am dead!"

Joseph Henry Green, 1863
British doctor, after checking his own pulse: "Stopped."

General John Sedgwick, 1864
In the American Civil War, Sedgwick was shot by a sniper as he remarked: "They couldn't hit an elephant at this distance."

Viscount Palmerston, 1865
British Prime Minister: "Die, my dear doctor? That's the last thing I shall do."

Billy the Kid (aka William Bonney, Henry McCarty), 1881
American outlaw, before being shot by Sheriff Pat Garrett: "Who is it?"

Marie Antoinette, 1893
French queen, who accidentally trod on her executioner's foot as she went to the guillotine: "Pardonnez-moi, monsieur." (Pardon me, sir.)

Oscar Wilde, 1900
Opinions differ about the Irish writer's last words. Some people claim he said: "Either these curtains go/that wallpaper goes, or I do."

Prince Philippe

Prince Philippe, heir to the French throne, was killed when his horse tripped over a pig in the streets of Paris in 1131.

Pliny the Elder

Roman writer Pliny was choked by the fumes of the erupting volcano Vesuvius in AD 79.

Sir Thomas Urquhart

Urquhart was the Scottish author of books with extraordinary titles such as *Logopandecteision*. He died laughing when told of the Restoration of King Charles II in 1660.

William III

This British king died in 1701, after a fall from his horse when it stumbled over a molehill. His opponents drank a toast to the mole, calling it "The little gentleman in black velvet".

See also

Volcanic eruptions: page 46

Joan of Arc, 15th-century French heroine who was burned at the stake aged 19

Poster for Houdini show

Do Spirits Return?

HOUDINI

SAYS NO - AND PROVES IT

3 SHOWS IN ONE

MAGIC-ILLUSIONS-ESCAPES = FRAUD MEDIUMS EXPOSED

LYCEUM THEATRE

PATERSON

THURS. FRI. SAT. SEPT. 2·3·4

MATINEE SATURDAY

Queen Victoria, 1901

British queen: "Oh, that peace may come." (a reference to the war at the time in South Africa). "Bertie!" (her husband, Prince Albert).

Captain Lawrence Oates, 1912

Oates was a member of Scott's expedition to the South Pole. He was terribly injured from frostbite and went to his death rather than hold up his companions. When he left the tent he said, "I am going outside and may be some time."

Anna Pavlova, 1931

Ballerina: "Get my swan costume ready!"

Lytton Strachey, 1932

English writer: "If this is dying, then I don't think much of it."

Douglas Fairbanks Sr, 1939

American film actor: "I've never felt better."

Heinrich Himmler, 1945

Nazi leader, as he committed suicide by taking poison: "I am Heinrich Himmler!"

H.G. Wells, 1946

English novelist, author of *The Time Machine*: "I'm all right."

John F. Kennedy, 1963

Moments before he was shot, Kennedy replied to "You certainly can't say that the people of Dallas haven't given you a nice welcome, Mr President" with his final words, "No, you certainly can't."

www.findagrave.com

search

Entertainment lasts

Shakespeare's last play
Most people agree that *The Tempest*, 1611, is the last play Shakespeare wrote, although some think he may have written a later play that has been lost. Shakespeare died in 1616, and *The Tempest* was first published in 1623.

Charles Dickens' last story
The Mystery of Edwin Drood was Charles Dickens' last novel. It was published in monthly episodes, but ended, unfinished, when Dickens died in 1870.

Beethoven's last symphony
Ludwig van Beethoven's Ninth Symphony was the last he composed before his death in 1827. He promised the London Philharmonic Society that he would write his Tenth Symphony for them, but died before he could begin work on it.

The last Beatles concert
The Beatles last played together in public at Candlestick Park, San Francisco, on 29 August 1966. Their last publicly performed song was "Long Tall Sally".

The last silent film
The Four Feathers (1929) was the last silent film released by a major studio. The 1976 film *Silent Movie* does contain one word, "Non!" (French for no), which is spoken by Marcel Marceau, a mime artist.

The sixth and last Star Wars film
Star Wars: Episode III – Revenge of the Sith was released in 2005. It made almost $850 million worldwide, bringing the total for the series, which started in 1977, to $4.3 billion.

Crime and punishment lasts

Last executions for witchcraft in America
On 22 September 1692 seven women and one man were hanged for witchcraft at Salem and other places in New England.

Last beheading in the UK
On 9 April 1747, 80-year-old Simon Fraser, Lord Lovat, was beheaded for treason at Tower Hill, London.

Last person to be burned at the stake in England
Catherine Murphy belonged to a gang of coiners (coin forgers). She was strangled and then burnt at the stake at Newgate, London, on 18 March 1789.

Last public hanging in the UK
Michael Barrett was hanged outside Newgate Prison, London, on 26 May 1868 for the murder of Sarah Ann Hodgkinson. She was one of several victims who died from a bomb he had planted.

Last witness to the assassination of Abraham Lincoln
Samuel James Seymour, who died on 13 April 1956, was the last surviving witness to the assassination of the American president. Seymour was only five years old when he saw John Wilkes Booth shoot Abraham Lincoln at Ford's Theatre, Washington DC, on 14 April 1865.

Last person executed by guillotine
The last person to be executed in public was the murderer Eugene Weidmann who had his head cut off at Versailles, France, on 17 June 1939. The last official use of the guillotine in France was on 10 September 1977, when Hamida Djandoubi was executed for murder at Baumetes Prison, Marseilles.

Last prisoner of Alcatraz
Alcatraz Island, in the Bay of San Francisco, USA, was a prison for over 100 years. Surrounded by freezing water, it was considered impossible to escape. Armed rober Frank Clay Weatherman was its last prisoner. He left the island on 21 March 1963, after which Alcatraz closed.

Last Aztec emperor
Montezuma II was removed from power by Spanish invaders and killed in June 1520.

Montezuma II, the last Aztec emperor

Last men on the Moon
US *Apollo 17* astronauts Eugene A. Cernan and Harrison H. Schmitt spent three days on the Moon, blasting off to return to Earth on 14 December 1972. This was the last day on which any human walked on the surface of the Moon.

Royal lasts

The last Egyptian pharaoh
Cleopatra VII ruled from 69 BC, when she was 17 years old, until 30 BC, when Egypt became a province of the Roman empire.

The last Roman emperor
Romulus Augustus was about 14 when he was removed from power in AD 476. The Roman empire split into western and eastern divisions.

The last British king killed in battle
Richard III was killed at the battle of Bosworth on 22 August 1485.

The last British king born abroad
George II was born in Hanover, Germany, on 10 November 1683.

The last king of France
Louis-Philippe (1773–1850) reigned from 1830 until 24 February 1848, when he gave up his throne. Disguised as "Mr Smith", he travelled to England where he lived until his death.

The last emperor of China
Hsüan T'ung gave up his throne on 12 February 1912 and later took the name Henry Pu-yi. The film *The Last Emperor* (1987) is about his life.

The last tsar of Russia
Nicholas II was removed from power by the Russian Revolution of 1917, and murdered with his family at Ekaterinburg in July 1918. Their remains were reburied in St Petersburg in July 1998.

Pharos of Alexandria

Last of the Seven Wonders

The last of the Seven Wonders of the world to be built was the 124 m (406.9 ft) Pharos (lighthouse) of Alexandria, Egypt, which was completed in 279 BC. It was partly knocked down by invaders and later destroyed by an earthquake. The only one of the Seven Wonders that survives today is the Great Pyramid at Giza in Egypt.

See also

The Seven Wonders of the ancient world: pages 206–7

Transport lasts

The last stagecoach
Horse-drawn stagecoaches carried passengers and mail in Britain from the 17th century until the 19th century, when they were gradually replaced by trains. The Royal Mail between Inverness and Thurso, Scotland, last operated in October 1874.

The last horse-drawn London bus
The last horse-drawn bus ran in London on 25 October 1911.

The last Model T Ford
The Model T, first produced in 1908, was one of the most popular cars of all time. The last US-made Model T (number 15,007,033) rolled off the production line on Thursday 26 May 1927.

The last Routemaster bus
The Routemaster double-decker bus was introduced in London on 8 February 1956 and was a familiar sight in the capital for almost 50 years. The last Routemaster service ran on Friday 9 December 2005, although there are still two heritage routes in operation.

Last flight of Concorde
Concorde was the world's only supersonic airliner. It was in service for 34 years until it made its last commercial flight, from New York to London, on 24 October 2003.

Last voyage of the Titanic

The last voyage of the *Titanic* was also its first. It sank on 15 April 1912 after striking an iceberg, killing 1,517 people.

Prow of the wreck of the *Titanic*

See also

Shipwrecks: page 218

R

racquet sports 290–1
Radcliffe, Daniel 156
radio 275
rail transport 214–15, 218
rail tunnels 205
rain gauges 45
Rainforest Pyramid 201
Rambert, Dame Marie 261
Ratatouille, film 271
Realism 242
recording timeline 250, 251
recycling and rubbish 72–3
Red Crescent Movement 111
Reformation 102
refrigerators 189
religions 160–9
religious buildings 162, 200
Renaissance 102, 198, 242
reptiles and amphibians 62–3
Rezazadeh, Hossein 293
Richter Scale 47
rivers and lakes 38–9
road disasters 218
road tunnels 205
roadkill recipes 98
robberies 184
Robin Hood 171
rock music 254–5
rockets, space 29
rocks and minerals 34–5
rococo style 198, 242
rodeo 300
Rolls Royce 212
Roman building style 198
Roman empire 106
Roman gods 161
Roman numerals 82
Romanesque building style 198

Romania 129
Romanticism 242
Rome, foundation of 104
roofs and domes 201
Roosevelt's Four Freedoms 111
Routemaster bus 307
rowing 294
Rowling, J.K. 230, 232
royal "lasts" 306
Royal Observatory, Greenwich 26
Rubáiyat of Omar Khayyám 234
rubbish and recycling 72–3
rugby league 287
rugby union 287
rulers and leaders 108–9
running (athletics) 284
Russia 137
Russian Revolution 105
Rwanda 134

S

sacred texts 164–5
Sagrada Familia Cathedral 200
sailing 294, 295
saints 167
Salt Lake City 163
Samoa 143
San Marino 126
Santiago de Compostela 163
Santorini volcano 46
São Tomé and Príncipe 133
satellites 29
Saturn 23, 24
Saudi Arabia 137
Scarlatti, Domenico 67
Schlumpf brothers 246
schools 240, 241
Schulz, Charles 67

Schumacher, Michael 297
science and technology 74–89
science of life 48–73
scientific crime detection 185
Scott, Sheila 152
Scottish law 182
scouts and cub scouts 157
Scrabble 191
Scream, The (painting) 242
screen legends 272
sea battles 181
sea life 56–7
sea water elements 79
seas and oceans 40–1, 56–7
seconds (of time) 14, 15
security uses of animals 65
sedimentary rocks 35
semaphore 226, 227
Senegal 131
Serbia 129
Serengeti national park 221
Seuss, Dr 233
Seychelles 141
Shakespeare, William 150, 306
sharks 56, 57
Shaw, George Bernard 155
sheep 64
ships 210–11
shipwrecks 218
shrapnel 178
Sidis, William James 156
Sierra Leone 132
sign language 227
signs and symbols 226–7
Sikhism 164
silk 65
Simpsons 270
Sing Sing Prison 185
Singapore 140
singing and songs 251, 252
singles, top-selling 254
Sir Gawain and the Green

Knight (poem) 234
skeleton (of humans) 93
ski-jumping 299
skin, human 93
skins of animals 65
SkyDome 201
skyscrapers (buildings) 202–3
skyscrapers (flags) 210
sleep 96
Slovakia 128
Slovenia 129
snakes 62, 63
snooker 293
snowboarding 298
soap operas 275
soccer 288–9
sodium 79
solar energy 195
Solar System 22–5
solids (mathematical shapes) 83
Solomon Islands 142
Somalia 131
songs and singing 251, 252
sound barrier 217
sound levels 77
South Africa 135
South America 122–3
South Korea 139
space 18–31
space exploration 28–31
space tourism **31**, 220
space walks 31
spacecraft 28, 29, 31
Spain 126
Spanish Armada 218
Spanish language 224
species of animals 52
spectrum colours 77
speed measurements 84
speed of animals 53
speed of light 20, 21
speed of water transport 210
Speke, John Hanning 153

Author's acknowledgements

318

The author would like to thank the following people, organizations and publications for kindly supplying information for this book.

Whitaker's Almanack 2008

Academy of Motion Picture Arts and Sciences (AMPAS)*
American Film Institute
American Forests
Amnesty International
Association of Leading Visitor Attractions
Alexander Ash
Caroline Ash
Nicholas Ash
Box Office Mojo
BP Statistical Review of World Energy 2007
Richard Braddish
Thomas Brinkhoff
British Broadcasting Corporation (BBC)
The British Council
British Film Institute
British Library
British Museum
British Phonographic Industry (BPI)
Carbon Dioxide Information Analysis Center
Central Intelligence Agency (CIA)
Richard Chapman
Christian Research
Christie's
Computer Industry Almanac
Department for Environment, Food and Rural Affairs (DEFRA)
Death Penalty Information Center
Earth Impact Database
The Economist
Emporis
Energy Information Administration
Ethnologue
Euromonitor
Federal Bureau of Investigation
Food and Agriculture Organization of the United Nations (FAO)
Global Education Digest (UNESCO)
Global Forest Resources Assessment (FAO)

Gold Fields Mineral Services
Nathalie Golden
Golden Raspberry Award Foundation
Russell E. Gough
Monica Grady
Robert Grant
Greyhound Racing Association of America
Hollywood Reporter
Home Accident Surveillance System (HASS)
Home Office
Human Development Report (United Nations)
Imperial War Museum
International Centre for Prison Studies
International Federation of Audit Bureaux of Circulations
The International Institute for Strategic Studies, *The Military Balance 2007–2008*
The International Institute for Strategic Studies, *The Military Balance 2006–2007*
International Olympic Committee (IOC)
International Telecommunication Union (ITU)
International Union for the Conservation of Nature (IUCN)
Internet Movie Database (IMDb)
Internet World Stats
Inter-Parliamentary Union
London Zoo
Dr Benjamin Lucas
Mattel, Inc
Chris Mead
Mike Melvill
National Aeronautics and Space Administration, USA (NASA)
National Basketball Association, USA (NBA)
National Football League, USA (NFL)
National Statistics
Natural History Museum
AC Nielsen
The Nobel Foundation
Organisation for Economic Co-operation and Development (OECD)
Organisation Internationale des Constructeurs d'Automobiles (OICA)
Felicity Page

Parker Brothers
Patent Office
Periodical Publishers Association
Tony Pattison
Population Reference Bureau
Recording Industry Association of America (RIAA)
Dafydd Rees
Louise Reip
Royal Astronomical Society
Royal Observatory, Greenwich
Screen Digest
Screen International
Robert Senior
Sotheby's
Time magazine
Tree Register of the British Isles
United Nations (UN)
United Nations Children's Fund (UNICEF)
United Nations Educational, Scientific and Cultural Organization (UNESCO)
United Nations Environment Programme
United Nations Population Division (UNPD)
US Census Bureau International Data Base
US Geological Survey
US Mint
US Patent Office
Variety
Lucy T. Verma
Ward's Motor Vehicle Facts & Figures 2007
WebElements
World Association of Girl Guides and Girl Scouts
World Association of Newspapers
World Bank
World Christian Database
World Gazetteer
World Health Organization (WHO)
World of Learning
World Organization of the Scout Movement
World Tourism Organization (WTO)

population data
© by Stefan Helders
www.world-gazetteer.com

Country names
The following abbreviations are used for country names on page 285
BUL: Bulgaria
CHN: China
CUB: Cuba
CZE: Czech Republic
DEN: Denmark
ETH: Ethiopia
FRA: France
GBR: Great Britain
GDR: German Democratic Republic (1955–90)
MAR: Morocco (Maroc)
QAT: Qatar
ROM: Romania
RUS: Russian Federation
UKR: Ukraine
USA: United States of America
USSR: Union of Soviet Socialist Republics (1922–91)

Picture acknowledgements

L = left, R = right, C = centre, T = top, B = bottom

Page 2 Flirt Collection/Photolibrary; 4 Robert Harding Travel/Photolibrary; 8 Robert Harding Travel/Photolibrary; 10 Roberto Schmidt/ AFP/Getty Images; 11T Jeremy Swinborne/iStockphoto; 12C Jeremy Horner/Corbis; 14TL Eileen Tweedy/The Art Archive; 15B David Taylor/Getty Images; 16C Charles & Josette Lenars/Corbis; 17TR REGIS MADEC/Thaiworldview.com; 18 NASA/EPA/Corbis; 19B NASA; 19TC NASA; 20TR NASA; 20BR NASA; 20C NASA; 20CR NASA; 22BL NASA; 22CL NASA; 22CR NASA; 22C NASA; 22TR NASA; 23BL NASA; 23BC NASA; 23BR NASA; 23TL NASA; 24CL Gianni Dagli Orti/Corbis; 24C NASA; 24TR NASA; 24TC NASA; 25CL NASA; 25C NASA; 26CL Roger Ressmeyer/Corbis; 26TR Bettmann/Corbis; 27C NASA; 28R NASA; 29TL NASA; 30CL NASA; 30C NASA; 31TR NASA; 32 Mark Webster/Oxford Scientific/Photolibrary; 34C Charles & Josette Lenars/Corbis; 35T Timothy Ball/iStockphoto; 36BL Theo Allofs/ ZEFA/Corbis; 36TL iStockphoto; 37CL Robyn Glover/iStockphoto; 38B Andre Klaassen/iStockphoto; 38T Frank Leung/iStockphoto; 40T Daniel Leclair/Reuters/Corbis; 41C Stewart Westmorland/Corbis; 41BL John Pitcher/iStockphoto; 44TR Shaun Lowe/iStockphoto; 44TC Clint Spencer/iStockphoto; 46B Gary Braasch/Corbis; 47T Koch Valerie/iStockphoto; 48 Marian Bacon/Animals Animals/Photolibrary; 50TR Peter Fuchs/iStockphoto; 51BL Frans Lanting/Corbis; 51C Jon Rasmussen/iStockphoto; 52CR Richard Nowitz/Corbis; 53TR Brad Thompson/iStockphoto; 54TL Jim Jurica/iStockphoto; 55R iStockphoto; 55BL iStockphoto; 56CL Amos Nachoum/Corbis; 57TR Will Burgees/Reuters/Corbis; 57CL Don Bayley/iStockphoto; 58TR Tim Davis/Corbis; 58BL Anastasiya Maksymenko/iStockphoto; 59B Tim Davis/Corbis; 60TL Thomas Bedenk/iStockphoto; 61CL Dan Guravich/Corbis; 61TR Will Schmitz/iStockphoto; 62B Jeremy Edwards/ iStockphoto; 63TR Steve Geer/iStockphoto; 64CR Jose Carlos Pires Pereira/iStockphoto; 65TR Wolfgang Kaehler/Corbis; 66B Nico Smit/ iStockphoto; 66TR iStockphoto; 68T Christoph Ermel/iStockphoto; 69BR Jameson Weaton/iStockphoto; 70TR Wayne Lawler/ Ecoscene/ Corbis; 70B Loic Bernard/iStockphoto; 72B Roger Milley/iStockphoto; 73BC Marcelo Wain/iStockphoto; 73CR Nathan Watkins/ iStockphoto; 74 Maximilien Brice/CERN/ Science Photo Library; 75TR Les Cunliffe/iStockphoto; 76TR Liz Van Steenburgh/iStockphoto; 76CR Liz Van Steenburgh/iStockphoto; 78CR Bettmann/Corbis; 78CL Donall O Cleirigh/iStockphoto; 80L Strauss/Curtis/Corbis; 81T Alexander Kolomietz/iStockphoto; 84TL Hulton-Deutch Collection/Corbis; 84R Carole Gomez/iStockphoto; 85TR Nogues Alain/Corbis/ Sygma; 86L iStockphoto; 87TL Bettmann/Corbis; 87C Courtesy of Apple; 89TL Bettmann/Corbis; 89TR Courtesy of Apple; 90 Jens Neith/ ZEFA/Corbis; 91TR Carol Munoz/iStockphoto; 92TR Stephen Sweet/iStockphoto; 93C Maria Boytunoa/iStockphoto; 94C Bettmann/Corbis; 95R Bettmann/Corbis; 95BL Corbis; 96TL Maria Bibikova/iStockphoto; 97TR David Pollack/Corbis; 97L Roberta Casaliggi/iStockphoto; 98TL SwimInk2/LCC/Corbis; 98CR Kelly Cline/iStockphoto; 99TR Mary Evans Picture Library; 100 Claudia Daut/Reuters/Corbis; 102CR iStockphoto; 102TR Jose Marafona/iStockphoto; 103R David Lewis/iStockphoto; 104CL Falk Kienas/iStockphoto; 104C Eliza Snow/ iStockphoto; 105T Bettmann/Corbis; 106B Karim Hesham/iStockphoto; 107TR Jivko Kazakov/iStockphoto; 107TL Francisco Orellana/ iStockphoto; 108TR Jack Tzekov/iStockphoto; 108CL John Woodworth/iStockphoto; 109L Palazzo Baberini. Rome/Dagli Orti/The Art Archive; 109C John Steele/iStockphoto; 110TL Corbis; 110CB Wally McNamee/Corbis; 111TR Natalia Bratslavsky/iStockphoto; 112 Dimitar Dilkoff/AFP/Getty Images; 116BR Bob Krist/Corbis; 116T Arne Thaysen/iStockphoto; 117BR Ivan Mateev/iStockphoto; 118B James Rabinowitz/Corbis; 119T Yann Arthus-Bertrand/Corbis; 120TL Randy Mayes/iStockphoto; 121B Steven Miric/iStockphoto; 122BL Fabian Guignard/iStockphoto; 122BL Dennis Sabo/iStockphoto; 124TC Mike Morley/iStockphoto; 124BR Emilia Kun/iStockphoto; 125TC Rob Broek/iStockphoto; 126TL iStockphoto; 126B Stephen Hoerold/iStockphoto; 127TR Ekatrina Fribus/iStockphoto; 128TL Klemen Demsar/iStockphoto; 128BR Marisa Allegra/iStockphoto; 129TR Mark Weiss/iStockphoto; 130T John Woodworth/iStockphoto; 131BR Alan Toby/iStockphoto; 132BL Paul Almasy/Corbis; 132TL Andrew Cribb/iStockphoto; 133BL Steven Tilson/iStockphoto; 134BR Torleif Svensson/Corbis; 134TR iStockphoto; 135TR Michel de Nijs/iStockphoto; 136TL iStockphoto; 136CR John Sigler/iStockphoto; 137TR iStockphoto; 138B iStockphoto; 139TR iStockphoto; 140TL Stefan Tordenmalm/iStockphoto; 140B Ondrej Cech/iStockphoto; 141C Andy Green-AGMIT/iStockphoto; 142B Lisa Kyle Young/iStockphoto; 142TR Felix Mockel/iStockphoto; 143C Matthew Scholey/iStockphoto; 144 Brian Snyder/Reuters/Corbis; 145TR Sandra O'Claire/iStockphoto; 146TL Frank May/DPA/Corbis; 147CR Bettmann/Corbis; 148TR Gianni Dagli Orti/Corbis; 148BL Nik Wheeler/Corbis; 149LC Dave Wirtzfeld/iStockphoto; 149LC Dave Wirtzfeld/iStockphoto; 149LC Dave Wirtzfeld/iStockphoto; 150TL Historical Picture Archive/Corbis; 150CR Bettmann/Corbis; 150CL Peter Spiro/iStockphoto; 151B iStockphoto; 152TL Bettmann/Corbis; 153C Jim Sugar/Corbis; 154TL NASA; 155C Shannon Stapleton/Corbis; 155BL The Scotsman/ Corbis/Sygma; 156T Alison Wright/Corbis; 156BL Nancy Kaszerman/Zuma/Corbis; 157B Edward Parsons/UN/EPA/Corbis; 158 AFP/Getty Images; 160B Sandro Vannini/Corbis; 161C Richard A. Cooke/Corbis; 162C Bennett Dean/Eye Ubiquitous/Corbis; 163R Ashwin Kharidehal Abhirama/iStockphoto; 164TR Corbis; 164L Nancy Louie/iStockphoto; 165C Elio Clol/Corbis; 166C Fred de Noyelle/Godong/Corbis; 167TR Robert Young/iStockphoto; 168BL Earl & Nazima Kowall/Corbis; 169TR Reuters/Corbis; 169C Nikhil Gangavane/iStockphoto; 170L iStockphoto; 170TR Pam Wardlaw/iStockphoto; 170C Geoffrey Hammond/iStockphoto; 172C Christine Balderas/iStockphoto; 172L iStockphoto; 173B Sharon Dominick/iStockphoto; 174B Jiri Vatka/iStockphoto; 175L Joza Pojbic/iStockphoto; 176 Stuart Price/AFP/Getty Images; 177TR Lise Gagne/iStockphoto; 178C Owen Franklen/Corbis; 178T Vladimir Melnik/iStockphoto; 180C The Dmitri Baltermants Collection/Corbis; 181T Fine Art Photography Library/Corbis; 182R Jeff Gynane/iStockphoto; 183L Tim Wright/Corbis;

320

ACKNOWLEDGEMENTS

183T Dan Mason/iStockphoto; **184T** Gerald French/Corbis; **184C** Dusty Cline/iStockphoto; **185B** Reuters/Corbis; **185T** Achim Prill/ iStockphoto; **186** Jonathan Hordle/Rex Features; **187T** Joel Blitt/iStockphoto; **188CL** Sandro Vannini/Corbis; **188R** Bettmann/Corbis; **190BL** Christie's Images/Corbis; **190LR** Neema Frederic/Corbis Sygma; **192R** Tim Graham/Corbis; **192CB** Sascha Burkard/iStockphoto; **192L** iStockphoto; **193R** Archivo Iconografico, SA/Corbis; **194B** Eliza Snow/iStockphoto; **195CR** Eric Foltz/iStockphoto; **196** OMA/EPA/ Corbis; **198L** Asier Villafranca Valasco/iStockphoto; **198B** Jim Jurica/iStockphoto; **199TC** Andrea Jemolo/Corbis; **199TR** Paul Hardy/ Corbis; **200B** Roger Antrobus/Corbis; **201T** Pawel Libea/Corbis; **203T** Paul Cheyne/iStockphoto; **204T** iStockphoto; **205C** Donall O'Cleirigh/iStockphoto; **206B** Liu Liqun/Corbis; **208** Car Culture/Corbis; **210B** Tony Arruza/Corbis; **212C** Aston Martin; **213T** Bill Nation/ Corbis Sygma; **214C** Tim Wimborne/Reuters/Corbis; **215TL** Thomas Hottner/iStockphoto; **215CR** Robert Churchill/iStockphoto; **216B** Underwood & Underwood/Corbis; **216T** Bettmann/Corbis; **217CR** Bettmann/Corbis; **218TL** Eileen Tweedy/Magdalene College, Cambridge/The Art Archive; **219BR** Hulton Deutsch Collection/Corbis; **219R** Reuters/Corbis; **220B** Jaques Langevin/Corbis; **220CL** Allison Marles/iStockphoto; **221T** Duncan Gilbert/iStockphoto; **222** MGM/Album/AKG-Images; **223T** Catherine dée Auvil/ iStockphoto; **224BL** Alison Wright/Corbis; **224T** Andres Balcazar/iStockphoto; **226C** Ian Poole/iStockphoto; **226TL** Robert Dawson/ iStockphoto; **228CR** Seth Joel/Corbis; **228T** iStockphoto; **229B** Amazon.com; **231TR** The Estate of C.S. Lewis, 1950; **232C** Blue Lantern Studio/Corbis; **234T** Blue Lantern Studio/Corbis; **235CL** Marisa Allegra Williams/ iStockphoto; **235BR** Rey Rojo/iStockphoto; **236R** Marvel Characters Inc./Corbis; **238** Danny Lehman/Corbis; **239TR** iStockphoto; **240C** Joseph Sohm; ChromoSohm Inc./Corbis; **241T** Michael S Yamashita/Corbis; **242CR** Gillet Luc/iStockphoto; **242TL** Adrian Beesley/ iStockphoto; **243TR** Archivo Iconografico, SA/Corbis; **244C** Laryn Bakker/iStockphoto; **244BR** Matej Michelizza/iStockphoto; **247TL** Gabe Palmer/Corbis; **247CR** iStockphoto; **247BR** Olga Shelego/iStockphoto; **248** Michael Ochs Archives/Getty Images; **250TR** Dave Bartruff/Corbis; **251C** Bettmann/Corbis; **253TR** David Lees/ Corbis; **253C** Corbis; **254CR** Bettmann/Corbis; **254CL** Courtesy of Apple; **255C** Bettmann/Corbis; **255TR** Henry Dilz/Corbis; **256B** Jonathan Drake/Reuters/Corbis; **256BR** Luke Daniek/iStockphoto; **258TL** Sunset Boulevard/Corbis; **258C** Josef Philipp/iStockphoto; **259R** Fernando Mañoso/EFE/Corbis; **260B** Robbie Jack/Corbis; **261TL** Robbie Jack/Corbis; **261R** Diane Diederich; **262** Paramount/Everett/Rex Features; **264TL** Swim Ink 2/LLC/Corbis; **265CR** Yann Arthus-Bertrand/Corbis; **266TR** Trapper Frank/Corbis Sygma; **267TR** MGM/United Artists/Sony/The Kobal Collection; **267BL** Warner Bros/The Kobal Collection; **268CR** RKO/The Kobal Collection; **269CR** Michael Goulding/Orange County Register/Corbis; **270CR** Disney/The Kobal Collection; **271T** Album/AKG-Images; **272C** Michael Caronna/ Reuters/Corbis; **272TL** Bettmann/Corbis; **273TR** RKO/The Kobal Collection; **274TL** iStockphoto; **275C** Dan Herrick/iStockphoto; **276** George Tiedemann/GT Images/Corbis; **277TR** Tracy Hebden/iStockphoto; **278B** Duomo/Corbis; **279TR** Bettmann/Corbis; **280BR** Historical Picture Archive/Corbis; **280CL** Historical Picture Archive/Corbis; **281T** iStockphoto; **282BR** Karl Weatherly/Corbis; **282C** Karl Mathis/EPA/Corbis; **284TL** Tim de Waele/Isosport/Corbis; **284C** Jorge Delgado/iStockphoto; **285R** Duomo/Corbis; **286TL** Tomasso DeRosa/Corbis; **286BR** Simon Bruty/SI/Newsport/Corbis; **287TR** Jeff Lewis/Icon SMI/Newsport/Corbis; **288TR** AFP/Getty Images; **289CR** Matt A. Brown/Newsport/Corbis; **290T** Susan Mullane/Newsport/Corbis; **290CR** Jim Sugar/Corbis; **290CL** Jolande Gerritsen/iStockphoto; **291C** Jolande Gerritsen/iStockphoto; **292TR** Bettmann/Corbis; **292BL** Duomo/Corbis; **294BL** Andy Clark/Reuters/Corbis; **294TR** David Gray/ Reuters/Corbis; **295BR** Maggie Hallahan/Corbis; **296BL** Pichon P/Corbis/Sygma; **296TC** Eric Gaillard/Reuters/Corbis; **297T** Bryn Lennon/ Getty Images; **298TR** Olivier Marie/EPA/Corbis; **300BL** Kevin R Morris/Corbis; **300TR** Kelly-Mooney Photography/Corbis; **301CR** Steve Boyle/Newsport/Corbis; **302** Universal Studios/Kime French/AKG-Images; **304CR** Gianni Dagli Orti/Corbis; **305TR** Corbis; **306CR** Archivo Iconografico, SA/Corbis; **306BC** Ralph White/Corbis; **307TL** Bettmann/Corbis